A FRAGILE

A FRAGILE BALANCE

Re-examining the History of Foreign Aid, Security, and Diplomacy

Louis A. Picard

and

Terry F. Buss

Kumarian Press
An Imprint of Stylus Publishing

A Fragile Balance: Re-examining the History of Foreign Aid, Security, and Diplomacy
Published in 2009 in the United States of America by Kumarian Press
22883 Quicksilver Drive, Sterling, VA 20166-2012 USA

The text of this book is set in 10/12.5 Sabon

Proofread by Publication Services, Inc.
Index by Publication Services, Inc.
Production and design by Publication Services, Inc.

Printed in the United States of America by Thomson-Shore, Inc.
Text printed with vegetable oil-based ink.

∞ The paper used in this publication meets the minimum requirements of the American National Standard for Information Sciences-Permanence of Paper for printed Library Materials, ANSI Z39.48-1984

Library of Congress Cataloging-in-Publication Data

Picard, Louis A.
   A fragile balance : re-examining the history of foreign aid, security, and diplomacy / by Louis A. Picard and Terry F. Buss.
      p. cm.
   Includes bibliographical references and index.
   ISBN 978-1-56549-295-0 (pbk. : alk. paper) — ISBN 978-1-56549-296-7 (cloth : alk. paper)
   1. Economic assistance, American—History—20th century. 2. Economic assistance, American—History—21st century. 3. United States—Foreign relations—20th century. 4. United States—Foreign relations—2001-2009. 5. National security—United States. 6. United States—Military policy. I. Buss, Terry F. II. Title.
   HC60.P495 2009
   327.73— dc22
                                              2009010986

Louis A. Picard dedicates this book to the memory of
H. Charles Hooks and E. Brian Egner.
They never met each other, but they should have.
He also thanks his wife, Pauline Greenlick,
for all of her love, advice, and support.

Terry Buss dedicates this book to his
precocious children, Abby and Nathaniel,
of whom he is exceedingly proud.

TABLE OF CONTENTS

PART III. Contemporary Aid in Historical Perspective and Beyond

PREFACE

The focus of this book is on US foreign aid policy and its relationship to foreign policy issues. The book has a historical focus, placing foreign aid within the context of diplomacy and foreign policy going back to the eighteenth century and beyond but continuing to the present time, with the last two chapters examining foreign aid and foreign policy in the post–September 11 world.

The book tries to demonstrate and simplify the complex world of foreign aid with all its diversity and range of definitions. In the end, however, our position is that foreign aid, like defense and security policy, is a subset of foreign policy. Our goal was to write a book accessible to an undergraduate university audience and general reader but which also presents new ideas, debates and information that will be of interest to foreign policy specialists.

This book, though it aspires to be fair and accurate, does have a point of view that we try to make clear throughout: foreign aid (grants, sub-market loans, and nonmonetary transfers of resources) can be used to provide social services, and develop human resources and democratic institutions. It is not, by itself, the best tool to promote economic growth. Our use of sources is broad and includes nonsocial science materials, both to make the manuscript interesting to the reader and also because we think it provides a broader perspective. It does not shy away from the polemic or the rhetorical but tries to use it to understand the diversity in our understanding of foreign aid at a time when foreign policy choices have gotten out of control.

ACKNOWLEDGMENTS

Several generations of graduate students in Louis Picard's class in foreign aid have suffered through earlier versions of this manuscript. Others have maintained the Picard newspaper archives and wondered whether or not he ever read the clippings they have cut and filed. The answer is: sometimes.

For student support and advice over the years, the authors are extremely grateful. The GSPIA students' frank comments have contributed immensely to preparation of the completed manuscript. A number of foreign assistance practitioners helped in gaining access to research materials, including Ed Connerley, Bob Groelsema, Jeanne North, Haven North, and the late Wendell Schaeffer.

In addition, we acknowledge the influence and support received over the years from Steve Morrison, Ken Kornher, and many others who are currently or formerly with the US Agency for International Development. Picard is grateful for the support of Al Zuck, formerly the director of the National Association of Schools of Public Affairs and Administration (NASPAA) between 1984 and 1987. Financial support to Picard for this book came from GSPIA. Picard is grateful for the sabbatical granted to him by the University of Pittsburgh from January through August of 2007. Financial support during this period came from the African Center for Strategic Studies of National Defense University.

PART I

BACKGROUND

Custodian of the values of civilization and history, [the colonialist] accomplished a mission; he has the immense merit of bringing light to the colonized's ignominious darkness. The fact that this role brings him privileges and respect is only justice; colonization is legitimate in every sense and with all its consequences.

Albert Memmi, *Colonizer and Colonized*

Americans are barely aware of our history, much less anyone else's.

Mark Hertsgaard, *The Eagle's Shadow*

1

FOREIGN AID POLICY IN THE TWENTY-FIRST CENTURY

[F]or the friendship which is gained by purchase and not through grandeur and nobility of spirit is bought but not secured.

> Niccolo Machiavelli, "The Prince"

However, here we have a "hen and egg" puzzle.

> Barbara Ward, *The Rich Nations and the Poor Nations*

Foreign policy decisions are in general much more influenced by irrational motives.

> Barbara W. Tuchman, *The March of Folly*

Our Approach

For the third time in a generation, the United States is embroiled in a war in a developing country based on false information and faulty decision making. More than forty years ago, the United States escalated its involvement in Vietnam. In October 2001 and March 2003, the United States invaded Afghanistan, then Iraq, respectively, becoming entangled in one of the longest military engagements in US history. Commentators often note the uncanny similarities among the three conflicts. Each shows the triangulation of foreign policy, then military intervention, followed by foreign aid, all for the worse. In all three, though one hopes for a better future, US diplomacy has taken a global beating that might take decades to repair; the military faced a situation where it could not gain a decisive victory and became mired in nonmilitary actions for which it was neither designed nor prepared to execute; and aid found itself serving goals that were more supportive of military objectives rather than development goals that were largely unattainable in a war zone.

3

Our book examines US foreign aid from a public policy perspective. Our approach concurs with the view of Vernon Ruttan, who states, "Changes in US [foreign] assistance policy respond to and are constrained by domestic political and economic interests and concerns."[1] Our approach uses history as its methodology. Understanding the history and context of foreign aid within foreign and security policy is as important as understanding technical formulas or narrow calculations of cost-benefit analysis.

The international assistance story "is full of entertaining and penetrating commentaries about the ironies—as well as the historic failure—of foreign aid."[2] Along with the irony, there is also a great deal of sadness and lost opportunity in the enterprise. Our book analyzes failures and successes as lessons for future foreign assistance approaches. Although we hoped to find more successes than failures, that was not the case in foreign aid.

The book assesses US foreign aid policy at this critical juncture—immediate post–September 11—to contribute to the policy debates about future US foreign and security policy. It looks at decision policies and processes, placing each in a historical, social, and economic context. Our view is that foreign aid, foreign policy, and security policy reflect broad political values of government and society, and understanding these is not only an empirical exercise but also a normative one.

Richard Neustadt and Ernest May warn us about the danger of ignoring the past and assuming that the world is new and that "decisions in the public realm required only reason or emotion, as preferred."[3] Our approach places foreign aid within the context of diplomacy, as well as foreign and security policy beginning in the eighteenth century and extending to the post–September 11 world. Foreign aid appeared to many observers to begin in 1948 as a blank canvas swept clean by the carnage of World War II. In reality, what seemed a new approach carried excess baggage from past events, values, and assumptions that originated centuries earlier. Our book's goal is to examine that baggage and link it to decisions made at critical points in history, from the beginnings of the Cold War to post–September 11.

We do not intend for this book to be merely a work of abstract social science.[4] It addresses both academic debate and practical perceptions as reflected in the normative discussions about foreign aid. Rather than leaving foreign and security policy to the "purity" of the academy, it takes political, journalistic, activist, and normative debates seriously. It treats all sources as proximate, and, while social science research is important, the approach here assumes that foreign and security policies are too important to be relegated to armchair debates.

Motivated by the tragedies of Vietnam, Afghanistan, and Iraq, the focus of this book is on US foreign aid policy and its relationship to foreign and security policy issues. Foreign aid cannot be separated from either foreign or security policy, in spite of the propensity of many analysts to do so; however, all three can be reconstructed in ways that emphasize one over the other at any point in time. This is important in light of the current emphasis on bringing together foreign, defense, and international assistance policies (the so-called triangulation of US international policy). Some have dubbed triangulation the three D's: diplomacy, defense, and development.[5]

Our goal is to examine various influences on foreign aid over time and discuss the context and process of policy making on and implementation of aid policies and their impact on international relations. A conceptual framework for understanding foreign aid reflects on the search for an enlightened but realistic optimism that deals equally with commercial, security, and humanitarian concerns in a manner nonthreatening to nations receiving aid.

If there is a causal relationship involved in foreign policy and foreign aid, it is a simple, if not profound, one: politics and implementation should be examined historically because past events are always antecedents of future events. There is no single explanation of foreign aid policy decisions in terms of a realpolitik, economic determinism, or religious obligation. Different elements weigh in differently at different times. Neustadt and May call for the "placement" of events in a weighted timeline to understand both patterns and processes of decision making.[6]

We believe there is no single explanation for state behavior, whether it acts diplomatically, militarily, or through international assistance. Foreign aid, like foreign policy as a whole, reflects a multitude of influences on group dynamics and individual decisions, cultural, social, and economic, which combine over time to influence the policy and implementation of international assistance.[7] Some aid decisions are made by people in power; many are reflected in actions by people working on the ground.

Our goal was to write a book accessible to students while also presenting new ideas, debates, and information of interest to foreign policy specialists and informed citizens. This book does not shy away from policy debates but tries to use them to understand the diversity of the issues and our understanding of foreign aid at a time when foreign policy choices may have gotten out of control.

Correctives are important, and self-correction is a part of the process of policy debate.[8] Our book has been influenced by what Robert Cowley calls "counterfactual" history, that is history that might have been but is not but which can "cast a reflective light on what did [occur]."[9] This book is a commentary and, perhaps, a corrective.

Understanding Foreign Aid

Paul Mosley defines foreign aid correctly, though narrowly, as "money transferred on concessionary terms by the governments of rich countries to the governments of poor countries."[10] In this sense, there was some government financial or humanitarian assistance prior to World War II, though the first broad transfer of funds on a worldwide basis in peace time occurred with the Marshall Plan.

Unlike most writing on foreign aid, however, we look at the earlier period of international assistance prior to 1948 because it defined values and boundaries of contemporary foreign assistance and helped to establish processes under which it would be granted.

The definition of aid is important when one places the United States within the context of its *isolationist* and *expansionist* history represented in the nineteenth century by the notion of Manifest Destiny. This, as we will see in the next several chapters, resulted in a *messianism* defined by isolationism prior to World War II and *unilateralism* in the late twentieth and early twenty-first century, with the United States increasingly willing to go it alone in foreign and security policy after 1989.

Foreign aid is one tool for achieving foreign policy goals. In addition to foreign aid, this pool of potential actions includes:

- Threat and use of force
- Covert operations and proxy interventions
- Intelligence gathering and information dissemination
- Diplomacy
- Propaganda
- Cultural exchanges (visits and exchanges)
- Economic threats and promises and trade policies (sanctions and tariffs)

Foreign aid should be seen in the context of historical patterns of international assistance—private or public.[11] *International assistance* is the transfer of any resources (grants of money and concessionary—less than market rate—loans), the provision of goods and services, and technical assistance, including military assistance (in 2007, the Department of Defense and its Defense Security Cooperation Agency administered one-fifth of US assistance). Some observers also include debt forgiveness in foreign assistance. International assistance comes from private foundations and philanthropists, as well as publicly funded assistance: government-to-government and government-to-nongovernmental organizations (NGOs).

 aid as a political tool

Use of the term *foreign aid*, as a subset of international assistance here, means the subset of government (donor) economic and financial transfers—directly or indirectly. Foreign aid as it evolved after 1948 was an extension of diplomacy and an alternative to sanctions, conflict, intervention, and war.[12] Along with Carol Lancaster, we see foreign aid as a "voluntary transfer of public resources, from a government to another independent government, to an NGO, or to an international organization with at least a 25 percent grant element."[13]

Technical assistance is the provision of expert assistance more often than not on a temporary basis to government agencies (and sometimes to NGOs).[14] This includes technical assistance provided to the private sector or NGOs and interest associations. Technical assistance includes consulting, service support, education, and training.[15]

Specifically, such technical assistance provides technical specialists, civilian and sometimes military, on direct contract with government agencies or with private businesses and NGOs or foundations that provide services. Often technical assistance concerns institution or capacity building. Consulting, both long- and short-term, constitutes the heart of technical assistance. The technical assistance expert is responsible to the client, but it is not always clear who the client is: the host country, its leadership and its program managers, or the donor agency and its contracting and program officers.

This book tries to demonstrate and simplify the complex world of foreign aid with all its diversity and meanings. Given the complexity of aid, discussion is necessarily selective and incomplete. In the end, foreign aid like trade, defense, and security policy "may productively be viewed as a microcosm of nation-states' broader efforts in foreign affairs."[16]

The most common form of international aid is the transfer of economic resources for political, social, and economic development. Often incorporated into foreign aid is international technical assistance. *Military* and *security assistance* is also a subset of foreign aid in some cases, as is eradicating illegal drugs exports and interdiction of illegal migrants—"boat people."

Traditionally, foreign aid focuses on at least four primary objectives:

- Broadly based economic growth
- An effective attack on poverty and disease
- An end to the destruction of the physical environment of the world
- The promotion of democracy and governance (increasingly common since the end of the Cold War)[17]

Following from this there are four components to foreign aid policy visible through time:

- Physical infrastructure development
- Support for social and economic development
- Humanitarian and security assistance
- Support for good governance, conflict resolution, and political development

Democratic governance and political development have become particularly important in the last fifteen years. As early as 1950, advocates made it clear that democratic governance was essential for development aid to succeed.[18] Increasingly since 1989, there is concern for the establishment of legitimacy for democracy and good governance, which predominates, at least conceptually, in aid debates; however, if aid is inappropriately provided, this can make governance problems much worse. Funding opposition political parties with assistance may create political instability, for example.

In the twentieth century, foreign assistance served a multiplicity of purposes: diplomatic, security, cultural, developmental, humanitarian relief, and promotion of commerce. After the Cold War, promotion of economic and social transitions in former socialist countries, the support for democratic governance, mediating conflicts, managing postconflict transitions, addressing environmental problems, and fighting international terror are increasingly important.

Our book has a point of view: foreign aid can be used to provide social services, develop human resources, and promote democratic institutions, but it is not in itself the best tool to promote economic growth or redistribution of resources. Again, if used injudiciously, aid can also do great damage.

While not always an independent policy, foreign aid is a tool of foreign and security policy, and it also serves as a strong symbol and signal to the international community. Since the 1950s, foreign aid and technical assistance were "established on the premise that the developed world possessed both the talent and the capital for helping backward countries to development."[19] Since 2000, observers have questioned the validity of that assumption.

An Overview

We organized our material in three parts, the first focusing on the background necessary to understanding foreign aid's antecedents for the United States. Chapter 2 examines the relationship between foreign aid and foreign and security policy, focusing on the ways the United States uses foreign aid and international assistance to further its international interests. Interpretations of foreign assistance include viewing aid as part of an exchange system, assistance as a humanitarian response and international assistance as part of a policy of trade and commerce. For some there is also a moral dimension to the debates about foreign aid.

Worldwide imperial systems defined much of foreign policy in the last 300 years. These empires still resonate on foreign policy today. In Chapter 3, we analyze foreign aid within the context of the values and processes that characterized these worldwide governance mechanisms. Missionaries, traders, and military occupiers—British, French, Dutch, Belgian, Portuguese, and Spanish—all left their mark on international relations and foreign assistance prior to 1950.

Part II analyses the somewhat distinct epochs in the history of aid, diplomacy, and security policy. Chapter 4 looks at United States foreign policy and its involvement in imperial expansion and international assistance prior to World War II. Origins of many foreign aid processes and assumptions lay in the US interventions in Latin America, Asia, and Africa prior to World War II, and in their competition with the European colonial powers, particularly in parts of East Asia. The Monroe Doctrine and the self-defined role in the Western Hemisphere are components of that legacy.

Contemporary foreign aid begins with the US entry into World War II. Chapter 5 looks at the way international relations between the wars, assumptions made by President Franklin D. Roosevelt, and requirements of international assistance as part of the war effort defined foreign aid parameters. The quasi-military nature of foreign aid procedures and links between military and civilian assistance are testament to that period. After World War II, foreign aid went through a number of periods, beginning with the initial assistance to Greece and Turkey under the Truman Doctrine and the Marshall Plan.

Chapter 6 begins with the origins of foreign aid targeted to less developed countries (LCDs) that began under President Harry Truman during the Cold War, examines its first decade and establishment of US Agency for International Development (USAID). In Chapter 7, we examine the Vietnam War, the way that foreign aid was changed by the disastrous intervention in Vietnam in the 1960s and 1970s, and how the war shaped foreign aid and technical assistance after 1975, foreshadowing involvement in Iraq in 2003.

Beginning with post-Vietnam reforms, Chapter 8 goes on to examine the Ronald Reagan presidency, structural adjustment requirements, and the end of the Cold War in 1989. Decline in support for foreign aid, sometimes referred to as donor fatigue, reached its nadir during this period. This donor fatigue has left many foreign aid watchers pessimistic about the future. Chapter 9 discusses the changing environment of foreign aid at the end of the twentieth century, the way in which foreign aid is carried out, and how efforts at institutional development and capacity building have evolved. The chapter concludes with an analysis of the presidencies of George H.W. Bush and Bill Clinton and their impact upon foreign aid policy to 2000.

Chapter 9 also focuses on the remilitarization of foreign aid, the quagmire of Iraq and Afghanistan, and the role foreign aid played in the Iraq War. Chapter 10 recounts a most unusual development in foreign aid: the co-optation of foreign aid by the military. General David Petraeus, recent past commander of forces in Iraq, articulated a major revision of aid policy in which the military would take the lead in nation-building—"armed social work." At the same time, the Pentagon established the Africa Command that would not only create a military presence in Africa but would also pursue diplomatic and development activities displacing aid agencies and individual states.

Part III takes the historical antecedents of aid in the context of foreign policy and security and analyzes not only how they play out contemporarily, but also what it might suggest for effective aid policy in a post-September 11 world. Chapters 11 and 12 focus on the processes that define and constrain foreign aid and technical assistance, examining the ways in which the United States and LDC clients perceive one another, interact, and in many cases misunderstand each other. Chapter 11 identifies institutional factors that influence foreign aid processes, including the contracting out, grants processes and processes of capacity building. Chapter 12 discusses stereotypes, motives, and individual dilemmas that are all a part of the complex decision processes that constitute foreign aid policy and the standard operating procedures often central to misunderstandings surrounding foreign aid. The chapter concludes with a discussion of the budgeting process and the relationships between donors and the recipient country managers. Chapter 13 provides an overview of several contemporary debates about foreign aid policy, including unilateralism versus multilateralism, the importance of human security, support for democracy and governance, and links between foreign aid and trade and investment policy.

Chapter 14, by way of concluding, peers into the future of foreign aid as the United States moves further into the twenty-first century. While there have been limited successes in foreign aid policy, when foreign aid fails, as it did, for example, in post-Saddam Iraq, consequences can be catastrophic. The book ends on a cautiously optimistic note. Foreign aid can be successful from developmental, diplomatic and humanitarian perspectives, but only if one understands the limits of foreign aid and the potential contradictions between foreign aid and the other components of foreign and security policy.

Notes

1. Vernon W. Ruttan, *United States Development Assistance Policy: The Domestic Politics of Foreign Economic Aid* (Baltimore: Johns Hopkins University Press, 1996), p. 8.

2. Robert D. Kaplan, "Far and Away." Book Review of *Dark Star Safari* by Paul Theroux, *Book World*, March 30, 2003, p. 8.

3. Richard E. Neustadt and Ernest R. May, *Thinking in Time: The Uses of History for Decision-makers* (New York: The Free Press, 1986), pp. xi–xii.

4. See Samuel P. Huntington, *The Clash of Civilizations and the Remaking of World Order* (New York: Simon & Schuster, 1996), p. 13. One does not have to agree with Huntington to admire the skill and clarity with which he has presented his polemic.

5. See, for example, Reuben E. Brigety, *Humanity as a Weapon of War: Sustainable Security and the Role of the U.S. Military* (Washington, DC: Center for American Progress, June 2008).

6. Neustadt and May, *Thinking in Time,* pp. 203–206.

7. This view has been influenced by John D. Steinbruner's important and challenging book, *The Cybernetic Theory of Decision: New Dimensions of Political Analysis* (Princeton, NJ: Princeton University Press, 1974).

8. Emory Roe calls on the writer "to think counter-intuitively [and] to conceive of a rival hypothesis or set of hypotheses that could plausibly reverse what appears to be the case, where the reversal in question, even [though] it proves factually not to be the case, nonetheless provides a possible policy option for future attention because of its very plausibility. See Emery Roe, *Except-Africa: Remaking Development, Rethinking Power* (New Brunswick, NJ: Transaction Publishers, 1998), p. 9.

9. Robert Cowley, "Introduction," in *What If? America: Eminent Historians Imagine What Might Have Been,* ed. Robert Cowley (London: Pan Books, 2003), p. xiii.

10. Paul Mosley, *Overseas Aid: Its Defense and Reform* (Brighton, UK: Wheatsheaf Books, 1987), p. 3.

11. See Carol Lancaster, *Transforming Foreign Aid: United States Assistance in the 21st Century* (Washington, DC: Institute for International Economics, 2000), p. 9.

12. George Liska, *The New Statecraft: Foreign Aid in American Foreign Policy* (Chicago: University of Chicago Press, 1960).

13. Thus including concessionary loans. Carol Lancaster, *Transforming Foreign Aid,* p. 9.

14. Rowland Egger, "Technical Assistance at Home and Abroad," in *Institutional Cooperation for the Public Service: Report of a Conference* (Chicago: Public Administration Service, 1963), p. 47.

15. Ferrel Heady, "Report," in *Institutional Cooperation for the Public Service: Report of a Conference* (Chicago: Public Administration Service, 1963), p. 58.

16. Steven W. Hook, *National Interest and Foreign Aid* (Boulder, CO: Lynne Rienner, 1995), p. 34.

17. Ralph H. Smuckler and Robert J. Berg, "New Challenges New Opportunities, U.S. Cooperation for International Growth and Development in the 1990s" (East Lansing: Michigan State University), p. vi.

18. William Vogt, "Point Four Propaganda and Reality," *American Perspective,* iv, no. 2 (Spring 1950): pp. 125. The entire article is on pp. 122–129.

19. Judith Tendler, *Inside Foreign Aid* (Baltimore: The Johns Hopkins University Press, 1975), p. 10.

2

International Assistance, Foreign Policy, and Security Policy

Where . . . avenues are closed—where the economic system will not give people bread, or where the political system will not permit them a hearing, or where the prestige arrangements afford them no chance of dignity—men will appeal to the sword.

Edmund Stillman and William Pfaff, *Power and Impotence*

Each [colonial] station should be like a beacon on the road towards better things, a center for trade of course, but also for humanizing, improving, instructing.

Joseph Conrad, *Heart of Darkness*

Interpreting Foreign Aid

Motives underlying foreign aid policy are complex and multifarious. In this chapter, we examine some of these, placing them within the context of diplomacy and security policy. Four different views of foreign aid are common:

- Exchange theory, a version of which is sometimes referred to as realpolitik
- Financial imperatives and commercialism
- Humanitarian impulses
- Moral imperatives for giving

We examine each in turn.

We begin with a caution. There is no single motivation explaining foreign aid policy. Rather, different motives are explicitly defined by elites and implicitly motivate those who advocate for and implement foreign aid policy over time. Since World War II, communications equipment has been linked to military alliances while commercial concerns have influenced food assistance. Increased support for HIV/AIDs victims has been supported by humanitarian groups. Following from this, there is no single source of foreign and security policy values. Though the executive branch—including the White House, Departments of State (State) and Defense (Defense) and other federal agencies—account for much decision making, Congress is a major actor in foreign aid, and inputs into policy come from NGOs and other interest groups, foreign service officers, and other administrators, contractors, and the public. Additional pressures emanate externally from allies, international organizations, and advocacy groups.

Foreign Exchange as a Form of Diplomacy

The realist school of foreign aid sees development assistance as statecraft and an economic instrument of power politics.[1] Nations exchange money, goods, and services to influence behavior of other states. Historically, policymakers are informed by their view of national interest, and exchanges are made with the leadership of other nations to further that interest. Subsidies (either as grants or loans at sub-market rates) are a reliable means of influencing international behavior.

As a foreign policy, subsidies go back at least to Athens (and its rivalry with Sparta) and its system of allies during the classical Greek period (between 650 and 362 BC). In 402 BC, Thucydides argued that relations with other governments had to be based on self-sufficiency, even if it included economic exchanges. Exchange, as a pattern of interaction, evolved into the imperial system of the Roman Empire, a model that influenced both land-based imperialism and overseas colonialism after 1500.

Technical assistance, likewise, has a long history as an extension of social exchange among nations.[2] In 300 AD, in an early example of overseas technical assistance, Japan sent a number of Koreans to China to teach the art of weaving and preparing silk for production. Alexander the Great (336–323 BC) offered Egypt technical assistance during the founding of the great port city of Alexandria.

The earliest recorded instance of humanitarian assistance occurred in 226 BC when a huge earthquake devastated Rhodes. In response, nations around the Mediterranean sent food aid and other assistance to victims. There are examples of interterritorial assistance designed to solidify unity (and placate the gods) within the Roman Empire in times of war, famine, or natural disaster, such as droughts in Palestine, floods in Gaul, or the eruption of Mount Vesuvius.

During the Renaissance (1400–1600), steady exchanges of technical and cultural information throughout Europe cemented alliances and ensured support in war and trade. By the fifteenth and sixteenth centuries, the Medicis and the Tudor kings created alliances based on financial support as an instrument of diplomacy.[3] Niccolo Machiavelli, creator of realpolitik, advocated use of both the carrot and stick in international affairs.

The princely states of Italy—Milan, Venice, and Genoa—were characterized by stability and diplomatic astuteness that would latter define the European nation-state system arising out of the Enlightenment (1650–1789). Exchange was central to that system. As Steven Hook points out:

> Foreign assistance was not unknown to diplomats of the eighteenth or nineteenth centuries. Developed countries had long supplied allies with military equipment on concessional terms, and states often transferred funds overseas for disaster relief or other purposes. For example, French and Dutch aid to the United States was critical to U.S. success, in the Revolutionary War against Great Britain.[4]

Foreign aid, as a form of subsidy, presents not only a burden but also a privilege of leadership and power in world affairs. The subsidy relationship is "that of a quid pro quo; a subsidy relationship without reciprocity was unthinkable."[5] There is, as we will see in Chapter 3, a strong connection between the impact of foreign aid and Western imperialism.

Loans under preferential conditions came to life as an instrument of foreign policy after the 1850s. Loans meant a country would be admitted to a group with foreign securities deemed reliable enough to be listed and traded on major foreign exchanges. Access was often controlled by major powers through their national banks.

During the premodern period, specie money—precious metals such as gold and silver—undergirded the international monetary system. From the late 1700s, subsidies still meant cash in gold, not long-term credits.[6] Foreign loans were later used to build railroads and other capital construction projects in North America, Eastern Europe, Latin America, Asia, Africa, and the Middle East. The United States adopted British models of lending, which changed it from a debtor to a creditor nation after World War I.

War and the threat of war—often defined in imperial terms overseas, especially in Europe—have long characterized perceptions of unequal exchange. Loans and subsidies were an extension of the spoils of war, functioning as a form of state bribery, and serving as an alternative to armed conflict. According to George Liska, "Modern foreign aid derives from subsidies and loans to allies in fluid political and military conditions."[7]

Subsidies of absolutist statecraft in the 1600s and 1700s crystallized in the political economy of the nineteenth and twentieth centuries. Foreign loans in the liberal diplomacy of the pre–World War I era came next but did not replace subsidies. After World War I, both reparations and subsidies became part of the peace process, combining with other elements of what came to called foreign aid. These became tools of the Western countries after 1945.

Financial Inducements and Commercialism

From a political economy perspective, foreign aid is a support mechanism for the donor country's trade and commercial interests. There is the neo-Marxist school that extends this logic and sees foreign aid as part of a historical underdevelopment process that impoverished underdeveloped countries. For many critics, foreign aid is, at best, little more than a palliative that furthers the current international economic system. Use of financial inducements in international relations goes back hundreds of years in diplomatic intercourse. By the 1850s, technical assistance was a way to gain a foothold in the markets of Asian, African, Caribbean, and Latin American countries.

At the end of World War II, foreign aid would become one of several tools available to promote foreign policy. "What we call foreign aid," according to Hans Morgenthau, "stands largely in direct succession to what in previous periods of history, went by the name of subsidies."[8] Having seen reparations against the Axis powers destroy the peace twenty years after the Treaty of Versailles, focus after World War II was on reconstruction in Europe, a process that refined the principles of foreign aid. We will explore this in Chapter 5 when discussing the origins of international assistance in the wake of World War I.

It is no doubt true that the "development objectives of aid programs have been distorted by the use of aid for donor commercial and political advantage."[9] When donors offer official development assistance, they often use aid to compel support for their own interests. Donor countries often require that foreign aid be used to purchase their own services and goods, a procedure known as *aid tying*.

To many, it was the precepts of the "Protestant ethic" through economic reforms that would be central to the success of foreign aid.[10] That said, economic interests probably do not always constitute a dominant influence in foreign aid policy; rather, they are a continuous secondary concern. Commercial and trade interests have been a part of the broader political and security environment of foreign aid.

Humanitarian Impulses

Charity as a motivation retains a role in international assistance and foreign aid "even in a world with aid re-conceptualized in 'development compacts' or regimes of human rights" (as defined in democracy and governance programs).[11] Many scholars focus on issues of charity, religion, and humanitarianism. Motivations of those in the field, as well as the average citizen, often frame foreign assistance from a philanthropic, or in some cases, religious (faith-based) perspective.

Humanitarian concerns were important justifications for international assistance after World Wars I and II. Carol Lancaster points out that foreign aid after 1948 was also justified as a "response to world poverty which arose mainly from ethical and human concern[s]."[12] Humanitarianism began with the early influence of charity and compassion on international assistance in the 1700s through 1800s.

Initial concern for international assistance was on humanitarian and religious assumptions of philanthropic organizations of the sixteenth century. Humanitarian and development assistance had its origins in the eighteenth century and the Enlightenment, where many of the assumptions about underdevelopment, culture, and international ethics were formed. Many of these also evolved from the imperialism of the 1800s and early 1900s in which the United States had a tangential but significant role.

It was religion, and specifically proselytizing Christianity, that linked humanitarianism with missionary work into the twentieth century. From its modern origins in the early nineteenth century, and harkening back to the antislavery movement, it was philanthropy and NGOs that defined international assistance agendas until 1945.

Until after 1919, government-sponsored aid addressed humanitarian problems essentially charitable in their assumptions. Those who identified charity and philanthropy as motivations saw these as "grounded in puritan . . . concerns with self-improvement through self disciplining and partial renunciation" of worldly goods.[13]

Policymakers in more developed countries—especially the United States—tended to see their actions as generosity and justified foreign and military aid, including the use of force, to meet Cold War ideological and developmental goals. This trend continues in post–September 11.

A Moral Imperative

There has been one constant defining foreign aid for the last fifty years. At least part of the motivation for foreign aid has been ethical or moral in nature: to help people who have suffered economically through war, natural disaster, or structural underdevelopment.

The idealist school sees foreign aid as a moral issue, arguing that the developed world has an obligation to assist underdeveloped countries. Foreign aid was considered a moral obligation after World War II, although few scholars have examined foreign aid from an ethical viewpoint.

The key policy and ethical issue facing advocates of foreign aid is the extent to which it can and should be used to promote income redistribution, egalitarianism, or social equity.[14] Foreign aid's presumed influence on income distribution has been largely normative.[15] Recent evidence suggesting that foreign aid can assist the middle class and the working poor but not the poorest of the poor contradicts this. The bottom end of the social system is largely untouchable in the foreign aid process. At issue is whether support for the middle class in a developing country is enough to justify foreign economic and social assistance.

A related controversy revolves around values. To many, idealism is based on a more optimistic view of the world, as developed by Immanuel Kant (1724–1804) and later Woodrow Wilson (1856–1924). Following World War II, it was still the eighteenth-century Kantian views that influenced thinking on foreign aid. These assumed that the highest level of development required democratic societies with developing economies, freedom of dissent, and the protection of political rights and freedom of conscience.

Ultimately, policy problems and moral ambiguities have plagued aid, especially technical assistance, since 1945. These are rooted in the evolution of foreign aid policy during the last half-century but also in ethical, economic, and cultural assumptions, antecedents of government-to-government foreign aid. Thus, the next four chapters of this book go back to the period prior to 1948 to examine these antecedents.

Conclusion

Several factors have had an impact on the foreign aid process during the last two hundred years. Going back to the origins of the nation-state, there was always statecraft and commercial motives involved in international humanitarian assistance. In international relations, there are both a "realist paradigm in international relations theory . . . and cosmopolitan, cooperative, or altruistic strains" based on idealism, which operate in tandem.[16]

There are two broadly defined schools of foreign policy and foreign aid: a "hard" school and a "soft" school. The hard school focuses on security assistance and commercial concerns, and it is both costly and politically risky. The soft school takes the classical path of foreign aid with soft power being more effective than the use—or threat—of force in securing influence in international relationships.[17]

Soft power calls on well-endowed states to improve public health and education; introduce modern agricultural technologies; encourage small-scale industries; and carry out a wide range of agrarian reform, from land redistribution through the organization of cooperatives and provision of rural credit and farm inputs.

Foreign aid humanitarian and development goals sometimes become distorted through the use of aid by donor countries for commercial, military, and other political purposes. Prior to 1989, foreign aid, in large part, centered on Cold War influences between and among the super-powers. In the post–Cold War period, foreign aid often was offered as a carrot to tempt conflicting sides in civil strife into accepting mediation or as a component of the war on terror.

Beyond security concerns, all nations, large and small, have links between foreign aid and trade policies, and the private sector plays an important role in providing both commodities and services to foreign aid recipients. Humanitarian, and even moral arguments, justified foreign aid, but in the end, it was systems of international intercourse that framed the parameters of foreign aid. All of these factors, as perceived by political leaders, interest groups, and administrators in the field, helped define foreign aid into the twenty-first century.

For almost 500 years, it was the imperial system that began in the fifteenth century and the industrial revolution beginning in 1800 that defined global international relations and political economy. We turn to these issues next.

Notes

1. The classic is Hans J. Morgenthau, *Politics among Nations: The Struggle for Power and Peace* (New York: Alfred A. Knopf, 1948).

2. The next two paragraphs are taken from Carol Lancaster, *Foreign Aid: Diplomacy, Development, Domestic Politics* (Chicago: University of Chicago Press, 2007).

3. George Liska, *The New Statecraft: Foreign Aid in American Foreign Policy* (Chicago: University of Chicago Press, 1960), p. 37.

4. Steven W. Hook, *National Interest and Foreign Aid* (Boulder, CO.: Lynne Rienner Publishers, 1995), pp. 5–6. On the impact of nineteenth-century diplomacy see Henry Kissinger, *Diplomacy* (New York: Simon and Shuster, 1994).

5. Liska, *The New Statecraft*, p. 341.

6. See Robert Gilpin, *The Political Economy of International Relations* (Princeton, NJ: Princeton University Press, 1987), pp. 119–120 and Albert Fishlow, "The Debt Crisis in Historical Perspective," in *The Politics of International Debt*, Miles Kahler, ed. (Ithaca, NY: Cornell University Press, 1986), pp. 37–70.

7. Liska, *The New Statecraft*, p. 24.

8. See Hans J. Morgenthau, "Forward," in Liska, *The New Statecraft*, p. viii.

9. Peter Hjertholm and Howard White, "Foreign Aid in Historical Perspective, Background and Trends," *Foreign Aid and Development: Directions for the Future,* Peter Hjertholm, ed. (London: Routledge, 2002), p. 3.

10. See Max Weber, *The Protestant ethic and the spirit of capitalism* Translated by Talcott Parsons (New York, Scribner, 1958).

11. Des Gasper, "Ethics and the Conduct of International Development Aid: Charity and Obligation," in *Forum for Development Studies* (Oslo), 1, no. 1 (1999), p. 54. Entire article, pp. 23–57. Gasper of the Institute of Social Studies in The Hague has taken on the analysis of the ethnical debate over foreign aid.

12. Carol Lancaster, *Foreign Aid: Diplomacy, Development, Domestic Politics* (Chicago: University of Chicago Press, 2007), p. 4.

13. Ibid., pp. 38.

14. Terry F. Buss and Usama Ahmed, "Social Equity and Development," in James Svara and Norm Johnson (eds.), *Justice for All* (Armonk, NY: ME Sharpe, forthcoming).

15. Paul Mosley, *Overseas Aid: Its Defense and Reform* (Brighton, UK: Wheatsheaf Books, 1987), p. 156.

16. Ibid., p. 5.

17. See Joseph S. Nye, *Soft Power: The Means to Success in World Politics* (New York: Public Affairs Books, 2004), pp. 60–61.

3

HISTORICAL ANTECEDENTS

Mrs. Jellyby . . . is a lady of very remarkable strength of character [who] is at present (until something else attracts her) devoted to the subject of Africa, with a view to the general cultivation of the coffee berry—and the natives—and the happy settlement, on the banks of the African Rivers, of our superabundant home population.

Charles Dickens, *Bleak House*

"Why," she said, "it's natural to the folks here to be indolent. . . . They just haven't got any hustle in them."

Agatha Christie, *Murder on the Orient Express*

Today it is hard to believe that, as late as 1947, the Union Jack still flew over more than a quarter of the human race.

Christopher Booker, *The Neophiliacs*

A Half Millennium of Imperialism

Those who write about foreign aid usually assume that it is a post–World War II development. Stephen Browne, for instance, argues that overseas assistance "grew out of several processes unfolding in the immediate postwar era, and is thus about half a century old."[1] The view here differs, assuming a much longer legacy.

Antecedents of foreign aid, prior to 1948, are important. The history of international assistance provides an understanding of definitions, purpose, assumptions, motivations, and methods of government-to-government, government-to-business sector, and business-to-business assistance as they evolved since the 1950s. As we will see, use of public resources for humanitarian relief began in the eighteenth century. Development funds for European colonies began between the two World Wars, and the United States, partially in response to the Nazi influence in the Western

21

Hemisphere, began to assist its de facto Latin American dependencies in the 1930s.

European empires defined foreign aid after 1500. The Spanish and Portuguese, and later the French, British, and Dutch, followed by the Germans, Belgians, Italians, and even the Americans, all dabbled in empire building. All found themselves financially responsible for wide swaths of territory around the globe which would, though all tried to be parsimonious, drain the exchequer.

In this chapter we examine the legacy of 500 years of colonialism on international relief, foreign aid, and technical assistance. The terms "colonialism" and "imperialism" are so overused and abused by both dependency theorists on the left and religious nationalists on the right that it is easy to forget these real transnational systems of government were in place, though fading, when today's baby boomers were born. The year 1960—when many less developed countries (LDCs) became independent and Prime Minister Harold MacMillan made his "winds of change" speech in South Africa announcing the end of European dominance in Africa, and the imperial order—is significant.[2]

Several threads characterize imperial and financial history: state-to-state power relationships, state-to-nonstate concessional arrangements, and the evolution of humanitarian NGOs. Imperial systems required money, and in part, this money had to come from the "mother country." Though Europe has a history separate from the United States and other European settler countries, its history is an important factor in the evolution of the international system and US foreign aid policy, and overseas territories financial policy in the nineteenth and twentieth century.

Critics of foreign aid make three claims about the origins of foreign aid. First, development policies originated in the colonial systems that ruled most of the world prior to 1948. Second, foreign aid and international charity are an industry, as a component of organized religion and, ultimately, a commercial self-serving system. Third, no LDC ever transformed from starvation to food self-sufficiency through international charity. To the critics of international assistance, implications of this legacy were clear: "charity and development work are political [and] doing relief and development work in the context of oppression is counter-productive."[3] Promotion of development, if it is to transform systems, could well threaten political leaders of donor and recipient countries. Undertaking development work, moreover, can and to some should be a subversive activity! Thus, there are internal contradictions within the constructs of the international assistance system as it has evolved out of the last two centuries. Those advocating foreign assistance have to grapple with that dilemma.

The Missionary Factor

Historical processes and values of foreign aid go back to religious and cultural expansion. In 1095, Pope Urban II called for a crusade of Christian nations to wrest Asia Minor and the Levant from the Muslim Arabs. The Crusades ended in 1291 with the expulsion of the West from the Near East. This was the first phase of a religious and imperial struggle that, to some, continued down to and through the twentieth century. Some suggest that the conflict continues today, pitting the West against East.[4]

Religious conversion motivated the Crusaders and their descendents—seventeenth-, eighteenth-, and nineteenth-century missionaries. Furs, food, minerals, and trade goods were also targets of opportunity. Moreover, during the Crusades in the twelfth century, Europeans plundered Islamic holy sites and massacred Muslims in the name of God, pocketing the wealth they found.[5]

Conversion remained at the heart of the missionary influence in Asia, Africa, and Latin America from the beginning. But by 1700, Christians also saw themselves as agents of virtue, and in the 1800s, they tried to save Africans from slavery, give Asians access to health and education, and encourage subsistence farmers to move away from subsistence agriculture to commerce.

"Humanistic service and the philosophy behind it," as Ian Smillie notes, "is neither new, nor does it emerge from a particular place and time."[6] Historically, there were several components to the religious origins of international assistance and eventually foreign aid, including, for example, tithing—the requirements for charity and religious involvement in the organization of schools and hospitals. The tithing issue has resurfaced symbolically in the foreign aid debate of the late 1990s, when UN administrators asked developed countries to tax themselves even more to assist poor nations.

Tithing goes back at least 3,000 years in Jewish law, and in the Middle Ages, European churches, using parishioners' donations, became the dispenser of charity, provided hospitals, schools, and general welfare. Islam prescribes charity as one of the five pillars of wisdom.

The mission became part of overseas expansion of Europe in the fifteenth century. Many European NGOs trace their origins to missionary organizations and antislavery movements. One of the oldest was Les Soeurs de la Congregation de Notre-Dame, founded in 1653.[7] Sulpicians opened up North America for the French, and the Jesuits much of Asia. Overseas missions of the great European powers helped to define imperialism throughout its 400-year history.

Values and processes of international assistance, as opposed to subsidies and exchange, probably go back more than 300 years. Historically, for more than 200 years, voluntary organizations played a role in technical and humanitarian assistance. In both Europe and the United States, voluntary agencies date back to at least the 1830s and began to operate internationally by the 1850s. with one of the first efforts being that of Henry Dunant, founder of the International Committee of the Red Cross (ICRC) at the Battle of Solferino in the Austria-Sardinia War in 1859.

Voluntary organizations, antislavery societies, and religious groups defined the need and scope for international voluntary and social action groups from the late 1700s. In continental Europe, many NGOs became involved in international welfare efforts by the mid-nineteenth century, focusing on humanitarian and war relief, social reform, and charity.

Humanitarianism and relief efforts were important in time of war. Florence Nightingale, Mary Seacole, and Clara Barton led groups of volunteers to nurse the wounded in the Crimea and the American Civil War,[8] along Henry Dunant in the wake of the Crimean War. Dumont's ICRC, "dating from 1863, has through its disaster relief operations indirectly contributed to the spread of technical [and] administrative methods" of international assistance throughout the world.[9]

Impacts of Imperialism on International Assistance

More than in any other empire, the British Raj defined colonial rule and international development, eventually becoming a model for the United States.[10] In the British Empire—with Imperial India as the jewel in the British crown—international assistance began in the early 1800s, "with a handful of humanitarians driven by urges often half hidden from themselves."[11]

Abolitionist and missionary movements' efforts to end slavery were major forces in the imperial system. In much of Europe and North America, origins of international humanitarian involvement in Africa, the Americas, and the Indian Ocean reside in the antislavery movement of the late eighteenth and early nineteenth centuries.

Reformers in England founded the Anti-Slavery Society in 1787. This occurred as part of a set of missionary impulses that ironically would stimulate colonial expansion. European empires justified this as part of a "moral mission, with antislavery as its flagship."[12] To the abolitionist movement, ending the Atlantic and Indian Ocean slave trades rationalized European intervention in Africa and elsewhere.[13]

From the early 1800s, the missionary "of the old breed [was] an educator, not an evangelist, someone who had come to Africa to serve, to call it home, and to die in the bush."[14] Moreover, colonial missionaries were a nineteenth-century phenomenon with implications for the twentieth century. The educator, medical missionary, and humanitarian worker reflected the softer side of foreign policy.

Both the French and British sent missionaries to North America by the end of the eighteenth century. At the end of the Victorian period, European countries argued that colonialism was a beneficial process and would help to bring a backward world into the light of the modern age.[15] There were built-in contradictions to colonialism, however. The reality for French critics was that colonizers saw this humanitarian romanticism as a serious mental illness threatening the French empire.[16]

Throughout much of the 1800s, British colonial policy placated the ever-increasing demands of liberal missionaries, cloaking their Victorian social change policy in religion.[17] Imperial historians, pre–World War II, often ascribed philanthropic motives to British colonialists in the 1800s. Colonial administrators, in the 1800s Exeter Hall[18] tradition, "protected" the African population from European settler greed and avarice.

The Exeter Hall liberals of the Aborigines Protection Society, Society for the Extinction of the Slave Trade, and Civilization of Africa group challenged customary traditions of slavery from the Cape to the Caribbean and questioned the foundations for segregation and later apartheid in South Africa that would define the British imperial custom by the twentieth century. Nineteenth-century missionary schooling provided the "oppressed" with the skills "to put forward a refined political argument in English."[19]

Nineteenth-century missionary societies were the aid organizations of the Victorian period, "the old ladies of Clapham."[20] However, as the *Economist* puts it, looking backward, "The brave souls who spread the Lord's word in the 19th century often found the natives uncomprehending and hostile."[21] These misunderstandings have their counterparts in twentieth century international assistance.

By the mid-1800s, David Livingstone, as Niall Ferguson only partly tongue in cheek points out, "had become a one-man NGO: the nineteenth century's first medicin sans frontieres."[22] Albert Schweitzer and the American medical missionary Dr. Tom Dooley played a similar role at the dawn of the foreign aid era.[23]

There were more than 12,000 British missionaries in the field throughout and beyond the British Empire in 1900, representing more than 360 missionary societies and other organizations. One hundred years later, they and their counterparts from other counties were still there. At the start of the twenty-first century, the "modern equivalents of the mission-ary societies campaigned earnestly against 'usages' in far-flung countries that they regard as barbaric: child labour, [human trafficking] and female circumcision."[24] Victorian NGOs were not that different from their twenty-first-century counterparts.

Europeans and North Americans traveling to Africa and elsewhere in the late nineteenth century and early twentieth century often "were instilled with a sense of technological and moral superiority as they worked with indigenous peoples."[25] Some missionaries thought little of conversion but focused instead on health and education. Others used social services as bait to convert patients, students and their parents.

Missionaries often severely disturbed traditional social values in once socially and economically self-sufficient communities. This was so deftly demonstrated in Nigeria by Chinua Achebe in his acerbic novel, *Things Fall Apart*.[26] The wreckage of this community collapse resulted from incompat-ibility between stable, closely integrated folk cultures and an ever-changing machine civilization represented by the trader, soldier, and missionary.

The missionaries' goal was to save natives of the tropics, though many had few converts. Instead, missionaries taught by example, accepted as different by Christians, Moslems, Hindus, and Animists alike. In Africa, as in many other parts of the world, the seed of the European missionary had "not sprouted, and now it was decayed and moribund."[27]

Legacy of Colonialism

As late as 1947, Britain governed 25 percent of the world's population. Large chunks of Asia, Africa, and the Caribbean fell under the French, Dutch, and Belgians. The United States boasted a considerable de jure and de facto empire of its own. Along with the empire, many British settlers, missionaries, and colonial officials aspired to export their culture overseas.

Governance in the British and the other empires was only possible by co-opting the leadership of the oppressed. The key to creation of an Indian elite was British education. There were contradictions between metropolitan values and settlers and colonial officers in the field. Imper-ial beliefs at home had "paternalistic liberalism" embedded in them because the Victorians believed all men should have equal rights, regard-less of skin color.

The Anglo-Indians and white settlers in Africa, however, "preferred a kind of apartheid, so that a tiny white minority could lord it over the mass of 'blacks.'"[28] Colonialism perpetuated under the great trading compa-nies, the Dutch East Asia Company, British South Africa Company, and others that dominated colonial trade in the 1700s and 1800s. Settlers managed trading companies throughout the empire, engaging in agriculture, trade, and manufacturing production in the process.

The Empire divided people in Britain and those in the colonies into a class-based pyramid, with the upper classes in both countries having more in common with each other than with fellow countrymen. Links between elites among the colonizers and colonized, characterized by a common love of court fashion, uniforms, medals, pith helmets and other claptrap, has been described by one apologist for imperialism as "ornamentalism."[29]

International relations in the late nineteenth and early twentieth century, as directed toward the non-Western world, reflected the strange logical convolutions of Social Darwinism.[30] Racial and cultural imperialism were never far from the surface in imperial views of the non-Western world. Historically, both European and American policymakers found it difficult to overcome a black-and-white view of Asia and Africa.[31]

This colonial view of non-Western society remained with many Westerners as they interacted with the developing world throughout the twentieth century. Frances FitzGerald, writing about Southeast Asia explains:

> Unable to understand the natives, the French colonialists of the nineteenth century, along with their American counterparts in the rest of Asia [as well as the rest of the non-Western world] invented all of the racist clichés that have passed down into the mythology of the American soldier: that Orientals [and Africans and Arabs] are lazy, dirty, untrustworthy, and ignorant of the value of human life.[32]

Until the 1950s, most British policymakers, as well as those in continental Europe and the United States, carried "the prevailing attitude toward subject peoples. . . . Regardless of their history, they were not considered 'ready' for self-rule until prepared for it under Western Tutelage."[33] The League of Nations confirmed this, in that most former colonial dependencies of Germany, because they were located in Africa, were considered second-class mandates and not worthy of preparation for independence.

Throughout the colonial period, attitudes toward people in Asia and Africa were reflected in such words as "nigger," "wogs," "kaffers," "slopeys," and "gooks."[34] And yet, at the heart of the imperial system, was a claim that colonial officials, settlers, traders, and missionaries all had a "civilizing mission" in the dependent territories. More than anything else, no doubt because of these racial attitudes, one of the patterns of aid administration inherited by developed countries from the colonial period was an unofficial policy of benign neglect.

Victorious powers after World War I, at least temporarily, found they administered much of Europe, more permanently the Middle East, virtually all of Africa, and the Pacific, topped up by de facto control of Asia, the rest of Africa, and especially Latin America. At the same time, many of the post–World War I leaders—and most clearly Woodrow Wilson—feared leaving a poisoned legacy unfulfilled nationalism in their wake.

The World War I Allies promoted changes throughout Central Europe and, to a lesser extent, parts of the Middle East (though not in Asia and Africa) where a "modern ethnic nationalism superimposed itself on an older different world" of land-based imperialism.[35] Ethnic and religious nationalism were legacies of the imperial world of the 1800s, which would plague the twenty-first century.

In their memoirs, whites in sub-Saharan Africa often perpetuated an image of the "dark continent" and a "heart of darkness," suggesting gloom and alienation. In the view of some imperialists and missionaries, Africa symbolized the dark passions of the human soul of sinners in contrast with the efficiency and technology produced by rational and scientifically advanced Europe.

Colonialism's image etched itself in the memory of the generation that grew prior to World War II, and because "aloneness is the human condition, a stark example of the perfect stranger was the white man in black Africa, alone at his post, odd man out."[36] African savagery represented victory of passion over reason. In turn, indigenous peoples absorbed this hostility and returned it. The words "faranji" or "Aferingi," meaning the foreigner, describe the alien nature of the European presence in North Africa and the Middle East.[37]

The colonial model of foreign intervention initially concerned the notion of an "external protectorate." For their own well-being, indigenous peoples were barred from managing their own affairs to protect them from themselves and their neighbors. Dependence, and a sense of inadequacy, resulted from colonialism but was not its cause. In the end, colonial intervention destroyed and distorted indigenous institutions and left many colonized societies out of the mainstream in ideas, technology, and economic progress. It then became a challenge for foreign aid and technical assistance to put colonized peoples back into the mainstream.

"Cultural comfort," representing this mainstream, being culturally safe for language, custom, and dress—thus having indigenous peoples adopt Western behavior—was important both to missionaries and other Western officials, including aid workers. African women in Victorian dress and men in dark suits and ties (the Worried Oriental Gentlemen of memoirs and aspersion) in the tropics became symbols of Westernization. The first line of defense of the colonized was to change the dress, lighten the skin, or in some way change the physical appearance to become more like the colonial model. Such an image of cultural comfort fits well for aid workers, technical assistance specialists, and even in some cases Peace Corps volunteers.

From the beginning Europeans tended to interact with those they could trust, who were honest and trustworthy, and above all who could speak English or the other colonial languages.[38] What began as a search for cultural comfort ended by spreading European languages, particularly English, and Christianity. Resentment within administrative and settler communities was also a legacy of colonialism. Those in expatriate and settler communities who believed in empire saw it collapse first with horror, then with apathy.

In the immediate post-colonial period, Europeans and the United States looked to wield influence in their former colonies, neocolonies and protectorates. Many ex-colonial officers went into international development work after 1960. North-South relationships became institutionalized in the post-war period, and at the end of the colonial period, these institutions determined the role of the colonized and their relationship with the colonizer. Colonial society tended to be a managing/controlling law-and-order society and worked hard to give that appearance.

Much of the admitted stereotypes of Westerners, fitting into theories of modernization and development, have dominated foreign aid during the past sixty years. In the territorial unit, the colony had a limited recruiting ground from which to draw administrators. Those officials chosen to maintain the system contributed more vigor to its defense and often transformed themselves into foreign aid administrators when colonialism finally ended, reinforcing long-standing institutionalized North-South relationships.

Impacts of Imperialism on International Assistance

Origins of empire lay not in missionary or colonial impulses alone. The intersection of economic and commercial motives, political imperatives, and international relations combined to create the British and European empires—and Japanese and American empires—in the eighteenth and nineteenth centuries. This is not the place to review that history. Suffice it to say that in the British and other empires seeds were sewn for theories of modernization and developmentalism that would raise international assistance to national policy by the late 1930s.

International assistance to ex-colonies or neocolonies was a by-product of colonialism. Foreign aid policy and processes, including voluntary NGOs, was a product of the systems of empire that governed the non-Western world prior to 1960. "The Victorians had . . . elevated aspirations," according to Niall Ferguson, "and they dreamt not just of ruling the world, but of redeeming it. . . . Like NGOs today, Victorian missionaries believed they knew what was best for Africa."[39] The reality of superiority and inferiority, defined during the colonial period, remains prevalent today.

From the 1850s, it was common practice among Britain, France, Belgium, Holland, Germany, and even the United States to transfer money on concessionary terms to their colonies, protectorates, and dependencies. By the 1920s, the British and French used public funds for expansion of infrastructure, development of health services, and funding of education in their colonies. Treasury departments in home countries, of course, often resisted concessions because they drained the bank. Terms used to describe this process prior to 1940 were "infant colony subsidies," "grants-in-aid," and "budget supplements." As revealed in the next chapter, the United States developed similar patterns of financial intervention in its spheres of influence, particularly in Central and South America.

International assistance in part evolved out of de facto and de jure colonialism. Foreign aid and technical assistance schemes had antecedents in British, French, and other colonial rule. The British developed their Colonial Development and Welfare Fund in 1929, and France had similar programs in its Asian and African Empires. Even smaller and less developed colonial systems—Belgium, Holland, and Portugal—gave lip service to developmentalism in their colonial areas. The United States, as we will see Chapter 4, had foreign aid and technical assistance programs for its de jure and de facto colonies by the 1920s.

From the beginning, colonialism's goal was one of modernization and Westernization, because, according to one early advocate of development, in traditional society all desire for modernization was lacking. Traditional, underdeveloped societies were rural and poor. Developed societies were urban, industrial, and rich. Barbara Ward described what she called the positive elements of imperialism, "colonial rule abolished local wars and . . . modern medical science and modern sanitation began to save babies and lengthen life."[40] For Ward the next step was a Keynesian approach to economic development in the non-Western world.[41]

Institutionally, there was nothing apart from a few river commissions that could properly be called international administration until after the 1850s. Prior to World War I, however, some fifty public international organizations carried out development administration in many fields.[42] Organizations required the services of only a few hundred people and cost relatively little. Costs and personnel involved in international activity multiplied several-fold between the two world wars. Much of this international administration was indirect, however, funneled through colonial systems and, after 1918, the League of Nations mandates established after the War.

Conclusion

Government and administration "in most of the countries of Asia and Africa and more distantly, Latin America, [were] conditioned by their colonial pasts."[43] There was seldom significant delegation of authority or significant local self-government.

Colonialism defined authority in most of what we call the developing world until well after the 1960s and much of the practice of foreign aid and technical assistance grew out of that heritage. Understanding that legacy is important in any attempt to define the mixed legacy and the moral ambiguities that frame international assistance after 1960. These values remain an important factor in influencing foreign aid.

It is our contention that many of the characteristics of the colonial period—in terms of administration, development policy and normative values, some for better, many for worse—carried over to both bilateral and multilateral aid programs.

Our book does not argue that a history of colonialism and imperialism is the only driver of aid, security, and diplomacy in the twenty-first century. Much would occur in the evolution of foreign aid policy that was not a product of that history. Yet, to reiterate: three components of international assistance—economic exchange, commercial development, and religion-based humanitarian impulses—converged in the 1850s as the European powers, along with Japan and the United States, created worldwide empires. To what extent this convergence continues to define world governance is a focal point here.

Also at issue is to what extent there are similarities between Britain in the early twentieth century and the United States since 2000. In the latter case, the United States was overloaded with misused foreign aid and was made a pawn of its "attempts to secure that indefinable and ultimately unattainable thing [called] 'national security.'"[44] We will revisit this issue at various points in this book.

Notes

1. Stephen Browne, *Beyond Aid: From Patronage to Partnership* (Aldershot, UK: Ashgate Publishing, 1999).

2. Lawrence James, *The Rise and Fall of the British Empire* (New York: St. Martin's Griffin, 1994), pp. 615–616.

3. Michael Maren, *The Road to Hell: The Ravaging Effects of Foreign Aid and International Charity* (New York: Free Press, 1997), p. 88.

4. See Anthony Nutting, *The Arabs: A Narrative History from Mohammed to the Present* (New York: Mentor Books, 1965), pp. 171–180.

5. For an interesting perspective see Paul Theroux, *Dark Star Safari: Overland from Cairo to Capetown* (New York: Houghton Mifflin, 2003), p. 104. See also Robert Fisk, *The Great War for Civilization: The Conquest of the Middle East* (New York: Knopf, 2005).

6. Ian Smillie, *The Alms Bazaar: Altruism Under Fire: Non-Profit Organizations and International Development* (London: IT Publications, 1995), pp. 22–23.

7. Sisters of the Congregation of Notre Dame.

8. A.N. Wilson, *The Victorians* (New York: W.W. Norton & Company, 2003).

9. Walter R. Sharp, *International Technical Assistance* (Chicago: Public Administration Service, 1952), p. 8.

10. Niall Ferguson makes this argument. See his *Empire: The Rise and Demise of the British World Order and the Lessons for Global Power* (New York: Basic Books, 2003).

11. Deborah Scroggins, *Emma's War: An Aid Worker, A Warlord, Radical Islam, and the Politics of Oil—A True Story of Love and Death in the Sudan* (New York: Pantheon Books, 2002), p. 18.

12. Ibid., p. 45.

13. Michela Wrong, *In the Footsteps of Mr. Kurtz: Living on the Brink of Disaster in Mobutu's Congo* (New York: Harper Collins, 2001), p. 39.

14. Theroux, *Dark Star Safari*, p. 288.

15. Joseph N. Weatherby, *The Other World: Issues and Politics of the Developing World* (New York: Longman, 2000), p. 23.

16. Albert Memmi, *The Colonizer and the Colonized* (Boston: Beacon Press, 1991), p. 21.

17. The Victorian mission saw nineteenth-century Victorian England as an ideal model for a civilized society for Asia and Africa. See A. N. Wilson's wonderful book, *The Victorians*.

18. Exeter Hall was the celebrated gathering place in the Strand for the missionary and humanitarian societies that represented liberal thought in Britain. See for example, C. W. de Kiewiet, *The Imperial Factor in South Africa: A Study in Politics and Economics* (Cambridge, MA: Cambridge University Press, 1937).

19. See also Antjie Krog, *Country of My Skull; Guilt, Sorrow and the Limits of Forgiveness in the New South Africa* (New York: Random

House-Times Books, 1998), pp. 46–47. Also personal communication. Letter from Professor D. A. Kotze, then Professor, Department of Development Administration, University of South Africa, to one of the authors (Picard), June 28, 1985.

20. Clapham was the area in London where the various antislavery movements were located.

21. "The Missionaries' Position," *The Economist,* (April 24, 1993), p. 36.

22. Ferguson, *Empire,* p. 131.

23. Schweitzer established a hospital in Gabon, while Dooley worked in Vietnam.

24. Ferguson, *Empire,* p. 131.

25. David E. Apter, *Ghana in Transition* (Princeton, NJ: Princeton University Press, 1972), p. xv. Paul Theroux in *The Mosquito Coast* (New York: Penguin, 1982) vividly captures this process.

26. Chinua Achebe, *Things Fall Apart* (London: Heineman, 1962).

27. Theroux, *Dark Star Safari,* p. 320.

28. Ferguson, *Empire,* p. 204.

29. David Cannadine, *Ornamentalism: How the British Saw Their Empire* (Oxford, UK, and New York: Oxford University Press, 2001).

30. Richard Hofstadter discusses the links between Social Darwinism and American imperialism in his *Social Darwinism and American Thought* (Boston: Beacon Press, 1955), pp. 170–200.

31. See Wu Xinbo, "To Be an Enlightened Superpower," in *What Does the World Want from America? International Perspectives on U.S. Foreign Policy* Alexander T. J. Lennon, ed. (Cambridge, MA: MIT Press, 2002), p. 4.

32. Frances FitzGerald, *Fire in the Lake: The Vietnamese and the Americans in Vietnam* (New York: Vintage, 1972), p. 371.

33. Barbara W. Tuchman, *The March of Folly: From Troy to Vietnam* (New York: Alfred A. Knopf, 1984), p. 235.

34. Ibid., p. 241.

35. Margaret MacMillan, *Paris 1919: Six Months That Changed the World* (New York: Random House, 2003), p. 240.

36. Theroux, *Dark Star Safari.* See his prescient "Tarzan Is an Expatriate," republished in Paul Theroux, *Sunrise with Seamonsters: A Paul Theroux Reader* (Boston: Houghton Mifflin, 1985).

37. William Easterly, *The White Man's Burden: Why the West's Efforts to Aid the Rest Have Done So Much Ill and So Little Good* (New York: The Penguin Group, 2006).

38. Harlan Cleveland, Gerard J. Mangone, John Clarke Adams, *The Overseas Americans* (New York: McGraw-Hill, 1960), p. 34.

39. Ibid., p. 116.

40. Barbara Ward, *The Rich Nations and the Poor Nations* (New York: W. W. Norton, 1962), p. 42.

41. Ibid.

42. Quincy Wright, "Forward," in William C. Rogers, *International Administration: A Bibliography* (Chicago: Public Administration Service, 1945), p. iii.

43. Edward W. Weidner, *Technical Assistance in Public Administration Overseas: The Case for Development Administration* (Chicago: Public Administration Service, 1964), p. 7.

44. Caleb Carr, "William Pitt the Elder," in *What If? America—Eminent Historians Imagine What Might Have Been*, ed. Robert Cowley (London: Pan Books, 2005)

PART II

EPOCHS OF AID, DIPLOMACY, AND SECURITY POLICY

Behind the foreign expert lies a long tradition of white colonial exploitation.

> Ralph Linton, "An Anthropologist Views Point Four",
> *American Perspective*

The supply of good [educational] programs [in Asia] reflects . . . the long history of American missionary and business relationships in China and Japan.

> Harlan Cleveland, Gerard J. Mangone, and John Clarke Adams,
> *The Overseas Americans*

4

MANIFEST DESTINY AND AMERICAN EXPANSIONISM

Night after night McKinley paced the floor of the White House, and knelt beside his bed to pray.

Margaret Leech, *In the Days of McKinley*

With God's help, we will lift Shanghai up and up, ever up, until it is just like Kansas City.

John Franklin Campbell, *The Foreign Affairs Fudge Factory*

America is what everyone here wants to be like.

Mark Hersgaard, *The Eagle's Shadow*

American Expansionism

US imperial expansion was part of the country's perceived manifest destiny virtually from the nation's founding. This chapter examines the relationship between the cultural and political assumptions of manifest destiny and the origins of foreign aid and technical assistance. After examining early manifestations of international assistance, we look at US involvement in the Western and Eastern Hemispheres. The United States joined other industrial nations in the grab for land, all justifying their imperialism through assumptions about modernization, missionary activity, and technological superiority. These assumptions, in turn, contributed to foreign aid as the handmaiden of foreign and security policy in the twentieth and twenty-first centuries.

Manifest Destiny

Manifest destiny as a process began prior to the American Revolution when colonists from Virginia, New York, and Pennsylvania forced their

37

way into the Ohio Valley, touching off the French and Indian War. It continued with the new national government decisions after 1789 to push Native Americans off most of their lands. The Louisiana Purchase from Napoleon in 1803 doubled the size of the nation.

In 1823, President James Monroe asserted the Monroe Doctrine, stating: there would be no further European colonization in the Western Hemisphere; Europe would not be permitted to intervene militarily in Latin America; and the United States would not become involved in European affairs.[1] Most importantly, the Doctrine declared that the United States had a right to control other countries in the Western Hemisphere.[2]

The term "manifest destiny" was first used in the 1840s to promote expansion into Texas and California. For the United States, manifest destiny included cultural, social, and political values exportation, as well as geographical expansion. Manifest destiny would continue to affect foreign policy and foreign aid even after 1948. For most of the 1800s, expansion was continental and incorporative and—except for expropriation of Native American nations and the status of slavery—territorially egalitarian. Territories eventually became part of the Union.

Up to the 1850s, many leaders assumed the United States would eventually incorporate Canada and Mexico, not to mention parts of Central and South America and the Caribbean Islands. The Doctrine initially impacted US policy in the US-Mexican War (1846–1848), which brought the southwestern third of Northern America forcibly into the United States.

Large swatches of territory, Spanish Florida and related territories, such as the Mississippi Territory, were bought. The Indian Wars (1835–1842) incorporated the central plains into the Union. Treaties with Britain and continued conflict with Native American nations completed the conquest of what became the continental United States. With the purchase of Alaska from Russia, the United States began to look beyond the continent to fulfill its ambitions.

Next steps included expeditions of exploration out into the Pacific and, in some cases, conquest to Hawaii, the South Pacific, Japan and China.[3] Following the expansion of manifest destiny overseas, the Roosevelt Corollary (1904) to the Monroe Doctrine proclaimed that the United States "should prohibit incursions by foreign creditor nations into the hemisphere by undertaking preemptive invasions and occupations of those Latin American countries that failed to honor their debts."[4] The United States used this principle to intervene in many states in the Caribbean and Latin America well into the twentieth century.

US foreign policy from the 1890s was isolationist; however, the policy was not lacking in strong, positive assertions of authority in the Caribbean or Far East in an attempt to protect commercial interests.[5] Business and church leaders were among those who saw an obligation to guide less fortunate people and territories, to bestow upon them the enlightenment of stable institutions and culture—in short, exporting American values.

The United States annexed Hawaii in 1893 after a bloodless coup by American settlers against Queen Liliukalani. American settlers distained the native Hawaiian population, and from the beginning, they pressed for outright annexation.[6] Expansionists viewed Hawaii as a gateway to the Far East.

From the early nineteenth century, expansionists had demanded that Cuba either be given its independence from Spain or be purchased by the United States. Resistance to Spanish rule in Cuba simmered from the 1850s, especially after the insurrection of 1895, until the United States invaded the island in 1898. The success of the Spanish-American War defined American foreign policy for the next half century.

The Impact of the Spanish-American War

The Spanish-American War was fought until an armistice was declared on August 12, 1898. The War was steeped in emotion, from the sinking of the Maine (February 15, 1898) to Admiral Dewey's capture of Manila Bay, which caused a "delirious celebration" in the United States.[7] Secretary of State John Hay called it "a splendid little war."[8]

With victory over Spain, the United States was ripe with excitement and "dizzy and drunk with glory, and prostrate in admiration"[9] for President William McKinley, Admiral Dewey and the other instant heroes generated by this brief, and seemingly easy, war. The war validated manifest destiny in the Western Hemisphere. The "yellow journalism" of William Randolph Hearst and Joseph Pulitzer effectively called out for imperialism.

The United States had become a colonial empire by the turn of the century. In addition to annexing the Midway Islands in 1867 and Hawaii in 1893, the United States acquired the Philippines, Guam, and Puerto Rico as colonies. Cuba became a protectorate.[10] In 1898 and 1899, the United States annexed Johnson Island, Wake Island, and Palmyra Island as naval outposts. It also leased the Canal Zone from Panama (1903) and purchased the Virgin Islands from Denmark (1916). Policymakers often used the term "protectorate" rather than colony to describe the territories controlled, defining the empire more as a trusteeship. People in the colonies probably were not always understanding of the distinction. (See Table 4.1 on the US Protectorate System.)

With its new empire extending East and West, the United States constructed the Panama Canal between 1903 and 1914, not only for commercial but also military purposes. The canal became a model for high-cost international construction projects well into the twentieth century.[11]

Table 4.1 The US Associated States and Territories in the
Twentieth Century[12]

Name of Territory	Current Status	Population (2000 unless otherwise noted)
Republic of Palau	Associated State	19,129
Federated States of Micronesia	Associated States	107,000
Republic of the Marshall Islands	Associated State	50,840
Commonwealth of the Mariana Islands	Associated State (Commonwealth)	60,000
US Virgin Islands	Territory	120,000 (1999)
Guam	Territory	151,968 (1997)
American Samoa	Territory	59,000 (1995)
Commonwealth of Puerto Rico	Commonwealth Associated with US	3,897,960 (2004)
District of Columbia	Federal District	575,000
Republic of Philippines	Independent	86,241,697 (2004)
Panama Canal Zone	Incorporated into Panama	62,000 (1979)
Cuba	Independent	11,308,764 (2004)

Officially, the United States claimed its administration in the Philippines
was temporary until the eventual establishment of a free, prosperous, and
democratic government. But first it had to fight a protracted war with the
Philippines independence movement led by Emilio Aguinaldo from 1899 to
1901. Thereafter, US officials, in the 1920s and 1930s, pursued humanitarian and developmental programs to help establish a democratic government and rule of law. The Philippines only received its independence on
July 4, 1946.[13]

During 1898, factions debated whether the United States should annex
Cuba outright rather than pacify it or set up an autonomous government
under a protectorate. Both sides portrayed US involvement as a moral
issue and part of a crusade to further civilization. Policymakers advocating a protectorate prevailed with the Platt Amendment.

The Platt Amendment, sponsored by Senator Orville H. Platt, was
a rider to the US Army Appropriations Bill of 1901. It transferred
Guantanamo Naval Base to the United States in perpetuity and stipulated
that Cuba not transfer its land to any other foreign power. Until 1934,
the Platt Amendment mandated conditions for military and administrative intervention in Cuba.

Cuba under Platt could not contract foreign debt without US supervision, and Platt provided for US intervention in Cuban affairs whenever a
US administration deemed it necessary. The Platt Amendment was incorporated into Cuba's "independence" constitution. The United States

intervened several times in Cuba under Platt,[14] and in effect, Cuba remained a US protectorate until 1934, when Platt was repealed although US de facto intervention continued until the end of Cuban Revolution in 1959.

Buoyed by the Cuba experience, President Theodore Roosevelt (1901–1909) asserted that the United States could prohibit incursions by foreign creditor nations into the Western Hemisphere and occupy any hemispheric country that did not honor its debts. Then, Secretary of War (and later President) William Howard Taft announced in 1905 that henceforth the United States would practice "Dollar Diplomacy," controlling territories in its sphere of influence through guaranteed investment and financial control.

The American Empire included three groupings of countries: an inner group of colonies and protectorates that were de jure US territories; a second group that were de facto protectorates where the United States regularly intervened; and a third group where the United States had special interests and economic and political influence.

The Philippines, Puerto Rico, the Virgin Islands, Guam, and the Pacific territories were de jure protectorates. For many, the Philippines would be the cornerstone of a new American Empire in the Pacific. Hawaii, Cuba, and the Canal Zone also were administered at various times as protectorates or trust territories.[15] Countries where there was significant US involvement and rights of intervention and protection included Panama (from the US Canal Zone), Haiti, Nicaragua, Honduras, the Dominican Republic, and in Africa, Liberia. Throughout the first half of the twentieth century, the United States intervened in Latin American countries dozens of times to protect its interests. Other territories, where the United States had significant interests and intermittent involvement and, in some cases, intervention privileges, included El Salvador, Costa Rica, Bolivia, Ethiopia, Paraguay, Peru, Turkey, Persia, Siam, and China. It was in China that foreign policy defined an "open door" for US interests there.

What was different about these overseas dependencies, from the earlier expansion across the continent, was conquered territory—except for Hawaii—would never become part of the Union or enjoy federal status. New territories would have a subordinate relationship with the United States. This was a departure from the earlier continental expansion in Texas, California, the Louisiana Purchase, and Alaska.

The Republican Party under McKinley "had launched the ship of state on the crowded lanes of empire."[16] The United States, as it entered the twentieth century, was a worldwide sea power with pride and aspiration that would define it to the present day. Except in the very narrow sense of military alliances in continental Europe, prior to World War I and in the interwar period, the country was no longer isolationist. US foreign assistance motives and policy had much of their origins in the American "Empire" prior to 1939, just as British foreign aid devolved out of the British Empire. It is to these historical antecedents that we now turn.

Historical Antecedents of International Assistance

Well into the nineteenth century, the United States was essentially a developing country, seeking loans, credit facilities, and military assistance from Europe. US commissioners, including Benjamin Franklin and John Adams, sought both financial and military assistance from France and Holland during and after the Revolutionary War.[17] Loans from the Netherlands and France were important in sustaining the fledging republic.[18] American leaders looked to Britain and Europe for financial assistance throughout much of the 1800s.

As a developing country, the United States, because of its ethnic and racial diversity, is one that had appeal internationally.[19] In a fundamental way, foreign aid policy in the United States is as old as the republic. As John Montgomery has noted:

> The idea that America has a special mission in the world—to be the city on the hill that shows other countries how a republic ought to be governed—is old enough to be a part of the national heritage. . . . [The US appeared to have a] special calling to save the world.[20]

Origins of US state-supported foreign aid date back to the late 1700s and the first years of the republic. In 1793, Americans provided shelter and assistance to refugees displaced by revolution in Santo Domingo (now Haiti). In 1812, Congress passed a program of relief and assistance to victims of an earthquake: The 1812 Act for Relief of the Citizens of Venezuela. In the 1820s, the United States provided aid to Greek nationalists in their fight against the Ottoman Empire. Aid assisted starving families in Ireland during the Great Famine of 1847–48. Though Congress rejected public money for Ireland, private money assisted victims and the Navy transported assistance to Ireland.

Prelude to US Intervention

After 1800, the United States developed political and financial links with countries in Africa, Asia, and the Near East, in addition to historical links with Liberia, Turkey, Siam (now Thailand), and most importantly with China. Persia (now Iran) likewise utilized services of financial and economic advisers, American as well as British, in the late nineteenth and early twentieth century.[21]

US missionary impulses began in the 1800s in Africa and Asia and continued throughout the early part of the twentieth century.[22] In 1911, for example, a missionary opened a mission in Nasir, Southern Sudan, a center that would later be associated with the long-running Sudanese civil war in the twenty-first century. Missionary and humanitarian organizations distributed food surpluses in Europe and the Near East after World War I. Historically, there was an evangelistic flavor to protestant missionary work that Latin American intellectuals often labeled American "cultural imperialism."

Rivalry with Europe was never far from the surface in technical assistance to the Near East, Africa and Asia; however, at "the same time that the world was becoming aware of American preeminence in sanitation and public health and was turning to it for advice, it was also becoming familiar with the special emphasis that American education played on practical approaches and on training for the actualities of vocational and social living."[23]

As a great power, the United States continued foreign aid during World War I, much in the form of loans or the new "dollar diplomacy." In Europe, repayment of war loans was a part of all postwar negotiations on the future of Europe and was one of the causes of World War II.

International aid was one tool in the US foreign policy toolbox during the interwar period and provided a model for technical assistance after World War II. Despite this increased activity, until World War II, the United States had no systematic training beyond language teaching for overseas officials, diplomatic, technical, or economic.

NGOs and the Great Foundations

Throughout the 1800s, policymakers targeted foreign aid toward Latin America. Many of the antecedents of international assistance involved NGOs, many of which were faith-based. After 1899, creation of the American protectorate system—what we now call foreign aid and technical assistance—intensified within the US sphere of influence, often linked to what Patterson et al. called "financial supervision" interventions like those in Haiti, Cuba, the Dominican Republic, and Nicaragua.[24]

The United States mounted a full-scale assistance program in health, education, and public works in the Philippines after it defeated the Philippine rebels. Private sector economic involvement was important in Liberia, particularly in how Firestone Rubber affected the rubber extraction process.

In the American context, foreign and international aid became an act of charity, or at least philanthropy.

Andrew Carnegie was the first to distinguish between charity and philanthropy: charity involves giving to those in need (aligned to humanitarian assistance), while philanthropy provides money to assist those who wish to help themselves. This paternalistic distinction has defined development practices since the early 1900s.[25]

Privately endowed foundations, built on the fortunes of the early captains of industry, were among the forerunners to modern foreign aid. According to David Sogge, speaking of the nineteenth century origins of major foundations (Ford, Rockefeller and Carnegie):

> From the onset of their work in the first two decades of the twentieth century, they shunned conventional philanthropy, that is, charity via small-scale, short-run activities with palliative intent. Instead, they pursued what John D. Rockefeller called wholesale philanthropy: longer term, substantial support to activities with constructive or preventive intent by way of strategic institutions, particularly those creating and transforming policy. They saw themselves in the business of applied rationality, science and public uplift through social planning.[26]

Humanitarian assistance derives from charitable giving as defined in the nineteenth century. Development assistance, and in particular technical assistance, evolved out of philanthropy and involves the establishment of institutions (e.g., the famous Carnegie Libraries) and processes (teams of experts) to assist countries, organizations, and people to help themselves. Private foreign advisers and consultants worked directly with foreign governments.[27] They would remain active into the twenty-first century.[28]

Much overseas assistance was once the responsibility of large private foundations: Ford, Rockefeller, and Carnegie being the most famous. The Near East Foundation and the American Friends Service Committee were established after World War I, while the Unitarian Service Committee, the Brethren Service Commission and the Mennonite Central Committee were created after World War II (with the Gates Foundation established in the 1990s).

US missionaries continued to be active in Latin America and the Caribbean, Africa, Asia, and parts of the Middle East throughout the twentieth century, establishing schools, health clinics, social service centers, and demonstration farms. Ultimately, however, though private foundations and NGOs continued to play a role, US government-centered support of economic and social (and political) development in less developed countries

(LDCs) became important after 1930 (especially in Latin America) and dominated the post–World War II world.

Early Technical Assistance

In 1954, Merle Curti and Kendall Birr published a remarkable book on foreign aid covering the period, 1838–1938, stating,

> In this study we have concentrated on American technical missions abroad which have been in one way or another government-sponsored. We have used "technical" in a broad sense of the word; as used here it includes virtually all kinds of useful knowledge or scientific information which can aid in the conduct of human affairs. We have included knowledge which is relevant to the solutions of social as well as physical problems.[29]

Throughout the nineteenth century, the United States, through private and public funds, sponsored a number of scientific and exploratory expeditions around the world. Such missions were "less [than] dramatic in character, the coast, geodetic, and topographical surveys in other countries executed by American government agencies were, in a sense, technical missions."[30]

Technical cooperation activities had their origins in nineteenth-century patterns of involvement that combined exploration, investigation, and the gathering of technical information. In this sense the Louis and Clark expedition (1804–1806) was typical.[31] American exploration began in the Western Hemisphere and (in competition with European explorers) expanded to Africa, Asia, and the Pacific by the 1830s (with the voyages of the British scientists, Charles Darwin among the most famous). Many of these missions and expeditions were technically very successful. It is important to keep in mind, however, that unlike claims made in the twentieth century, motives for technical assistance often were explicitly commercial rather than philanthropic; there was little or no connection between these activities and philanthropy. Often, foreign countries paid expedition and technical mission costs.

It was common for the United States to receive a request for technical mission to a country in Latin America, the Near East, or Asia. International technical assistance was part of a process of expansion, based on economic interest, on national pride, and sometimes on humanitarian zeal. The pattern seldom varied.

By the 1870s, a number of foreign governments had turned directly to the United States for aid and assistance in solving their technical, local, or internal problems. Many of the earliest requests for American technical aid came from Latin Americans. The recipient group included European, Latin American, and Asian countries.

In the late nineteenth century, there was significant competition among the Western powers to provide technical assistance, particularly to Asian countries. This meant that over time the role of the technical adviser was as much to promote the donor country's products and equipment or its strategic interests as it was to provide assistance, a pattern followed in later foreign aid. By the 1890s, agricultural and other technical missions tied to the sales of products had become increasingly common.

From a US perspective, these technical missions were official ventures designed to serve the needs of the American economy and to ensure business access to underdeveloped areas. By the twentieth century, it had become "increasingly clear . . . that other countries were finding it profitable to look to America for expert assistance in solving their varied problems and were finding the technical mission to be a suitable instrument. . . . [Technical assistance] was, in the eyes of the one American observer, a remarkable combination of philanthropy and sound business."[32]

There were a number of examples of cultural differences between those giving technical assistance and those receiving it. Often, advisers, as a result of cultural chauvinism, assumed they knew better than those advised. Many experts, however, concluded that in comparison with Western standards, work done in the recipient country amounted to very little. Interestingly, nineteenth century experts—scientists, educators, or engineers—like their twentieth century counterparts, often doubted their contribution to LDC development.

Education became a major component of early international assistance. As a result of nineteenth-century technical assistance and international aid:

> European and American universities became centers of instruction for foreign students. Europeans and Americans sometimes became teachers in foreign lands. Missionaries carried with them information useful for life in the here as well as in the hereafter. Engineers, colonial governors, businessmen, and philanthropic foundations all lent a hand in carrying on this trade in ideas.[33]

The initial technical assistance and foreign aid focus, prior to 1940, was on Latin America, as well as other nations where the United States had historical interests. The remainder of this chapter examines this historical experience because it is seldom discussed in contemporary debates on foreign aid policy. Focus is on processes and values of international assistance that evolved out of this period. We discuss cases of

US international assistance from the founding of the republic into the early twentieth century. This period is important to understand because values, structures, and processes that later became entrenched in foreign aid had their origins here. Beginning by examining Western Hemisphere incursions, this chapter then looks at US involvement in the Eastern Hemisphere prior to World War I.

Interventions in the Western Hemisphere: The Latin American Conundrum

Hemispheric Technical Assistance

US foreign aid developed first in the Americas. In Central and South America, the United States, asserting the Monroe Doctrine, dominated the hemisphere in political terms, though a number of European powers, especially Britain, had significant financial influence. "For the family of American nations (exclusive of Canada)," according to Walter C. Sharp, "an evolving regional system, the origins of which date back to 1890, has long been a focus for cooperative assistance in the cultural, economic, and technical domain."[34]

Early on, Mexico came to the attention of explorers and scientists. The US-Mexican War stimulated information-seeking and exploratory activities in countries south of the Rio Grande. Before the war's end, a team of army engineers had surveyed the valley of central Mexico and prepared reports essential for completion of railway projects in the Southwest. Expansionism led to annexation of more than a third of Mexico by the United States. Resentment over annexation persists to this day.

Mexico continued to attract explorers, scientists, and miners from the United States throughout the 1900s. An American local government practitioner,

> [Henry] Bruere, who had been director of the New York Bureau of Municipal Research and Chamberlain of the City of New York . . . [during his stint as financial adviser in Mexico] successfully discharged broad responsibilities for studying and improving administrative organization and procedure.[35]

After 1900 the majority of US assistance missions went to Latin America (with some going to the Far East). At the end of the Spanish-American War, Cuba and the Philippines were the two anchors of the new American Empire. Nor was it an accident that American technical missions became more prominent at the turn of the twentieth century. By then the United States had become a world power, and requests for American missions became more frequent. American motives, in some cases, were not always clear to the recipient countries.

Prior to World War II, much foreign aid and technical assistance coincided with periods of US formal intervention in Latin America and its other client states.[36] During these interventions, there was concern about efficient and effective administration, especially financial management. In Central America, the United States tried to build model Caribbean republics in Cuba, Haiti, and Nicaragua.

Interventions, whether in Latin America or elsewhere, grew out of a combination of economic interests, humanitarian sentiments and strategic considerations. In Central and South America, the United States was much more deeply committed to occupation than it had ever envisioned.

The basis of this early excursion into nation-building was that the United States, in its spheres of influence, developed many of its plans on American middle-class standards, goals, and assumptions and on the moral certainties of Protestantism. City planners were prominent among advisers from the beginning. The search for middle-class patterns of governance was never fully achieved in Central America but remained a long-term goal of foreign aid, not only in Latin America but throughout the world.

Cuba: The Model Protectorate

Nowhere is nation-building under the American protectorate better represented than in Cuba. Nor have the consequences been more important and the experiment been so tragic. As was the case later in China, Liberia, Iran, and Vietnam, the closer the US field administration got to the situation on the ground, the greater the extent policymakers knew what was best for the country. In the end, aid failed and relations deteriorated into anger and frustration on both sides after 1959.

Cuba is worth examining in some detail because it offers an example of a fumbling experimental approach that eventually led to a fairly coherent development policy that would be replicated in other parts of Latin America. Not surprisingly, the protectorate period in Cuba bears some semblance to that in Iraq at present.

Leonard Wood, a doctor, was the military governor of Cuba from 1899 to 1902. Wood used his medical experience to introduce improvements to health care and sanitation in Cuba and to exterminate communicable diseases, especially yellow fever. To execute his task, self-described as the building of a Cuban nation, General Wood

> devoted himself to a series of reforms designed to develop a sound financial system, a prosperous nation, a healthy and literate people, a good judicial system, and a sound constitutional

government. To achieve these ends he had at his command a military government and an extraordinary amount of personal energy.[37]

The early administration of Cuba was a mixed bag. Anglo-Saxon legal techniques (such as trial by jury) and American electoral laws were not very successful. The occupation often used services of Americans who may or may not have spoken Spanish. Some people trained in Cuba, however, formed the nucleus of a growing colonial service that moved around the world and would merge into the aid bureaucracy after World War II.

In Cuba, Wood's top priority was the creation of an American-style education system to transform and Americanize Cuban culture. At the time, fewer than half of the children of school age were enrolled in school. This was not acceptable to the American occupiers. Education specialists who were brought in concluded that the existing situation failed to provide for adequate inspection of schools, books, and resources and it neglected teacher examinations. The occupation government wrote a new education law based on Ohio, where the American-appointed director of education had taught for several years.

What was needed, according to the American advisers, was practical education designed to help rural Cubans adapt to their agricultural environment. The Cuban occupation introduced locally controlled school boards. Cuban school board members proved to be either incompetent or corrupt. School board elections were often fraudulent, and teaching appointments became political footballs. School boards often were extravagant or dishonest with their funds. The situation was difficult because American policymakers concluded that literacy was a prime requisite of stable democratic government, the purported aim of the short formal occupation.

The administration purchased or accepted donations of textbooks in wholesale lots. Books were Spanish translations of American texts as there were few good Spanish or Cuban textbooks. The administration's policy was to support human resource development and use of US educational institutions to support social and political development. Donation of books (and health equipment), still standard fair for USAID, dates back to the Cuban experience.

Beyond political control issues, disease control was a primary area of concern for health specialists in Cuba, with physical sanitation efforts linked to this as well, as other aspects of what the US Army called its cleanup campaigns. Yellow fever, malaria, and cholera were continual targets. The public works campaign was massive and had a major impact on Cuba's economy.

The US intervention in Cuba was more comprehensive than all but a few aid programs in LDCs after World War II. The downside of this was that Cuba was overadministered, undergoverned, and controlled by a series of local dictators eventually beholden to the American mafia. In the aftermath of World War II, the mob ran Cuba as a tourist mecca for gambling and prostitution until the last American-backed Cuban dictator, General Fulgencio Batista y Zaldívar was overthrown by Fidel Castro on January 1, 1959.

The Haiti Example

Throughout the nineteenth and twentieth centuries, interventions in Haiti demonstrate a second pattern of US involvement[38] more episodic than Cuba. While Haiti was nominally independent after the revolution led by Toussaint Louverture in 1791, US involvement continued throughout the nineteenth century, intensified after the Spanish-American War, and continued throughout the twentieth century to the present. The United States occupied Haiti continuously between 1915 and 1934 in response to political instability, rioting, and threats to American commerce.

In 1914, as Haiti edged closer to bankruptcy and with each succeeding government becoming increasingly unstable, Secretary of State William Jennings Bryan under President Woodrow Wilson sought a customs receivership arrangement similar to that in other Central American countries. This would allow the United States financial control over the territory and the authority to appoint a financial czar.

The United States intervened in Haiti in 1915 after a great deal of revolutionary turmoil and the collapse of extended negotiations between the parties in Haiti. This intervention made the United States a protectorate authority over Haiti, and while the presence of the American Marines freed the government from the influence of the revolutionaries, it also made Haiti dependent upon American aid for its continued existence.

This US intervention in Haiti lasted until 1934, and while restoring some semblance of law and order, it had made the country formally a US dependency for close to twenty years. Influence in Haiti in the 1940s and 1950s remained deep, and for many years, the United States propped up Haiti's long-term dictator, "Papa Doc" Duvalier. In the wake of civil disorder, the United States intervened again in 1994 and 2004, first to restore former president Jean Aristide to power after a military coup, then to maintain order after the second overthrow of Aristide a decade later.

The long-term goal of the United States in Haiti was to introduce financial reforms, establish law and order, and provide development funds to implement expanded American-financed development programs. Throughout the twentieth century and into the twenty-first, these hopes appeared doomed to disappointment, leaving Haiti, one of the poorest countries in the world, in the grips of rigid, violent dictatorships or weak civilian regimes, utterly dependent upon international welfare and remittances from overseas Haitians.

The Eastern Hemisphere

Unlike the situation in Latin America and the Caribbean, US involvement in the Eastern Hemisphere was hesitant, uncertain, and intermittent. Nonetheless, as the 1890s progressed, the United States increasingly became part of the imperial system that governed Asia, the Middle East, and Africa. It came to play a major role in African and Asian countries that escaped formal imperialism but functioned as *de facto* colonies during the imperial age: Liberia, Ethiopia, Afghanistan, Persia, Thailand, and most importantly, China.

Requests for assistance came from many other parts of the world where the United States had special interests prior to World War II. In Africa and Asia, however, the United States was in direct competition with the great imperial powers, particularly Britain, to a much greater extent than in Latin America, though for much of the twentieth century it would cooperate with the European powers on security matters. Eventually, the United States would take a critical attitude toward European imperial systems (under Franklin Roosevelt), less for humanitarian reasons than for the economic exclusionary practices of what came to be called colonial or "imperial preference."

In Asia, policymakers called for an "open door" to American influence and trade in European spheres of influence while they developed spheres of influence of their own. In practice, however, patterns of involvement in nominally independent states, such as Persia, Ethiopia, and Afghanistan, were similar to those in the Western Hemisphere. In the remainder of this chapter, we look at one case study from Africa—Liberia—and two from the Middle East—Turkey and Persia. We conclude with a brief discussion of US foreign assistance activities in Asia prior to World War II.

Liberia

Freed American slaves arrived in Liberia in 1821. Between 1821 and 1847, the United States, through the government-sponsored American Colonization Society, was the de facto protectorate power in the country. Robert Finley established the Society in 1816 to afford abolitionists (philanthropists and clergy) a vehicle to free slaves and provide them and their descendants with a way to repatriate to Africa.

American white governors, who were US federal government agents, governed Liberia on behalf of the Society.[39] In 1822, the US government appropriated $100,000 to support the Society, one of a series of grants, "to assist in the purchase of land, the construction of homes and forts, the acquisition of farm implements, the payment of teachers, and the carrying out of other projects necessary to the care, training and defense of the settlers."[40] Little of this money ever reached Liberia.

In 1847, white governors handed over Liberia to the returned ex-slave settlers and the country became a nominally independent republic. Though the United States was parsimonious in its financial assistance in the 1900s, cultural links between the black republic and the United States remained close. During this period, the territory suffered internal strife, occasionally causing the United States to display its naval power off the Liberian coast.

In 1850, the United States published the report of the Reverend Ralph R. Gurley that concluded "Liberia lacked the financial means to develop its harbors, its agricultural resources, and its educational agencies."[41] The implication was clear: the United States should provide the financial support for Liberia to develop its infrastructure.

About 1900, the United States became more involved in Liberia. Patterns of intervention bear some resemblance to its involvement in the Caribbean and Central American states. European encroachment on Liberia, potentially threatening US investments, eventually became a concern. As a result of increased security concerns:

> Liberia's army was created in 1907 [and] President William Howard Taft sent the first US training officers to help out in 1912. . . . The [Liberian] army fought twenty-three brutal wars against indigenous uprisings, and the United States intervened directly in nine of them.[42]

Liberia was the site of some US technical assistance activity prior to World War I. In June 1908, for example, when the Liberian government became convinced that British mentorship would not assist Liberia and might threaten the independence of the country, a special commission was sent to Washington to urge it to help maintain the independence of the republic and to assist it in the creation of an efficient government. Speaking of Liberia, Curti and Birr note:

> Putting its cards on the table, the Liberian government at the start made it clear what it hoped for from the United States: a guarantee of its independence and territorial integrity; a customs receivership comparable to that of Santo Domingo; American

aid in policing the frontier; assistance in vocational education; and a research center for the promotion of public health and for the development of the republic's resources. The center was to be staffed with American experts.[43]

There were several attempts after World War I to induce the United States to provide financial support for Liberia, but it remained limited. In 1923, however, Firestone Rubber decided to intervene in the country in order to protect its investments. A US-guaranteed loan allowed the country to build up its infrastructure to support the rubber plantation dominated mono-export economy.

During this period, friction and racial tension between Liberians and Americans heightened because many of the latter came from the American South. World War II and its aftermath brought Liberia into the mainstream of international diplomacy, professionalized foreign aid workers, and increased access to aid. As other African countries became independent after World War II, US aid policy in Liberia came to resemble its intervention in former French and British colonies. The country was no longer considered a preserve of the American South.

Liberia continued to be a client state throughout the 1950s and 1960s, receiving significant amounts of educational assistance (in return for US military and communication privileges), though the country's rigid social system separating Americo-Liberians was sometimes compared with apartheid. Unfavorable comparisons have often been made between Liberia and Haiti, the two American-dominated "black republics." Until the collapse of the Americo-Liberian oligarchy in 1980, Liberia remained a US client state. Liberia became a pawn of the Cold War in the 1980s under ruthless military leadership before collapsing into military chaos and two gruesome civil wars in the 1990s. It ended up effectively in international trusteeship at the end of the millennium.[44] Liberia and its neighbor Sierra Leone became symbols for failed African states.

Modernization of Turkey and Persia

In 1846 the State Department received a request from the progressive-minded Sultan of Turkey to recommend two or three scientific agriculturists to him. Their role was to introduce improved cotton culture into his realm. There was much prestige awarded to such a request, and President James Polk regarded it as a "flattering mark of confidence." Polk's secretary of state, James Buchanan, went to great pains to find suitable people to send to Turkey. This request began a remarkable process of transformation that brought Turkey to the verge of European Union membership at the beginning of the twenty-first century.

In the 1870s, the Ottoman Empire, though collapsing, sought to modernize through importation of Western ideas, foreign investment, and professional advisers. In 1876, under a group of young leaders styled the "Young Turks," the Ottomans introduced a Western-style constitution and brought European and American advisers to the country.

Technical skills were important in the late 1800s. Often, the receiving country would pay for the expenses of the personnel, as did Turkey. Nonetheless, facilitating the provision of skilled professionals was a part of the diplomatic responsibility of the State Department and became a specialized function of its missions abroad.

Because of the Ottoman Empire's alliance with Germany and Austria-Hungary, the relationship between the United States and Turkey was negative during and immediately after World War I; however, by the mid-1920s US investors again became a significant presence in the country, and international financial managers, including Americans, provided financial advice given the massive Ottoman inherited debt.

President Muskafa Kemel Ataturk, Turkey's post–World War I strongman, is said to have modeled his republican Turkey on the United States. Ataturk made a conscious decision to modernize Turkey, adapting the Latin alphabet and Western clothes, and promoting a Western educational system, utilizing centralized personal direction to impose his will on the country. Turkey was to be a secular state without ethnic identification.

In 1928 Turkey invited a well-known international economist, Professor Edwin F. Kemmerer of Princeton, and six senior experts to advise it on fiscal matters. Their mission deserves special note both because Professor Kemmerer was associated with it and also because it was broader in scope than most technical missions.

After remaining neutral during World War II, Turkey received military assistance from the United States and Britain and later joined NATO. The country remains more or less true to the secular traditions of Ataturk. US technical assistance continued to be a part of this process of modernization during the post-war period.[45] The country continued to receive US military and financial assistance following September 11.

Technical assistance in Persia goes back to 1886 when the Shah inquired about technical support and economic investment in minerals, agriculture, and railroad development. At the time, Britain and Russia were the dominant influences in Persia, and the Shah saw the United States as a counterbalance to European dominance. Neither the British nor the Russians were sanguine about US involvement.

In 1910, Persia requested mining engineers, financial experts, and railroad experts to examine the situation in Persia. Ultimately, President Taft authorized the dispatch of a group of five public finance specialists headed by a financial adviser with experience in Cuba, W. Morgan Schuster, who, while employed by the Persian government, would be supported by the US Treasury. The group assisted in the reform of the tax, fiscal, and administrative systems in Persia; however, the group ran into corrupt practices and resistance to their efforts within the Persian bureaucracy and from British and Russian advisers entrenched in the public sector.

In 1921, the United States provided an adviser on financial matters to recruit capital investment for the country. Again there was friction between the reforming adviser from the US Treasury, Dr. Arthur Millspaugh, and the Persian government. Despite the friction, other missions in the 1920s and 1930s followed with advisers in agriculture, city planning, mining, and transportation.

In August 1941, Russia and Britain with US support invaded Persia and overthrew the pro-German Shah, Reza Shah Pahlavi, replacing him with his young son, Shah Mohammad Reza Pahlavi, who would control Persia (with the support of the CIA in the overthrow of Prime Minister Mohammed Mosaddeq on August 19, 1953) until the Iranian Islamic Revolution in 1979. In the post-war years, aid and technical assistance became a flood, leading the United States to support, among other things, the Shah's secret police.[46] Collapse of the US-Iranian relationship and the bitterness that followed bears some similarity to the tensions that developed with a number of other US client states in the twentieth century.

Thailand and the Philippines

The Philippines, as the largest territory in the US colonial system, received the lion's share of US assistance after the end of the Spanish-American War and the Philippine rebellion. In 1901, more than 500 young idealistic Americans (a prototype Peace Corps) arrived in Manila to help the Philippines develop. Eventually, several thousand young Americans went to the Philippines to teach in primary and secondary schools. There was, however, a "moralism" to their commitment and to those who followed.[47]

Education and health were high on the priorities of the US assistance program in the Philippines. The United States introduced a land reform program and tax reform. US investment led to a modicum of economic growth. US political and bureaucratic institutions were established.

Overall, it was the stated American goal to inculcate Filipinos with an American ethos. The American university and Western education had significant influence over patterns of higher education in the Philippines, Southeast and East Asia, and in other parts of the world. Walter Sharp suggests:

> The regional influence of certain American-sponsored educational institutions abroad has been far reaching. On any list of the scores of such institutions Robert College, Istanbul; the American University of Beirut; Yenching University, Nanking University, and St. John's University; Yale-in-China; the Booker Washington Institute, Liberia; and Santiago College, Chile, would deserve a high place.[48]

Physically, the Philippine Islands, at least superficially, came to resemble tropical American communities. The United States spent a great deal of money on transportation, agricultural assistance, and water reticulation. Despite foreign assistance, the Philippines remained one of the poorest countries in Asia, with half of the country's 88 million people living below the poverty line. In 2007, the United States still maintained a significant foreign aid program of $65 million annually.

Siam, now Thailand, was an early recipient of technical assistance prior to World War II. The country had avoided colonization in the nineteenth century but was under the influence of Britain and France. In Siam, modernization of the administrative and judicial systems was possible largely with the aid of Western, including American, advisers. During the interwar period, nearly all of the Siamese national ministries employed advisers, including British, American, Danish, German, Swedish, and French specialists. In many cases, these early technical assistance specialists acted as the de facto heads of the government departments. All the countries above had significant commercial interests in Thailand.

After 1930, with the advent of the constitutional regime and rising Siamese nationalism, the practice of employing foreign advisers declined; however, after Japanese occupation, Thailand became a US ally. By 1954, only four advisers remained out the more than fifty who had served the Siamese government. In the post-war period, Thailand would see the return of advisers and technical assistants in large numbers, including many Americans, in part because of the conflict in Indo-China.

Opening Up of East Asia

With the intervention of Commodore Matthew Perry of the US Navy on March 31, 1854, the United States forced the opening of Japan to the West. In the last half of the nineteenth century, Japan sought out technical assistance and international access to educational techniques and professional development. To further Japan's goals, special Japanese ambassadors went abroad to observe, to pave the way for young Japanese to study in the West, and to invite specialists to Japan. The responsibility of those traveling and studying abroad was to train future leaders; to help modernize communications, administration, education, agriculture, and industry; and to advise the Japanese government.

Expatriate Americans did much to promote the American educational model, legal institutions, and judicial reform in nineteenth and early twentieth century Japan. In visits to Japan, expatriate representatives argued that Japan could profitably borrow almost unchanged the American educational system. US emissaries were appointed to promote American commercial interests in Japan. The United States competed vigorously with European countries to provide technical assistance, gain influence, and, in turn, gain a commercial advantage in Japan as well as in other Asian countries.

Until 1940, US initiatives served as a model for an industrializing and developing Japan. Significant numbers of Japanese went to the United States to study during the interwar period and American ideas in education and agriculture were important influences. The United States, Germany, and Britain all provided technical experts to Japan during the interwar period.

World War II in the Pacific had elements of a "cousin's war" in the sense of a loss of friendship that many on both sides, Japan and the United States, felt given their history since 1854. The US occupation (1945–1952) brought American officials back to Japan in a second opening of the country. The dramatic development of post-war Japan, coming out of the US occupation as the world's second strongest economy, symbolized the assimilation of Western skills but within the context of an Eastern economy and culture.

The China Experience

China became a major recipient of US technical assistance in the last half of the nineteenth century, and by the 1890s, the United States had established a fully developed mission, the outcome of which transformed China on the one hand, but more importantly would impact the United

States on the other. In 1887, Chinese leaders, appreciative of the advantages offered by improved Western agricultural methods, were determined to establish a model farm and school based on the American example in which the latest and best appliances, technology, and methods might be made the basis of Chinese scientific agriculture. With US assistance, by the 1930s, China had committed itself to the improvement of agricultural production and begun to modernize its education and health systems, some of which continued to affect China after the communist takeover.

US involvement in China would have significant implications for foreign aid policy in Asia after World War II. In China, technical assistance followed the missionaries, who had already established a presence there. Missionary activity, as early as the nineteenth century, targeted education and health issues in China. As Walter Sharp has noted:

> Since the turn of the century, the medical and educational phases of Christian foreign missions appear in some areas (e.g. China) to have dwarfed in importance their accomplishments in religious evangelism. Mission schools, for better or for worse, have opened the door for Western knowledge for the young intellectuals of Asia and Africa.[49]

Among the many technical enterprises that the United States financed, China Foundation (founded in 1911 in the aftermath of the Boxer Rebellion) promoted what was an intense soil survey, entrusted to the National Geological Survey of China.[50] Efforts in China after World War I represent an early example of popular education as a development tool. US voluntary associations sent tractor teams to China in the 1930s to teach the populations there the techniques of mechanized agriculture.

In China, as in many other countries, privately funded technical assistance continued to play a role between the two world wars. Other technical missions were sponsored by American private foundations. Technical assistance in China, despite the ravages of the civil war, focused on a number of social and economic issues in the 1930s and 1940s.

Y. C. James Yen was born in 1893 out of a Christian family and was US-educated at Princeton. He was recruited by the YMCA to work with Chinese rural peasants sent to France during World War I. James Yen, whose name is linked with popular education in Asia, created the people's school approach in the 1920s. After the first World War, Yen returned to China convinced that adult education was the key to development. Several of Yen's colleagues were also American-educated. In 1928, Yen was able to raise $500,000 from donors in the United States. People's education, a form of popular adult education, provided a mission for China's rural residents.

In 1935, the Rockefeller Foundation announced a program of annual support for rural reconstruction in China. Yen helped found the Chinese-American Joint Commission on Rural Reconstruction funded jointly by the American and Chinese governments to finance projects in agriculture, irrigation, cooperative organizations, public health, literacy, and land reform after World War II. When China fell to the communists, Yen's experiment in China ended, but he later established similar centers in Taiwan and the Philippines. Political advisers became common in the early twentieth century. In China, between the two world wars, Professor Frank J. Goodnow, who was a distinguished political scientist at Johns Hopkins University, accepted a post as constitutional adviser to the Chinese government. Goodnow effectively wrote the first constitution of Republican China in 1914 and influenced governance in China as one of several major civilian players in the China theater. Frank Goodnow left a deep impression on many of the Chinese leaders, some of whom later applied his ideas to Taiwan. As an intellectual conservative, Goodnow took an active part in what would later become the Chinese Lobby in the debate about US policy toward the Chinese civil war and later the communist takeover.

The end was tragedy for the China Lobby, however. Three years after the end of World War II, the fall of China to the communists was the most traumatic of all Cold War events for diplomats, missionaries, and the American international assistance missions in Asia. Establishment of communist rule in October 1949 shocked those who had invested so much there. In response, the United States worked to isolate China from the world community until the visit by Richard Nixon and Henry Kissinger in 1972, proving the way for a return to capitalism in China and the development of an economic rival to North America and Europe in Asia and Africa.

Conclusion

One can learn much about foreign aid policy during the period prior to 1948. It's all there: missionaries, concern with terms of trade, professional specialists, idealism, balance-of-power calculations, and even military support. Technical assistance played an important role in US involvement in international assistance prior to 1940. Motives were varied: technical specialists were sometimes missionaries, sometimes had commercial ties, and often defined their roles in moral or even ethical terms.

What was not there was the volume of financial transfers that would come into being after 1948 with the Marshall Plan and Truman's Point Four Program. Nor would one find the bureaucratization and "projectization" that would all but eliminate flexibility and creativity as components of US foreign aid. Both would begin in the postwar period with the announcement of the Point Four Program.

What preceded World War II and the beginning of the Cold War were the developmental dilemmas and moral ambiguities built into the Western modernization concept, pushed by both colonialists and developmentalists alike. It was these dilemmas that would deepen as the United States entered the period of modern foreign aid after 1945. The development of modern state-sponsored foreign aid and technical assistance was ultimately, however, a product of the two World Wars and the Cold War sequel. It is to these developments that we now turn.

Notes

1. Joseph N. Weatherby, et al., *The Other World: Issues and Politics of the Developing World* (New York: Longman, 2000), pp. 124 and 191.

2. Robert G. Patterson, J. Garry Clifford and Kenneth J. Hagan, *American Foreign Policy: A History to 1914* (Lexington, MA: D. C. Heath and Company, 1983), p. 85.

3. Tom Wicker, "'His Accidency' John Tyler," in *What If? America: Eminent Historians Imagine What Might Have Been*, Robert Cowley, ed. (London: Pan Books, 2005), p. 63.

4. Weatherby, et al., *The Other World*, p. 125.

5. This point was made by Margaret Leech, *In the Days of McKinley*, p. 97. The next two paragraphs are based upon her masterful book on what the American people called the martyred president.

6. For a discussion of this see Stephen Kinzer, *Overthrow: America's Century of Regime Change from Hawaii to Iraq* (New York: Times Books, 2006), pp. 9–30.

7. Ibid., p. 206.

8. Frank Freidel, *The Splendid Little War* (New York: Dell Publishers, 1962), p. 9. The Peace Treaty with Spain was signed in Paris on December 10, 1898, and ratified by the United States Senate on February 6, 1899. The treaty came into force on April 11, 1899.

9. Leech, *In the Days of McKinley*, p. 209.

10. Legally Cuba was a protectorate between 1898 and 1934 and effectively until 1959.

11. David McCullough, *The Path Between the Seas: The Creation of the Panama Canal 1870–1914* (New York: Simon and Schuster, 1977).

12. Most figures come from the 2000 US Census. Statistics on US dependencies provided by the Office of Insular Affairs, US Department of the Interior Web site and other US government sources. Areas without Federal status include commonwealths, incorporated and unincorporated states, and associated states. The table excludes unpopulated areas. Associated states are independent, but the US controls their foreign and defense policy; territories are dependent states with partly representative institutions; the commonwealth status represents a situation similar to that of a state but lacking certain privileges and is similar to an associated state. Independent countries are internationally recognized as such and have United Nations representation.

13. See Stanley Karnow's important book, *In Our Image: America's Empire in the Philippines* (New York: Ballantine Books, 1990), for a discussion of the US administration in the Philippines.

14. For the historical significance of the Platt Amendment, see Herbert L. Mathews, *Castro: A Political Biography* (Harmondsworth, UK: Penguin Books, 1969), pp. 40–41.

15. American settlement, territorial status, and statehood effectively changed Hawaii's status as a dependent territory, but this does not change its colonial origins.

16. Leech, *In the Days of McKinley,* p. 290.

17. David McCullough, *John Adams* (New York: Simon & Shuster Touchstone Books, 2001).

18. See Gore Vidal, *Imperial America: Reflections on the United States of Amnesia* (New York: Thunder's Mouth: Nation Books, 2004) for an amusing discussion of this.

19. Most importantly Ira Sharkansky, *The United States: A Study of a Developing Country* (New York: David McKay, 1975).

20. John D, Montgomery, *Aftermath: Tarnished Outcomes of American Foreign Policy* (Dover, MA: Auburn House Publishing Company, 1985), p. 121.

21. See Stephen Kinzer, *All the Shah's Men: An American Coup and the Roots of Middle East Terror* (New York: John C. Wiley and Sons, 2003).

22. See Daniel Bergner, "The Call: The Post-Colonial Missionary," *New York Times Magazine* (January 29, 2006).

23. Curti and Birr, *Prelude to Point Four,* p. 196.

24. Thomas G. Paterson, J. Garry Clifford, and Kenneth J. Hagan, *American Foreign Policy: A History to 1914* (Lexington, MA: D. C. Heath and Company, 1988), p. 55.

25. Waldemar A. Nielsen, *The Golden Donors: A New Anatomy of the Great Foundations* (New York: E. P. Dutton, 1989) provides a discussion of this.

26. David Sogge, *Give and Take: What's the Matter with Foreign Aid?* (London: Zed Books, 2002), p. 144.

27. Philip M. Glick, *The Administration of Technical Assistance: Growth in the Americas* (Chicago: University of Chicago Press, 1957), pp. 4–5.

28. See Daniel Bergner, "The Call," for a discussion of missionaries in lesser developed countries in the early twentieth century.

29. Merle Curti and Kendall Birr, *Prelude to Point Four: American Technical Missions Overseas* (Madison, WI: University of Wisconsin Press, 1954), p. 8.

30. Ibid., p. 16.

31. Stephen E. Ambrose, *Undaunted Courage: Meriwether Lewis Thomas Jefferson and the Opening of the American West* (New York: Simon and Schuster, 1996).

32. Ibid., pp. 79 and 146.

33. Ibid., p. 4.

34. The Pan American Union itself, later the Organization of American States, was founded in 1889–90 and began as a bureau to compile commercial statistics and data on customs laws. See Walter R. Sharp, *International Technical Assistance* (Chicago: Public Administration Service, 1952), p. 11.

35. Ibid., p. 160.

36. Kinzer, in his book on US interventions around the world, *Overthrow,* tells the story of US interventions in Hawaii, Cuba, the Philippines, Nicaragua, Honduras, Iran, Guatemala, South Vietnam, Chile, Greneda, Panama, Afghanistan, and Iraq.

37. Sharp, *International Technical Assistance,* p. 84.

38. For a history of foreign aid to Haiti, see Terry Buss, *Haiti in the Balance: Why Foreign Aid Has Failed and What to Do about It* (Washington, DC: Brookings Institution Press, 2008).

39. Bill Berkeley, *The Graves Are Not Yet Full: Race, Tribe and Power in the Heart of Africa* (New York: Basic Books, 2001), p. 29.

40. J. Gus Liebenow, *Liberia: The Evolution of Privilege* (Ithaca, NY: Cornell University Press, 1969), pp. 3–4.

41. Curti and Birr, *Prelude to Point Four,* p. 66.

42. Liebenow, *Liberia,* p. 30–31.

43. Curti and Birr, *Prelude to Point Four,* pp. 69–70.

44. Blaine Harden, *Africa: Dispatches from a Fragile Continent* (Boston: Houghton Mifflin, 1990), pp. 236–237.

45. Dankwart A. Rustow, *Middle Eastern Political Systems* (Englewood Cliffs, NJ: Prentice-Hall, 1971), pp. 79–85.

46. See John L. Seitz, "The Failure of U.S. Technical Assistance in Public Administration: The Iranian Case" *Public Administration Review* 40, No. 5 (September–October, 1980), pp. 407–413.

47. Karnow, *In Our Image,* p. 197.

48. Sharp, *International Technical Assistance,* p. 2.

49. Ibid.

50. The China Foundation remains very active in China sponsoring health and education projects particularly in the rural areas. The China Foundation works both in China and Taiwan.

$$\underline{5}$$

THE IMPACT OF TWO WORLD WARS

Roosevelt recognized that the prime minister [Winston Churchill] was "pretty much a 19th century colonialist," as the diplomat Averell Harriman put it, and "that the old order could not last." The war [World War II] was a fault line.

Rick Atkinson, *An Army at Dawn*

Behold, we the American holy warriors have arrived. . . . We have come to set you free.

Radio Broadcast, quoted in Rick Atkinson, *An Army at Dawn*

Wars and the Origins of Foreign Aid

For many years, missionaries, traders, abolitionists, philanthropists, educators, and businessmen all carried out international aid and technical assistance and contributed to the complex of values and assumptions in the motives of individuals, organizations, and countries as they interacted with the developing world.

At the governmental level, by 1940, the United States operated a fully developed technical cooperation program in Latin America in agriculture, education, and health.[1] There were overlapping, if not competing, activities in Latin America where a dozen or more agencies engaged in multiple aid initiatives, some of them dating back to the 1930s.

Elements of foreign aid and technical assistance flourished in China, Persia, and the Philippines. The US also provided assistance to Liberia and Ethiopia in Africa and in Iran, Turkey, and Thailand in Asia during the interwar period; however, prior to World War II, it is fair to say that foreign assistance was somewhat unstructured.

This chapter examines foreign aid's modern origins during the interwar period, beginning with post–World War I efforts to reconstruct Europe.

The chapter then discusses Roosevelt's Good Neighbor Policy in Latin America, the wartime assistance of US allies by the "arsenal of democracy," and ends with a discussion of the Cold War's beginning and the massive Marshall Plan effort between 1948 and 1954.

Humanitarian Assistance

The United States' entry into World War I and the peace negotiations that followed reflected both change and continuity in the country's world view. "The United States' entry into the war," according to Margaret MacMillan, "became a crusade, against human greed and folly . . . and for justice, peace, and civilization."[2] From the war's outbreak in 1914, the need for humanitarian assistance came to the fore as Europe plunged into its first continental war in 100 years. Even prior to US participation, during the first 15 months of the conflict, more than 250 American nurses served in European countries under the direction of ICRC, and educational institutions, particularly Harvard, dispatched relief and medical aid missions.[3]

In August 1914, Herbert Hoover became the chairman and chief adviser of the Commission of Relief in Belgium. He continued to play the role of relief czar throughout the war and after, first in the nonprofit sector and then as a senior government administrator.[4]

Technical collaboration became increasingly significant for NGOs in Europe during World War I.[5] Of importance from a humanitarian perspective was the role played by NGOs, according to Walter Sharp:

> The overseas work of the Young Men's and Young Women's Christian Associations, the Unitarian Service Committee, and the American Friends Service Committee [was important]. The last-named group, established originally in 1917 as a relief agency, soon broadened its interests to include long-range rehabilitation work as well. Programs of famine relief and medical services were carried out in Russia, Poland, and Serbia between 1917 and 1931.[6]

After World War I, policymakers believed that American values were universal, and their government and society ought to be a model for the world. This included a faith in American *exceptionalism* that on occasion led to a

> certain obtuseness on the part of Americans, a tendency to preach at other nations rather than listen to them, a tendency as well to assume that American motives are pure where those of others are not. And [President Woodrow] Wilson was very

American. He came to the Peace Conference, said Lloyd
George, like a missionary to rescue the heathen Europeans
with his "little sermonettes" full of rather obvious remarks.[7]

Europeans came to resent reminders that the United States contributed
the bulk of Europe's relief and that it promoted its own economic interests—
for example, dumping American pork products and severely undercutting
European producers. Resentment between Europeans and Americans as
donors had a contemporary ring.

Allies feared that without postwar relief in Europe there would be complete social collapse. In 1918, the United States sent 6.2 million tons of
food to Europe. Throughout Europe in early 1919, reports came in from
public agencies and NGOs about the existence of millions of unemployed
people, desperately trying to feed themselves and their families on stale
bread, dried beans, and rotten cabbage. Hoover estimated that 200 million
people worldwide faced famine. Politics was salient: Hoover's motivation
for rapid response to refugees was, in part, fear that the poor and huddled
masses of Europe would fall to "communism, the 'collectivist infection.'"[8]

Hoover's American Relief Administration (ARA), in operation in
1919, represented a pioneering effort at large-scale relief. The ARA was
a complex organization with offices all over Europe—running railways,
supervising demining operations, and waging "war on lice, with thousands of hair clippers, tons of soap, special baths and stations manned
with American soldiers."[9] It was supported by special congressional
appropriations through the US Food Administration.

The ARA shipped millions of tons of food to Russia and Eastern Europe.
Hoover hoped that the prompt delivery of food aid to Russia, Hungary, and
Germany would calm down social unrest. To critics, aid in the form of surplus food also provided a potential dumping ground for America's 18 million tons of agricultural surplus. One important humanitarian and technical
support mission led by Hoover was to Russia in 1921. Though the mission
failed to end communist control, it was an instance of a growing tendency
to use official technical support missions in international crises.

In the interwar period before the Great Depression, patterns of foreign
assistance were similar to those in the prewar era. The formation of the
League of Nations, however, represented a new internationalism that
engaged the United States, despite the failure of the US Senate to ratify the
Treaty of Versailles ending the war.

Three legacies of World War I would have an impact upon the international assistance. First, the concept of self-determination, as defined by
Woodrow Wilson's "Fourteen Points" speech, became a watchword for
developing and transitional states. Second, patterns of humanitarian

assistance required NGOs from the victorious powers to feed the hungry and the displaced well after the end of the conflict. By 1933, under the Agricultural Adjustment Act and subsequent progams, the United States sold (at subsidized rates) or sent food shipments outside of emergency situations to poor countries in and beyond Europe. Third, national governments would, because of the problem's enormity, provide significant financial support to international organizations.

There were sporadic foreign aid activities organized directly by Americans and Europeans; however during the interwar period, the principal "carriers of technology and technical assistance . . . [remained] the missionary societies, private industrial firms, an impressive number of individuals directly employed by foreign governments, and a number of educational and philanthropic organizations."[10] At the same time, as the Europeans (and Asians) became dependent on international assistance, the United States postured *universalism* and humanitarianism efforts despite its propensity for isolationism.

Early Foreign Aid

Though it defined the foreign aid and foreign policy debate briefly during and after World War I, the United States remained "a particularly parochial society with a poor record of deep or comprehensive interest in other societies."[11] The United States, except for the last few years of the Woodrow Wilson administration, continued to be isolationist until the end of 1941.

Between 1920 and 1940, American and other religious, philanthropic, educational, and business groups all over the world had carried out foreign aid and technical assistance using US government, International Labor Organization and League of Nations financing; however, focus often was on Europe because the bulk of the rest of the world was still ruled under colonial systems, a responsibility of the mother country. After World War I, economists at the League of Nations paid little attention to the problems of poor countries. A 1938 League of Nations Survey made no mention of Africa or Asia and presented only one paragraph on Latin America.[12]

Internationally, most private sector humanitarian organizations originated during wars and/or natural disasters. The modern role of NGOs came to be shaped between 1919 and 1939. The Save the Children Fund was created in 1919, World University Service in 1920, and what is now Plan International in 1937. The volunteer-sending organizations owed their basic philosophy to the cross-cultural European work camps that sprang up after 1919.

Most of the interwar organizations "began with and retained a strong emphasis on emergency assistance."[13] Oxfam and Care (which was originally called the Center for American Relief in Europe) were founded in 1943. World Vision was formed after World War II. Within a decade (by the early 1950s), many of these organizations increasingly focused on development assistance, becoming dependent on governments to support their activities.

Influence, Values, and Stereotypes

In commenting on the missions to the ten Latin American countries, E. F. Kemmerer,[14] president of the American Economic Association in his 1926 presidential address, noted a precipitous decline in the traditional preference of Latin-American governments for European advisers. There was, he claimed, an increasing tendency to turn to the United States. During the interwar period, financial advisers "heralded the day when American financial and other economic experts were to play an even larger role on the world stage."[15]

International security, humanitarian missions, technical assistance, and diplomacy were closely intertwined during the interwar period. In Asia and Latin America, the United States sent military and naval missions to less developed countries (LDCs) during a time of crisis, despite the view that technical missions often had a more positive impact. These missions were similar to interventions after World War II.

Foreign aid and technical assistance, though increasingly important, faced considerable challenges. There was often the problem of press reports of corrupt practices in poor countries during this period. In one case, problems developed over the nature of patronage and corruption within US-supported international administration service systems. Some in authority had forced assistance workers to hand over a portion of their salary to their superiors to maintain their positions.[16]

Beyond this, technical assistance, for many critics of international aid, particularly in Latin America before 1939, was simple if not surprising; the background problem that impeded economic progress was imperialism. This in turn led to a nationalist reaction in many places that handicapped US efforts. *Authoritarianism* was seen by some as an inadvertent result of US (and other) interventions in Latin America, Africa, and Asia in the interwar period because an "American-trained constabulary in Santo Domingo and Liberia made easier the path of a dictator in the former and strengthened an elite in the latter. Educational reforms aided many people, but they generally favored urban over rural folks."[17]

Ultimately, recipient countries began to see aid as paternal, based on what Walter Lippmann called the "fatal universalism" of American thought.[18] The United States represented a more advanced society than could be replicated in poor countries through foreign aid. Advisers sent out to teach the "natives" between the wars were often portrayed in writing and in cartoons as older siblings or parents. Often, donors portrayed recipients of advice as a bad pupil.

Prior to World War II, the assumption was that "native" people in Africa, Latin America, and Asia were doomed to low standards of living because of their inability to handle machines.[19] Mechanization was a central assumption of white supremacy. Many academics and practitioners in the early days of aid saw the United States as central to a universal model of modernization that should inspire all people.

John Dewey's *instrumentalism* influenced technical assistance in the period between world wars, focusing on experiential activities of instrumentalism and pragmatism (searching for what works). In education, the Institute for International Education of New York (established in 1919), supported largely by foundation grants, sponsored fellowships and scholarships, facilitated overseas lecture tours for professors and journalists, and promoted international summer schools and student work schemes. After World War I, many universities became involved in international assistance work.

By the late 1920s, a series of welfare, educational, research, and development activities constituted an important feature of organizations engaged in foreign investment enterprises. The goal promoted joint activities in which American and local capital participated, emphasizing projects designed to improve living standards through education and training.

Those desiring a more imperial role for the United States after 1919 took a strong position on Eastern Asia but:

> did not explicitly recommend technical aid, but it did include among the arguments suggested in favor of assuming the mandate the statement that the Near East presents the greatest humanitarian opportunity of the age—a duty for which the United States is better fitted than any other—as witness Cuba, Puerto Rico, the Philippines, Hawaii, Panama, and our altruistic policy of developing people rather than material resources alone.[20]

There were two components of colonial and later foreign aid policy adopted by US administrators and specialists: modernization through trusteeship and need for accumulation of wealth from capital investment. Prior to World War II, social equity and political rights would have been inconsistent with the underlying division of labor and trading patterns within colonial preferential treatment areas. Rising expectations within developing countries only began with the end of the colonial period in the 1950s.

Foreign Assistance and the New Deal

The Good Neighbor Policy

Outside Latin America, prior to World War II, aid was largely rhetorical and dependent on private sources. Latin America was different. Implementation of the Good Neighbor Policy in Latin America during the Roosevelt administration brought the first sustained effort at foreign aid. Modern aid began in Latin America and according to Dennis Rondinelli:

> For more than a century, the United States [had] sent money and supplies abroad. . . . But beginning in the [late 1930s], with the initiation of the "Good Neighbor Policy" with Latin America, the United States embarked on a deliberate, albeit cautious policy of providing financial and technical assistance for promoting economic and social progress in foreign countries.[21]

Aid to Latin America has long been a priority for the United States. As part of the Good Neighbor Policy (the phrase was actually Herbert Hoover's), the United States established a full-fledged, though modest, assistance program for Central and South America that included support for private loans, provision of financial and technical advisers, creation of a favorable climate for investment, and establishment of the Export-Import Bank. Initially, it operated through unrelated requests by Latin American governments.

Ultimately, three organizations—the Intergovernmental Committee on Scientific and Cultural Cooperation (ICSSCC), the Institute of Inter-American Affairs (IIAA) and the Office of Inter-American Affairs (OIAA)—administered assistance programs in Latin America in which functionally overlapping units which eventually would become USAID and its allied Departments of Agriculture, Commerce, Labor and Education.

The ICSCC and IIAA, established in 1938, were authorized to use services of any department in their efforts. In 1940, ICSCC had a budget of almost $400,000. The budget jumped to $4 million annually after World War II. In 1950, its last year as a separate operation, it received $26 million.

Most of the aid projects focused on natural or social issues—agriculture, geological investigations, civil aviation, child welfare, and statistical services.

Many were advisory, with the U.S government providing salaries and expenses for experts. ICSCC activities remained piecemeal and short-term.

IIAA was a model for technical assistance that would be widely adopted in the postwar period. The IIAA was a nonprofit corporation without capital stock. Nelson Rockefeller was its coordinator. IIAA's mission was to provide technical support to address problems of "controlling contagious diseases, improving public health and sanitation, growing more food, and improving the facilities of elementary and vocational education."[22]

Congressional appropriations to IIAA and OIAA were $5 million (or more) between 1940 and 1950. Over that period the agencies actually spent some $75 million on cooperative action (the contemporary name for foreign aid). Through the program, more than 500 Latin American nationals arrived in the United States to study, carry out research, or participate in guided visits. In all, the United States spent $25 million on education during the ten years of its operation.

The IIAA established field offices in almost all Latin American countries and operated projects that would be taken over by the Point Four Program in 1950. Though designed as a partnership, IIAA was staffed almost exclusively by American civil servants. In its eight years, IIAA spent $63 million.

OIAA initially operated separately under the president's supervision but later was transferred to State after 1945. There was tension between the IIAA and ICSCC from 1942 and 1950, a tension not unusual during the Roosevelt administration.

In the wake of Roosevelt's Good Neighbor Policy, numerous agencies exchanged information and skills with foreign nations on a reciprocal basis. Latin Americans made increasing requests for technical, naval and military missions. The United States supported work of the International Health Board of the Rockefeller Foundation in San Salvador, Bolivia, Paraguay, Brazil, and other countries. The Public Health Service through State contributed effective help in several countries.

Throughout the 1930s, the United States and Latin Americans discussed the creation of an Inter-American Development Bank (IADB), to promote economic development in Central and South America. Early on, suspicions about foreign assistance policy (and its unwillingness to engage Latin America) were well entrenched among Latin American intellectuals and political leadership alike. IADB, finally established in 1959, would become a core regional institution of the World Bank system in the postwar era.

The Pan American Highway

During the 1930s, the United States increasingly undertook larger, more comprehensive activities. Between 1930 and 1950, US aid largely funded the Inter-American activities. It was President Coolidge's Secretary of Commerce Herbert Hoover who advocated the Inter-American Highway project and it was promoted by the Pan American Union and the Pan American Highway Commission. The United States provided matching funds to contributions from Latin American states, and the Army Corps of Engineers and private contractors carried out much of the actual construction. The United States had a veto over major decisions made about the construction of the highway.

The Inter-American Highway was a major US foreign aid project during the inter-war period. The project began in the 1920s. Responsibility for the project was initially located in the Central American Accounts section of the Division of the American Republics, located in the Department of State. Construction was managed by the Army Corps of Engineers and oversight was provided by the Department of Commerce. From its beginning in the early 1920s, the Pan American Highway took on philanthropic overtones. Throughout the 1920s, the highway remained embedded within the Department of State's Division of Latin America's bridge program. Contractors and suppliers did much of the actual work from the beginning.

The Pan-American Highway, as it was called by the Roosevelt administration, was plagued by a host of difficulties including the baggage of the past relationships between the United States and Latin America. These included perceptions of US cultural superiority, arrogance, mutual anger and resentment.[23] It was as complicated a foreign aid project as many implemented after World War II.

During the Roosevelt administration the supervisory responsibility for the project was taken over by the Bureau of Public Roads, then a part of the US Department of Agriculture and now a core division within the Department of Transportation. The project had domestic appeal especially as it evolved in the 1930s and became identified with Roosevelt's Good Neighbor Policy.[24] Roosevelt modeled the highway after his large domestic projects that reflected his vision of developmental government. Roosevelt successfully lobbied Congress for further appropriations in 1934. Its advocates consciously presented the road as a development activity and a potent symbol of US concern to increase the GNP of Central and South America.[25]

As World War II approached, Latin Americans feared that the road would be used as a military highway. By 1939, the United States is estimated to have provided 75 percent of the cost of the road. By the late 1930s, however, the project had bogged down and was unfinished at the beginning of the war. World War II renewed interest in the road as it was linked to hemispheric defense.

In 1942, Congress appropriated funding to complete the highway for security purposes. By 1945, the highway was 70 percent completed. This was the largest aid project to that time.

Construction was finally completed in 1957 by a combination of the US Army Corps of Engineers and numerous contractors, US and local. In the end, it had become a part of the Point Four Program announced by President Truman in 1950.

Impacts of Renewed War

Foreign aid in its modern form dates from 1940 to 1941 when the United States responded to Nazi aggression in Europe with lend-lease assistance to all of the European states fighting Germany. In early 1941, Lord John Maynard Keynes, representing the British Treasury, arrived in Washington to negotiate the British lend-lease agreement, setting the stage for an elaborate system of international assistance and the basis of postwar aid.

From the beginning of World War II, policymakers coupled foreign aid to military and foreign policy. Two important organizations were the Foreign Economic Administration, created in 1940, and the Office of Lend-Lease Administration, created in 1941. A third organization, the War Relief Control Board, established in 1942, and renamed the Advisory Committee on Voluntary Foreign Aid in 1946, coordinated and funded NGOs. From its beginnings in 1941, Lend-Lease left behind a formative legacy that affected Allied leaders for a generation.

World War II marked an American coming of age in security and diplomacy. "The truth was that," as Rick Atkinson points out in early 1942 "a callow, clumsy army had arrived in North Africa with little notion of how to act as a world power. . . . [T]he balance of the war . . . would require learning not only how to fight but how to rule."[26] With US entry into World War II in December 1941, the country became a global leader and as President Roosevelt called it, the "arsenal of democracy."

Food, economic, and military assistance, amounting to approximately $50.1 billion provided to the Allies in Europe and Asia, was the first large-scale foreign aid, military, and technical assistance program mounted by the United States. Foreign aid from the Roosevelt administration forward was part of the US transition to great power status and a prototype for assistance.

With the invasion of North Africa, the United States began to act like the senior partner in the Anglo-American alliance in military, diplomatic, financial, and strategic terms. Britain and the other great imperial powers slipped into a junior partner role, a process that would be completed at the war's end and subsequent decolonization of the underdeveloped world. There was "a subtle shift in the balance of power within the Anglo-American alliance;

the United States was dominant ... by virtue of power and heft, with consequences that would extend not only beyond the war but beyond the century."[27]

The Marshall Plan's origin lies in the Casablanca conference of Churchill and Roosevelt in late 1943, when the Allies demanded unconditional surrender, with physical occupation and reconstruction of the Axis and occupied powers. This decision had implications for the future conduct of the war, the occupation period afterward, and several generations of postconflict development strategies.

During the war, tensions developed between the United States and Britain over colonialism. President Roosevelt complained about European colonialism and called for the freeing of all the "backward" people from Europe's "backward" colonial policies. According to Rick Atkinson, "Roosevelt recognized that the prime minister [Churchill] was 'pretty much a 19th century colonialist,' as the diplomat Averill Harriman put it, and 'the old order could not last.' The war was a fault line."[28] Changes in foreign economic policy and international assistance would be part of the new postwar economic order.

Crisis in the Balkans and the Marshall Plan

Policymakers channeled US foreign assistance through the United Nations in anticipation of a peaceful nonconfrontational world; however, almost immediately after Germany surrendered in 1945, tensions with the Soviet Union developed, forcing the United States to send emergency aid to assist the devastated nations of Western Europe. "For two years after Germany surrendered in 1945," according to David Broder, "America ... sent emergency help to the devastated nations of Western Europe, both allies and adversaries."[29] Between 1945 and 1947, humanitarian assistance arrived in Europe through NGOs with funding from the United States.

Foreign aid after World War II had two goals. First, aid would target the redevelopment of human and economic resources worldwide during the transition to peace and contribute to the reconstruction of the War devastated countries of Europe. Second, aid would constitute the "first line of defense in the struggle against Soviet expansion."[30]

Assistance to Greece, Persia, and Turkey fit into the second goal as the United States feared the countries were at risk of a communist guerrilla takeover. At war's end, the Soviet Union had already taken over Eastern Europe, giving credibility to the threat. An early clash between Russia and the United States occurred in Iran, which came under American influence. Yugoslavia, though communist, would eventually declare itself neutral; however, between 1945 and 1948, Yugoslavia backed a communist insurrection in Greece. For three years, Greece suffered in a civil war between a national communist movement and a reactionary conservative government propped up by Britain. Turkey also faced a desperate economic situation and threats from the Soviet Union. In late 1946, the Labour Government in Britain announced that it could no longer support Greece economically or militarily.

On March 12, 1947, President Truman asked Congress for $400,000 for economic and security assistance to Greece and Turkey, under what came to be called the Truman Doctrine—a commitment to contain the expansion of Soviet influence in Europe and around the world. State ostensibly administered aid to Greece and Turkey to address problems of "economic instability, difficulty of reestablishing agricultural production, banditry and subversive pressure from the northern [communist] neighbors of Greece and Turkey."[31] The Truman administration also sent civilian and military personnel to Greece and Turkey to manage development and security programs and to train officials. The intervention institutionalized a process for international assistance in the postwar period and "involved the United States directly in the management of the countries' economic and military affairs much more deeply than had been initially intended."[32]

The Cold War defined foreign aid at the end of World War II. In large part, the Marshall Plan was a response to the communist takeover in Eastern Europe. As Judith Hoover points out, "From 1947 until the fall of the Soviet Union in 1991, the country was scared as hell about Soviet power and the threat of nuclear war."[33] Foreign aid for policymakers was at least nominally premised on the thesis that economic and social development, and democratic government was essential to national security. Advocates of foreign aid argued that "Communism [could] be checked only by systematic economic growth. . . . [However] some [went] so far as to believe that US economic programs [could] provide the basis for new more humanitarian principles and practices in international relations."[34]

As the Cold War sharpened in 1947 and 1948, "The underlying fear was that democratic governments would collapse, notably in France and Italy, where strong communist movements waited in the wings."[35] With the communist threat in the Balkans and Eastern Europe, policymakers granted bilateral assistance as part of the Truman Doctrine first to Greece and Turkey, and then to the rest of Western Europe under the Marshall Plan.

In June of 1947, Secretary of State George C. Marshall spoke at Harvard University, announcing his intention to reconstruct Europe and Japan. Two years later, as we will see in Chapter 6, President Truman announced the Point Four Program to extend support for Europe to much of the rest of the world. In 1950, the Mutual Security Act specified that foreign aid only be given if it strengthened the security and well-being of the United States.

After 1948, the Marshall Plan to Western Europe became the reference point for all foreign aid. Policymakers modeled early assistance to Japan, then Korea and Taiwan, and other Asian countries on the Marshall Plan. The Marshall Plan also provided assistance to Europe's colonies in Africa and Asia. Foreign aid, far from being based on nobility on the part of the donor, was predicated on the assumption that economic growth was essential to countering the growing communist threat in Europe and Asia.[36]

As the Marshall Plan developed, Truman and his advisers realized that Europe's postwar ruin made the prospect of communist takeovers in France, Italy, and perhaps other Western European countries likely. "What was needed," as David Broder put it half a century later, "Truman and Marshall understood, was a sustained effort of much larger scale, with unprecedented peacetime cooperation by governments on both sides of the Atlantic."[37] The success of the Marshall Plan was that it established broad policy decisions from the outset with respect to the assistance program. This made it possible to establish a clear assignment of primary responsibility to the aid administrators.[38]

Prior to the Marshall Plan, the State Department administered foreign aid outside of war zones. With the Marshall Plan targeted at war-torn Europe, policymakers transferred foreign assistance agencies outside the traditional foreign policy structure and linked it to security concerns. Foreign aid to Latin America, though, continued to be administered through State bureaus.

By the late 1940s, the Marshall Plan had funneled $13 billion in reconstruction money and technical assistance to sixteen European countries.[39] The Plan, "run by businessman Paul Hoffman . . . was a magnificent success. It came in under budget—$13.5 billion rather than the projected $17 billion. It put Europe back on its feet, frustrating the Communists' hopes."[40] Under the Plan, Korea, the Philippines, Taiwan, and Turkey also received $3 billion for a variety of humanitarian and development purposes. Ironically, the Plan, at the time, was seen as very risky.

A Model for Foreign Aid

The Marshall Plan contributed three antecedents to contemporary aid: the European Recovery Program (1948), the Mutual Defense Program (1949), and the Point Four Program (1950), discussed in Chapter 6. According to one observer, "A key factor of the Marshall Plan, and something which probably contributed to its success was that it operated on recipient-friendly terms so that it was up to the Europeans to manage and control the funds received."[41] In this way the Plan funds differed from later foreign aid schemes.

Organizationally, in April 1948, the State administered programs to Austria, France, Greece, Italy, Trieste, Latin America, and a few client states in Asia and Africa, but these were gradually subsumed under the Marshall Plan administrative apparatus.

Congress approved the creation of the Economic Cooperation Administration (ECA) on April 3, 1948, to administer the European Recovery Program. Within four months the organization was fully operational and US support in Europe alone would employ 630 Americans that year. By the beginning of 1949, there were 720 people working in the Washington office, 290 in the Paris office and 1,127 in the country missions. It was on the way to becoming a complex, difficult, and cumbersome operation. The foreign aid establishment grew rapidly from that time.[42]

ECA, having missions in each country served, screened funding requests and assisted in program administration throughout Europe and later Asia and would later administer the Point Four Program.

The Marshall Plan did get Europe back on its feet, but most importantly "also created new markets for American firms and weakened the appeal of Europe's communist Parties."[43] In the Plan, as in later foreign aid schemes, one object was to promote joint enterprises where American and local capital participated, with emphasis on projects designed to improve standards of living by reducing production and distraction costs in the agriculture and mining sectors. The Plan was economically Keynesian in its approach, designing foreign aid as part of a development planning process. The Plan was expensive: during a four-year period, it spent $13.5 billion or $87.5 billion in 1997 dollars.

Capital growth strategies predominated in the early postwar period, and "development specialists . . . tended to give the greatest priority to industry, as the sector that was most capital intensive."[44] The Plan was successful because it provided capital funds to reconstruct Europe's infrastructure. Europe possessed needed institutions, skills, and values despite destruction of its infrastructure.

That said, education and technical assistance remained a priority. In 1948, Congress recognized the importance of educational and technical exchange to promote better understanding between the United States and other parts of the world by establishing an Office of Educational Exchange, later called the Fulbright Program, after Senator J. William Fulbright.

The Plan seemed to transform Western Europe almost overnight. Japan quickly became a success story. There were a series of initial successes in building the economies of Korea, Taiwan, the Philippines, and a couple of Latin American countries. As a result, many experts assumed that the Plan might be transferable. In the 1950s, foreign aid assumed that there was no scientific or technical problem in the newly emerging nations that American professionals could not address.

ECA action outside the Marshall Plan countries of Europe and their dependent territories developed in an unsystematic, piecemeal fashion. The program began with the ill-fated effort to restore economic stability in China as reflected in the provisions of the China Aid Act of 1948. Under this measure, Congress appropriated of $450 million for economic assistance to the pre-communist Republic of China, including Formosa. Most of the money never made it to the mainland, but it did provide a base for the economic miracle played out in Taiwan in the 1950s.

Roosevelt's New Deal, extended by President Truman as the Fair Deal, spanned economic aid, information dissemination, and intelligence agencies, which came to dominate Cold War foreign policy. Many of those who worked as the first generation of international development specialists began by working in the military occupation of Germany and Japan.

As the occupation wound down, former members of the military occupation in Germany and Japan moved to the Marshall Plan, and on to Greece and Turkey under the Truman Doctrine. Civilian members of State's early foreign assistance efforts moved on to the huge foreign aid enterprises in Asia, Latin American, and by the early 1960s, Africa. The policymaking processes, programs, value systems, and contracting mechanisms often went with them.

Conclusion

While foreign aid and technical assistance in its modern form is only sixty years old, their antecedents go back well into the 1800s. The move to massive government-to-government aid represented a major shift in international assistance after World War II. Patterns of international assistance, however, did have their roots in the nineteenth and the first half of the twentieth century.

The Marshall Plan's legacy can still be seen in the world today. Most importantly, the aid scheme marked the beginning of a time when the United States first became permanently involved in the world. Ironically, for all its success, the Plan would become a reminder of US timidity in foreign aid terms as the Cold War dragged on. It became a marker of bolder times.

After 1948, for the first time, governments in more-developed countries assumed that the redistribution of wealth internationally was part of their responsibility. While private funds remained important, by 1970 voluntary private transfers of resources accounted for only 3 percent of the flow of resources into developing countries. We discuss creation of a more formalized foreign aid program in the postwar period, emanating from the Marshall Plan assumptions, in Chapter 6.

Notes

1. Edward W. Weidner, *Technical Assistance in Public Administration Overseas: The Case for Development Administration* (Chicago: Public Administration Service, 1964), p. 6.

2. Margaret MacMillan, *Paris 1919: Six Months That Changed the World* (New York: Random House, 2002), p. 6.

3. See Merle Curti and Kendall Birr, *Prelude to Point Four: American Technical Missions Overseas* (Madison, WI: University of Wisconsin Press, 1954), p. 150.

4. Walter Cohen, "Herbert Hoover Feeds the World," *The Trojan Horse: A Radical Look at Foreign Aid,* Steve Weissman, ed. (Palo Alto, CA: Ramparts Press, 1974), p. 151.

5. See Walter R. Sharp, *International Technical Assistance* (Chicago: Public Administration Service, 1952), p. 1.

6. Ibid.

7. MacMillan, *Paris 1919,* p. 14.

8. Cohen, "Herbert Hoover Feeds the World," in Weissman, ed., *The Trojan Horse,* p. 152.

9. MacMillan, *Paris 1919,* p. 62.

10. Philip M. Glick, *The Administration of Technical Assistance: Growth in the Americas* (Chicago: University of Chicago Press, 1957), p. 3.

11. Edmund Stillman and William Pfaff, *Power and Impotence: The Failure of America's Foreign Policy* (New York: Random House, 1966), p. 44.

12. William Easterly, *The Elusive Quest for Growth: Economists' Adventures and Misadventures in the Tropics* (Cambridge, MA: MIT Press, 2001), p. 30.

13. Ian Smillie, *The Alms Bazaar: Altruism Under Fire—Non-Profit Organizations and International Development* (London: IT Publications, 1995), p. 39.

14. Kemmerer was a distinguished monetary economist who between 1923 and 1933 led a series of missions to Latin America to assist governments in developing more effective systems of money and banking.

15. Both quotes from Curti and Birr, *Prelude to Point Four,* p. 186 and p. 188.

16. This problem is discussed in John M. Champion and John H. James, *Critical Incidents in Management: Decision and Policy Issues* (Scarborough, ON: Irwin Publishing, 1988).

17. Curti and Birr, *Prelude to Point Four*, p. 217.

18. As noted by John Franklin Campbell, *The Foreign Affairs Fudge Factory* (New York: Basic Books, 1971), p. 182.

19. Linton, "An Anthropologist Views Point Four," p. 114.

20. Curti and Birr, *Prelude to Point Four*, p. 154.

21. Dennis A. Rondinelli, *Development Administration and U.S. Foreign Aid Policy* (Boulder, CO: Lynne Rienner Publishers, 1987), p. 1.

22. Glick, *The Administration of Technical Assistance*, pp. 14–15.

23. Ibid., p. 182.

24. Sumner Welles, *The Time for Decision* (New York: Harper & Row, 1944), pp. 185–241 provides a firsthand account.

25. Kemp, *Highway Diplomacy*, p. 8.

26. Atkinson, *An Army at Dawn*, p. 159.

27. Ibid., p. 538.

28. Ibid., p. 299.

29. David S. Broder, "Recalling One of History's Great Successes," *Pittsburgh Post-Gazette* (May 30, 1997), p. A19.

30. Wallace S. Sayre and Clarence E. Thurber, *Training for Specialized Mission Personnel* (Chicago: Public Administration Service, 1952).

31. Speech by Arthur Z. Gardiner, Director United States Operations Mission in Vietnam, address given to the Saigon Rotary Club on September 22, 1960 (Washington, DC: Department of State and U.S. Government Printer, 1961).

32. Vernon W. Ruttan, *United States Development Assistance Policy: The Domestic Politics of Foreign Economic Aid* (Baltimore: The Johns Hopkins University Press, 1996), p. 39.

33. Quoted by E. J. Dionne., "Inevitably, The Politics of Terror," *Washington Post* (May 25, 2003), p. B1.

34. John D. Montgomery, *The Politics of Foreign Aid: American Experience in Southeast Asia* (New York: Praeger, 1962), p. 84.

35. Martin Wolf, "Marshall's Lasting Legacy," *Financial Times* (June 3, 1997), p. 12.

36. Severine M. Rugumamu, *Lethal Aid: The Illusion of Socialism and Self-Reliance in Tanzania* (Trenton, NJ: Africa World Press, 1997), p. 68.

37. Broder, "Recalling," p. A19.

38. James Grant, "Towards a More Effective Domestic Political Base for American Economic Assistance Abroad" (Unpublished Paper, 1961), p. 17.

39. Robert Dvorchak, "Hailing the Man Behind the Plan," *Pittsburgh Post-Gazette* (June 1, 1997), p. A1.

40. Broder, "Recalling," p. A19.

41. Nadia Minty, "The Mythology of Foreign Aid" (Unpublished Paper, Pittsburgh, GSPIA, University of Pittsburgh, April 17, 2003).

42. According to Herbert A. Simon, "Birth of an Organization: The Economic Cooperation Administration," *Public Administration Review,* 13, no. 4 (Autumn, 1953), pp. 227–236. These paragraphs are based on his personal history of ECA for which he worked during the formative period.

43. Hertsgaard, *The Eagle's Shadow,* p. 84.

44. Carol Lancaster, *Aid to Africa: So Much to Do: So Little Done* (Chicago: University of Chicago Press, 1999), p. 16.

6

POINT FOUR, USAID, AND THE COLD WAR

Americans not only don't know much about the rest of the world, we don't care.

Mark Hertsgaard, *The Eagle's Shadow*

In retrospect, however, foreign aid reached its peak in 1960s.

Larry Chang, "Foreign Aid and the Fate
of Least Developed Countries"

We aid other countries with whom our relationships may be more nearly correct than cordial, because we believe that it is in our interests to maintain friendly contacts with their governments and their people and to keep them from going behind the Iron Curtain.

Arthur Z. Gardiner, 1960 speech at the Saigon Rotary Club

Origins in the Cold War

Foreign Assistance to Lesser Developed Countries

Foreign aid to developing countries after 1945, as we have seen, did not develop in a vacuum. There was a 200-year legacy of state and nonstate action preceding it. Two themes have emerged as we examine the first decade of institutionalized foreign aid. First, there was a long history of financial transfer and exchange that defined diplomacy. Second, between 1500 and 1950, increasingly global colonial empires defined a system of international governance, including aid that affected international assistance for the past sixty years.

International assistance following World War II was intended to be humanitarian and temporary—supposedly completed in two to three years. Early foreign aid fell to postwar Europe and her colonies, China, Japan, and the Philippines, and a few others, members of the informal client-state system. US assistance was to finance the transition to peace throughout the world.[1] The international aid system gradually changed with the decision to expand foreign assistance worldwide after 1948, though its initial developers continued to view assistance as temporary.

After 1945, the United States developed "rules of the game" for its foreign aid.[2] Operations and commodity procurement rested on those rules developed in wartime and through Interim Aid Group operations in State and the Office of International Trade in Commerce. Much of the contracting mirrored military models, originating from World War II. Likewise, the grants process, which provided money for NGOs working internationally, had its roots in the early 1900s.

The Truman administration created the Economic Cooperation Administration (ECA) on April 3, 1948, to administer foreign aid under the Marshall Plan. The Plan relieved deficits in war-torn countries of Europe and Asia. Two aspects of foreign aid policy had their origins in the ECA: there would be strict scrutiny of all individual transactions and foreign aid regulations would require agencies to "buy American." ECA originally was to end in 1952.

International assistance would be humanitarian, providing at least minimum amounts of consumers' goods and raw materials, so that countries could reactivate agricultural and industrial production and restore communications systems. Secretary of State Dean Acheson promoted linkages between foreign aid and foreign trade.

After 1948, there were many components to foreign aid and technical assistance that were perhaps more naïve than growth-oriented approaches to foreign aid,[3] including the debates for and against the thought that development occurred through self-help, private enterprise, and individual initiative. Some development theorists focused on state-led development; however, to many development theorists, it was the absence of individual initiative that caused underdevelopment. Humanitarian aid needed to incorporate developmental principles for it to be successful. Wise guidance to indigenous peoples on the part of the change agent was built into this principle.

Prior to 1950, large-scale economic aid was only available to a few non-European countries, excluding China and the Philippines, in the form of loans provided by the Export-Import Bank, established in 1934, and from the International Bank for Reconstruction and Development (aka the World Bank) created in 1946.[4] By 1950, however, Allied policymakers began to hear clamors for foreign aid from the "underdeveloped nations of the earth who were already blaming their poor circumstances on the exploitation by the colonial powers and the industrialized countries."[5]

Assistance to the Philippines began again in 1946 in support of its independence. Other countries receiving foreign aid just after World War II included Morocco, Libya, Ethiopia, Tunisia, and Somaliland. In South

America, Colombia and Venezuela were early recipients. Taiwan, Korea, Thailand, and Indochina in Asia received support. US attitudes in the late 1940s and early 1950s "expressed a sense of omnipotent capacity with which the United States emerged from World War II."[6] As foreign aid policy developed, "what U.S. officials did in the reconstruction of Europe [and after] continued to follow the American's impulse to address other people's problems by concentrating on one-shot solutions, usually by applying their own experience to them."[7] It was an optimistic beginning.

Ethiopia as an Example

The early years of foreign aid continued patterns established in the inter-war period. In Ethiopia, for example, prior to World War II the United States had assigned a financial adviser, Everett A. Colson, who served from 1931–1935 and later assisted Emperor Haile Selassie in his unsuccessful appeal to the League of Nations after the Italian invasion of Ethiopia. The United States and Britain assisted Haile Selassie financially as he returned to power as part of the Anglo-Ethiopian agreement on December 19, 1944. There was a modest US assistance program to support the Ethiopian military during World War II.

By 1946, financial assistance and aid-related tax reforms allowed Ethiopia to double the size of its budget and professionalize its public administration. Ethiopia hired American and European teachers with the freed-up funding. In addition, in 1946, there was a Mennonite missionary group working in Ethiopia.

By 1948, foreign aid to Ethiopia still remained modest; however, despite good relationships between the United States and the monarchy, democratization faltered, even as the United States and Britain supported the incorporation of the former Italian Eritrea into Ethiopia. By the mid-1950s, though, the kingdom was a staunch ally in the fight against communism.

Assistance in health, education, and public administration continued until a Marxist-Leninist military junta, the "Derg" led by Mengistu Haile Mariam, overthrew the monarchy in 1974. After that, the United States isolated Ethiopia until a revolt brought Meles Zenawi and the Ethiopian People's Revolutionary Party (EPRP) to power. Meles, supported by US foreign and military assistance, became an American ally in the Horn of Africa, and in 2007, acted as a surrogate for the United States in occupying Somalia.

The Cold War and Point Four

Modern foreign aid policy began after World War II with an eye to contain communism and ultimately "win" the Cold War. In 1950 this was a realistic strategy for a real concern, even if it sometimes distorted aid's technical goals. Foreign aid policies, until 1989, kept military assistance and aid to less developed countries (LDCs) within the context of Cold War competition and sometimes subordinated economic assistance to US security needs.

The Point Four Program originated under President Truman as the fourth point in his January 20, 1949, inaugural address. Truman "called for a 'bold new program' for making the benefits of American science and industrial progress available to 'underdeveloped' countries."[8] Early assessments of Truman's Point Four speech made clear that "United States foreign aid has been a powerful instrument for strengthening orderly social processes in an era during which the exploitation of poverty, of bleak economic horizons, and of frustration of even modest national aspirations threatens both our own national security and the peace of the world."[9]

In 1953, in addition to Japan, the United States aided Taiwan, South Korea, Thailand, Indonesia, the Philippines, Indochina, and Burma. Direct assistance continued to Germany, Austria, and Japan until the mid-1950s. US-administered territories, including trust territories in the Caribbean and the Pacific, also received assistance.

Origins of Asian foreign aid lay in aborted Chinese and Korean rehabilitation programs. China had fallen to the communists in 1949. Of $230 million available by 1950, only $139.5 million was expended in Korea and Taiwan, and only $81 million when the mission to Korea ceased to function following the outbreak of the Korean War. The remaining $44 million funded new assistance programs in Burma, Indonesia, Thailand, and, of course, Laos, Cambodia and Vietnam. The United States would renew aid to South Korea and Taiwan after the Korean War.

In Formosa and the three Associated States of Indochina, Thailand, and the Philippines, ECA funding accompanied military assistance administered by Military Assistance Advisory Groups. To "operate the program in the field, ECA organized country staffs known as Special Technical and Economic Missions (STEMS). More than twice this amount ($535 million) was concurrently allocated for military assistance to the general area of China (including the Philippines and the Republic of Korea)."[10]

Concerned about the menacing spread of communist influence, the State Department, in the early spring of 1950, sent a survey mission to Southeast Asia to examine the potential for a US program of economic and technical aid. Unlike Western Europe after the war, Southeast Asia did not need support for imports, its capacity to absorb capital being limited. Rather, its needs lay in technical and managerial resources that would focus on reconstruction, rehabilitation, and development. This would be combined with military assistance for the French-controlled Vietnamese (Indochina) army.

Technical assistance, in its contemporary form, began with Point Four in 1950. As Paul Mosley points out, "It is in the early 1950s that one sees the beginning of aid in its present-day sense, as a transaction between sovereign states, with the beginning of the U.S. development program in Southeast Asia."[11] During the next twenty years, this program defined foreign policy and foreign aid in the postwar world and provided some success in Asia. In its first decade, foreign aid became a broad construct.

Aid-sponsored reform efforts inhibited new communist revolutions in Asia, Africa, and Latin America. The theory was that it would afford friendly leaders an opportunity to maintain their authority and legitimacy by delivering better services to their own citizens.[12] The intended outcome was greater political stability in Third World countries.

Not all developing country political leaders were happy with this. The United States considered left-wing movements to be threatening to ruling elites, and in some recipient countries substantial resistance to donor demands and conditions arose. There was also increasing resentment in recipient countries about the administrative mechanics of foreign aid that LDC policymakers felt were very cumbersome.

From the beginning, the major powers distributed aid to achieve short-term security and diplomatic objectives. A statistical analysis of aid disbursement by the United States, Britain, France, and Germany clearly demonstrated that the only significant pattern of distribution was the US foreign policy interests.[13] There were those who opposed aid as an instrument of foreign or military policy; however, foreign aid was "meant to influence the international behavior of the recipient."[14] Foreign crises almost always produced either a demand for foreign aid, or for critics of policy, a demand for the end of aid activities.

Point Four borrowed from prewar precepts of international assistance espoused by missionaries, private agencies, and State offices that administered aid prior to 1948.[15] The big difference after Point Four was the United States, and eventually most developed nations, would create huge aid bureaucracies to implement programs.[16] In 1950, in recognition of the need for specialized expertise in non-Western countries, the Truman administration established the Technical Cooperation Administration (TCA) to fund technical assistance.

Point Four emanated from the Marshall Plan experience. Policymakers linked assistance to ECA, but Point Four legislation created TCA to administer aid outside of Europe, European colonies, and former enemies of the United States. There was to be no duplication between the two programs.

Overall, the foreign aid industry was well developed by 1950. A bibliography of international administration published shortly thereafter noted that there were 215 organizations involved in international development work in 1950.[17] By 1951, foreign aid grants totaled $34 billion. Foreign aid employed 630 Americans and more than 800 Europeans in development and administration.[18] Supporters of Point Four suggested that missing from many developing countries were professional skills and that technical assistance should be the new program's focus. Only American know-how would fill the skills gap.[19]

Point Four shifted assistance from postwar Europe to the developing world. Foreign policy focused on the principles of modernization of the countryside which were, "an important part of so-called nation-building throughout the post-war period."[20] It also committed the United States to a policy of "enlightened self-interest" and moved the foreign aid system toward a more permanent and coordinated set of institutions. As Walter Sharp asks:

> What are the underlying assumptions of Point Four? First, that the United States should assume leadership in a cooperative effort to raise the living standards of more than a billion of the earth's peoples who are now the victims of undernourishment, disease, and ignorance. Second, through such an effort the economies of both advanced and underdeveloped countries can eventually be strengthened. Third, that technical assistance and capital investment can be combined in a program which will help the underdeveloped areas to attain a balanced economic development while avoiding the evils of exploitation and social disruption. Fourth, that the peoples of such areas can thereby be rallied to the cause of democratic freedom and against Soviet communism.[21]

Congress approved final legislation for Point Four on June 5, 1950. Initially, Point Four was intended to provide only technical assistance. Developing countries were to seek development financing from capital markets and the World Bank. Only a limited amount of nongovernment capital was available for Indochina and a number of dependent overseas territories. This proved unworkable, so development funding became a part of the TCA mandate.

The Cold War prolonged the tenure of ECA, and it merged with TCA and security assistance agencies to form the Mutual Security Administration (MSA) in 1951. The International Development Act of 1950 portended the centralization of military, economic, and technical assistance programs, entrusted to the MSA director under the Executive Office of the President. This reform reflected lack of confidence on the part of Congress in the ability of State to manage programs. MSA was initially designated the Foreign Operations Administration (FOA) under President Dwight D. Eisenhower.

By 1953, foreign aid policy stressed both political and military considerations and minimized purely economic and humanitarian motivations of aid. As a result of the Cold War, and, particularly, intervention in Korea, foreign aid increased significantly under Eisenhower. In July 1955, FOA became the International Cooperation Administration (ICA). In September 1961, the Foreign Assistance Act of 1961 created the US Agency for International Development (USAID).[22]

Assessing the First Decade

By the early 1950s, in addition to the Cold War, world leaders inherited the twin legacies of colonialism and imperialism that had defined technical assistance for more than a century. Entry of the United States into institutionalized foreign aid coincided with the disintegration of the old European empires and proliferation of newly independent Asian and African countries. A new alliance system, the North Atlantic Treaty Organization (NATO), appeared to challenge the Soviet Union.[23]

From the early postwar period, the assumption continued to be that technical assistance was temporary. As a result, aid underwent almost continuous reorganization. Agencies dispersed loans separately from grants and technical assistance, each of which also had different organizational structures. Special international jurisdictions were defined for the departments of Agriculture, Labor, Commerce, and Health, Education and Welfare.[24]

Throughout the Cold War, foreign aid, though low in terms of per capita assistance, remained large in absolute terms and often set the policy agenda among multilateral and bilateral organizations outside of the United States. The end of the Cold War in 1989 had an impact on the nature of the international system and foreign aid. As Madeleine Albright asserts:

> In colonial times, conflicts in Africa [and elsewhere] were settled through negotiations among the European powers. During the Cold War, outcomes were influenced by military assistance and proxy troops provided by one bloc or another. In the new era, there were no similarly potent external forces seeking to maintain order.[25]

Critics warned of impossible promises made in the Point Four speech; some called it both foolish in the modesty of the amounts promised and a "hoax" played on the poor nations of the world.[26] As the United States approached Point Four's implementation, Curti and Birr warned policymakers to learn from the past: "[If] American experience in the past is neglected or overlooked and the mistakes of previous missions are repeated, Point Four may turn out to be merely one more grand scheme that failed."[27]

By the late 1950s, foreign aid served as an extension of the ideological division between the East and the West. To its critics, "Western donors . . . [used] conditions attached to their aid as a means of forcing non-aligned developing countries with mixed economies away from socialism and public ownership and towards free market capitalism."[28] Criticism, at its most extreme, explained foreign aid as expanding the international capitalist system. Those of a more realist bent, saw international security as the primary motive.

Critics of foreign aid began to look back in history for lessons. There was the prewar experience with Latin America in the 1930s. Foreign assistance in Latin America was a disappointment. Among Latin Americans, by midcentury there were both disagreeable memories, as well as perceptions of continued US interference and political pressure in the hemisphere's internal affairs. Both were often cited as reasons for aid failures.[29] Everett and Helen Hughes, were blunt: "The exportation of technical skills and capital to unindustrialized areas is not a new thing under the sun. In the past its characteristic form has been the exploitation of colonial territories by imperialist powers."[30]

Despite these warnings, an optimism existed that defined foreign aid. "In an atmosphere of freedom and goodwill," Curti and Birr argued, "Americans can, through Point Four and its successive programs, be of great help in bringing some of the blessings of liberty and well-being to needy peoples of the world."[31]

In the early 1950s, ECA expanded its operations to Asia by combining commodity grants with specific technical assistance projects. These were, given the nature of the developing Cold War, not targeted just at economic development but also at production of strategic materials needed for security. With the United States' vastly superior bargaining power, it would be able to induce LDCs to accept economic aid on conditions designed to promote its foreign policy objectives, including increased production of strategic raw materials, favorable trade conditions, and an open investment climate. Needless to say, elites in LCDs resented this.

The early foreign assistance period was seen as a success. Despite criticisms, especially those linked to Latin American sensitivities, a broad consensus developed around foreign aid goals. Intellectually, as Barbara Ward noted in her classic lectures in the 1960s, foreign aid after Point Four "assumed progress." From this assumption came another: that developed country experts had unlimited ability to cope with LDC problems. By the end of the 1960s, however, the assumption of progress was no longer a given.

The early postwar world, as Stephen Browne points out, was thoroughly Keynesian. The goal under Point Four and subsequent aid programs was promotion of state-led economic growth and creation of a skilled labor force. As the Cold War evolved, however, foreign aid went from being a tool, though benign, of anti-communism, to include, as one Washington insider put it, a "social evangelism forming around the idea of American-financed economic development in the Third World. . . . Gradually, it dawned on wiser heads that our military assistance provided far less influence and leverage . . . than did our economic aid."[32]

Foreign aid policy became a part of the Cold War struggle. At the time, nearly all democratic theorists expected social reforms to preempt social revolution. Foreign aid became a weapon rather than a resource. As in World War II, the United States requested bases and staging areas in return for assistance.

During its early years, foreign aid had a state-centric focus among donors and aid recipients. The goal of international aid was to assist LDCs in what was called the "breakthrough," or takeoff stage, to higher levels of wealth creation.[33] In countries targeted for breakthrough, foreign aid and technical assistance would fill the gap. Concern overall was for capacity building, especially development administration. The private sector, however, was available to do some development work but often not incorporated in the development planning process.

During the first decade of the modern foreign aid era, technical assistance was very hands-on and "the administrators of the Technical Cooperation Administration programs [expected] most of their field employees to work with foreign people in villages and rural areas."[34] Modernization of rural sectors was important because "the spread of technology to economically backward regions of the globe [was] a by-product, if not a direct aim, of the overseas activities of religious, philanthropic, business and governmental organizations for a long time."[35]

Foreign aid institutions were still viewed as temporary by many political leaders, and they continued to function on a year-by-year basis. Even after the creation of USAID in 1961, policymakers considered foreign assistance as temporary. Because of uncertainties about the future, the foreign aid maxim within aid agencies such as USAID was to move money quickly.

The Eisenhower Legacy and Continued Criticism of Foreign Aid

By the end of the Eisenhower administration, foreign aid incorporated a series of contemporary (and security-focused) norms. Security assistance was on the ascendancy under MSA and its successor organizations. Southeast Asia was already of concern.

Eisenhower put his stamp on foreign aid when he established the ICA in July 1955. Aid under USAID became institutionalized. For the next forty years, there would be few structural changes.

By 1958, critics again noticed the self-serving nature of bilateral foreign aid. Indeed, in that year, almost 76 percent of all expenditures of ICA were spent in the United States. There was little evidence, according to State, that assistance programs directly built up economic enterprises or supported US economic activity, though it did often promote US marketing, expand trade opportunities, and protect US economic interests.[36] Leaders in the developing world shared this perception.

Debate about the utility of international assistance had become serious. As early as 1963, Edward Banfield warned against the fog of moralizing about aid[37]; however, doing nothing was not an option. As Mary Anderson would later put it "[I]t is a moral and logical fallacy to conclude that because aid can do harm, a decision *not* to give aid would do no harm. . . . By failing to support people engaged in a battle for justice, we support the status quo of injustice."[38]

As it evolved, foreign aid was much more complex than postwar aid to Europe. Donors, led by the United States, embarked on a vast program of international social engineering. In style, and sometimes in substance, the missionary model persisted into and beyond the Cold War period. Truman called US foreign aid workers, "technical missionaries," and according to James Thompson, "technocracy's own Maoists . . . have given new life to the missionary impulse" of US foreign policy.[39] There were similarities in background and worldviews of missionaries and colonial officers and the first generation of Peace Corps volunteers in the early 1960s.

It was in the late 1950s that a Republican-backed "Retrenchment in Aid" campaign began to criticize it as romantic and at a time when the economy was in recession claimed that, "American taxpayers [were] being fleeced to placate ungrateful nations."[40] The answer for advocates was to recognize the role economic assistance played as a tool of national security policy and to support commercial policies but also to argue it could and should be done more effectively and efficiently to promote development and support the national interest. By the end of the Eisenhower administration, foreign aid also suffered from lack of a domestic constituency. There was only a vague belief among some academics and practitioners that foreign aid was a quick fix to stimulate rapid and predictable economic growth.

There were two false assumptions predominating among advocates of foreign aid in retrospect. First, foreign aid is likely to lead to economic growth. Prior to 1960, observers identified the self-sustaining growth of economic institutions as a goal. Second, economic growth can and often will lead to politically developed and stable democratic societies. Both of these assumptions proved to be increasingly problematic.

Aid policy after 1960 was often characterized by fragmentary and contradictory goals. It was possible to distinguish between elite projects that allowed only an indirect impact on development and grassroots activities that would directly affect disadvantaged peoples. The latter were more difficult to implement successfully and difficult to support financially.

During the first decade of the foreign assistance era, development planners accepted macroeconomic planning theories as the basis for action. Conservative critics suggested that this brought command economics to development thinking. The assumption was a rationale for economic stability and growth, the twin goals of foreign aid, could be identified.

Economic growth assumed that countries ready for economic take off could be decisively influenced by massive amounts of foreign aid. Techniques included macroeconomic interventions. These new strategies assumed that economists could measure a country's needs by calculating capital investment opportunities and gaps in foreign exchange.

These macroeconomic assumptions replaced the technical assistance and bottom-up style of aid characterized under Truman and to some extent under Eisenhower; however, as John Franklin Campbell points out, "To preach a doctrine of minimum conflict and constant political stability on the one hand and fast economic growth and social change on the other is to insist on the most jumbled self-contraction."[41] This was so when resources were spread thinly around the world.

Following from this, and crucial to development, was the need within societies to reduce social tensions, mediate conflicts, and where possible, foster understanding between and among groups. Conflict resolution was at the center of discussions about political development and later governance. These have been constants for USAID policy since the 1960s.

There has long been support for private sector development within foreign aid circles; however, no strategy developed to stimulate growth for private sector in LDCs. Throughout the 1950s and into the 1960s, it was the philosophy of science that seemed to point the way for foreign aid. What was needed were technical people, engineers, and architects, not interested in politics but who could provide technical solutions to a country's development problems. For many practitioners, foreign aid was to be apolitical.

As foreign aid programs expanded, skepticism about implementation strategies grew, especially among program managers and planners in

LDCs as well as, for different reasons, conservatives in the business community in the United States and among international professionals. As a UN official put it, "No one [working in foreign aid programs] is seeing the forest from the trees in either UN or AID. Technicians are being sent over to do particular jobs, but these jobs do not have any relation to a meaningful whole."[42]

Institutionalizing Foreign Aid

The Situation in 1960–1961

ICA, created in 1955, became USAID in 1961. That name stuck. Earlier organizations were temporary and functionally specific. ICA/USAID operated on the assumption that the national interest required a longer-term international development program with greater operational flexibility.[43] Despite the creation of ICA, however, a negative image of foreign aid developed among political conservatives.

By 1960, aid programs included: military assistance, defense support, development and technical assistance, and the provision of mutual security funding. Foreign assistance also included the Public Law 480 (food security), the presidential contingency fund, nonmutual security foreign aid programs, and Export-Import Bank loans.[44] There were three components to PL 480: Title One, where US-produced, inexpensive (submarket-priced) food is sold on the private sector in LDCs; Title Two, emergency free food; and Title Three, food for development provisions, where food was delivered as part of development projects.

Of the whole, approximately 50 percent of US aid went for military assistance, 33 percent for defense support, 7 percent for development assistance and 14 percent for the rest, including administration. Coordination of foreign aid was at issue for policymakers from the beginning. There were several overlapping programs of varying geographical and substantive scope that reflected a mixture of emergency, midterm, and long-range objectives implemented by, at best, a loosely arrayed set of administrative arrangements. Some of the arrangements were of a "rather makeshift character."[45]

By 1960 foreign aid faced difficulties. From the beginning, there was little appreciation of what a foreign aid program was supposed to do in the minds of recipient country officials.[46] Not surprisingly, aid met up with the vagaries of political obstacles and "[d]ivergent views emerged as to where and how the line should be drawn between the exchange of technical knowledge and skills and the provision of capital investment (a kind of chicken and egg problem). Which should come first? Or should they go hand in hand?"[47] One of the factors slowing the foreign aid process related to congressional delays in appropriating funds. Walter Sharp comments:

> The difficulties, added to the regrettable delay with which Congress appropriated initial funds for Point Four operations, led to disillusionment over what were regarded as "unfulfilled" American promises. The sense of disappointment was heightened by the decided modest amount of money made available for the first phase of the program.[48]

During this period before mass communications, "the knotty problems of any headquarters-field relationships [were] multiplied by distance and compounded by cross-cultural misunderstandings."[49] A report submitted by the International Development Advisory Board under the chairmanship of Nelson Rockefeller, supported a similar thesis: "A unified agency with a new point of view is needed. A mere on-paper shift of existing agencies and functions will not suffice. Nor will it do simply to transfer additional functions to ECA."[50]

The decade between 1951 and 1961 became the high watermark of idealism for aid in what it would achieve in international development. In 1961 President Kennedy stated that the United States would give aid to the Third World, (the term normally used to describe the developing world at this time) "not to contain the spread of communism, not because other nations are doing it, but because it is right."[51] Kennedy's Alliance for Progress for Latin America appeared to represent a new dynamic in foreign aid.[52] Foreign policy claimed a moral component, resting on

> action rather than in the profession of remote, if high minded goals. . . . But the influence of the [policymaker] intervention-ist's naïve historicism is so large today that we see are increasingly ruthless with the obstacles we see as standing in the way of our irreproachable but distant goals."[53]

The Creation of USAID

The Foreign Assistance Act of 1961 created USAID. The agency is still in existence in 2009, forty-seven years later, perhaps a minor miracle. USAID, a "temporary agency," has managed the bulk of development assistance, with primary focus on support for health, education and training, transportation and agriculture, and economic development. Legislation called for the use of domestic federal agencies to support these activities.

After the creation of USAID, foreign aid took three forms:

- direct dollar aid to supply foreign exchange for the purchase of imports
- funds for economic and social development in the form of either loans and grants
- technical assistance provided by skilled professionals in residence for varying periods of time

Missions negotiated bilateral agreements with host countries either delivering support directly or increasingly through contractors and grantholders. USAID initially preferred large infrastructure projects. These allowed funding to be quickly expended, and results could be seen by the public.

USAID emphasized encouraging popular participation in democratic public, private, and local institutions that promoted economic and social development. USAID's goal was to support friendly foreign countries by promoting the development of their productive capacity and free market economic institutions and by eliminating or minimizing barriers to the flow of private investment capital.

USAID's creation reflected an upgrading of foreign aid, placing it in the hands of what the late David Halberstam ruefully called the "Best and the Brightest" of the foreign policy establishment.[54] By 1962 a basic mode of operation evolved that would change little through the present. Within the structures of USAID, the system operated on a virtual master plan, having standard organization systems, personnel systems, and procurement mechanisms. Unfortunately, the system came to operate with a rigidity that made adjustments to local situations difficult.

By 1963 USAID managed a $3.6 billion per year program, up from just under $1 billion in 1960[55]; however, the mid-1960s were a peak in foreign aid spending, tied as they were to the growing crisis in Southeast Asia. All too often, from 1961 through 1967, project grants and loans made by both bilateral and multilateral organizations were not part of an obvious coordinated development strategy.[56] By 1967 the foreign aid budget dropped to below $2 billion for the first time since 1960, and by 1968 it was down to $1.4 billion. By 1970, support for foreign aid had fallen off significantly with little protest from business, academics, or the public.

Kennedy Policy Reforms

Ideologically, advocates of foreign aid were divided between self-defined realists and moralists. There were increasing numbers of critics of foreign aid on both the left and the right. Domestic critics also expressed concern about whether foreign aid had a positive or negative impact upon the economy. Government reports often justified foreign aid because it helped the economy and international trade.

Foreign aid grew 24 percent under Kennedy. Though Kennedy projected an image of idealism, the aid goal became to resist Communist aggression in Asia.[57] After fifteen years of postwar foreign aid, Americans had a political mission under the new president. The goal was to ensure the security and welfare of the United States by educational, political, or even military methods.

Realists had become dominant at the policymaking level, linking foreign aid to the Cold War issues. Despite congressional criticism, the United States saw the Third World as an ideological battleground. Foreign aid's critics saw political actions, technical assistance, and aid projects as manipulative and interference in other people's business.

Beginning with Kennedy, the tone of speeches about the Soviet Union and communism became "much more secular, humanistic, scientific, and negotiable."[58] The goal was to use foreign policy to negotiate an end to the Cold War. The Kennedy administration became identified with a realist approach to security and foreign aid. As incoming Secretary of State Dean Rusk put it, "I think the principal point is that a change in administration gives us a chance to take a fresh look at a good many of our policies, to make fresh approaches, and to see whether we are going in the direction in which we as a nation really want to go."[59]

Though there were critical reappraisals of foreign aid during the Eisenhower administration, it was the Clay Report that jolted the international assistance community. In December 1962, Kennedy appointed General Lucius D. Clay, hero of the Berlin airlift, to head a "Citizens' Committee" to investigate foreign aid. Many described the report as "draconian," as having a "shock-effect" and as an attack on the romantic notions motivating international assistance.

The Clay Report raised crucial questions about aid, which led to increased focus on market economics. In augmenting the role of the private sector and free enterprise, the report introduced development loans, investment guarantees, and small business provisions. It also introduced a contracting process to utilize private enterprise in policy implementation. More than anything else, it recommended an agency machinery (through USAID) that defined foreign aid as an instrument of the State Department, with an implementation process modeled on the contracting that dominated defense and security agency practice.

To many advocates, the report created despair about foreign aid that began what would later be called "donor fatigue." There would be an increased emphasis on foreign policy and security as they relate to aid, as well as a decreased role in large-scale transfer of capital for development to recipient governments and an increased role for the private sector in policy implementation. Development was de-emphasized as a goal. The report, with its heavy stress on security and relegation of development, stimulated mistrust internationally.

From a security perspective, Kennedy's Alliance for Progress also illustrated the new emphasis on realism. It proposed an accelerated aid program for Latin America to ensure there would be no more "Cubas" in the Western Hemisphere. Moreover, the Alliance also worked to strengthen Latin American armies and defend American business interests. US policy, according to Latin American critics, helped Latin American elites stave off political reforms.

Military assistance again featured in foreign aid legislation. Despite Kennedy's rhetoric of realism, foreign aid came to take on an increasingly ideological and moral dimension. According to Stanley Hoffman, during the 1960s, "Foreign aid like foreign policy more generally became the orphans of [the policy of] containment."[60] At the same time, foreign aid experts were less and less sure of the formula for social and economic development, particularly assumptions about economic growth. Democratization, ideologically, began to appear in foreign assistance.

Conclusion

There is a tendency among Americans to believe that their values and needs are universal. On the whole, Americans have remained an optimistic society. Internationalism since the 1950s meant historical commitment, compromise, and recognition of the inherently political nature of the international process. This remained difficult for many policymakers who may see moral choices in international interaction. This perception can lead to difficulties in distinguishing between that which a country declares and that which is real.

During the immediate postwar period, the purpose of foreign aid was to restore war torn countries, strengthen the military and political defenses of "free" nations, and weaken the appeal of communism. There was a messianic element to the enterprise. By the end of the 1960s, however, foreign aid as reform "had lost its evangelistic tone and taken on a legal flavor."[61]

The shift toward government-to-government aid represented a major change in international assistance after World War II and was defined in the period between 1948 and 1961. Now, at least in theory, governments assumed that some redistribution of wealth internationally was part of their responsibility. The goal of policymakers in the 1950s was to create a foreign aid system that included a unified administration and policy formulation, long-term planning and financing, and integrated country-level programming.

Perceptions of foreign aid failure originated in strategic rather than developmental considerations during the Cold War. There may be a lesson here for those who see foreign aid as a part of a war on terrorism. As a result, it is not unlikely that there may be similar perceptions of failure in future as the US reaches into the twenty-first century.

Notes

1. See Jacob J. Kaplan, "United States Foreign Aid Programs: Past Perspectives and Future Needs," *World Politics*, 3, no.1 (October 1950), pp. 57–58. Entire article: pp. 55–71.

2. An important book on the origins of U.S. foreign aid is Steven W. Hook, *National Interest and Foreign Aid* (Boulder, CO: Lynne Rienner Publishers, 1995).

3. Edwin A. Bock, *Fifty Years of Technical Assistance; Some Administrative Experiences of U. S. Voluntary Agencies* (Chicago: Public Administration Clearing House, 1954), pp. 2–3 and 15.

4. Walter R. Sharp, *International Technical Assistance* (Chicago: Public Administration Service, 1952), p. 7.

5. Kaplan, "United States Foreign Aid Programs," p. 68.

6. Barbara W. Tuchman, *The March of Folly: From Troy to Vietnam* (New York: Alfred A. Knopf, 1984), p. 293.

7. John D. Montgomery, *Aftermath: Tarnished Outcomes of American Foreign Policy* (Dover, MA: Auburn House Publishing Company, 1985), p. 47.

8. David McCullough, *Truman* (New York: Simon & Schuster, 1992), p. 730.

9. Kaplan, "United States Foreign Aid Programs," pp. 55–71. Quote, p. 55.

10. Ibid., p. 49.

11. Paul Mosley, *Overseas Aid: Its Defense and Reform* (Brighton, UK: Wheatsheaf Books, 1987), pp. 2–23.

12. Montgomery, *Aftermath*, p. 65.

13. Severine M. Rugumamu, *Lethal Aid: The Illusion of Socialism and Self-Reliance in Tanzania* (Trenton, NJ: Africa World Press, 1997), p. 61.

14. George Liska, *The New Statecraft: Foreign Aid in American Foreign Policy* (Chicago: University of Chicago Press, 1960), p. 127.

15. *A Reference Volume on Technical Assistance Programs with Particular Emphasis on the Work and Responsibilities of Voluntary*

Agencies, Study Sponsored by the American Council of Voluntary Agencies for Foreign Service (Washington, DC: May 1953), p. 6.

16. See Steven W. Hook, "Preface," in *Foreign Aid Toward the Millennium*, Steven W. Hook, ed. (Boulder, CO: Lynne Rienner Publishers, 1996), p. viii.

17. Katrine R. C. Greene, *Institutions and Individuals: An Annotated List of Directories Useful in International Administration* (Chicago: Public Administration Service, 1953).

18. Martin Wolf, "Marshall's Lasting Legacy," *Financial Times* (June 3, 1997), p. 12.

19. As Milton J. Esman and John D. Montgomery laconically point out in "Systems Approaches to Technical Cooperation: The Role of Development Administration," in *Public Administration Review*, (September/October, 1969), pp. 507–539. Quote, p. 511.

20. Harvey Cleaver, "Will the Green Revolution Turn Red?" in Weissman, ed., *The Trojan Horse: A Radical Look at Foreign Aid* (Palo Alto, CA: Rampart Press, 1974), p. 179.

21. Sharp, *International Technical Assistance*, p. ix.

22. The story of the founding of USAID is ably presented by Vernon W. Ruttan, *United States Development Assistance Policy: The Domestic Politics of Foreign Economic Aid* (Baltimore: Johns Hopkins University Press, 1996).

23. Edmund Stillman and William Pfaff, *Power and Impotence: The Failure of America's Foreign Policy* (New York: Random House, 1966).

24. John D. Montgomery, *The Politics of Foreign Aid: American Experience in Southeast Asia* (New York: Praeger, 1962), pp. 152–153.

25. Madeleine Albright, *Madame Secretary: A Memoir* (New York: Miramax Books, 2003), pp. 450–451.

26. William Vogt, "Point Four Propaganda and Reality," *American Perspective*, iv, no. 2 (Spring 1950), p. 124. Article, pp. 129–138.

27. Merle Curti and Kendall Birr, *Prelude to Point Four: American Technical Missions Overseas 1838–1938* (Madison: The University of Wisconsin Press, 1954), p. 218.

28. Mosley, *Overseas Aid*, p. 38.

29. Daniel Cosio Villegas, "A Latin American View of Point Four," *American Perspective*, iv, no. 2 (Spring 1950), pp. 138 and 140–141. Article, pp. 138–145.

30. Everett C. Hughes and Helen M. Hughes, "Sociologists View Point Four," *American Perspective*, iv, no. 2 (Spring 1950), p. 129.

31. Curti and Birr, *Prelude to Point Four*, p. 218.

32. Both quotes from Townsend Hoopes, *The Limits of Intervention: An Inside Account of how the Johnson Policy of Escalation in Vietnam Was Reversed* (New York: David McKay Company, 1969), p. vi. and 43.

33. See Walt W. Rostow, *The Stages of Growth: A Non-Communist Manifesto* (Cambridge, MA: Cambridge University Press, 1960).

34. Wallace S. Sayre and Clarence E. Thurber, *Training for Specialized Mission Personnel* (Chicago: Public Administration Service, 1952), p. 23.

35. Sharp, *International Technical Assistance,* p. x.

36. *The United States Economy and The Mutual Security Program* (Washington DC: U.S. Department of State, April, 1959), pp. 6 and 16.

37. Ibid., p. 35.

38. Mary B, Anderson, *Do No Harm: How Aid Can Support Peace—or War* (Boulder, CO: Lynne Rienner Publishers, 1999), pp. 2 and 7.

39. Quoted by Campbell, *The Foreign Affairs Fudge Factory,* pp. 178 and 181.

40. Usha Maharajani, "Kennedy and the Strategy of Aid: The Clay Report and After," *Western Political Quarterly,* xviii, no. 3 (September 1965), pp. 656–668. Quote, p. 663.

41. Campbell, *The Foreign Affairs Fudge Factory,* p. 183.

42. Noted in Edward W. Weidner, *Technical Assistance in Public Administration Overseas: The Case for Development Administration* (Chicago: Public Administration Service, 1964), p. 46.

43. See H. Field Haviland, "Foreign Aid and the Policy Process: 1957," *American Political Science Review,* 52, no. 33 (September 1958), pp. 689–724.

44. Sidney Sonenblum and Herbert Striner, *The Foreign Aid Programs and the United States Economy, 1948–1957* (Washington DC: National Planning Association, May 9, 1958), p. 7.

45. Sharp, *International Technical Assistance,* p. 51.

46. United Nations, *Technical Assistance Administration, Training in Public Administration* (New York: 1958), pp. 33–34.

47. Sharp, *International Technical Assistance,* p. 25.

48. Ibid., p. x.

49. Gerald Harlan and John Cleveland, *The Overseas Americans.* (New York: McGraw-Hill, 1960, p. 151).

50. See Sharp, *International Technical Assistance,* p. 54.

51. Mosley, *Overseas Aid,* p. 27.

52. Hook, *National Interest and Foreign Aid,* p. 26.

53. Stillman and Pfaff, *Power and Impotence,* p. 169.

54. David Halberstam, *The Best and the Brightest* (New York: Fawcett Crest, 1972).

55. Edward K. Hamilton, "Toward Public Confidence in Foreign Aid," *World Affairs*, 132, no. 4 (March 1970), p. 287.

56. Carlos F. Diaz-Alejandro, "Some Aspects of the Brazilian Experience with Foreign Aid," (Center Paper No.177, Yale University Economic Growth Center, 1972), p. 467.

57. William Easterly, *The Elusive Quest for Growth: Economists' Adventures and Misadventures in the Tropics* (Cambridge, MA: MIT Press, 2001), p. 106.

58. Judith Hoover, "Ronald Reagan's Failure to Secure Contra-Aid: A Post-Vietnam Shift in Foreign Policy Rhetoric," *Presidential Studies Quarterly*, xxiv, no. 3 (Summer 1994), p. 536.

59. Dean Rusk, "A Fresh Look at the Formulation of Foreign Policy," Reprint from the *Department of State Bulletin* (February 20, 1961), p. 1.

60. Stanley Hoffmann, "What Should We Do in the World?" *The Atlantic Monthly* (October 1989), p. 85.

61. Montgomery, *Aftermath*, p. 72.

7

THE VIETNAM WAR

Thousands of pages of mimeographed reports and documents sent from Saigon have been piled haphazardly in out-of-the-way files in the University library, un-catalogued and unused.

Warren Hinckle, "The University on the Make"

"AID!" the farmer cried. "Look at you. . . ." He pointed, sweeping his finger from one charred remembrance of a home to another. "Here is your American AID!" The farmer spat on the ground and walked away.

Neil Sheehan, *A Bright Shining Lie*

We have "discovered that the need to influence these countries is far less than we imagined." We now know that the economic development of the poor countries will be "very slow."

John Franklin Campbell, *The Foreign Affairs Fudge Factory*

Foreign Aid and the March of Folly

The Cold War

There was a legacy of US policy in Vietnam, based on assumptions of modernization, industrialization, and individualism that had their origins, as we have seen, in nineteenth century Europe—and America—into what was still in 1950 called the non-Western world. This chapter hones in on the limitations of those assumptions and of unilateralism in foreign aid and foreign policy within the context of what Barbara Tuchman called the "March of Folly,"[1] a phenomenon characterized by the pursuit of policies contrary to a country's own interests.

By the 1960s, foreign aid was no longer a temporary solution but part of the arsenal of foreign and security policy tools available to the government; however, with this logic, as one critic puts it, "We have been conditioned by our social science training not to ask the normative question; we possess neither the inclination nor the means with which to question and judge our foreign policy."[2]

From about 1955 to 1965, until the US intervention became militarized, large numbers of foreign aid officers worked in South Vietnam. Efforts to promote social change and economic development became justification for US military intervention a decade later, and USAID became associated with the Vietnam War.

During the Cold War, a logical step was to link foreign aid to proxy wars, first in Korea and Indochina, and then throughout Asia, Latin America, and Africa. To critics of foreign aid, it was during the 1960s that foreign aid seemed to support "dangerous liaisons" between the United States and venal and violent dictators.[3] Foreign policy adviser, Jeane Kirkpatrick, is said to have noted, in response to criticism of support for Zaire's President Mobutu, that he may have been a bastard but that he was our bastard.

Foreign and military assistance in Vietnam and foreign aid policies that followed were part of this pattern as Robert McNamara so forcefully (if belatedly) demonstrated. Many aid policies became grounded in *unilateralism*.[4]

We give attention here to the legacy of Vietnam as it affected foreign aid between 1951 and 1975. Vietnam was a watershed not only in military but in foreign assistance terms. More than half of aid officials in the 1980s and 1990s served in Vietnam where military and aid policy intermingled. Similarly, the Iraq intervention is tainting and will taint foreign assistance efforts into the future.

The Early Years

The Vietnam War was a direct outcome of French colonial rule in Indochina. America's participation for more than fifteen years "originated from ignorance and excessive optimism and escalated even though officials became dubious of eventual success."[5]

Despite the anticolonialism of the Roosevelt and Truman administrations, in 1946, the assumed Communist domination of the Vietminh prevented the United States from treating the Indochina War as a colonial question. The Truman Doctrine compelled the United States to assist colonial and other governments—such as the British in Malaya—in fighting local Communist-inspired revolutionaries.

On February 2, 1950, Truman recognized the French-dominated protectorate in Indochina, providing economic and military aid to France in their fight against the Vietminh. From the beginning, there was congressional resistance to involvement among those who thought that anything proposed by France was colonial and oppressive. Resistance to involvement, either by Congress or within the administration was small until 1964.

The British successfully put down the Communist uprising in Malaya, the only successful counterinsurgency model sponsored by a Western power in Asia, and brought a rural revolt "the Mau Mau," under control in Kenya. The Malayan enterprise influenced US foreign policy and proved to be an unfortunate model for Vietnam.[6]

The United States defined its mission in Vietnam as *transformation* and modernization, of gaining control of the revolutionary process through a search for a third way between communism and colonialism. North and South Vietnamese, alike, spoke of freedom from colonial exploiters. Americans talked of good government and would complain that much of the foreign aid "trickled away into the pockets of profiteering officials."[7] There was no common understanding of the meaning of democratic governance in Indochina. That there was a shared concept of democracy worldwide was, for many critics, an American delusion.

Initially, in Indochina, focus was on humanitarian aid, food assistance, and resettlement of refugees from the north. Later, focus of the US Operations Mission turned to agricultural development, security assistance and land reform. During the Ngo Dinh Diem period, technical assistance addressed social reform and land tenure issues. US representatives attempted local reforms, including farming cooperatives, self-help projects, and village democratic elections. By 1960 the foreign aid team in Vietnam had provided some infrastructure assistance, malaria control, and relief for refugees. Little else seemed to stick on the ground.

Vietnam itself, prior to the military buildup was part of a golden age in foreign aid. During the period prior to the dustup of the Vietnam War in 1965, foreign policy agencies had excellent access to academics with development policy and administration interests. During the 1950s, academics spent significant time in the Southeast Asia region that had become aid laboratories. Many social scientists served with the US advisory team.

With the withdrawal of the French from Indochina, the United States embarked on nation-building exercises in South Vietnam—creation of a viable state with legitimate political authority, a functioning economy, and a sense of community. Among different social strata, religions, and ethnic groups, the dilemma was clear: How would it foster an independent South Vietnam that would not become totally dependent on American assistance?

To many but not all serving in ICA and later USAID in Vietnam, the real war "was with poverty and social backwardness, and with the selfishness of that minority of men who stand in the way of a 'world of freedom and opportunity for . . . the whole human race.'"[8] In the early 1950s, some of those administering the Vietnam assistance program possessed a missionary zeal, in searching for the third force between communism and colonialism. They attempted, with persistence, to dampen down each political crisis or use foreign aid to buy off non-communist revolutionary forces.

From the beginning, there was no attempt by the military or the civilian leadership to explain the conflict. According to journalist James Reston, what it was creating in Vietnam was an idealistic nation, while in practice, the United States, "was coming more and more to rely on pure power."[9] There was continuity between the 1960s and the present.

Political and military intervention in Vietnam represented a high watermark in the United States' impulse towards patterns of unilateral political-military intervention following 1945—that is, until post–September 11. Involvement in Vietnam assumed that Russia and China were, under Communist leadership, both expansionist, and the cause of the Communist revolutions in Asia.

Many of the early foreign aid programs in Southeast Asia, both humanitarian and developmental, appeared to contemporary observers to be successful. As a result of these early assessments, foreign advisers in Vietnam "were inserted into every part of the [government of Vietnam] bureaucracy with the authority not only to advise but to insist on the adoption of new programs."[10]

There were real successes in the 1950s. Charities, mainly religious NGOs such as Catholic Charities, Catholic Relief Services, and the International Relief Committee were heavily involved in what was called the "miracle" of relief work in South Vietnam in the 1950s. "Operation Exodus" moved hundreds of thousands of refugees (mainly Catholic) from North Vietnam to the South.

Support for military assistance and foreign aid were comingled during the Vietnam War in the Kennedy/Johnson period. The assumptions were simple. As David Maraniss points out in his remarkable book about the period, Souvanna Phouma (of Laos) once persisted in asking President Lyndon Johnson "whether he could get assistance for refugee care and defense needs, the president advised him to talk with Secretary McNamara."[11] Defense called the shots in foreign assistance policy in Vietnam.

In Vietnam in the 1950s, people were directed both by the tradition of the family and by the impact of the state. At the village level, focus was on community development. USAID's Civic Action Project was a rural development effort designed to encourage villages to rebuild war-damaged public facilities. With its community development focus, assistance became very retail.

Observers were initially optimistic about the US intervention. In 1960, Joseph Buttinger could claim, "Vietnam . . . is the first country in Asia where the West, by replacing imperialism with policies of aid, has stopped the 'Russians' without firing a shot." "War or Peace," Buttinger went on, "survival or annihilation, may depend on the skill with which we use, in Asia and elsewhere, the weapon of foreign aid in the pursuit of our political aims in the international arena."[12]

Kennedy, Johnson, and Vietnam

Vietnam-era US policymakers, whether in the military, foreign affairs, or foreign aid policy, were born prior to World War II and shaped by it—the age of Kennedy's Camelot. Many in the Kennedy generation were infused with the missionary idealism that had awakened in them. This generation went overseas full of illusions, for which the intoxicating atmosphere of those years was as much to blame as their youth.

Yet security issues were at heart of the intervention in Southeast Asia. In the Kennedy administration, "economic aid administrators of all ranks were required to take a 'counterinsurgency course' before being posted to underdeveloped countries."[13] "Pacification" would involve nothing less than politically managed counterrevolution in the interests of American-style democracy. Security assistance in Vietnam drew inspiration from hearts and minds theories of John J. McCuen, a lieutenant colonel in the US Army who advocated "counter guerrilla and 'middle group' support to counteract revolutionary forces."[14]

In 1961, the Cold War was real, and policy advisers such as Walt Rostow believed that Third World countries were a new battlefield in the war. In focusing on Southeast Asia, concern was that area's suffering "from the ravages of recent or incipient war and troubled by unsettled political conditions [that] have weak, inexperienced, and unstable governments woefully deficient in administrative and financial capacity."[15] Aid to Indochina, according to one USAID official, was not so much "a development program but, in effect, a battle field action where a certain amount of waste is inherent under the crisis situation."[16]

At the beginning of 1964, there was as yet no central guiding philosophy in foreign policy in Southeast Asia. Foreign policy leadership was pulled by the extremes of debate and "there seemed to be no logical stopping point between isolationism and globalism."[17] However, the United States, according to its critics, suffered from a missionary compulsion to guide the South Vietnamese toward its policy objectives. Above all, however, intervention meant *pacification*. Vietnam, as Frances FitzGerald wryly noted, became an archeology of pacification with strategic hamlets, new life hamlets, and finally "Really New Life Hamlets" being introduced.[18]

Intervention in military assistance and aid had rules of engagement. Though the original purpose was to manage and limit military engagement, the model would influence foreign policy and foreign aid from that time. Above all, as Caputo points out, within the rules of engagement, there "seemed to be a matter of distance and technology."[19] You could not go wrong if your mistakes were at great distance from their impact and if they involved sophisticated methodologies. At close range, "[t]here was no one out there to stop me from actually doing it [killing the innocent], no one and nothing except that inner system of moral checks called conscience."[20] Similar, though less dramatic, authority existed within foreign aid.[21]

Foreign aid rules, above all for political reasons, required speedy results, a quick fix. This was a pattern that stuck with USAID at the end of the war. In 1964, the Johnson administration committed to a three-year program of military and economic aid and established an unworkable program based on an advanced agreement with South Vietnam involving specific, measurable goals. This led to the infamous body-counts fiasco and became the basis of a quantifiable cost benefit analysis for US foreign aid.

The Anti-War Movement

For the first time after 1964, academics and intellectuals so linked to Democratic Party foreign policy began to question the moral implications of actions in Vietnam and other parts of the Third World as involvement in Vietnam deepened. Political unease became the source of increased moral outrage. This increased throughout the decade, as these same academics and other intellectuals became a central component of the antiwar movement. In September 1965, Senator J. William Fulbright broke with the Johnson administration, characterizing the intervention, as the "arrogance of power." Riots followed. Foreign aid policy was discredited both domestically and internationally in Vietnam. During the Vietnam War, a left-wing magazine, *Ramparts,* published an article revealing the extent to which Michigan State University (MSU) had become involved in US support for South Vietnam. This involvement became symptomatic of the intersection of foreign aid and military policy.

In 1955, Dr. Wesley Fishel, of Michigan State University established an extensive technical assistance program focused on public administration and security.[22] The MSU team consisted of some fifty academics, including public administration experts who came to assist in the reorganization of the police, the civil guard, and the public service. Prominent among the strategies was the creation of "agrovilles," protected rural development centers.

In June of 1955, a team of CIA specialists knowledgeable in solving intractable problems of a political nature arrived in Saigon. They, at least in part, came under the cover of a MSU advisory group funded by the ICA, the predecessor to USAID.[23] The intervention by MSU in Vietnam ultimately disturbed many at the university. According to *Ramparts*, "One lesser-known, and perhaps more unpleasant task of the MSU professors was to provide a front for a unit of the Central Intelligence Agency."[24] However, according to one participant, none of those directly involved were "significantly troubled by the fact that our Project had become a CIA front."[25]

Writing about the phenomenon of what *Ramparts* called "MSU and Madam Nhu," Walter Hinckle has noted the leaders of the project saw "the future of the social science in the world-wide scope of the 'action' projects [they are] now directing—in Formosa as . . . in Vietnam."[26] According to Ramparts, however,

> The same disastrous vacuum of information occurred in this country [Vietnam] only a decade before when the China experts, almost to a man, were purged as Reds and comsymps, and yahoos were all the public had left to hear. . . . The professors found their colleague [Wesley] Fishel and General Edward Landsdale of the CIA maneuvering furiously to consolidate Diem's support, an effort that culminated with the endorsement of Diem by the U.S. Security Council in the spring of 1955.[27]

Ramparts, despite the inaccuracies in its reporting, epitomized the anti-Vietnam position among academics and journalists. The magazine concluded:

> This residential ranking attests to [Wesley] Fishel's importance as head of the Michigan State University Group in Vietnam, an official university project under contract to Saigon and Washington, with responsibility for the proper functioning of Diem's civil service and his police network, the shaping up of the 50,000 man 'ragamuffin' militia, and the supplying of guns and ammunition for the city police, the civil guard, the palace police, and the dreaded Surete—South Vietnam's version of the FBI.[28]

By 1965 the United States dominated civil and military policy in Vietnam, a country that it claimed to want to make independent. This was a development that most policymakers at the time, both in Saigon and Washington, frankly were uncomfortable with. Policy elites in the South Vietnam government, in turn, came to take aid for granted. US expenditures on refugees alone came to $30 million a year. By the end of the 1960s, Vietnam received almost half of US assistance.

The reality was, however, that Robert McNamara's system of security-oriented performance budgeting had crept into USAID, and cost-effectiveness limited choices and narrowed options for programs. To its critics, US foreign policy was influenced by game theory and systems analysis pushed by "whiz kid" technocrats such as Alain C. Enthoven[29] and McNamara himself. On the ground, however, many Vietnamese saw the Americans "merely as the producers of garbage from which they could build houses."[30]

The Militarization of Aid

In 1965 Vietnam had both the largest aid mission and the largest military assistance program in the world. Despite this, and unlike the situation in Taiwan and Korea, most of the funding did not go for development. Approximately 90 percent of the entire USAID foreign aid budget every year went to military forces, the civil guard, and the intelligence services, and only a minute fraction went to industrial or agricultural development.

During the Lyndon Johnson years, in its public face "the foreign aid program was celebrated as a global war on poverty that in a short time could be expected to eradicate disease, illiteracy, and the other age-old problems of mankind."[31] The goal in its unilateral political and military interventions was overtly the realization of what it called a liberal, social, and political revolution. As early as 1966, Stillman and Pfaff identified this as the "near ultimate folly of American interventionism."[32]

Practical implications of involvement in Vietnam caused alarm as "billions in aid . . . poured untold quantities of every conceivable commodity into a simple, fragile economic system."[33] All of this was aggravated by half a million Americans spending incredible amounts of money. By 1966, military involvement had reached such a point that "[t]he shooting war on the ground . . . proceeded with full autonomy, subordinating by its sheer weight [and undermining by its sheer destructiveness] the political efforts aimed at pacification, reform, and nation-building."[34]

Critics of foreign policy in Vietnam suggested that the United States, "drawing upon [an] old missionary tradition, was obsessed by a zeal to improve Asia [and was] reanimated by the anti Communist crusade."[35] Policymakers also focused on the impact of individuals and personalities as the overthrow of Diem made clear.

During Vietnam, idealism of the Marshall Plan gave way to strings attached by Congress and the executive branch, whether of a political or a commercial nature. The operational framework in South Vietnam also had a colonial flavor to it. Planners in Washington continued to see "Vietnam as a source of raw materials and cheap labor and as an outlet for manufactured goods."[36]

The United States offered aid to North Vietnam at various times as a carrot to entice the enemy into peace negotiations. In April 1965, the United States proposed a $1 billion development project for Southeast Asia centering on the Mekong River. As the war Americanized, Vietnamese elites and the urban middle class, particularly in Saigon, grew more and more dependent on donor aid.

Most of the security concerns in Vietnam were naturally military not civil. Most importantly, as the war expanded, little aid trickled down to the village level, despite the fact that prior to 1965 community development was the most successful component of aid policy in Vietnam. The focus of foreign policy concerns by 1965 was on the threat of peasant rebellions. Poverty breeds communism, which was a "disorder caused by social evil, a parasitic growth feeding on injustice."[37] To quote President Johnson:

> The roots of . . . trouble are found wherever the landless and the despised, the poor and the oppressed, stand before the gates of opportunity seeking entry into a brighter land. They can get there only if we narrow the gap between the rich nations and the poor—and between the rich and the poor within each region.[38]

USAID eventually turned to retired military officers as a source of manpower for service in what was an increasingly risky country. USAID professionals, called the US Operations Mission in Vietnam, were fearful that their agency was being taken over by the military. By 1966, "USAID . . . [and the Public Affairs Office of the US Embassy] alone included hundreds of people ranging from agricultural experts to hospital administrators, film makers, sociologists, artificial limb manufacturers, and water pollution experts."[39] Many existed in the twilight between civilian and military activity.

In the late 1960s, John Paul Vann symbolized special operations in Vietnam. Overtly he was an USAID official in the office of Civil Operations and Revolutionary Development Support (CORDS). In 1965, Vann, who had served several tours in Vietnam in the military, approached senior officials in USAID to join the civilian pacification program, the Strategic Hamlet program. In 1966, Vann became deputy director of

USAID operations in north of Saigon. The strategy was to combine military control with social reform.

Ostensibly, Vann's job was to support community efforts in raising hogs, supporting refugees, and civilian pacification projects; in reality, he was a senior operative in special operations in Vietnam and managed the Vietnamese operations that tried to control the rural countryside. Vann, whose personal courage was well known, came to represent the duplicitous nature of intervention. Though technically a civilian, he covertly shared command over 158,000 South Vietnamese troops. He maintained his USAID cover until his mysterious death on October 9, 1972.

The Strategic Hamlet program was one of the products of foreign aid in Vietnam. The assumption was security had to be combined with social change. The Vietnamese needed schools and health facilities to restore the loyalty to embattled communities. USAID's role was to secure villages and train specialized teams of Vietnamese pacification workers, who wielded both carrots and sticks at the village level. After 1966, village elections were held in militarily secure areas in Vietnam. In the aftermath of the successes of the National Liberation Front (the Viet Cong), the bottom-up tactics of the guerrilla movement influenced community-based development management throughout the developing world.

The Legacy

By 1967, despite some disillusionment about the war, Vietnam became inundated with social scientists working under USAID or Defense. "In laying out the groundwork for the reorganization," according to FitzGerald, "groups of social scientists set out to research the economics and sociology of the Vietnamese as well as every aspect of Vietnamese government operations."[40] In the next eight years, USAID officials also came to sponsor the South Vietnamese police, security, and intelligence services. The answer to each new social or political problem appeared to be the introduction of new foreign aid workers. By the end of the 1960s, the United States

> had a small bureaucracy in each [province], comprising of pig experts, rice experts, market and gardening experts, AID administrators, International Voluntary Service workers, English teachers, city planners, accountants, doctors, police inspectors, welfare workers, handicraft consultants, psychological warfare and counterinsurgency experts.[41]

Vietnamese elite reaction to US foreign aid activity was a mirror image of US perceptions. Many concluded that the United States had designed its foreign and security policies to advance its own geopolitical interests. By the middle of the 1960s, the United States found itself in a quagmire in Vietnam. A turning point in the war, from a foreign aid perspective, was the September 1967 resignation of four staff members of the International Volunteer Service in protest against the war. They had come to realize that "the main efforts of the United States in Vietnam were destructive rather than constructive."[42] Antiwar protests, some of which, as Tuchman put it, were "mindless," tinged the whole image of foreign involvement in international development throughout the remainder of the century.[43]

The unpopularity and ineffectuality of the Vietnam government conditioned the effectiveness of assistance and ultimately neutralized any impact it might have had. Operationally, US officials initially were concerned about corruption in Vietnam; however, little was done to address the issue. Foreign aid professionals began to voice discouragement. Americans as they arrived in Vietnam "assumed a particular kind of relationship with the Vietnamese; they had expected the Vietnamese to trust them, to take their advice with gratitude, and to cooperate their mutual enterprise of defeating the Communists."[44] It just did not happen.

In 1971, aid had been available to "to the poor nations for nearly 20 years . . . but [had] become increasingly controversial"[45] as it became conjoined with American-defined international conflicts. It supported an international agenda in the definition of international development goals. After 1945, the United States opted for collective action, a multilateral approach based on collegial action among allies.[46] By 1975, elements of a more unilateralist approach (despite the Vietnam failure) began to appear in foreign aid policies. The shift between multilateralism and unilateralism patterns would continue to characterize foreign policy and foreign aid debates into the twenty-first century.

Ethical debates, as they apply to foreign aid, become difficult when looking from goals to policy. The dominance of interventionism and unilateralism beginning with the Vietnam War suggests that the United States emerged as "the last of the ideological [developed] nations."[47] Writing as early as 1966, Stillman and Pfaff suggest, "the United States [had] a tradition of political messianism, and of a conception of itself as different, and better, than other nations—as a 'redeemed' political society with a mission of redemption to others."[48] Such a unilateral interventionist policy, according to its critics, resulted in immoral and unethical actions. Unilateralism in the post–September 11 world perpetuated this problem.

Even as the United States withdrew militarily from Vietnam in 1973, it left behind thousands of civilian contract advisers and a massive foreign aid program, both committed to ensure that the Saigon regime survived.

This burden was short-lived given the collapse of the South Vietnamese regime on April 29, 1975. When the final evacuation took place, with helicopters perched precipitously on the roof of the American Embassy, USAID officials and advisers were among the last to leave. What remained in the minds of those who worked in Vietnam were the experiences, both good and bad, and the experimental nature of much aid on the ground.

From a foreign aid perspective, Vietnam in turn, had significant influence on foreign policy for a generation or more. This might not have been such a bad model had it not been part of the disastrous consequences of the Vietnam War. From a foreign aid perspective, Vietnam became a model both for what foreign aid could achieve and for the foreign assistance failures that seemed inevitable. Rural development and basic needs, as we will see in Chapter 8, were two aspects of foreign aid policy with origins in the Vietnam War.

Models developed in Vietnam influenced thinking about rural development in the 1970s. During their period in Vietnam, American aid officials focused almost exclusively on the development of public sector policies and programs and worked with organization and reorganization of the public sector. In part, this came "from the American—or Western—view of government as a complex machine."[49]

Foreign aid continued to include funding for security, supporting assistance to countries that played a strategic role in US foreign and security interests. By the mid-1970s, USAID estimated that more than a million foreign police officers had received training or supplies through its "public safety" program. After 1975, the United States came under increasing criticism for its training of police and security forces in repressive regimes.

An illustration is the disastrous end of US involvement in Iran, sometimes linked with Vietnam, with the holding hostage of 52 American diplomats and advisers for more than a year. Despite the authoritarian nature of the Shah's rule, the United States poured foreign aid into the country. In the 1960s and 1970s, assistance to Iran averaged more than $1 million a year. In addition to development aid, the United States supported state structures, the policy and security forces, and the defense structure. As a result, the post-Shah regime blamed the country's troubles, real and imaginary, on the United States.

In southern Africa during the 1970s and 1980s, aid consisted of cash grants, sector import loans, and physical infrastructure. USAID provided security assistance in the form of an Economic Support Fund (ESF).[50] In security-threatened areas, human needs issues tended to be overwritten by the need for dependable allies. In ESF countries, State, and in sensitive cases, the National Security Council, took a more direct role in setting country priorities.

Vietnam through September 11, from an ethical perspective, was perceived by many critics, domestic and international, as "acting stupidly—and cruelly: employing . . . immense strength in increasingly expedient ways, in pursuit of causes that are remote and intrinsically unserious—indefensible in terms of historically and political reality."[51] An outgrowth of the Vietnam War was an increased anti-Americanism in LDCs. From a foreign aid perspective, the legacy is perhaps more complex.

However, the involvement in Vietnam was tragic and folly. Often, the Johnson administration appeared confused. At various times the administration appeared to fear the left-dominated antiwar coalition. At other points, the government "reacted to intimidation by the rabid right at home and the public dread of Communism that this played on and reflected. . . . [In this reaction] lie the roots of American policy in Vietnam."[52]

Ultimately, the foreign aid problems coming out of Vietnam were institutional and reflective of a more general pattern. The high-level officials in the US mission "had created a system by which they could receive no bad news."[53] Since that time, USAID reports, assessments, and evaluations have often reflected a good-news view of the world. As FitzGerald has put it in describing technical assistance in Vietnam, "The officials of AID obviously believed . . . that the United States could win the war and 'modernize' the country to the point where it would pass the 'phase' [of the] rural insurgency movement. They had, it appeared, learned nothing and forgotten nothing."[54]

Conclusion

With the end of the Vietnam War and the related collapse of Iran on February 5, 1979,[55] foreign aid concerns shifted toward basic needs although still influenced by many of the assumptions established in Southeast Asia. The United States began withdrawing rather than expanding foreign aid and technical assistance, a withdrawal that would continue until September 11, 2001. This shrinkage was the first time that had occurred since the end of World War II.

Vietnam's legacy for the Third World was to solidify, in the minds of LDC intellectuals and elites, an image of the West that made no distinction between the United States and the Western European former colonial powers. Both Europe and the United States were seen as "colonial exploiters," rich and white. As the Vietnam War illustrated, in both isolationism and interventionism, the United States has needed an evangelical vision and a moral role in reforming and developing the lesser developed parts of the world.

As a result of Vietnam, both in terms of foreign and development policy, the United States veered away from the very concept of playing a global role as a country, leaving much of foreign aid in the hands of international organizations and a handful of European nations. Withdrawal would have significant consequences, and debate as to whether Vietnam was a foreign policy or military defeat would continue through the end of the twentieth century.

With a much less global foreign aid policy, LDC elites became suspicious of the twin goals of stability and modernization that had defined foreign aid through so much of the Cold War. The fateful events of September 11 would restore US concern for international affairs, if not development management concerns.

Notes

1. See Barbara Tuchman's important book, *The March of Folly: From Troy to Vietnam* (New York: Alfred A. Knopf, 1984).

2. Hinckle, "Introduction" to "The University on the Make," pp.11–22. Quote, p. 13.

3. For example, see David Sogge, *Give and Take: What's the Matter with Foreign Aid?* (London: Zed Books, 2002), p. 11.

4. See Robert S. McNamara, *In Retrospect: The Tragedy and Lessons of Vietnam* (New York: Random House Times Books, 1995).

5. Robert D. Schulzinger, *A Time for War: The United States and Vietnam, 1941–1975* (New York: Oxford University Press, 1997), p. 30.

6. See Philip Caputo, *A Rumor of War* (New York: Ballantine Books, 1977).

7. Tuchman, *The March of Folly,* pp. 256–257.

8. Reinhold Niebuhr quoted in Edmund Stillman and William Pfaff, *Power and Impotence: The Failure of America's Foreign Policy* (New York: Random House, 1966), p. 13.

9. Quoted in David Maraniss, *They Marched into Sunlight: War and Peace, in Vietnam and America, October 1967* (New York: Simon and Schuster, 2003), p. 194.

10. Frances FitzGerald, *Fire in the Lake: The Vietnamese and the Americans in Vietnam* (New York: Vintage, 1972), p. 154.

11. Maraniss, *They Marched into Sunlight,* p. 445.

12. Both quotes from Joseph Buttinger, "Fact and Fiction on Foreign Aid," *Dissent,* vol. 6, no. 3 (Summer, 1959), p, 339 and p. 351.

13. Townsend Hoopes, *The Limits of Intervention: An Inside Account of how the Johnson Policy of Escalation in Vietnam Was Reversed* (New York: David McKay Company, 1969), p. 14.

14. John J. McCuen, *The Art of Counter-Revolutionary War: The Strategy of Counter-Insurgency* (Harrisburg, PA: Stackpole Books, 1966).

15. Walter R. Sharp, *International Technical Assistance* (Chicago: Public Administration Service, 1952), p. 47.

16. James Grant, "Towards a More Effective Domestic Political Base for American Economic Assistance Abroad," (Unpublished Paper, 1961) p. 14.

17. Hoopes, *The Limits of Intervention*, p. 16.

18. FitzGerald, *Fire in the Lake*, p. 185.

19. Caputo, *A Rumor of War.*

20. Ibid.

21. A point clearly demonstrated by Sheehan, in *A Bright and Shining Lie.*

22. Schulzinger, *A Time for War*, p. 89.

23. Sheehan, *A Bright Shining Lie*, p. 187.

24. Ibid., pp.11–22. Quote, p. 14.

25. Sheinbaum, "Introduction" to "The University on the Make," *Ramparts*, pp. 11–22. Quote, p. 13.

26. Hinckle, "The University on the Make, p. 22.

27. Ibid., pp.11–22. Quote, p. 17.

28. Ibid., pp.11–22. Quote, p. 14.

29. See Alain C. Enthoven, and K. Wayne Smith, *How Much Is Enough?: Shaping the Defense Program, 1961–1969* (New York: Harper and Sons, 1971).

30. FitzGerald, *Fire in the Lake*, p. 5.

31. Campbell, *The Foreign Affairs Fudge Factory*, p. 73.

32. Ibid., p. 175.

33. Hoopes, *The Limits of Intervention*, p. 118.

34. Ibid., p. 62.

35. Tuchman, *The March of Folly*, p. 302.

36. Banning Garrett, "Post-War Planning for South Vietnam," in *The Trojan Horse: A Radical Look at Foreign Aid*, Steve Weissman, ed. (Palo Alto, CA: Ramparts Press, 1974), p. 137.

37. Stillman and Pfaff, *Power and Impotence*, p. 12.

38. Ibid., p. 51.

39. FitzGerald, *Fire in the Lake*, p. 335.

40. Ibid., p. 107.

41. FitzGerald, *Fire in the Lake*, p. 435.

42. Ibid., p. 452.

43. According to Tuchman, *The March of Folly*, p. 323.

44. FitzGerald, *Fire in the Lake*, p. 368.

45. Sarah Jackson and Joe Kimmins, "Thunder from the Left: The Radical Critique of Development Assistance," *Communique on Development Issues* (Washington, DC: Overseas Development Council, no. 4, January 1971), p. 1.

46. Akio Watanabe, "First among Equals" in *What Does the World Want from America? International Perspectives on U.S. Foreign Policy*, Alexander T. J. Lennon, ed. (Cambridge, MA: MIT Press, 2002), p. 18.

47. Stillman and Pfaff, *Power and Impotence*, p. 179.

48. Ibid., p. 225.

49. FitzGerald, *Fire in the Lake*, pp. 34–35.

50. For a discussion of this see Caleb Rossiter, *The Bureaucratic Struggle for Control of U.S. Foreign Aid: Diplomacy vs. Development in Southern Africa* (Boulder, CO: Westview Press, 1985), pp. 2–3.

51. Stillman and Pfaff, *Power and Impotence*, p. 181.

52. Tuchman, *The March of Folly*, p. 269.

53. FitzGerald, *Fire in the Lake*, p. 454.

54. Ibid., p. 545.

55. See Robert Fisk's discussion of this calamitous event in his monumental book, *The Great War for Civilization: The Conquest of the Middle East* (New York: Alfred A. Knopf, 2005), pp. 92–138.

8

BASIC NEEDS, STRUCTURAL ADJUSTMENT, AND THE COLD WAR'S END

Foreigners have not helped us. . . . We have had many bad experiences. First the Spaniards, then the Russians and the Chinese. Now the United Nations and the French and the World Bank.

Robert Klitgaard, *Tropical Gangsters*

The economy was in disarray. It would be a big success just to get production back to where it was twenty years ago.

Robert Klitgaard, *Tropical Gangsters*

Wonderful people. Terrible government. The African Story.

Paul Theroux, *Dark Star Safari*

The Search for New Models

The Vietnam War ended in 1975. In the three decades since, foreign aid has evolved into its modern form. This chapter examines the way foreign aid policy evolved through 1999. We look first at agriculture, food aid, and rural development, all antecedents of Vietnam. After a brief overview of "basic needs," we discuss the apparent about-face by the Reagan administration as it implemented structural adjustment and policy reform. Lastly, we assess impact of the Cold War on foreign policy and the lethargy that developed within the foreign aid establishment in the 1990s.

Agriculture, Food Aid, and Rural Development

Scientific farming made Americans efficient producers of food. Food aid has long been a part of foreign aid, and historically it has been used as a tool to influence foreign policy. The Green Revolution dates back to the

119

early 1940s in Mexico and later in India, focusing on miracle grains through capital-intensive farming. With the Green Revolution, the United States had a model for agricultural development based on years of research, an effective extension support, and advanced agricultural education. Through foreign aid, LDCs became consumers of US food products on the one hand, and food exporters through US technical assistance on the other.

In 1954, with the passage of US Public Law 480, food became a major component of foreign aid policy and part of domestic subsidies for US agriculture. Food assistance, as a companion to agricultural and rural development policy, disposed of domestic farm surpluses while creating future markets for agricultural exports.

In the first ten years of its foreign aid program, the United States distributed agricultural commodities worth $1.5 billion. Food was a powerful weapon: in the postwar period, the United States seemed to have the power to decide who lived and who died when famine struck in Asia, Africa, and Latin America.

From the beginning of the postwar period, there were few interest groups in support of foreign aid with the exception of agricultural lobbyists, the Land Grant Universities, and the Farm Bureau Federation.[1] A 1957 assessment of foreign aid explained the subsidies from a domestic perspective: "It seems certain that, had large purchases for foreign aid not been made during these years, governmental expenditures under the price-support legislation would have increased markedly, and large stocks would have been acquired [and stored]."[2]

Over time, long-term provision of food aid may have been destructive to LDC agricultural economies.[3] By the end of the 1950s, much concern about foreign aid focused on the negative impact food aid on economic growth and indigenous agricultural productivity given the input of free or submarket foodstuffs into LDCs. Despite this caution, however, increased LDC food production, because of the ability of farmers to produce surpluses, should be considered a partial success for foreign aid.

Part of the rural development mission, of course, was to "break up old, economic and socially self-sufficient small village groups in LDCs." The result, as Linton recognized very early, was economic wreckage in the rural areas that was "due to fundamental incompatibility between stable, closely integrated folk cultures and an ever-changing machine civilization."[4]

Issues have not changed. According to a 2002 *New York Times* article, "The criticism has nothing to do with famine relief, but with American farmers selling their subsidized grain below cost to the rising middle class overseas, much like countries that the United States accuses of dumping their under priced steel here."[5] Beyond food production, however, impact on rural development in the 1950s and 1960s was minimal; nor were conditions much improved in urban areas.

Rural development failures meant widespread migration to cities. For those living in LDCs in the 1980s, although urban employment was "better than what a rural farmer makes, but basically what a $200 a month job does is it provides a person with maybe an office, telephone (which in many countries does not work anyway), and a place of operations where they can conduct their own private business."[6]

The Shift to Basic Needs

In the late 1960s, the World Bank's strategy for reducing poverty came to include what was called meeting *basic needs*—targeting the poorest of the poor. Economists recognized that growth strategies and commercialized agriculture would do little to address the causes of poverty. By the mid-1970s, food aid and development had become a central focus of the debate over what was to be called "integrated" rural development—combination of technical assistance to farmers with the delivery of social services to rural villages. Integrated rural development was a center point to the basic needs approach advocated by the World Bank.

Robert McNamara brought his basic needs and Keynesian planning focus with him from the Department of Defense to the World Bank in late 1967, where he "implemented a system of annual lending quotas that is still in existence."[7] Both basic needs and rural development were keystones. Although meeting basic needs was a World Bank approach, USAID readily accepted it as a priority. President Jimmy Carter (1977–1981) adopted basic needs as part of his policy.

Basic needs goals were sometimes defined differently because "the content of the bundle of goods and services that satisfy basic needs varies from one country to another, [although] there is a common core that includes nutrition, education, health, water and sanitation, and shelter."[8] Pinpointing the meaning of basic needs has been a perennial problem in international development.

Basic needs policy developed out of a concern for poverty within the Congress and among development experts, not to mention the rising influence of foreign aid policy from Third World nations through their calls for a New International Economic Order—the idea that developed countries were obligated to help the poor countries because of past wrongs such as slavery, underdevelopment, and colonialism. Under basic needs, the Congress directed that future bilateral assistance focus on critical problems that affect poor majorities, including food and nutrition, population planning, education and health, and human resources development.[9]

In many poor countries, public investment programs in basic needs, small-scale agriculture, and integrated rural development were overwhelmingly the aggregation of what individual donors wanted to finance. Results often were poorly designed public investments in rural industrialization. There was too little attention paid to peasant agriculture; too much public sector involvement in areas where LDCs lacked technical, managerial, and entrepreneurial skills, and there was too little capacity and effort to foster grassroots development.[10]

Major donors found linkages between social service delivery and technical assistance for increased productivity difficult to achieve. Specifically, donors could not program through "forward and backward linkages" that could displace one of the most crucial aspects of rural development—*institution building*—something normally not subject to tight programming.[11]

As Robert Cassen pointed out, very little aid, even food aid, had been "directed at or had any effect [positive or negative] on the very poorest people, though these people appear to have gained indirectly from aid projects that reduced their food costs."[12] Despite the efforts of rural development specialists, there was little progress on the production of grains and tubers throughout the developing world—plantains and tubers in Africa, potatoes in Andean South America, or rice in Southeast Asia. By 1987, one study found close to half of the completed rural-development projects financed by the World Bank in Africa had failed.[13] Agriculture projects alone failed one-third of the time in West Africa and half the time in East Africa. "The main empirical result," as Paul Mosley pointed out, "is a negative one, namely that there appears to be no statistically significant correlation in *any* post-war period, either positive or negative, between inflows of development aid and the growth rate of GNP in developing countries."[14]

The basic needs programming roughly ran from 1970–1980, though some components of the policy linger on. By the early 1980s, a shift in development priorities away from the integrated social service and rural development models began, though concerns with agricultural development remained. After 1983, except in human or natural crisis areas, basic needs were no longer a priority.

A US-initiated Africa Food Security Initiative (AFSI) in the 1990s, stimulated by chronic drought and starvation on the continent, showed renewed support for some basic needs principles because AFSI was to reduce prenatal and childhood malnutrition by increasing rural people's incomes.[15]

Criticism of US food policies continues today. As a *New York Times* report notes: "In Rome, at a United Nations conference on hunger, developing countries pointed . . . to the huge new subsidies to American farmers as one of the biggest obstacles to creating vital opportunities for their own farmers and enabling them to climb out of poverty."[16] We will return to this issue when we discuss trade issues in Chapter 11.

The Poverty Debate

From 1948 through to 2009, two views about the nature of poverty within the donor community predominated. One view sees the origins of poverty as endemic to LDCs, caused by indigenous cultural norms, lack of education, poor political leadership, or poor economic and social policies, not to mention corruption as a central problem. International donors often blame fraud as the reason for donor fatigue both among legislators and the public.

The other view sees poverty as part of a malfunctioning global system. From this perspective, "[n]early half a century after colonial empires began to crumble and dozens of new countries were born with high hopes of ending dependency and deprivation, a significant number of those nations have seen growth stall and desperate poverty grow instead."[17] Critics blame unfair global economic endowments and comparative advantages. Following from this, dependency theorists conclude that the vested or class interests in LDC governments are often hostile to the development values and strategies of experts called in to advise them.

The problem according to the American new left was that foreign aid programs were not really designed to help poor countries or their people catch up with their rapidly growing needs. At best, foreign aid was little more than a palliative, Band-aids applied to serious wounds. At worst, foreign aid was a charitable red herring designed to divert the attention of developing world leadership, while permitting powerful more developed country economic interests to increase their hammerlock on the global economy.

Neither polar position captures the complexity of global poverty. Many of the significant disagreements about poverty are ethical and philosophical. One issue involves the responsibility of the international community to poverty alleviation because the search for poverty reduction may find it is the internal dynamics of a LDC that have to be addressed. A related issue involves individual responsibility and how that intersects with the nation-state system and global economic processes.

Other ambiguities revolved around what basic needs should be provided either by the state, or failing that, by the donor community. Increasingly, critics concluded that to define an absolute income poverty line, one should begin by trying to understand what the important needs, requirements, or capabilities of human beings are.

Despite the definition and standards defined by the international donor community, there are wide divisions as to how to measure poverty. The World Bank often uses a formula based on one US dollar per day as a minimum. The so-called dollar-a-day *threshold* was based on what a single dollar buys at 1990 prices. The future is adjusted for differences in prices among less-developed countries. To its critics, the World Bank based its calculations on things that most poor people could never afford to buy. An alternative approach is *prioritization*—any measure should place greatest weight on the economic plight of the very poorest people.

There is a middle position: *selectivity,* suggesting that aid should be given only to countries adopting sound economic, good governance, and democratization policies. Foreign aid, other than humanitarian assistance, should be withheld from countries that are undemocratic or are making little effort to tackle corruption.[18] If that middle position is found, according to one observer, "Something more momentous may result, perhaps an alliance between liberals and conservatives to launch a fresh assault on global poverty using less softheaded approaches than in the past."[19] It is the selectivity argument that would later be adopted in the Millennium Challenge Account (MCA), a program we discuss in Chapter 13.

Policy Reforms and Structural Adjustment

Reagan's New Foreign Policy Agenda

When President Ronald Reagan came to office in January 1981, he launched aid policy reforms that would define his presidency internationally. By the early 1980s, the internal origins thesis of poverty predominated in the US donor community. Reagan administration economist John Williamson coined the term "Washington Consensus" to describe a shift in American foreign aid policy away from the global dimensions of poverty.[20] It was a short step from there to a focus on policy reform, structural adjustment, and international financial stability.

During the first Reagan term, foreign policy shifted to Central America and to anti-communist proxy wars in Africa. In his rhetorical stance, Reagan distanced himself from the internationalism of previous administrations, creating a kind of "prophetic dualism" based on unilateralism in foreign aid and foreign policy. The focus on policy reform demonstrated that realism:

- return to support for economic growth, particularly in Asia,
- new emphasis on democracy and governance, except where Cold War concerns required support for authoritarian rulers
- concern for access to energy and other natural resources

Above all, the struggle was to contain and roll back international communism. Foreign aid became a vehicle.

To its critics, the Reagan administration came to personify the arrogance of erratic unaccountable power, the disasters of Cold War intrigue, and proxy wars in marginal nations.[21] The Reagan administration to its critics was marked by its appeals to fear and selfish motives: nowhere was this more clear than in the intervention in Central America, particularly assistance to the anti-communist Contras in Nicaragua.

Throughout the Cold War, there had been elements of unilateralism in US foreign policy. The Reagan years saw a surge in unilateralism that would be the basis of post–September 11 responses to international relationships by neoconservative policy analysts, many of whom garnered foreign policy experience under Reagan.

Reagan and his successors directed foreign aid at middle income Asian countries presenting good opportunities for success. Private investment followed. The Asian successes would later be identified as justification for MCA. As Stephen Greenhouse pointed out, "Not surprisingly, the lion's share of new investments has gone to some referred to as 'middle class' countries—like South Korea, Mexico and Argentina—many of which were avoided by private investors a few years ago because of their debt crises and economic policies."[22]

In the 1980s, the United States shaped foreign aid to encourage energy efficiency, renewable energy, and natural resource management. Its overseas face, however, did not always complement its energy and environmental policy at home.

Democratization was part of the new foreign aid process. In some places it was an important element, and even took on what Reagan called a "moral imperative." Failure of democracy, Reagan officials argued, could lead to conflict, and ultimately the likelihood of millions of refugees, many of whom would eventually find their way to the United States and other developed countries. In reality, for some critics, democracy and governance seemed to take second place to economic reforms and the free market.

More than anything, the Reagan administration would reshape foreign aid to address international debt and the way it was treated by financial institutions. Four sets of interrelated reforms were developed: *debt, structural adjustment, conditionality,* and *privatization.*

Debt, Structural Adjustment and Privatization

Debt was a critical factor in aid debates as early as the 1960s. "When the 1960s are compared as a whole with the 1950s, if one uses aggregate balance of payments statistics, the main accomplishment of this increase in development loans and grants appears to be a tidying up of the Brazilian foreign debt."[23] By 1970, the debt burden in many developing countries had become an urgent problem that had been foreseen but unfortunately not addressed at that time.[24] By 1980 LDC debt was a top priority for donors.

Debt crushed LCD economies, and debt management dealt a crippling blow to many countries, especially in Africa. Africa at the time spent close to four times as much servicing its debt as it did on health and education and paid out more in interest on the debt than it received in trade, foreign aid, and other forms of financial transfer. For critics, indebtedness made foreign aid to many countries close to meaningless. There were almost no prospects of escape from debt.

The year 1981 is an important one in the history of foreign aid: Robert McNamara stepped down at the World Bank. International development policy began to focus on structural adjustment and public sector reform and away from basic needs and rural development. Jamaica became one of the first countries to come under *structural adjustment*. Structural adjustment consisted of seven reforms:

- Fiscal discipline
- Reordering and reducing public expenditures
- Tax reforms
- Trade liberalization
- Liberalization of foreign investment
- Privatization
- Deregulation

Under structural adjustment reforms, what was needed to complete "the top down reforms [was] a new class structure with an empowered and diverse bourgeoisie made up of business men and women."[25] From this perspective, middle class "control of the government or the state must therefore be, and is, a fundamental issue in [debates about] the orthodoxy of 'dependence' analysis."[26] Structural adjustment meant that neo-orthodox versions of free market capitalism had become the global norm in foreign aid. Foreign aid would be given to countries that were both well governed and had adopted market-oriented economic policies to provide a boost to their development.

The goal of structural adjustment policies was to open up a country's domestic economy and move it away from indigenous, import substitution commodities toward imported goods, services and investments. According to the Reagan administration, structural adjustment policies supported by the IMF and the World Bank would allow debtor LDCs to grow out of debt.

Specifically, structural adjustment called for reforming the Washington Consensus in a way that tied development money to structural adjustment conditions, including market deregulation, privatization of state-owned enterprises, reduction of the size of government, and trade liberalization by recipient countries. The way foreign aid loans were used was important. According to Robert Cassen, "Aid receipts were once thought to be associated with reduced domestic savings, but some recent research which distinguished aid for consumption from that used for investments—as most other studies failed to do—found that countries with higher investment-aid receipts did achieve relatively high domestic savings rates."[27]

Under structural adjustment, donors adjusted loans and allowed LDCs to borrow more money to pay back loans. According to Frank Conahan, "The United States frequently conditioned its balance-of-payments assistance in recipient countries by requiring them to obtain and/or comply with [International Monetary] Fund programs."[28] In most collapsed states, not only was the debt crisis severe but also much of the foreign aid never arrived. Foreign aid designed to structurally adjust LDC institutions often disappeared to overseas creditors and international contractors.

During the 1980s, rather than training public managers and supporting government programs, as was the case a decade before, donors trained business managers and entrepreneurs, and supported regional and national business councils, as well as civil society organizations. Often, they used the same bag of tricks as they had to support public sector activities since the 1960s.

In both the public and the private sectors, management skills continued to be the weak link in the development policy chain. What transformed the picture under structural adjustment was "dividing countries according to the quality of their economic policies."[29] Changes in these economic policies became a second component of the Reagan foreign aid revolution.

Conditionality and Policy Reform

Structural adjustment, as practiced by the United States, was based on *conditionality* and imposed on LDCs in three ways: *condition precedents,* actions the United States requires a recipient government to take before disbursing aid; a *covenant,* actions the United States requires a government to take before, during, or after assistance is provided but is not tied to the disbursement of the funds; or a *prior action,* an understanding—not written in any formal agreements—about actions the host government will take prior to the disbursement of aid.

Policy reform advocates assumed that conditionality was essential to foreign aid success and would only have a major impact after countries progressed in reforming their institutions and policies.[30] Direct attempts to improve living standards would succeed but only if fully implemented under policy reforms. There were complications. In the late 1980s, according to Stanley Hoffman, numerous LDCs continued "to face the problem of the debt . . .; here what [was] needed, in the short term, [was] extensive relief measures that [would] allow developing countries to concentrate on exports and to afford imports, rather than having to spend their resources on servicing their debt."[31] It was up to the multilateral organizations and large bilateral donors to set conditions for debt servicing adjustments.

Ownership and competition were critical. To advocates of structural adjustment in the Reagan administration, central planning had impoverished millions of people. Structural adjustment redefined the way LDCs looked at development. Questions were familiar: What, we ask ourselves, should we strive for? "Regrettably," according to one critic, "it has long been a convenient notion to identify development merely with economic growth."[32] One of the architects of privatization said: "For developing countries to achieve rapid growth in today's global economy, they must embrace private, rather than state, ownership of business. They must be receptive to foreign trade, technology, ideas and investment, and they must have governments that accept the rule of law and curb corruption."[33]

At a policy level, the United States appeared to place a high priority on the development and implementation by the LDC of effective and efficient economic growth policies. The United States and its European partners opposed what the Organization for Economic Co-operation and Development (OECD) called inappropriate subsidies, price and wage controls, as well as prohibitive tariffs, overvalued exchange rates, and interest rate ceilings. Of concern was interference with market solutions that would impede economic performance.

Structural adjustment conditionality also targeted public service, as well as rule of law and property rights. By the 1990s, structural adjustment conditions included demands for stable and democratic political institutions, decentralized governance, and the acceptance of the activities of civil society organizations. Weakening LDC state structures became a part of the policy reform process.

Privatization has been widely supported since 1981. According to one USAID official in the early 1980s, "It is time to shift to an emphasis on working through the private sector, both profit and non-profit . . . As we are now seeing in Eastern Europe and have seen in the past in Mexico, Spain, Asia, and elsewhere, political weakness leads to fundamental [policy] reform."[34] Privatization was central to the reform process in Greece, Turkey, Portugal, Spain, and Ireland, essentially started under the Marshall Plan and continuing through the 1980s.[35]

The question asked by some critics was should countries that had bad policies simply be left to their fate? According to NGO advocates, by no means should they be abandoned.[36] Donors should still help by spreading development knowledge through the intercession of NGOs. In addition, social support projects should be given to NGOs in this situation, but no money should to be given to the corrupt state. Beyond this, however, there should be no support directed at state structures prior to the implementation of policy reforms.

Privatization and contracting out each became an increasing part of foreign aid in the 1980s because of ideological compatibility with structural adjustment and because of the impact of domestic US personnel ceilings under Reagan. Delegation of authority for foreign aid to international and national private sector for-profit and NGOs created opportunities for advisers to play multiple, sometimes conflicting, and ambiguous roles. As a result, they were able to facilitate, frustrate, or even damage the processes of development and nation-building. While undertaking activities that serve their personal and/or their professional interests, such advisers may have inadvertently undermined key developmental goals.

The carrot offered for policy reforms and donor conditions was the Heavily Indebted Poor Country (HIPC) program.[37] HIPC and social and municipal funds targeted at the delivery of services were meant to address hardships imposed by policy reform—structural adjustment with a human face. HIPC allowed LDCs to use debt payments for economic and social development activities, thus reducing their debt obligations. Debt burden of poor countries came about because of lending by the International Monetary Fund, the World Bank, bilateral donors, and most importantly, private banks seeking bailouts on their loans. At the same time, self-serving aid or misinformed donor agents often gave LDC policymakers and the public false hopes because the message of structural adjustment was that the reforms advocated were a ticket to economic growth and development.

Economic development and policy reforms depended on a country's institutional and political characteristics. LDCs may have good macroeconomic policies as a result of structural adjustment initiatives, but ineffective public service delivery and democratic governance mechanisms. If there was a will to correct this problem, then assistance was possible. In such circumstances, assistance should be directed at the creation of an effective public sector. Public sector development was often difficult. When not possible, bilateral donors should be more willing to cut back their financing to countries with consistently low-quality public sectors.

Critics suggested that victims of structural adjustment were the poor and, perhaps, elements of the middle class. As Frank Conahan puts it:

"Reductions in government spending usually result in cutbacks in expenditures for power plants, roads, education, and other infrastructure investment. Complementary private-sector investment dependent on public investment may also be cut."[38] Nonetheless, the main lines of structural adjustment continue to define aid policy.

Toward Mediocrity

While it appeared that the Reagan administration had introduced a new foreign aid policy, for many critics, reality was somewhat different. From a fiscal perspective, there was continuity to foreign aid from 1965 through to 2000. It took the shock of September 11 to jolt the United States out of its complacency and standard operating procedures in its international assistance policy. It is to that continuity that we now turn.

Donor Fatigue

By the late 1960s, aid flows produced a complex web of large and competing bureaucracies in Washington, within recipient states, as well as a diffuse spectrum of policy objectives and expectations.[39] Organizationally, USAID has often been a part, albeit a minor part, of the endless interagency struggle for control over the foreign and security policy process. Over the years, USAID has been worn down by criticism from the executive branch, Congress, press, and public, not to mention LDCs and fellow donors.

There is a determinism to the aid institutions relating to tasks, environment, and organization. Aid bureaucracies have fragmented authorities that function within a complex system, making policies unstable and inflexible. Organizational weakness and duplication of effort is a reality. As John Franklin Campbell pointed out years ago:

> A desk officer of State, who follows U.S. relations with one small African country, has recently calculated that while in theory he is the focal point of all Washington efforts concerning "his" country, in fact there are sixteen other people in Washington just like him, working on the same country in different chains of command.[40]

Beyond this are the numerous task forces our foreign service officers participate in. These are designed to bypass normal bureaucratic processes but they increase duplication and complexity of aid processes. It was the complexity introduced by the conduct of the Vietnam War that shaped the future of foreign aid and foreign and security policy for the next forty years.

To its international critics, Vietnam had caused the "collapse into nightmare" of the American Dream, what Booker called the "most powerful image of the twentieth century."[41] The Western world reeled at the collapse of US Vietnam policy: "Above all, [the Vietnam War] consumed the nation [the United States] in anger, disillusion and self-doubt. Shock waves generated in the 1960's never fully abated, and appear today in the rhetoric of political correctness and neoconservatism."[42]

By the late 1960s, donor fatigue had set in. There were calls for more collaboration in organizing foreign aid. Esman and Montgomery called for "joint teams of host national and American professionals to administer innovative and experimental development activities."[43] Little came of these suggestions.

The weight of LDC debt exacerbated donor fatigue in the 1970s. As costs of servicing old loans increased, commercial lending decreased drastically, and foreign aid fatigue hit donors, primarily in the United States.[44] Increasingly, as Martin Wolf noted: "There were . . . skeptics about aid, among them Peter [now Lord] Bauer. But his arguments made him something of a pariah. Experience proved chastening. Academic studies confirmed what practitioners could see with their own eyes; there was no connection between aid and alleviating poverty."[45]

By the middle of the 1970s, foreign aid was based in large part on strategic and ideological concerns rather than on developmental considerations as the Cold War deepened. Perceived problems with the Vietnam War and its ignominious end rubbed off on development assistance.

LDC population growth was a factor in donor fatigue because "[n]o other phenomenon, the Pearson Commission [the 1968 World Bank Commission on International Development chaired by Canadian Prime Minister Lester Pearson] said, 'casts a darker shadow over the prospects for international development than the staggering growth of population.'"[46] Foreign aid in much of Africa, Latin America, the Caribbean, and parts of Asia and the Middle East remained ineffective, and until the HIV/AIDs pandemic intervened in the 1990s, LDCs overall had very high population growth.

The gap between what policymakers decided to do and what bureaucrats did had widened to a chasm by 1970.[47] Foreign aid policy was as much a bureaucratic process as it was a political product, as Edward Horesh notes, "[w]ithin the bureaucracy itself, different departments of state have different interests and that political and policy debate is carried out within these departments and between them."[48]

Richard Nixon's Task Force on International Development of 1970, led by Rudolph Peterson, chairman of the Bank of America, recommended that a series of specialized agencies replace USAID, greater use be made of multilateral organizations, and a more relaxed and flexible approach to development management be taken. As Peterson noted in March 1970:

> The international organizations could roughly double their present rate of lending—from $2.5 billion a year to $5 billion a year—over the next several years while continuing to follow sound practices and maintain high standards. An increase in International Development Association [IDA] lending is critical to establishing an international framework for development. In view of the debt-servicing problem in a number of the developing countries, concessional lending on IDA terms is badly needed. Furthermore, IDA lending is the foundation for international participation in some of the major development programs.[49]

No action was taken on the Peterson recommendations, though under President George W. Bush there was a tendency to hive off development functions to agencies outside of USAID.

Every year from 1970 on, Congress would slash USAID's budget and often would threaten to abolish the organization as a separate entity. For the next thirty years, appropriations for foreign aid continued to decline. Despite this, policymakers were not able to admit that the United States lacked the resources and the will to do more for LDC social and economic development. Discussion of reforms in foreign aid began again in the early 1970s. By then, foreign aid, and foreign policy processes more generally, had become seriously outdated. This meant that more than two decades of institutions, procedures, and personnel operated relatively unchanged in a changing world.[50] As a result, "Disenchantment with foreign aid [was] shared by both donor and recipient countries. . . . [One can see] some of the sources of this [negative] mood in the case of one large country, Brazil, which during 1964–1967 ranked only behind India, Pakistan, and South Vietnam as a recipient of net official aid flows."[51]

By the middle of the 1970s, USAID suffered from both overadministration and excessive expansion; however, by 1975 the United States and a number of other donors had lost confidence in the ability of foreign aid to promote economic and social development.[52] During the next decade, this confidence weakened within USAID and among the major bilateral donors. The result was annually reduced budgets for both bilateral and multilateral agencies despite suggestions that multilateral assistance would be a better option development.

In the middle of the 1970s, a Carnegie Foundation Report called aid programs "lethargic, negligent and crippled by bureaucracy."[53] By 1975, USAID was weak and in trouble. It had no domestic champion and had become a whipping boy of Congress. Implications of this sobered those who advocated a role for international assistance within foreign policy. This refocused debate on foreign aid policy toward organizational imperatives.

There were characteristics of USAID that were unique in their impact on international assistance. As Judith Tendler wrote in 1975, "although the agency's [USAID] organizational environment was more conducive than most to adaptation and innovation, criticism of its performance has often focused on its unadaptive and uninnovative behavior."[54]

During the 1970s, the United States and other donors openly and cynically traded aid for political support; however, often those using foreign aid to buy political support got very little for their aid money.[55] "This ambitious U.S. role," in the 1970s, according to Rudolph Peterson, "required a prominent U.S. presence in some countries; and friction with some governments resulted from attempts to influence sensitive areas of their national policy related to development."[56] US policies remained government-oriented, and the funds were based on the expectation that the transfer of US resources, education, and technology would bring immediate results as had occurred under the Marshall Plan. The term "graduation" date came to be laid on the mystique of a quick ending of foreign assistance.

While there was little support for government-to-government assistance, private contributions to international charities were different, and while "Americans historically have given generously to such efforts, fundraisers fear[ed] that all the calamities [both human made and natural disasters] coming together are proving to be too much of a bad thing."[57] In debates about foreign aid, the United States often complains, not entirely without justification, that "unflattering comparisons between America's aid budget and those of more generous Dutch and Scandinavians unjustly exclude private donations stimulated by U.S. tax incentives."[58]

Throughout the lesser-developed world, according to Paul Theroux, it appears that social concerns such as health, community development, and education were dealt with by foreign volunteers and technicians with little apparent involvement of LDC nationals. "Whenever I saw a town that looked tidy and habitable I saw the evidence of foreign charities."[59] Privately managed foreign involvement in social development became a fixture of domestic political life throughout the developing world.

Budgetary Stagnation and Standard Operating Procedures

In 2000, Americans remained uncomfortable with foreign aid, particularly because "most people seem to think that foreign aid accounts for 15 per cent of the budget, when it's really less than 1 per cent"[60] Lack of domestic support, according to Sebastian Mallaby, meant that of all "Washington's powerbrokers, hustlers and 'decision-makers,' the appropriators are most aware of the uneasy relationship between domestic priority and international policy."[61]

Debate about aid spending had two components. The first concerned amounts to be given. According to the Peterson Report:

> U.S. lending under such a system [was to be] be concentrated in selected countries, in selected programs—particularly in agriculture and education—and in multinational projects where long-term development is of special interest to the United States. . . . U.S. lending, however, would be made strictly on the basis of development criteria.[62]

The second focused on the choice between loans and grants. We will return to this issue in Chapter 11.

To later critics, aid administrators sometimes were caught up in their own self-promotion and in their public relations efforts designed to create an illusion of efficiency and effectiveness.[63] Internally, bureaucratization and careerism increased.

The structure of foreign aid needed to change to prevent a deterioration of conditions and to initiate a movement toward more effective approaches to international development. Lack of a strategy for institutional development is the key to many of USAID's critics. Fred Riggs has asserted, "Surely the development of institutional memories, both in developing countries and in AID itself, is an important facet of development administration."[64]

By 1969, to be sustainable, aid should have been pegged at $3 billion to promote a sustained growth at which point official aid could have peaked. This did not happen, and according to Christopher Booker, the West internationally suffered from "exhaustion and loss of momentum . . . [and a] 'fading into reality' of the collective dreams of the Fifties and Sixties."[65] To Neil Lewis, quoting a Red Cross official, "Americans 'just [got] tired of seeing starving people on television. . . . The needs are overwhelming and people who would ordinarily donate just get confused as to where to give money. . . . They end up just turning the television off."[66]

Foreign aid going to LDCs in 1970 was less than 20 percent of what the annual aid to Europe had been at the height of the Marshall Plan.

Much of the assistance went in the form of loans, 90 percent of which was used to purchase equipment from developed countries and contribute to LDC debt. The rest went to purchase commodities for relief, training, and technical assistance, and it was tied to donor-designed projects. About 85 cents of every dollar of foreign aid stayed in the United States during this period.

Prior to 1980, technical assistance alone appeared a weak strategy for international development because "aid can still do little more than leave the American advisor to his own devices in this difficult area of guided social change."[67] For its advocates, foreign aid was most useful in capacity building and human resource development rather than in managing and growing the economy. In addition, aid worked best when it was introduced incrementally into countries that had developed systems and policies to manage that aid. It was this long-term and incremental process that best justifies continued support for foreign aid and technical assistance.

Allocation and management of technical assistance was not, as Paul Mosley points out, "a rational optimizing process."[68] Rather, the goal of foreign aid focused primarily on the reduction of uncertainties for themselves and their governments. Donor rules were complex. In the early 1980s, the US Foreign Assistance Act listed thirty-three separate objectives to which all US-supported projects ostensibly must conform. Sometimes these were in conflict with each other. In addition, "donor aid schemes [were] almost always expensive, top-heavy, and require[d] lots of literate administrators."[69]

International assistance, Lord (Peter Thomas) Bauer suggested, created an artificial support system. Foreign aid can be a barrier to development because it brings on a variety of repercussions that adversely affect the basic conditions for development.[70] According to one World Bank official, "Aid can make a big difference but only when there is also a domestic constituency for change."[71] Over time, however, academic criticism of the foreign aid process increased in volume.[72] By the early 1980s, donors recognized the need for sensitivity of aid officials to the stakeholder needs of their counterparts in recipient countries; however, there continued to be a gap between this recognition and the need to identify a mutuality of interests.

By rejecting the findings of the Peterson Commission, USAID became even more rigid in the 1980s and beyond. At the same time, "the . . . cumbersomely managed USAID . . . had 58.6 percent of its personnel engaged in administrative tasks."[73] This was a level of inefficiency duplicated in African states considered by specialists to be inefficient. Organizationally, foreign aid would get worse.

By the early 1980s, donor fatigue deepened further, foreign aid policy-makers lost faith in the LDC state, and lethargy developed within the foreign aid policy process at the federal government level. In 1980, "[i]n the absence of a FY80 aid appropriations bill, foreign aid programs [were] being funded by a continuing resolution which maintains the monetary levels established by the FY79 bill—approximately $7.5 billion."[74]

University involvement with foreign aid became increasingly problematic. USAID, for example, reassessed its support for the Midwest University Consortium on International Activities (MUCIA) at the end of the 1960s and decided to cut back "both its funding for public administration training and for research and technical assistance in administrative reform and institution-building."[75] USAID's cooperative agreement with the National Association of Schools of Public Affairs and Administration (NASPAA) ended. By the early 1990s, university based technical assistance had declined dramatically.[76]

In the 1970s, the foreign aid budget, adjusted for inflation, fell by nearly 50 percent. Regional figures reflect these trends. Throughout the 1980s, the United States

> provided between $1 billion and $1.6 billion annually, in constant 1992 dollars, for bilateral (country-to-country) aid to Africa through a variety of programs. U.S. assistance to Africa [had] peaked in the mid-1980s, reflecting the high levels of foreign affairs spending characteristic of the period and the special attention given to famine conditions in some African countries.[77]

Aid spending declined between 1985 and 1990. By 1990, an international debate raged over the amount and the nature of donor funding among OECD countries.

Since 1985, foreign aid "has not just stagnated, but it has actually declined in real terms."[78] The long-term spending trends showed that "between 1970 and 1991 the volume of ODA [Overseas Development Assistance] rose from US$28 billion to US$54 billion (at 1990 prices). But the increase over 1970 to 1980 was greater than the rate of increase during 1981 to 1991, marked by an increase of only $11 billion."[79]

Between 1945 and 1997, the United States spent more than $1 trillion on foreign aid. Because of this, foreign aid failure rates shook policymakers. The foreign aid story in Africa was particularly bleak. Sub-Sahara Africa was the continent most dependent on foreign aid in 1990. The region had only 12 percent of the world's population but received nearly a third of the world's foreign aid, which amounted to 14 percent of black

Africa's GDP in 1987. It was by far the least-developed continent, and as the millennium approached, it was getting worse.

Toward the End of the Century

George H. W. Bush and the End of the Cold War

By 1976 the Soviet Union had declined as a military and economic power, and the United States was de facto the single superpower in the world. By that time, the United States developed a strategy, *globalism,* a form of interventionism based on the assumption that any crisis can be solved. Less clear was that, beginning in the 1970s, the source of crisis would be ethnic and religious conflict and social disruption. The Bush and Clinton administrations, despite their policy differences, provided a bridge of multilateralism in foreign aid and foreign policy that ran from the collapse of the Soviet Union down to September 11, 2001.

Throughout the Cold War, the solution to the problem of international competition with the Soviet Union was social reform promoted by foreign aid that would align LDC countries to the West; however, both isolation and globalism—that is, interventionism—shared a "moral fervor that is fundamentally theological in its origins."[80] Interventionism, and particularly unilateralism, is fundamentally isolationist in its interaction with the world. Emotionally and morally, the United States has remained largely an isolated nation, despite its alliances, since the 1990s.

Nineteen-eighty was a marker in terms of international development. By then, the Soviet bloc was no longer a significant alternative aid donor, dropping its contributions to 8 percent of the total global aid budget, down from 31 percent in 1961. As the Cold War receded, predominance in foreign aid began to move from government programs to the nonprofit and private sector. After 1989, it should have been possible to prioritize on the substantive issues of development, ignoring previous concerns of the great powers to consolidate their political-ideological camps. In reality, in the light of terrorist threats, these concerns continued to cloud both the intent and the content of development assistance.

Though Soviet power was diminished by 1985, it still largely defined foreign aid policy under both Reagan and Bush. The reason for foreign aid failures during this period, according to John Montgomery, was that policymakers "were unwilling or unable to keep track of the consequences of their decisions that had characterized their performance in . . . previous encounters with large-scale foreign policy operations."[81]

The Berlin Wall fell on November 9, 1989. With the collapse of communism, a "whole spectrum of American opinion, from Richard Nixon leftward, [was] in agreement that Russia must be helped. But wait: help means money. And where, in these deficit-cutting times, is America supposed to find that?"[82]

There would be no new Marshall Plan for Eastern Europe or the collapsing Soviet Union. The problem for the Bush administration was where to find the money. By the end of the Cold War, "aid fatigue was palpable at . . . annual IMF/World Bank meeting[s]. . . . Nobody should be surprised that the pressure to cut aid budgets has emerged so soon after the absorption of communist countries into the capitalist order."[83] For Russia and Eurasia, in particular, a historic opportunity may have been lost for some observers.

To some critics, George Herbert Walker Bush had all the makings of a foreign policy president. He had long experience in international and security policy. His people were "exceptional; he was such a contrast to the 'stand tall' and 'how we are neglected' stuff that Reagan and others spread."[84] As Stanley Hoffman put it in 1989:

> Also, the new thinking [in the George H. W. Bush administration] corresponds to a realistic reading by many Soviet leaders and experts of an international system in which the traditional Soviet mode of behavior—the attempt to impose political control and ideological conformity on others by force—yields limited results, often at exorbitant cost; in which the arms race and the logic of "absolute security" lead only to a higher, more expensive plateau of stalemate and to new forms of insecurity; and in which, in particular, the contest with the United States for influence in the Third World has turned out to be extraordinarily unrewarding.[85]

There had been little aid to Eastern Europe or to the Soviet Union prior to 1989. It was in Eastern and Central Europe that the first Bush administration had the chance to define new policies. President Mikhail Gorbachev implored the industrial nations for "extensive aid," according to Steven Greenhouse, "but they turned him down, saying his reforms were too half-hearted. Many Sovietologists said the West's failure to give Gorbachev billions in aid that he could proudly take back to Moscow was an important factor behind his downfall."[86] Failure to support Gorbachev with international assistance may have been a big mistake.

Foreign aid to Eastern Europe, however, began in earnest under the Bush administration. In 1989, the incoming Bush administration asked Congress to provide $455 million in aid for Poland and Hungary during a three-year period. Congress then voted to provide $837.5 million to the two former communist countries on a three-year schedule.[87] As the Eastern

European challenge developed, "[c]aught between limited resources and philanthropic instincts, Congress [was] preparing a re-examination of foreign aid programs, but most lawmakers [were] unwilling to deal with a choice as stark as the one . . . presented."[88]

For Bush, the priority in Eastern and Central Europe was clear: in 1992, he stated: "To this end, I would like to announce today a plan to support democracy in the states of the former Soviet Union."[89] By 1992 the leaders of the Big Seven industrial democracies had committed to a $24 billion, one-year program to help move Russia toward democracy, including a contribution from the United States of nearly $4.5 billion; however, the devil in the details was the money.

A majority in Congress opposed a Marshall Plan-style approach to Eastern Europe. Thinking at the time was "with the traditional, anti-communist rationale behind much of U.S. assistance fast losing relevance . . . the government needs to rethink the goals and criteria for overseas aid or face a taxpayer revolt against the $15 billion annual bill."[90] The neglect was devastating to former Soviet bloc countries.

Interest in foreign aid to Eastern and Central Europe was short-lived. Ultimately, it was the European Union and European countries that defined the future of Eastern Europe and the former Soviet Union. The usual combination of aid, policy reform, trade, and investment, combined with carrot-and-stick policies (and no little cronyism linking donor agents with ex-communist capitalists) drew Eastern and Central Europe, outside of the Balkans, toward the European Union.

As the millennium approached, both policy elites and the public had disengaged from world affairs and become increasingly interested in domestic affairs, drugs, crime, and the legal and moral shortcomings of American celebrities, "sex, drugs and rock and roll" as the old song said. And there was the O. J. Simpson trial. As Tim Weiner noted, "Foreign aid dropped off sharply after the cold war ended."[91] In foreign policy and foreign aid, it was assumed that the "only consistent factor [was] that invariably it is the United States that sets the tone."[92] Later US involvement in Southwest Asia was based on that policy.

There had been a number of attempts to define a new foreign policy during the first Bush administration. On January 29, 1991, USAID Director Ronald Roskens invited three foreign aid specialists to chair three teams that would plan and shape the restructuring of USAID.[93] Bush's loss in the 1992 elections cut that process short, however, and little came out of these deliberations. The United States and other industrialized countries transferred fewer donor resources to official development assistance in 1993 than in any previous year since 1973, and in Eastern Europe and the former Soviet Union, the US Information Agency and later the State

Department's Bureau of Public Affairs supplanted USAID after 1996. Further cuts took place in 1994 and 1995.[94] It would be left to a new Democratic administration to grapple with foreign aid issues.

Bill Clinton

In 1993 the incoming Clinton administration encountered a US foreign assistance program largely in disarray. The Clinton administration defined five broad areas of emphasis for its development assistance: health and population control, environment, democracy and governance, humanitarian relief, and economic growth. Support for education was downplayed during the Clinton years. Despite emphasis on reinventing government in domestic policy, there is little evidence that the Clinton approaches had any significant impact on the processes of foreign aid programming or on USAID in organizational terms.[95]

At the end of the Cold War, according to Madeleine Albright, there was increasing danger that the United States would take on the role of a world policemen.[96] This appeared to occur in Somalia in 1992 when the US-led UN humanitarian intervention resulted in a brief but horrific war between the United States and one of the clan factions in Mogadishu.[97] Reaction to the failures in Somalia was immediate. The United States withdrew from the scene and left Somalia without a government and vulnerable to religious fanaticism. Using Ethiopia as a proxy, US influence returned to a severely weakened Mogadishu in 2007.

The Clinton administration's approach to foreign and security policy was hesitant and conservative. Structurally, under Clinton in more than one case, what started as a humanitarian intervention by donors later led to full-scale peacekeeping interventions—for example, Somalia, Kosovo, and Bosnia. Somalia taught the United States a lesson. In the end, NGOs, UN peacekeepers, and many journalists, with more than a little shrillness, invested heavily in the idea that the developing world at the end of the Cold War would be one of violence and chaos. The neglect of the crises in Rwanda, the Congo, Sierra Leone, Haiti, and Liberia followed.

The Clinton administration hesitated about peacekeeping because it feared being bogged down as in Vietnam, which until Iraq was the classic example of an intervention feared by American presidents. The lessons of foreign policy crises, of course, are hard to learn because each case is different. As Secretary Albright noted, "Tragically, the lessons we thought we had just learned in Somalia simply did not apply in Rwanda." Each country, she went on, "has its own history, culture, and language; [and] its own pantheon of heroes and adversaries."[98]

Clinton was a cutback president in foreign aid as in domestic policy—in part at least forced by Congress. In 1993, USAID announced that twenty-one missions serving thirty-five countries and territories would be phased out over three years as part of a series of program cutbacks.[99] Domestically, foreign aid was under attack throughout the Clinton administration. Well into Clinton's first term, *New York Times* reported

> Secretary of State Warren Christopher warned . . . of "a new generation of isolationism" emerging in Congress and said the State Department could not sustain more budget cuts without seriously undercutting American foreign policy around the world. . . . Mr. Christopher said a steady decline in foreign-affairs spending had already forced the United States to close consulates and even embassies and to shortchange efforts in some parts of the world in order to address immediate crises in others.[100]

Clinton seemed to support multilateralism. USAID quickly aligned its objectives with the UN, World Bank, and other international organizations and pledged to use future aid flows to promote democracy and sustainable development in the underdeveloped world. Although the administration had made humanitarian intervention a centerpiece of its foreign policy promises, the United States often did a poor job of delivering emergency aid to those in need.[101] Clinton argued that foreign aid needed a second chance.[102]

The Clinton administration did expand foreign assistance to Eastern Europe and the former Soviet Union, as the concept of a transitional country developed; however, the Eastern Europe and the Eurasian situation appeared

> to reflect long-brewing resentment over the presence of a U.S. aid program initially designed to help developing countries [in Africa and Asia]. While many communities across this vast country welcome the Peace Corps volunteers, some officials grumble that Russia is treated as if it were simply another impoverished Third World backwater and that the American volunteers are ill-prepared for their assignments in this former superpower.[103]

Two developments illustrated the vulnerability of Clinton's foreign aid policy in his second term. First, Clinton wanted return to the practice known as *aid tying,* where the United States would give development aid to poor countries only on the condition that they use the assistance to purchase American goods and services. Second, "[a] day after Mr. Clinton presented a budget that included a modest increase in spending on foreign aid, [the new Secretary of State Madeline Albright] also argued that after four years of a declining foreign-affairs budget, the United States was 'steadily and unilaterally disarming ourselves'"[104] from a foreign and foreign aid policy perspective.

By 1997, former Soviet bloc countries came back to haunt policymakers. On May 20, 1997, USAID suspended a $14 million contract with Harvard University's Institute for International Development (HIID). Money was to aid financial-market development in Russia. According to the *New York Times*, "The agency suspended the grants, the last part of a $57 million contract . . . after an investigation uncovered what the officials described as evidence that the advisers, Andrei Shleifer and Jonathan Hay, had misused the money."[105]

Privatization and democratization were somewhat naively welcomed by Western policymakers and the public alike as key components of success attained by Russia during the 1990s. As a result, according to Eugene Rumer, "Advisers funded by USAID were deployed throughout key Russian government agencies, while NGOs funded by USAID offered democracy-building advice to political parties and local governments."[106] The closeness of US cooperation to the scandals that followed assured the United States would be identified in Russia with corruption, inefficiency, and economic decline.

Foreign Aid Spending and the End of the Cold War

Despite declining amounts of aid, pressures to spend rather than ration resources did not impart to LDCs a sense of scarcity about the supply and management of donor funds. From the perspective of the donor program manager, the rule is, move the money. By 1990, the scarcity was real, however, and "cutbacks [in US foreign aid] would involve an embarrassing inability by the administration to make good its foreign aid pledges, many of them to countries where the United States has important base rights" or lingering Cold War obligations.[107]

In 1991, as Congress was reluctant to approve a comprehensive aid package, US lawmakers once again allowed most projects to be financed with repeated short-term appropriations and continuing resolutions, a pattern that would continue over the next decade.[108] The foreign aid budget, at about $10 billion, had not been increased for a decade. As a percentage of the overall economy, it was at its lowest point since World War II.[109]

By the early 1990s, as a result of donor fatigue in the United States and a number of other OECD counties, donors found it very difficult to respond to disasters.[110] This was particularly true of a natural and incremental disaster like the HIV/AIDS crisis. "This [was] a very big moment for HIV/AIDS and foreign aid," said J. Stephen Morrison, director of the Africa Program at the Center for Strategic and International Studies and a State Department official under President Clinton.[111] Under both Clinton and George W. Bush, however, foreign aid failed to fully address the HIV/AIDS crisis—though the Bush administration dramatically increased funding to combat HIV/AIDs through his President's Emergency Plan for AIDS Relief (PEPFAR).

US spending patterns continued apace through the 1990s. In 1992, with USAID foreign aid funding running out, Congress again voted to extend the current level of spending through the end of the fiscal year.[112] In April 1992, President George H. W. Bush "signed into law a stopgap six-month extension of US foreign aid that include[ed] money for United Nations peacekeeping and potential aid for the former Soviet Union."[113] In 1994, bilateral assistance exclusive of the security-based Economic Support Fund was $2.5 billion less than the 1966 sustainable figure.

Financially, Clinton operated on continuing resolutions in foreign aid for most of his two terms. There was nothing unusual about not passing the bill to authorize foreign aid. In 1994, Congress had not approved a foreign aid bill since 1985, though it went on to pass less conspicuous continuing resolutions and appropriations bills to spend aid money in any event.

By 1995, in absolute terms though not as a percentage of GDP, foreign aid remained the largest in the world, and it had "produced a large and complex institutional framework."[114] The result was a bureaucratic tangle. Under Clinton, USAID depended almost entirely on a variety of intermediaries, contractors, NGOs, or (though decreasingly) universities to deliver technical assistance and training.

Throughout the 1990s, foreign aid spending reflected levels of foreign affairs spending characteristic of the early post–Cold War period, and there was special attention given to famine and other humanitarian conditions in a number of African and Central American countries. Foreign aid spending often distorted priorities in LDCs. Martin Wolf said:

> What you see is not what you get. It is impossible to find a way around the obstacles created by a poor environment through targeted assistance to high-priority areas. Money is fungible: a government can offset aid by adjustments in where it spends its own money. Aid — including debt relief — always finances the

marginal priorities of the government, be these palaces, prisons
or primary schools (or tax cuts, for that matter).[115]

Some critics argued that the "downward trend in US development
assistance appropriations should be reversed"[116] because the US decline in
spending set the trend in other developed states. For example, as Michael
Peel pointed out in 1995, the "21 members of the OECD gave an average
of 0.27 per cent of GNP, down from 0.34 per cent in 1990."[117] During the
past twenty years, and taking into account growth of the economies of
the advanced democracies and the depreciation in the value of money
because of inflation, the more developed nations had fallen further and
further short of their defined aid target of 1 percent of GNP.[118]

Increasing bureaucratization aid and the drop in foreign aid and technical assistance during the past thirty years has meant that even if US
foreign aid were 100 percent effective, it would not promote sustainability. In 1996, USAID spending accounted for only 0.27 percent of GDP.
The United States was at the bottom of OECD members in terms of spending, and the 1996 statistics stood at the lowest level recorded since com-
parable statistics began in 1950.[119]

During the Clinton administration, consolidation of foreign policy and
foreign aid agency was a goal of the Republican-controlled Senate. In the
late 1990s, Senator Jesse Helms "proposed abolishing USAID and transferring its $7 billion in annual aid to a quasi-governmental foundation
that would deliver grants to private relief groups."[120] While USAID was
not abolished, in 1997, the Clinton administration, acting on the basis of
congressional mandates, reorganized foreign affairs structures with the
State Department and clumsily incorporated the US Information Agency
into State, which assumed closer responsibility for USAID's budget. This
reorganization presaged further integration of USAID into State in 2006.

Despite increasing criticism of foreign aid, on February 12, 1996, Clinton
signed the FY1996 Foreign Assistance Appropriations Act (P.L. 104–107).
The foreign aid allocation in 1996–1997 provided $12.1 billion for for-
eign assistance programs and operations. That was "18 percent below the
administration's FY 1996 request of $14.8 billion and 11 percent below
the FY 1995 enacted level of $13.6 billion."[121] Policymakers fretted over
the downward spiral of their budgets and lack of results. Many began seriously rethinking their efforts since the halcyon days of the development
aid era began in the 1960s.[122]

In 1997, with an operating expense request level of $495 million,
USAID had $60 million less for operations in FY97 than it had in FY96.
The years 1998–1999 were a turning point of sorts because after "years
of decline, rich governments [including the US] spent 9% more on aid in

1998 than in the year before."[123] By 2000, concessional aid transfers involved more than $50 billion annually. It represented, however, a fraction of what was needed for sustainability, and "most aid packages were [still] tied to the procurement [of] U.S. goods and services."[124]

By 1999, foreign aid, which amounted to much less than 1 percent of the federal budget, had been in freefall for fifteen years. In that year, Congress authorized some $13.5 billion in expenditures for overseas assistance, an amount that remained relatively stable through September 11. In 2002, USAID funding declined, and the $10 billion aid budget remained the lowest among rich nations as a percentage of the total economy (though it would increase dramatically after that time). Nor was there any agreement to devote any major new funding to international debt reduction efforts in LDCs beyond covering $1 billion in shortfalls in the debt management current program.[125]

Haggling over the foreign aid budget is a congressional tradition and pastime; however, as the millennium approached, what was at stake to aid advocates "was the fate of the sole superpower's $13 billion foreign assistance budget for 1998. All congressional staff could do was to bet on how long the haggling would take before a foreign aid bill was passed."[126] By 2000, the US "ranked dead last among the advanced nations in the share of income that it allocated to foreign aid."[127] There was little support for foreign aid in Congress. Throughout the decade, foreign policy and foreign aid institutions had faced attack from their congressional foes. In one case involving USAID, Congress "recommended that the agency limit overhead costs to 15 per cent of the total amount an organization receives from the U.S.I.A. for a program."[128] The information agency was later abolished. Only September 11 staved off a similar fate for USAID.

During Clinton's presidency, the overall foreign aid budget declined from $14.1 billion in 1993 when he took office to $13.5 billion in 1999. The decline was all the more dramatic after factoring in inflation. The aid budget would decline even further in the first two years of the George W. Bush administration. USAID support staff was cut during the same period by about a third, down to 7,000, including both foreign service and domestic civil servants.

Conclusion

Throughout the 1990s under structural adjustment, the United States and other donors increased support to promote in their bilateral programs politically sensitive, restrictive, and intrusive policies and actions that would encourage conservation measures, such as energy efficiency, renewable energy, and forest management. Such action often advocated policies that would not be acceptable to the United States and other countries at home. As Severine Rugumamu has noted, "the institutional and organizational capacities of the recipient states [came to be] considered as critical intervening variables in explaining the aid relationship."[129]

Throughout much of the developing world there existed a continuous tension between the humanitarian functions of foreign aid in trying to improve social welfare conditions in LDCs and the narrower imperatives of self-interest. In 2000, neither concern appeared to be important to the American public. During the 2000 presidential campaign, foreign aid had reached its nadir. Candidate George W. Bush would attack nation-building and overseas assistance. Bush wanted to focus on domestic affairs.

Overall, as the millennium approached, interest in foreign aid waned. Except for a few bankrupt African countries, USAID no longer represented a significant transfer of resources to LDCs relative to the size of their economy. By the end of the twentieth century, the path to apathy about international development was clear. Despite the acceptance of structural adjustment by many LDCs, by the mid-1990s, foreign assistance levels continued to plunge.

September 11, however, would change all of that: policymakers became concerned that impoverished people fed by fundamentalist religions and living in failed states would offer sanctuary and become a breeding ground for terrorists. As a result, foreign aid budgets would surge with allocations, more than doubling in ten years. We will turn to those developments in the next two chapters.

Notes

1. H. Field Haviland, "Foreign Aid and the Policy Process: 1957," *American Political Science Review,* 52, no. 33 (September 1958), p. 700.

2. Staff Report, *The Foreign Aid Programs and the United States Economy,* 1948–1957 (Washington, DC: National Planning Association, May 1958), p. 37.

3. Stephen Browne, *Beyond Aid: From Patronage to Partnership* (Aldershot, UK: Ashgate Publishing, 1999), p. 93.

4. Ralph Linton, "An Anthropologist Views Point Four," *American Perspective,* iv, no. 2 (Spring 1950), p. 119. Article, pp. 113–121. See p. 119 for quotes.

5. Elizabeth Becker, "A New Villain in Free Trade: The Farmer on the Dole," *New York Times* (August 25, 2002), p. A10.

6. Interview, USAID official, Kinshasa, Zaire, April 1989. Author's Research Diary (April 28, 1989).

7. Jack Willoughby, "Save the World. Sell the Mercedes," *Financial World* (March 3, 1992), p. 44.

8. Mahbub ul Haq and Shahid Javed Burki, "Meeting Basic Needs: An Overview," *World Bank Poverty and Basic Needs Series* (Washington DC: World Bank, 1980), p. 6.

9. Frank C. Conahan, "Foreign Assistance: U.S. Use of Conditions to Achieve Economic Reforms," *GAO Report to U.S. AID* (August 1986), p. 8.

10. Pierre Landell-Mills, Ramgopal Agarwala, and Stanley Please, "From Crisis to Sustainable Growth in Sub-Saharan Africa," *Finance & Development* (Johannesburg: December 1989), p. 26.

11. E. Philip Morgan, "Why Aid Fails: An Organizational Interpretation" (Public Lecture, Institute of Development Management, July 19, 1979), p. 18.

12. Robert Cassen, "The Effectiveness of Aid," *Finance & Development* (Johannesburg, South Africa: March 1986), p. 12.

13. "Aiding Africa," *Economist* (November 25, 1989), p. 47.

14. Paul Mosley, *Overseas Aid: Its Defence and Reform* (Brighton, UK: Wheatsheaf Books, 1987), p. 139.

15. USAID, "Implementation Report on the *Africa: Seeds of Hope Act*" (Washington DC: August 1999), p. 6.

16. Elizabeth Becker, "Raising Farm Subsidies, U.S. Widens International Rift," *New York Times* (June 25, 2002), p. A1.

17. Barbara Crossette, "Givers of Foreign Aid Shifting Their Methods," *New York Times* (February 23, 1992), p. A2.

18. Paul Blustein, "The Right Aid Formula This Time Around?" *Washington Post* (March 24, 2002), p. A27.

19. Paul Blustein, "Treasury Bonds with Bono," *Washington Post* (June 4, 2002), p. C1.

20. Dirk Olin, "Washington Consensus," *New York Times Magazine* (May 25, 2003), pp. 21–22.

21. Bill Berkeley, *The Graves Are Not Yet Full: Race, Tribe and Power in the Heart of Africa* (New York: Basic Books, 2001), p. 69.

22. Steven Greenhouse, "Third World Markets Gain Favor," *New York Times* (December 17, 1993), p. C1.

23. Carlos F. Diaz-Alejandro, "Some Aspects of the Brazilian Experience with Foreign Aid," Center Paper No.177, (New Haven, CT: Yale University Economic Growth Center, 1972).

24. Rudolph A. Peterson, et al., "U.S. Foreign Assistance in the 1970s: A New Approach," (Washington, DC: Report to the President from the Task Force on International Development, March 4, 1970), p. 10.

25. M.D. Shoen, Special Adviser, USAID Africa Bureau, Oral Interview, Author's Research Diary, (June 6, 1991).

26. Gerald K. Helleiner, "Aid and Dependence in Africa: Issues for Recipients," in *The Politics of Africa: Dependence and Development* (London: Longman, 1979), p. 223. Entire article, pp. 221–245.

27. Robert Cassen, "The Effectiveness of Aid," *Finance & Development* (March 1986), p. 11.

28. Conahan, "Foreign Assistance," p. 2.

29. Ibid.

30. Martin Wolf, "Aid, hope and charity," *Financial Times* (November 11, 1998). The citation is quoted from the World Bank report, *Assessing Aid,* published November 10, 1990.

31. Stanley Hoffmann, "What Should We Do in the World?" *Atlantic Monthly* (October 1989), p. 95.

32. Wolfgang P. Teschner, "The State of Education Development in the Region," Panel Review Meeting of Asian Development Bank (March 14–15, 1988), p. 1.

33. Jeffrey D. Sachs, "When Foreign Aid Makes a Difference," *New York Times* (February 3, 1997), p. A17.

34. M.D. Shoen, Special Adviser, USAID Africa Bureau, Oral Interview, Author's Research Diary, (June 6, 1991).

35. For example, "From 1975 through 1992, U.S. economic assistance to Portugal, managed by USAID, was $1.3 billion, including refugee and disaster assistance, agriculture, schools and rural education, health, low-income housing and housing guaranties, basic sanitation, consultants and training, balance-of-payment loans, PL 480 loans, and Economic Support Funds (ESF) cash transfers." Background Notes: Portugal, June 1997 Released by the Bureau of European and Canadian Affairs, http://dosfan.lib.uic.edu/ERC/bgnotes/ eur/portugal9706.html. Accessed June 2, 2007.

36. Terry Buss, *Haiti in the Balance* (Washington, DC: Brookings Institution Press, 2008).

37. See the Web site of the International Monetary fund on HIPCs accessed on October 17, 2008. http://www.imf.org/external/np/hipc/doc.htm.

38. Frank C. Conahan, "Foreign Assistance," p. 17.

39. Steven W. Hook, *National Interest and Foreign Aid* (Boulder, CO: Lynne Rienner Publishers, 1995), p. 28.

40. Ibid., p. 17.

41. Christopher Booker, *The Neophiliacs: A Study of the Revolution in English Life in the Fifties and Sixties* (London: Fontana Books, 1970), p. 311.

42. Ronald Steel, "Would Kennedy Have Quit Vietnam?" *New York Times* (May 25, 2003), p. E1.

43. Milton J. Esman and John D. Montgomery, "Systems Approaches to Technical Cooperation: The Role of Development Administration," *Public Administration Review,* (September/October 1969), pp. 507–539. Quote, p. 508.

44. Ralph H. Smuckler and Robert J. Berg, "New Challenges New Opportunities, U.S. Cooperation for International Growth and Development in the 1990s" (Occasional Paper, Michigan State University, August 1988), p. 4.

45. Martin Wolf, "Aid, hope and charity," *Financial Times* (November 11, 1998), p. 12.

46. Rudolph A. Peterson, et al., "U.S. Foreign Assistance in the 1970s: A New Approach," Report to the President from the Task Force on International Development (March 4, 1970), p. 26.

47. I.M. Destler, *Presidents, Bureaucrats and Foreign Policy: The Politics of Organizational Reform* (Princeton, NJ: Princeton University Press, 1972).

48. Edward Horesh, "Academics and Experts or the Death of the High Level Technical Assistant," *Development and Change,* 12, no. 4, (October 1981), p. 615.

49. Peterson, et al., "U.S. Foreign Assistance in the 1970s," p. 24.

50. Richard Holbrooke, "The Machine That Fails," *Foreign Policy,* no. 1 (Winter 1970–1971), pp. 65–77. Quote, p. 65.

51. Carlos F. Diaz-Alejandro, "Some Aspects of the Brazilian Experience with Foreign Aid," Center Paper No. 177, Yale University Economic Growth Center, 1972, p. 443.

52. Stephen Browne, *Beyond Aid: From Patronage to Partnership* (Aldershot, UK: Ashgate Publishing, 1999), pp. 27.

53. Steve Talbot, "Food as a Political Weapon," in *The Trojan Horse: A Radical Look at Foreign Aid,* Steve Weissman ed., (Palo Alto, CA: Rampart Books, 1974), p. 167.

54. Tendler, *Inside Foreign Aid,* p. 8.

55. Paul Mosley, *Overseas Aid: Its Defence and Reform* (Brighton, UK: Wheatsheaf Books, 1987), p. 38.

56. Peterson, et al., "U.S. Foreign Assistance in the 1970s," p. 9.

57. Celia W. Dugger, "International Disasters Tax America's Compassion," *New York Times* (May 12, 1991), p. A9.

58. Sebastian Mallaby, "Visions of U.S. Aid," *Washington Post* (April 19, 2004), p. A19.

59. Theroux, *Dark Star Safari,* p. 192.

60. Bruce Clark, "When life is at stake," *Financial Times* (April 11, 1998), p. 18.

61. Mallaby, "Visions of U.S. Aid."

62. Peterson, et al., "U.S. Foreign Assistance in the 1970s," p. 16.

63. T. Dichter, *Despite Good Intentions: Why Development Assistance to the Third World Has Failed* (UMass Press Book Review Announcement, February 3, 2003).

64. Fred W. Riggs, "Memorandum: Suggested Discussion Topics Based on Dennis Rondinelli, *Development Administration and Foreign Aid Policy*" (University of Hawaii, March 1987).

65. Booker, *The Neophiliacs*, p. 311.

66. Neil A. Lewis, "String of Crises Overwhelms Relief Agencies and Donors," *New York Times* (May 4, 1991), p. A5.

67. Esman and Montgomery, "Systems Approaches to Technical Cooperation," p. 509.

68. Mosley, *Overseas Aid*, p. 65.

69. Harden, *Africa*, p. 197.

70. Quoted in Larry Chang, "Foreign Aid and the Fate of Least Developed Countries," (Unpublished Paper, 1986), p. 5. Lord Peter Bauer is still considered out of the mainstream. Michael Prowse, "The Twilight of Foreign Aid," *Financial Times* (Sept. 28, 1992), p. 5.

71. Stephanie Flanders, "Foreign Aid Has Little Impact, says World Bank Study," *Financial Times* (April 14, 1997), p. 18.

72. Ivan Eland, *The Empire Has No Clothes: U.S. Foreign Policy Exposed* (Oakland, CA: The Independent Institute, 2004), William Easterly, *The Elusive Quest for Growth: Economist's Adventures and Misadventures in the Tropics* (Cambridge, MA: MIT Press, 2001), Easterly's *The White Man's Burden: Why the West's Efforts to Aid the Rest Have Done So Much Ill and So Little Good* (New York: Penguin Press, 2006), and John Perkins, *Confessions of an Economic Hit Man* (San Francisco, CA: Berrett-Koehler Publishers, 2004).

73. Peterson, et al., "U.S. Foreign Assistance, p. 132.

74. Robert J. Cabelly, "US Aid to Zimbabwe?" *African Index*, March 20, 1980.

75. Dennis A. Rondinelli, "Development Administration and American Foreign Assistance Policy: An Assessment of Theory and Practice in Aid," *Canadian Journal of Development Studies*, 6, no. 2, 1985, p. 221.

76. Vernon Ruttan, *United States Development Assistance Policy: The Domestic Politics of Foreign Aid* (Baltimore: Johns Hopkins University Press, 1996), pp. 219–220.

77. Raymond W. Copson, Brenda M. Branaman, and Ted S. Dagne, "Africa: U.S. Foreign Assistance Issues," *CRS Issue Brief* (June 2, 1992), p. 2.

78. Quoted in Chang, "Foreign Aid and the Fate of Least Developed Countries," p. 2.

79. Clay Wescott and Abdul Majid Osman, "International Resources and Policies" (New York: United Nations Development Program, Unpublished Paper, 1992), p. 3.

80. Edmund Stillman and William Pfaff, *Power and Impotence: The Failure of America's Foreign Policy* (New York: Random House, 1966), p. 15.

81. John D, Montgomery, *Aftermath: Tarnished Outcomes of American Foreign Policy* (Dover, MA: Auburn House Publishing Company, 1986), p. 88.

82. "Kind Words, Closed Wallet," *Economist* (March 27, 1993), p. 26.

83. Michael Prowse, "The Twilight of Foreign Aid," *Financial Times* (September 28, 1992), p. 30.

84. Donald Stone, Personal Note to Louis A. Picard, February 1988. Author's Research Diary.

85. Stanley Hoffmann, "What Should We Do in the World?" *Atlantic Monthly* (October 1989), p. 91.

86. Steven Greenhouse, "Bush and Kohl Unveil Plan for 7 Nations to Contribute $24 Billion in Aid for Russia," *New York Times* (April 2, 1992), p. A1.

87. Ferdinand Protzman, "Bonn Giving Poland Aid of $1 Billion," *New York Times* (October 26, 1989), p. A1.

88. Susan F. Rasky, "State Dept. Backs Dole on Foreign Aid," *New York Times* (January 17, 1990), p. A1.

89. "Excerpts from Bush's Talk on Aid: Allied Nations 'Must Win the Peace,'" *New York Times* (April 2, 1992), p. A7.

90. "Foreign Aid Not Remotely Popular with Voters, Congressmen Say," *Pittsburgh Press* (November 24, 1991), p. B5.

91. Tim Weiner, "More Entreaties in Monterrey for More Aid to the Poor," *New York Times* (March 22, 2002), p. A1.

92. Jonathan Power, "Breath of Fresh Air in Aid Policy at Last," *The Star* (Johannesburg, September 1, 1997), p. 14.

93. "AID/W Notice; Subject: Transition Teams," Office of the Administrator, USAID, January 29, 1991.

94. Ian Smillie, *The Alms Bazaar: Altruism Under Fire–Non-Profit Organizations and International Development* (London: IT Publications, 1995), p. 19.

95. Carol Lancaster, *Aid to Africa: So Much to Do: So Little Done* (Chicago: University of Chicago Press, 1999), p. 108.

96. Madeleine Albright, *Madame Secretary: A Memoir* (New York: Miramax Books, 2003), p. 153.

97. Mark Bowden, *Black Hawk Down: A Story of Modern War* (New York: Penguin, 2000).

98. For both quotes see Albright, *Madame Secretary,* pp. 154 and 166 respectively.

99. "U.S. Agency for Development Plans to Cut Aid to 35 Nations," *New York Times* (November 20, 1993), p. A6.

100. Steven Lee Myers, "Christopher Says Budget Cuts Point to 'a New Isolationism,'" *New York Times* (January 16, 1997), p. A5.

101. Jane Perlez, "State Dept. Faults U.S. Aid for War Refugees as Inept," *New York Times* (May 9, 2000), p. A8.

102. Michael Prowse, "The Twilight of Foreign Aid," *Financial Times* (September 28, 1992), p. 30.

103. Peter Baker, "Russia Ousting Dozens of Peace Corps Workers," *Washington Post* (August 12, 2002), p. 12.

104. For both quotes see "Linking Exports to Aid," *New York Times* (October 19, 1993), p. A14.

105. Steven Lee Myers, "A.I.D. Suspends Harvard Grant, Saying Money Was Misused," *New York Times* (May 20, 1997), p. A8.

106. Eugene B. Rumer, "Not Another Soviet Union," *Washington Post* (September 24, 2004), p. A25. The USAID gopher allows browsing of development, project, procurement, public affairs and administrative information via gopher.info.usaid.gov. See "Information at Your Fingertips," *Front Lines* (Washington: USAID, April–May 1996), p. 10.

107. John M. Goshko, "State Department Budget Faces New Cuts," *Washington Post* (April 27, 1987), p. A6.

108. "Foreign Aid Not Remotely Popular With Voters, Congressmen Say," *Pittsburgh Press* (November 24, 1991), p. B5.

109. Joseph Kahn, "U.S. Rejects Bid to Double Foreign Aid to Poor Lands," *New York Times* (January 29, 2002), p. A1.

110. "U.N. Vows to Step Up Aid Efforts," *New York Times* (September 13, 1992), p. A12.

111. Elizabeth Becker, "With Record Rise in Foreign Aid Comes Change in How it is Monitored," *New York Times* (December 7, 2003), p. A6.

112. "House Extends Foreign Aid, Kills Defense Fund Switch," *New York Times* (March 25, 1992), p. A1.

113. "Foreign Aid," *Pittsburgh Post-Gazette* (April 2, 1992), p. A10.

114. Hook, p. 127.

115. Wolf, "Aid, hope and charity."

116. Peterson, et al,, "U.S. Foreign Assistance in the 1970s," p. 36.

117. Michael Peel, "Aid to poor falls to lowest level," *Financial Times* (July 23, 1997), p. 4.

118. "How the European Community is Helping the Developing Countries" (Brussels: *European Development Aid,* Commission of the European Communities, n.d.), p. 5.

119. Graham Bowley, "Rich National make sharp cuts in aid," *Financial Times* (February 6, 1997), p. 5.

120. Eric Schmitt, "Helms Stipulates Private Channels for Foreign Aid," *New York Times,* January 12, 2001.

121. O'Sullivan, "President Signs FY 1996 Foreign Assistance Appropriations Act," p. 2.

122. Howard W. French "Donors of Foreign Aid Have Second Thoughts," *New York Times* (April 7, 1996), p. A5.

123. "Measuring Up For Aid," *Economist* (January 8, 2000), p. 98.

124. Ibid., p. 133.

125. Karen DeYoung, and DeNeen L. Brown, "G-8 Approves an Aid Package for Africa," *Washington Post* (June 28, 2002), p. A19.

126. Ibid.

127. Matthew Miller, "Thinking Big," *U.S. News and World Report* (June 9, 1997), p. 8.

128. Amy Magaro Rubin, "Senate Panel's Plan Would Limit Use of USIA Funds," *Chronicle of Higher Education* (August 8, 1997), p. A44.

129. Severine M. Rugumamu, *Lethal Aid: The Illusion of Socialism and Self-Reliance in Tanzania* (Trenton, NJ: Africa World Press, 1997), p. 13.

9

SEPTEMBER 11 AND THE IRAQ WAR

> Maybe you just had to assert the obvious: that this was a war, that this was the Green Zone, and that this was America.
>
> William Langewiesche, "Welcome to the Green Zone"

> The U.S. government went into Iraq with scant solid international support and on the basis of incorrect information—about weapons of mass destruction and a supposed nexus between Saddam Hussein and al Qaeda's terrorism—and then occupied the country negligently.
>
> Thomas E. Ricks, *Fiasco*

George W. Bush and Unilateralism

The Changing Environment

Foreign aid levels had plunged in the mid-1990s from $12 billion in 1993 to $9 billion in 1996, and they would continue to be low until the second year of the George W. Bush administration. The changing international environment after September 11, 2001, would have an immense impact on foreign aid policy. This legacy is especially poignant post–September 11, and the quagmire of US military and civil involvement in Iraq and Afghanistan.

This chapter examines moral ambiguities and uncertainties of foreign aid post–September 11 and the assumptions that defined the US response to the attacks. The foreign aid debate increased after September 11, with positions both for and against unilateral versus multilateral approaches to foreign and security policy. Of particular concern is the shift in emphasis from economic development policy to conflict resolution, security concerns, and regime reconstruction and governance within the context of the War on Terror.

When he arrived in the White House in January 2001, George W. Bush had no plans to restore aid funding and appeared to have modest ambitions

155

on foreign policy.[1] He would be a domestic president. He and his advisers talked about "a more 'humble' America that didn't tell countries how to conduct themselves inside their borders."[2]

During the presidential campaign, George W. Bush stated "I don't think our troops ought to be used for what's called nation building."[3] Bush, in his debates with opponent Al Gore, argued against interventions in places such as Bosnia and Somalia and promised there would be no more nation-building on his watch. While international trade and security were important issues, democracy, governance, and institutional development were not. After the January 20 inauguration, however, there were shades of a *neo-isolationism* in the early Bush presidency that would revert to a unilateralism that had long been brewing within neoconservative foreign policy circles.

Observers initially viewed Condoleezza Rice, Bush's national security adviser, and in the second administration, his Secretary of State, as a realist rather than an ideologue on foreign policy. Rice made a compelling argument that the United States could not afford to become involved in developing country nation-building efforts because this would "degrade the American capability to do the things America has to do."[4]

Overall, the Bush administration seemed to view international relations as a mixture of economic and military power. In looking at the Middle East, the Bush administration saw it in regional terms as part of an internal war within Islam. This meant the characteristics within a single country, in effect, were less important than the totality of the Middle East conflicts. What little attention that was paid to foreign aid focused rhetorically on an expanded role for faith-based organizations in international development activities and a concern about health programs that promoted birth control and/or tolerated abortion.

The Bush Premises and September 11

On September 11, planes struck the World Trade Center in New York City and the Pentagon near Washington, DC. A fourth plane crashed near Shanksville, Pennsylvania, while heading toward Washington to strike either the White House or the Capitol. September 11 was a wake-up call for both the Bush administration and the country in the foreign policy and foreign aid context. As a result of the terrorist attacks, foreign aid and military assistance spending over time would begin to increase precipitously. It would also stimulate more interest among policymakers for foreign interventions, in the process shifting the country toward unilateralism and restoring nation-building, democracy, and governance to prominence in foreign aid policy. Most importantly, in Iraq, it would lead to the most serious military and foreign policy disaster since Vietnam.

Terrorist attacks had three effects on the American people. First, there was a surge of patriotism and a neomilitarism. Secondly, popular attitudes after September 11 evolved into "an unseemly inferiority complex" in international relations.[5] And thirdly, the United States began to stray significantly from its founding ideals involving constitutional rights, torture, and the like. US foreign policy became what one commentator called a "condominium of power," a model based in part on the international rule of law and international organizations, or alternatively, failing that, use of unilateral coercive economic or military action.[6]

Pre–September 11, according to Bob Woodward, the United States, though it had "inconceivable scenarios [for countries all over the world], had no plans for Afghanistan, the sanctuary of bin Laden and his network."[7] That would change rapidly. The Bush administration, in its pursuit of the Taliban and bin Laden, declared a "crusade," a word which would have extremely negative connotations in the Islamic world.

According to Woodward, this "was all consistent with Bush's belief that he [was] an agent for change—that he must state a new strategic direction or policy with bold, clear moves. And because it would be the policy of the United States, the only superpower, the rest of the world would have to move over, would adjust over time."[8] To the Bush administration, the intervention in Afghanistan and later Iraq had become part of America's moral mission in world affairs.

Within the Bush administration, the "ideological opposition to any participation in what is called nation building . . . disappeared."[9] The declared goal, at least in principle, was to "support the growth of democratic movements and institutions in every nation and culture."[10] Nation-building came back onto the foreign aid agenda with a vengeance.

So-called civilian leadership in the Bush administration micro-managed the interventions in Afghanistan and then Iraq. Many, such as former Deputy Secretary of Defense Paul D. Wolfowitz, were "essentially idealistic interventionists who believed in using American power to spread democracy."[11]

For State's policymakers, the promise of a generous package of aid and debt relief was an important tool for allies such as Pakistan, which helped in the war against Osama bin Laden. In the wake of the attack, Bush "committed himself to some of the largest nation-building efforts since the Marshall Plan, from Iraq to Afghanistan and perhaps, if his vision is realized, elsewhere in the Middle East" and parts of Africa.[12]

In 2002 there was some increased support for foreign aid within the public, if it was linked to the anti-terrorism campaign. This "broad support was surprising because [a public opinion] survey indicated that most Americans think the United States spends 20 times more on foreign aid than it does."[13] In 2003 Congress approved "$1 billion for the new aid program and $2.4 billion for AIDS."[14] The Bush administration also promised to ask the Republican-led Congress to nearly double the amount of aid given to Africa.

Foreign aid became part of the political rhetoric prior to the 2004 elections. In 2003, a book by Wesley K. Clark, a retired Army general then running for president, called for a major expansion in foreign assistance and called for the establishment of a Department of International Assistance to manage the initiative.[15] In that same year, a few days after he announced a major initiative in order to fight global AIDS, President Bush turned his attention again to the AIDS crisis and stated he would request $16 billion for AIDS prevention, care, and treatment in his 2004 budget to Congress.[16] Under the Bush scheme, according to Rachel Swarms, most "of the money for the projects will come from existing programs . . . [and] critics condemned the plan as an attempt to divert attention from the reluctance of wealthy nations to reduce trade subsidies, which many economists say hurt farmers in poor countries."[17]

Ultimately, foreign aid did not receive much of a short-term bounce coming out of September 11. According to a 2003 *New York Times* report, "Mr. LaVergne, a Republican, and Mr. Cannon, a Democrat, [were] strongly critical of President Bush's request for $87 billion to finance military and reconstruction projects in Iraq and Afghanistan."[18] Their reaction was not atypical.

On October 7, 2001, the United States launched an invasion of Afghanistan to overthrow the Taliban regime, capture Osama bin Laden, and destroy al Qaeda. The US coalition quickly put into place an interim government headed by Hamid Karzai. While the initial phases of the operation went quickly, the coalition, later turned over to NATO, was a low-cost, under-manned force that failed to capture bin Laden or control much of the country. By 2008, the war in Afghanistan threatened to go out of control. Afghanistan continued to be a significant problem for the NATO coalition in 2009, eight years after September 11, with bin Laden still at large.

The United States operated with less than superpower resolve regarding assistance for the new government in Afghanistan and in the search for terrorists. According to Scott Anderson, to bring various natural and human-made crises to an end, and with more and more and more of the world's wars resulting in the wanton slaughter of civilian populations, "aid organizations are increasingly involving themselves directly in social, political and even, at times, military matters."[19] And they were doing so with fewer funds.

Understanding Iraq

Return to the Quagmire

From the beginning, the Iraq war was to be executed as a US-only unilateral invasion, unlike the Gulf War or Afghanistan. The United States, in invading Iraq, to use Woodward's words, "would be taking down a regime, would have to govern Iraq, and the ripple effect in the Middle East and the world could not be predicted."[20] Given the expectation that the war would be short, policy experts worried about the governance and development components of Iraq policy. Almost no planning had been undertaken, however.

The debate concerned the extent to which the United States was able to "Americanize" its intervention in Iraq and foreign aid programs in the Middle East given the absence of any significant allies other than Britain. Moreover, the political nightmare of the loss of Vietnam haunted many in the Bush White House. Though there were elements of a governance policy in Iraq that might prove useful, there was strong concern among critics such as Larry Diamond that the Iraq model ultimately would be a negative one.[21] In situations of conflict, one cannot operate without the military, but that often skews the reconstruction and development process. Internationally, as a result of the invasion and occupation of Iraq, around the world, "fear and distrust of the U.S. government increased."[22]

Bush, according to Woodward, never did create a political development plan for postinvasion Iraq, an issue that concerned many of Bush's military and civilian advisers. A prewar British memo that expressed concern that the United States lacked any plans to occupy, reconstruct, and govern Iraq or promote economic and social development confirmed this. Bush administration officials were virtually silent on Iraq's postwar future despite concern expressed by the British that the occupation of Iraq would be a major nation-building exercise.[23] In Iraq, according to Bob Woodward:

> Much has been made of the lack of planning that preceded the invasion, but it was . . . [international] isolation afterward that turned out to be as great a problem . . . . The occupation [was] characterized by a lack of institutional memory and expertise. Moreover, though there [were] some specialists involved, and a few non-native Arabic speakers, for ordinary officials no knowledge of the region [or the language was] required.[24]

The Iraq intervention, among other things, illustrated that foreign policy decisions face historical barriers between idealism and realism because the intelligence services "don't do a very good job trying to understand the soft side of societies—how well the government is working and the fundamental attitudes of the people."[25] The United States had stumbled "blindly into Baghdad."[26] To its critics, the Bush administration was not prepared after the end of the first phase of the Iraq war to undertake nation-building on a large scale.

Those recruited to work in Iraq soon became part of the problem. In Iraq, "there were a lot of young people who came in, particularly in the governance and policy area. [They were very] nice, very personable people—nothing against them. But they had no knowledge whatsoever of Iraq, very little of the region, and absolutely no prior experience in post-conflict operations."[27] Within the Bush administration, decision makers did not understand the massive undertaking they had taken on in Iraq. By the end of 2002, officials in the Pentagon recognized that planning for postwar Iraq was "all screwed up."[28]

From the beginning, the occupation of Iraq was unreal. There were conflicts between the military, USAID, and State over management of assistance.[29] Communication and consultation was nonexistent. There was also a sense of isolation within the American headquarters in Iraq, the infamous Green Zone. In the Green Zone, "[o]n the inside were the Americans who if anything were too secure—spoiled by wealth and national power, self-convinced, and softened by the promise and possibility of safe lives." William Langewiesche quoted a Green Zone resident who noted: "People came to the CPA [Coalition Provisional Authority], never spoke to an Iraqi, and just launched these projects." Langewiesche went on, "For related reasons, once the projects were launched there was a tendency within the Green Zone to believe that therefore progress had been made—often despite strong evidence on the outside that it had not."[30] This was an extension of a broader pattern in foreign aid where the assumption is made that once a policy decision has been made the deed is done. Implementation issues never enter the picture.

There was never a philosophy of occupation developed within Defense even though by the end of 2006, when Secretary Donald Rumsfeld resigned on November 8, 2006, the United States had been in Iraq for close to four years. The White House Deputies Committee, who had responsibility for planning, assumed a lengthy occupation of Iraq would be routine, leisurely, and peaceful. Iraq's people would greet the US troops with their bubble gum and chocolate bars in much the same way the people of postwar Europe had done in 1945.

Within Defense, policymakers assumed that the occupation could be worked out, as they went along with a small group lodged in the secretary's office. Aid to Iraq would be paid for through oil revenues. The occupation was not an issue that was referred to the leadership of Defense or the executive branch. On the ground, problems would be addressed only when the United States opened up an office of postconflict reconstruction in Baghdad.

The occupation of Iraq was a throwback to an earlier time. As a place, as an occupied country, and as an image in the occupiers' minds, Iraq contained "romantic elements of foreign adventure as well—of colonial plantations and compound life, of military posts throughout the world, and of the war that swirls just outside the gates."[31] According to William Langewiesche, speaking of the US administrators in Iraq:

> It is true that most of the rank and file [in the beginning] had supported the invasion, and continued to believe that they were contributing to the struggle against terrorism, but they were not ideologues so much as ordinary, overconfident, mildly presumptuous college graduates—freshly scrubbed Americans of the sort who inhabit Washington, DC, nestling up to power.[32]

During the first year of the occupation, the Iraq proconsuls, Jay Garner and Paul Bremer, had the "responsibility for all of the tasks normally run [in the US] by national, state and local government."[33] Even within the Bush administration, there was fear of what Stephen Hadley, the Bush second-term national security adviser, called "the imperial option."[34] According to an administration critic:

> There were excesses, as might be imagined. The hiring of the senior CPA staff was steered by Donald Rumsfeld and his conservative deputies at the Pentagon, who, by insisting on rigid agendas, effectively ruled out some of the more worldly officials and diplomats who might otherwise have been willing to intervene. In their place came zealous amateurs, often from the private sector, whose chief qualifications seemed to be their Republican credentials and their eagerness to get involved. To their credit, most of them eased off the ideology once they faced the practical realities of Iraq. They muddled through and sometimes got something done before getting out; they left no marks. A few of the most zealous, however, refused to back down, and, indeed, upon arriving in the Green Zone seemed to think of Iraq as a living laboratory, a testing ground for their ideas.[35]

In Iraq, the Green Zone became a significant problem for the military, the foreign service, and foreign aid officials alike.[36] It soon became clear that "[t]he decision to install the occupation government in the center of the city and to base it in the very same buildings that had been used by the recent dictatorship was a serious blunder—one of several such blunders rooted in the arrogance of Yankee know-how, and in the strange failure to anticipate the end of the honeymoon, and the hostility that even enlightened invaders would soon elicit."[37]

Except for some in State, the other principals in the White House and Defense were more interested in war than in humanitarian assistance, support for democratic governance, or economic development. Defense's initial approach to the humanitarian issue was to get USAID to make a series of strategically placed airdrops of food and emergency supplies. Neither USAID officials nor its contractors were able to get outside of the Green Zone for any significant time in order to begin developing policies.[38] Within Defense, "[w]eeks into the war, more and more paper was flying around Rumsfeld's office and the Pentagon about how to organize the aftermath."[39] However, as Woodward points out, Rumsfeld and his colleagues at Defense just were not interested in the occupation and simply could not recognize that they faced a task of full-blown nation-building.

Rumsfeld originally had not wanted to commit the United States to nation-building. Woodward quoted President George W. Bush as saying, "I oppose using the military for nation building. Once the job is done, our forces are not peacekeepers."[40] In reality, however, Defense became firmly involved in the nation-building process in a number of countries, including the botched effort in Iraq that led to Iraqi collapse into full-scale civil war by 2006.

Major Isaiah Wilson, a researcher for the US Army's Operation Iraqi Freedom Study Group assessed the planning process in Iraq in 2006 and concluded that because "of the failure to produce a plan . . . the U.S. military lost the dominant position in Iraq in the summer of 2003 and has been scrambling to recover ever since."[41] With the end of the military invasion, "what [the US] didn't plan for was the possibility that hundreds of thousands of soldiers would just go home, that the workforce to rebuild the country would melt away."[42] Then the real conflict began. By the end of 2006, the United States had virtually lost control of Iraq, and the reconstruction efforts were largely sidelined.[43] A temporary surge of forces in Iraq at that point postponed but did not address the governance and development problems faced by this besotted country.

A Foreign Aid Surge

Initially, under Bush, foreign aid spending patterns remained what they had been during the past decade. By early 2002, spending had stagnated at about

$10 billion; however, as a percentage of the American economy, foreign aid had fallen from close to 3 percent in 1946 to 0.1 percent in 2001."[44] By 2003, the foreign aid budget surged, "fed by concerns that impoverished and failing societies could offer breeding ground or havens for terrorists."[45]

On November 3, 2001, as Congress neared completion of a "$15.1 billion foreign aid spending bill, it [walked] a tightrope between staying true to long-held positions and showing support for several autocratic regimes [such as Pakistan] that are cooperating with the U.S. war on terrorism."[46] In assessing the Bush administration's second term, Elizabeth Becker noted that Congress was ready to increase foreign aid to the world's poorest nations by nearly $2 billion. This would be the biggest increase in development assistance since 1962, three years after President Kennedy created the Peace Corps and USAID and established Alliance for Progress in South America.[47]

In March 2002, the Bush administration made its foreign aid pledges bigger, more urgent, and more up front and center than it did in the administration's first year in office, and the president said he would ask Congress "to increase American aid to poor nations by 50 percent over the next three years to $15 billion in 2006, and to try to start the money flowing within months, not a year or two."[48] According to Woodward, however, "American values, democracy and human assistance programs [were] the softer [and neglected] side of Bush's agenda."[49] As one former senior USAID official sarcastically put it, defense and security in the Bush administration was manly work, while foreign aid was for "girly girls."[50]

Iraq and Afghanistan, not surprisingly, were high on the list for additional foreign aid money as the United States intervened; however, other foreign aid recipients were also affected. In 2002, the policymakers announced they planned to spend more than $1 billion to improve water efficiency on farms and in factories, to provide electricity to the urban poor, to help rural communities combat deforestation, and to ease hunger in Africa over the next four years.[51]

In the aftermath of the Iraq invasion, policymakers worried that the United States would win the initial conflict in Iraq but lose the occupation and peace. The reality began to dawn that it was foreign aid that was expected to ensure the peace. Thus far, this was not to be, and the danger warnings at the time were not heeded.

The War on Terror changed approaches to foreign policy and foreign aid. The changes were at least partly fiscal. The 2002 foreign aid program contained proposals by President Bush to increase spending to fight HIV/AIDS through PEPFAR and reduce hunger overseas; this would raise foreign assistance to more than $18 billion by the 2004 fiscal year. The foreign aid budget would continue to grow.

US interventions in Afghanistan and later Iraq (as well as earlier in Bosnia and Kosovo and in several states in northeast and west Africa) began to promote processes of institutionalization, democratic governance, and the rule of law. After 2001, President Bush redefined his foreign aid policy on reducing poverty and ending repression with statements about moral and strategic purposes. These would include "[d]emocracy, free markets and the rights of women."[52]

Yet, despite the surge of foreign aid funding, a number of traditional foreign aid areas remained on the chopping block. To quote Elizabeth Becker: "In one of the first signs of the effects of the ever tightening [2005] federal budget . . . the Bush administration [had] reduced its contributions to global food aid programs aimed at helping millions of people climb out of poverty."[53] To its critics, the Bush administration was less concerned about LDC poverty alleviation and development, and more concerned about its own national security needs. There was also a fear that poverty reduction and long-term development goals, the traditional concerns of USAID, would be overwhelmed by the demands of short-term strategic concerns.[54]

There were calls for new spending to support democracy and governance and to ensure transitions to secularism, particularly in the Middle East and northern Africa; however, there continued to be significant resistance in Congress to increasing the foreign aid budget. In 2002, according to Paul Blustein, "congressional appropriators appear[ed] poised to approve hundreds of millions of dollars less than the president requested for foreign assistance next year."[55]

In 2005, the Bush administration, asked for $2.8 billion for the HIV/AIDS fund and announced that it was "gearing up to meet the president's goal of $15 billion [in foreign aid] over five years, though some Congressional Republicans concede[d] that budget deficit concerns [would] probably scale back both initiatives."[56] By 2006, the proposed foreign aid budget was greater than $20 billion. USAID alone was to handle $14 billion. The amount channeled through USAID continued to drop, however, and by 2008 it managed only 40 percent of the aid portfolio.

In 2007, the Bush administration proposed a foreign aid budget of $23.7 billion. With much of that money aimed at combating the AIDS virus and creating a new economic development program, Africa would be the main beneficiary of this latest expansion in foreign aid activity, consuming 45 percent of US foreign assistance.[57] HIV/AIDS and the Millennium Challenge Account (see Chapter 13) became the two major foreign aid priorities of the Bush administration in its second term

Humanitarian and development concerns remained secondary. Midlevel planners from USAID had to convince the military that they should specify "no air strike" sites in Iraq such as health clinics, water plants, and the electric grid. They also advocated humanitarian aid for food and relief after the Iraq invasion. USAID officials were not entirely successful in either of these requests.

Iraq and Foreign Aid

To Secretary Rumsfeld, who had his supporters within USAID, foreign aid was entirely about feeding people. Governance and development to many observers appeared to be secondary to military control. Afghanistan with its international coalition began reconstruction through US and other bilateral and multilateral aid. Though there was a resurgence of Taliban resistance in the southern part of the country, Afghani foreign aid and security policy remained firmly multilateral in scope with bipartisan support in the US Congress.

According to critics, no money had been earmarked for democracy and governance prior to the invasion. Elisabeth Rubin, speaking of people in Hilla, Iraq, made the point: "This is a country of 23 million people, and we're there with no plan for what we're going to do. So [aid workers] just started figuring it out" themselves.[58] In 2003, USAID Administrator Natsios estimated that the rebuilding of Iraq would cost the United States $1.7 billion. By the middle of 2006, the United States had already spent over $250 billion on Iraq. Almost nothing had been done to reconstruct the social and political structures of the country.

The situation could verge on the ridiculous, according to Rachel Roe, who was a reservist and a lawyer assisting in rebuilding the legal system in Najaf. One legal specialist "showed up in the palace in Baghdad looking for the head of democracy and human rights to see what's the plan and found some 21-year old political appointee who had no idea what was going on."[59] US personnel in Iraq, understandably, lacked the language skills and cultural sensitivity to perform their duties effectively and had "little experience with complex overseas interventions to restore and maintain order."[60] According to Thomas Ricks, the "U.S. civilian occupation organization was a house built on sand and inhabited by the wrong sort of people."[61] The Iraqi bureaucracy lost its capacity to govern during the occupation.

International support for Iraq from Europe or the oil-producing Arab states was at best tepid. Tragically, after three and a half years of occupation, the Iraq Study Group would conclude in late 2006 that the "Iraq government is not effectively providing its people with basic services: electricity, drinking water, sewage, health care, and education."[62] Coordination of reconstruction between the senior management of Defense, State, and USAID remained ineffectual.

In the Iraq occupation, the Bush administration faced three problems:

- They had to find payment for public sector employees.
- They had to rapidly issue contracts for economic development and reconstruction.
- The occupation administration had to reconstruct the security forces.

The administration was ineffective in solving any of the three problems at least four years into the occupation. Security, service delivery, infrastructure, and governance remained unsolved. Iraqi public service was dysfunctional, and most social and economic development projects had come to a complete halt.

Governance and oil did not mix well in Iraq. According to Jonathan Weisman, in the debate on the 2004–2005 budget, "Senate Republicans proposed . . . to convert nearly half of President Bush's $20.3 billion Iraqi reconstruction program into loans underwritten by that nation's oil, and even some of the president's sharpest defenders said Congress [was] likely to significantly change the administration's vision for rebuilding Iraq."[63] For the next several years, even in the context of the collapse of security in Iraq by early 2007, many in Congress and some in the administration continued to assume that oil revenues would fund the US occupation of Iraq.

By 2005, US foreign aid to Iraq, most of which flowed through the Defense Department, was pegged at $21 Billion. This assistance was targeted at "governing and developing a democracy, help to provide essential services such as electricity, water, sanitation and schools; help to strengthen the economy, assist in strengthening the rule of law and civil rights; increase international support and communicate to Iraqis and promote a 'free, independent and responsible Iraqi media.'"[64] It was a wish list for US foreign aid around the world.

As late as 2006, some Republicans in Congress continued to talk about using Iraq's oil money to rebuild the country. According to David Firestone, "In explaining how it proposed to spend $20.3 billion to restore a civil society to Iraq, the administration has prepared a virtual travelogue of the country's descent into destruction and chaos."[65] Sensitivity over democracy was high in Iraq. According to Dana Wilbank:

> White House officials were steamed when Andrew S. Natsios, the administrator of the U.S. Agency for International Development, [had said in 2003] that U.S. taxpayers would not have to pay more than $1.7 billion to reconstruct Iraq—which turned out to be a gross understatement of the tens of billions of dollars the government now expects to spend. Recently,

however, the government has purged the offending comments by Natsios from the agency's Web site.[66]

Despite these failures and USAID efforts to direct support for long-term social and economic development, there was increasing resistance in Congress for the provision of reconstruction support. The Iraq Study Group concluded that technical assistance support for Iraq was essential and recommended that U.S. economic assistance alone be increased to $5 billion per year.[67]

Coming out of Iraq was a contracting model, a Defense Department process that would be transferred to another plane (in terms of scale) in smaller countries. The Iraq intervention took outsourcing to its limits. As part of the occupation process,

> The military's reliance on [Iraqi and overseas] civilians to serve as interrogators and translators in Iraq is now so great that many people are being sent abroad without complete background investigations or full qualifications for the positions. . . . Once on the job, [in Iraq] several experts said, many of the contractors are barely supervised.[68]

As a result, not surprisingly, there was widespread waste and corruption in Iraq contracts.[69]

Contracting in Iraq became analogous with the Civil Operations and Rural Development Support Program (CORDS)—the hearts and minds strategy that provided social services and infrastructure support to rural dwellers in Vietnam. Increasingly, the government's business was done through sole sourcing, without any threads of competitive bidding. From a foreign aid perspective, US allies had to assure delegates at a two-day conference of international donors in New York that the billions of dollars in foreign aid contracts financed by Iraq's oil revenue would be put out to competitive bidding.[70]

With the influx of aid, there were increased dangers and threats to foreign aid contractors in Iraq, as well as Afghanistan and other parts of the Middle East. In Iraq, the bulk of the foreign civilian deaths were contractors, and "[t]he chaotic nature of civil conflict is a major reason aid workers face greater danger more often."[71] According to Elizabeth Rubin, in discussing another Iraq foreign aid casualty, stated: "In a way [Fern Holland's] story slipped effortlessly into a parable about American exceptionalism. Headstrong, reckless, idealistic, Americans have always believed in the power of will—that one man or woman with enough faith and tenacity can at some moment pull off his or her vision."[72]

Eventually, a great majority of foreign aid workers in Iraq, fearing they had become targets of the postwar violence, had "quietly pulled out of the country . . . , leaving essential relief work to their Iraqi colleagues and slowing the reconstruction effort."[73] By the end of 2006, relief, reconstruction, and development efforts had come to almost a complete stop. What remained was a huge industry of private security contractors who came to dominate the international assistance process in Iraq. Though the military surge—and to some extent, foreign aid activities—provided a respite from the crisis mode, somehow the United States had to get out of Iraq. During the same period, the United States was, as we will see in the next chapter, applying the Iraq model—and its concern for oil—to the Horn of Africa and the Sahel.

Conclusion

The fallout from September 11 demonstrated the limits of multilateralism and the dangers of unilateralism in foreign aid, security, and foreign policy. There was still an absence of a clear strategy to deal with the some fifty or so weak and fragile states that were not Iraq.[74] With a new administrator of USAID in early 2006, the concept of fragile states was dropped as concern increased over short-term conflict resolution. The fragile and collapsed states metaphors may have reminded the political leadership too much of the problems in Iraq and Afghanistan.

In late 2008, the Iraq story remained unfinished. The popularity of President Bush was at an all-time low, 33 percent or less. The Iraq Study Group had released its devastating critical report. Rumsfeld had resigned. Midterm elections in 2006 had returned the Democrats to power in the House of Representatives and the Senate, and on November 4, 2008, Barak Obama won the presidency.

Yet despite all of the criticism, focus in Iraq remained on the military situation and the success or failure of the surge. Much more needed to be understood of the long-term consequences in terms of foreign aid and security assistance policy in the post–September 11 era. Unilateralism had, at least for the moment, been debunked. But could the United States return to the multilateralism that had allowed it to muddle through the Cold War? It is to these issues that we turn in the next chapter.

Notes

1. Bob Woodward, *State of Denial: Bush at War, Part III* (New York: Simon and Shuster, 2006), p. 16.

2. David E. Sanger, "Hawk Sightings Could Be Premature," *New York Times* (November 21, 2004), p. A1.

3. Ricks, *Fiasco*, p. 25.

4. Quoted in Sanger, "Hawk Sightings."

5. Mark Hertsgaard, *The Eagle's Shadow: Why America Fascinates and Infuriates the World* (New York: Picador Books, 2003), p. 19.

6. Joseph N. Weatherby, et al., *The Other World: Issues and Politics of the Developing World* (New York: Longman, 2000), pp. 320 and 328.

7. Bob Woodward, *Bush at War* (New York: Simon & Schuster, 2002), p. 25.

8. Ibid., p. 281.

9. Carlotta Gall, "More G.I.'s to Go to Insecure Afghan Areas to Permit Aid Work," *New York Times* (December 22, 2003), p. A8.

10. Woodward, *State of Denial,* p. 378.

11. Ricks, *Fiasco,* p. 22.

12. Sanger, "Hawk Sightings Could Be Premature," p. 1.

13. R.C. Longworth, "Poll Shows Wide Support for Foreign Aid," *Pittsburgh Post-Gazette* (March 22, 2002), p. A5.

14. Elizabeth Becker, "With Record Rise in Foreign Aid Comes Change in How it is Monitored," *New York Times* (December 7, 2003), p. A6.

15. Graham, Bradley, "Clark Wants More Foreign Aid, New Department to Handle It," *Washington Post* (September 29, 2003), p. A5.

16. Sheryl Gay Stolberg, "Bush to Seek $16 Billion for Epidemic of AIDS in U.S.," *New York Times* (February 1, 2003), p. A13.

17. Rachel L. Swarns, "U.S. Shows Off Aid Projects at U.N. Development Meeting," *New York Times* (August 30, 2002), p. A3.

18. Lynnette Clemetson, "Taxpayers Are Restless over Iraq Aid," *New York Times* (October 16, 2003), p. A12.

19. Scott Anderson, "What Happened to Fred Cuny?" *New York Times Magazine* (February 25, 1996), p. 47.

20. Bob Woodward, *Plan of Attack,* p. 270.

21. See for example his essay, "Foreign Aid in the National Interest—The Importance of Democracy and Governance," in Louis A. Picard, Robert Groelsema and Terry F. Buss, *Foreign Aid and Foreign Policy: Issues for the Next Half Century* (Armonk, NY: M. E. Sharpe, 2008).

22. Ricks, *Fiasco,* p. 430.

23. David E. Sanger, "Prewar British Memo says US Lacked Postwar Plans," *New York Times* (June 13, 2005), p. A10.

24. Langewiesche, "Welcome to the Green Zone," pp. 61–88. Quote, pp. 62 and 65 respectively.

25. Ibid., p. 281.

26. Stewart Patrick, "An Integrated U.S. Approach to Preventing and Responding to State Failure: Recent Progress and Remaining Challenges" (Unpublished Paper, Center for Global Development, April 19, 2006), pp. 1–9.

27. Langewiesche, "Welcome to the Green Zone," pp. 61–88. Quote, p. 74.

28. Woodward, *State of Denial*, p. 101.

29. Jane Perlez, "Pentagon and State Department In Tug-of-War Over Aid Disbursal," *New York Times* (April 1, 2003), p. B7.

30. All quotes from Langewiesche, "Welcome to the Green Zone," pp. 61–88. Quotes, pp. 62 and 82.

31. Ibid., pp. 61–88. Quote, p. 65.

32. Ibid., pp. 61–88. Quote, p. 74.

33. Woodward, *State of Denial*, p. 112.

34. Quoted in Woodward, *Plan of Attack*, p. 297.

35. Langewiesche, "Welcome to the Green Zone," pp. 61–88. Quote, p. 73.

36. See Rajiv Chandrasekaran, *Imperial Life in the Emerald City: Inside Iraq's Green Zone* (New York: Alfred A. Knopf, 2006) for a further discussion of this.

37. Langewiesche, "Welcome to the Green Zone," pp. 61–88. Quote, p. 62.

38. See Derick W. Brinkerhoff, "Building Local Governance in Iraq—Limits and Lessons," in Picard, et al., *Foreign Aid and Foreign Policy*, 109–128.

39. Woodward, *State of Denial*, p. 270.

40. Ibid., pp. 220 and 222. Quote p. 237.

41. Thomas E. Ricks, "Army Historian Cites Lack of Postwar Plan," *Washington Post* (December 25, 2004), p. A18.

42. Woodward, *Plan of Attack*, p. 343.

43. Three books define the magnitude of the Bush administration failure in Iraq between 2001 and 2006. They are Bob Woodward, *State of Denial: Bush at War, Part III* (New York: Simon and Shuster, 2006); Thomas E. Ricks, *Fiasco: The American Military Adventure in Iraq* (New York: Penguin Press, 2006); and most significantly James A. Baker III and Lee H. Hamilton, et al. (The Iraq Study Group), *The Iraq Study Group Report: The Way Forward—A New Approach* (New York: Vintage, 2006).

44. Joseph Kahn and Tim Weiner, "World Leaders Rethinking Strategy on Aid to Poor," *New York Times* (March 18, 2002), p. A4.

45. Robert McMahon, "Transforming U.S. Foreign Aid," *Council on Foreign Relations Publication no. 10176* (New York: Council on Foreign Relations, March 17, 2006) www.cfr.org/publications/10176

46. Dan Morgan, "Foreign Aid Tied to Terror Fight," *Pittsburgh Post-Gazette* (November 3, 2001), p. A1.

47. Elizabeth Becker, "With Record Rise in Foreign Aid Comes Change in How it is Monitored," *New York Times* (December 7, 2003), p. A6.

48. Tim Weiner, "More Aid, More Need: Pledges Still Falling Short," *New York Times* (March 24, 2002), p. A5.

49. Woodward, *State of Denial*, p. 127.

50. Author's Research Diary, October 14, 2008.

51. Rachel L. Swarns, "U.S. Shows Off Aid Projects at U.N. Development Meeting," *New York Times* (August 30, 2002), p. A5.

52. Woodward, *Plan of Attack*, p. 132.

53. Elizabeth Becker, "U.S. Cutting Food Aid that Is Aimed at Self-Sufficiency," *New York Times* (December 22, 2004), p. A3.

54. Larry Nowels and Connie Veillette, "Restructuring U.S. Foreign Aid: The Role of the Director of Foreign Assistance," *CRS Report for Congress* (Washington DC: Congressional Research Service, RL33/491, June 16, 2006), p. 10.

55. Paul Blustein, "U.S. Aid Plan Comes Up Short," *Washington Post* (June 22, 2003), p. A22.

56. Christopher Marquis, "New System Begins Rerouting U.S. Aid For Poor Countries," *New York Times* (February 22, 2004), p. 1.

57. Becker, "With Record Rise in Foreign Aid Comes Change in How It Is Monitored," p. 6.

58. See Elizabeth Rubin, "Fern Holland's War," *New York Times Magazine* (September 19, 2004), p. 71.

59. Rubin, "Fern Holland's War," p. 70.

60. James A. Baker and Lee H. Hamilton, et al., *The Iraq Study Group Report: The Way Forward-A New Approach* (New York: Vintage Books, 2006), p. 92.

61. Ricks, *Fiasco,* p. 202.

62. Baker and Hamilton, *The Iraq Study Group Report,* p. 20.

63. Jonathan Weisman, "GOP Senators Seek to Make Some Iraq Aid a Loan," *Washington Post* (October 2, 2003), p. A4.

64. Woodward, *Bush at War,* p. 410.

65. David Firestone, "Congress Gets a Hot Potato: Bush's Detailed Program to Rebuild Iraq," *New York Times* (October 5, 2003), p. A12.

66. Dana Milbank, "White House Web Scrubbing," *Washington Post* (December 18, 2003), p. A5.

67. James A. Baker and Lee H. Hamilton, et al., *The Iraq Study Group Report: The Way Forward—A New Approach* (New York: Vintage Books, 2006).

68. Joel Brinkley, and James Glanz, "Contractors in Sensitive Roles, Unchecked," *New York Times* (May 7, 2004), p. A12.

69. See Glenn Kessler and Bradley Graham, "Rice's Rebuilding Plan Hits Snags," *Washington Post* (January 15, 2006), p. A24. See also James Glanz, "Auditors Find Widespread Waste and Unfinished Work in Iraqi Rebuilding Contracts," *New York Times* (January 31, 2006), p. A12.

70. Colum Lynch, "Potential Iraq Donors Seek Greater Accountability from U.S. on Oil Plans," *Washington Post* (June 26, 2003), p. A16.

71. Karl Vick, "Aid Work in Growing Danger; Foreigners Targeted in Conflict Zones," *Washington Post* (May 23, 1999), p. A19.

72. Rubin, "Fern Holland's War," p. 74.

73. Ian Fisher, and Elizabeth Becker, "Aid Workers Leaving Iraq, Fearing They Are Targets," *New York Times* (October 12, 2003), p. A6.

74. "Fragile States Strategy" (Washington, DC: USAID, January 2005), pp. 1–18.

10

RECONSTRUCTION, CIVIC ACTION, AND AFRICOM

It seems as though Africa is a place you go to wait. Many Africans I met said the same thing, but uncomplainingly, for most lived their lives with a fatalistic patience. Outsiders see Africa as a continent delayed—economies in suspension, societies up in the air, politics and human rights put on hold, communities throttled or stopped.

Paul Theroux, *Dark Star Safari*

Many African countries suffer from feeble cabinets, paltry systems of policy making, and erratic decision making at the top.

Robert Klitgaard, *Tropical Gangsters*

The Policy Framework for Stability Operations

The Petraeus Model

In 2006, the new US Army manual on *Counterinsurgency,* co-authored by General David Petraeus, the military commander in Iraq and later Central Command (CENTCOM),[1] stated that once again nation-building was central to the military's mission in a post–September 11 world. The manual called for counterinsurgency strategies based on an "armed social work" nation-building model.[2] The Petraeus perspective has been applied not only in Central Command—encompassing Iraq and Afghanistan—but has become a strategic doctrine throughout Defense, especially in the newly created African Command (AFRICOM).[3]

Petraeus premised his doctrine on the notion of asymmetric war, wherein fragile and collapsed states' nonstate actors—religious organizations, ethnic-based NGOs, and ideological armed insurgents—act as spoilers within a country where they hope to benefit from lawlessness, economic chaos, and

173

political and social instability. The result is often state collapse and regional instability. To combat these nonstate actors, Petraeus asserts the need to reconstruct social, economic, and political institutions in collapsed states, using both military and civilian teams to implement reconstruction and post-conflict policies. Rather than asking the military to hand off a postconflict state to civilian foreign assistance agencies, the military remains in country as a senior partner to civilians.

The way to control these hostile nonstate influences, according to Petraeus, is by countering their political influence through support for civic action and community-based social development, using community change projects with heavy security support. An underlying assumption is that soldiers rather than—or in addition to—civil servants or NGOs development workers can be trained to carry out these civilian "social work" activities. State, supported by Defense, suggested that up to 80 percent of counterinsurgency efforts should go to civilian-administered political assistance, diplomatic activities, public information, and development, bringing into question the extent to which Defense should have a larger foreign assistance role.

In approaching counterinsurgency and reconstruction, Petraeus suggests that skills in anthropology (social roles and community dynamics) are as important as military tactics, logistics, or weaponry. Conflict mediation and human security issues are at the center of any intervention policy in fragile states, especially in collapsed states because people will side with the organization or force most able to offer them improved human security.

Civic action advocates will seek community support for medical aid, food, local infrastructure development, basic education, local democratic governance, training, public works, and health.[4] Also targeted are local justice systems—including policing, electoral support systems, and financial management systems—and the need to support to civil society groups to help entrench democratic governance.[5] Concern is with both the potential for success and failure of these self-help projects within the context of defense and security strategies.

This chapter clears away the brush on the civic action debates and examines the community development premise from the perspective of the creation, on October 1, 2007, of the new geographical command for Africa, AFRICOM, and the extent to which this security-based strategy for community development can contribute to the strengthening of fragile and collapsed states in Africa. Following from this, the focus here is on the lessons of prior US experience focused on community or civic action support and how those lessons and concerns might be applied to proposed AFRICOM security assistance activities. AFRICOM is important not only in itself, but also as a possible model for Latin America and Southeast Asia.

The Recent Context

Since 1991 with the collapse of the Soviet bloc, and especially after 2001, US foreign policy shifted toward management of low-intensity conflicts and conflict mediation. The assumption was that to succeed, there must be an increased emphasis on political, economic, and social development. Debate between multilateralism and unilateralism intensified during the same period. What security specialists call asymmetrical warfare has come to define US defense policies.

After September 11, foreign and security policy was more unilateralist, based on what President Bush called coalitions of the willing. Military solutions were not sufficient to address the challenges of insurgents motivated by deep social, religious, or ethnic concerns.[6] While intervention in Afghanistan was broadly multilateral in its origins (though led by the United States), the intervention in Iraq, by contrast, was criticized for its unilateralism and lack of effectiveness of the US occupation, lack of planning for the postwar occupation, and what many considered the United States' foreign intervention "on the cheap"—a strategy that turned out to be expensive both fiscally and in cost of lives.

The Bush administration's primary foreign policy concern was counterterrorism. From a security perspective, a key component was capacity building for conflict mitigation and peacekeeping. At issue was the extent to which support for civic action/community development activities could address the fundamental deficiencies of governance and civil society, which were perceived to challenge the some sixty fragile and collapsed states worldwide, two-thirds of which are in Africa.[7]

Foreign Aid, Policy Coordination and Security

Terrorism, needless to say, feeds on economic collapse, ethnic and religious conflict, weak governance structures, and excess political mobilization.[8] Also of concern among some policymakers was the recognition that in the fifteen years since the end of the Cold War, the United States failed to address the large-scale breakdowns in public order that had often occurred after international interventions.[9]

The challenge for US policymakers was the "archaic bureaucratic lines" that divide Defense, State and USAID (as well as other US agencies and departments, including the Central Intelligence Agency, the newly created Department of Homeland Security, and the Directorate of National Intelligence). These lines divide government both internally and between and among the great cabinet and subcabinet agencies that function throughout the federal system.[10] Across the developing world, this has suggested the use of a more holistic approach to defense and security issues within the context of the "increasing challenges and threats from the territories of weak and failing states."[11]

These changes reflected moves toward *whole-of-government* approaches to foreign and security policy. The methodology proposed could be used both unilaterally, such as in Iraq or multilaterally, as in Afghanistan. The lessons were to focus on "the post-invasion phase [that] has been characterized by continuing instability, intense counter-insurgency operations, and serious disruption to life on the ground."[12] Failures in Iraq in particular led to a debate about the future of US foreign and security policy in an asymmetrical world.[13]

In the whole-of-government approach, policymakers view implementation as an effort of the entire administration without fiscal, personnel, or organizational boundaries. According to OECD, the creation of joint budget lines, flexible pooled funding, and a panorganizational program management system are essential to foster integrated planning and management. Institutional, budgetary, and functional barriers between and among departments can stifle coordination, communication, and cooperation.

The challenge for donors and fragile states alike is adoption of a model of government that functions outside of normal departmental challenges.[14] Central to the management challenge is the presence of sufficient skilled staff, as well as flexible politics to implement whole-of-government activities. Within Defense, according to its Secretary Gates, officials need greater regional knowledge, language skills, and cultural understanding.

The challenge to conflict mediation and reconstruction is the widespread failure of governance at the state level and Defense's fixation about it.[15] The model envisioned requires an interagency, shared fiscal management process and a multiprofessional approach to program development and project management. At the heart of the problem is the need to "untangle lines of authority, [eliminate] overlapping lines of responsibilities and improve coordination of interagency . . . operations."[16] Such an untangling is easier said than done.

Creation of these out of department formal structures resembles those of the integrated project model with single-source funding, parallel organization funding, and a common understanding of economic management that crosses agencies. There is a need for an established, clearly defined coordinating agency and creation of incentives for collaborative working conditions in all stages of conflict mediation and reconstruction:

- External intervention
- Military stabilization
- Coordination

- Humanitarian support
- Capacity building

Poverty, Conflict, and Community Mobilization

Since September 2002 and the publication of Bush's *National Security Strategy*,[17] arguing that poverty, weak institutions, poor leadership, and corruption make countries vulnerable to terrorist networks and organized crime, there has been an increasing interest in the relationship between civilian and military intervention in collapsed and fragile states and microlevel strategies of mobilization. In the wake of the terrorist attack on the World Trade Center and the Pentagon, development, defense, and diplomacy became the three pillars of national security.[18] The methodology was to be collaborative and involved multiorganizational approaches to policy implementation at the subnational level.

For advocates of community-based civic action, foreign aid in the past decade was increasingly seen as a part of a whole-of-government process that is referred to variously as "Triangulation" or "The Three Ds" (Defense, Diplomacy and Development). The coordination and cooperation between and among government agencies, and between them, the NGO, and the private sectors, became essential to make this exercise work. It is difficult, and to some impossible, to achieve these goals within the reality of compartmentalized government.

The 2002 *National Security Strategy* assigned USAID a primary role in the national security mix (at both macro and micro levels) along with State and Defense,[19] much of this takes the form of international assistance in counterterrorism, counternarcotics, postconflict reconstruction, and humanitarian assistance. The future of the approach remains unclear. The overall issue is whether nation-building and democratic governance support will remain in civilian hands in the field or fall under Defense Department control.

Defense plays an increasing role in postconflict situations.[20] In December 2005, Bush called for the implementation of a community-level reconstruction and stabilization policy, focusing on countries that were at risk of conflict or civil strife.[21] Policymakers required collaboration between defense and security agencies, development organizations and diplomatic missions. The Bush administration identified peace, social action, and stability operations as a core mission of the military that was to focus on the rebuilding of subnational indigenous institutions within the context of asymmetrical conflict. On the foreign policy side, the Bush administration combined the role of administrator of USAID with a State Department position of Assistant Secretary and Director of Foreign Assistance in 2006.

On April 1, 2007, Secretary Gates committed Defense to improving interagency capacity to move to an integrated whole-of-government approach in all the geographic sectors, recognizing that a "significant impediment to greater interagency cooperation is the stove-piped nature of funding programming and decisions."[22] Gates is on record as advocating increased funding for both USAID and State.

The common thread is the use of community development to build capacity, leadership and institutional processes in governance systems, and a sensitivity to what is sometimes called "cultural mapping." These activities, of necessity, involve both interagency cooperation and nongovernmental organizations. Defense identified a "train-and-equip" program to promote civic action and community development. A major weakness of reconstruction efforts within the triangulation framework, however, is "the absence of a mechanism to monitor and evaluate the impact of U.S. foreign aid" to fragile and collapsed states.[23]

Cooperation among government departments relates to the difficulties of international collaboration given the climate of unilateralism during the past six years and relationships between donors, client states, and the purported beneficiaries of assistance policy. Making the process more conflicted is the requirement that coordination must also involve government personnel, contractors, nonprofits, and their grantees.

The dilemma is clear. According to Gates, the goal is "to achieve unified action and enhance the effectiveness of stability operations [and ensure] strategic planning for stability operations [as] a routine practice."[24] Above all, this coordination needs to include a quick response to crisis. Experiences of troops in Afghanistan and Iraq, and specifically Provincial Reconstruction Teams (PRTs) in both countries, are said to serve as a model for integrated foreign and security policy.

Increasingly, triangulation interventions involve direct involvement in crisis situations and involve national, regional, and subnational activities along the lines of these provincial transitional teams that have been used in both Afghanistan and Iraq.[25] Both the United States and other countries (Canada, Australia, and Britain) demonstrate the difficulty in Afghanistan of successfully integrating development aid and moving away from a military-dominated approach to provincial teams.[26] Results are less clear in the Iraq context. Even less clear was the role to be played by contractors and nonprofit grantees in the process, a mode of operation that was a source of criticism during the Bush Administration.[27]

People, Organizations, and Budgets

The Defense Security Cooperation Agency (DSCA), as a Defense agency, spent $50 billion in humanitarian aid in 2007. A significant concern of

DCSA is to build the capacity of US partners to fight the war on terrorism. All of this suggests a glaring financial mismatch between the authority and financial resources of State (and USAID) and Defense that could erode the role of State (and USAID) in foreign policy and international assistance.

In 2006, USAID created an Office of Military Affairs with a million dollars a year in seed money as the basis for placing USAID professionals in staff positions within the geographical commands. Long term, many foreign policy analysts believe (or fear) that USAID will be incorporated in State, which in turn would be dominated by DSCA, which administers close to a quarter of nonlethal assistance. In 2007 DSCA administered $12 billion in foreign military sales each year, had 900 security assistance personnel in more than one hundred countries, and supervised more than 14,000 overseas military students in the US. Disappearance of USAID as an independent development agency would also mean the loss of the institutional memory carried by the organization of community development techniques.

USAID established the Office of Conflict Management and Mitigation to complement OTI.[28] In 2004 a USAID *White Paper* defined its primary agency goal as transformational development going beyond the traditional focus on economic growth and social service development.[29] Between 2000 and 2005, official development assistance increased from $10 billion to $27.5 billion.

There are some eighteen foreign aid accounts in USAID and State. In addition there are several independent agencies such as MCC[30] and President's Emergency Plan for AIDS Relief (PEPFAR). On top of this is the dramatic increase in Defense's role in the nonlethal assistance process. By 2007, Defense managed over 22 percent of the foreign (nonlethal) aid, up from 7 percent in six years. This amount will likely increase to more than 25 percent in 2009 and 2010. The USAID administrator has little direct control over any of these accounts.

USAID's future remains uncertain. One school of thought suggests that USAID be elevated to a cabinet department with equal status to Defense and State. Another purpose is that it be absorbed in either State or Defense. To a large extent, this will be determined politically by the outcome of the 2008 presidential election and the election of Barack Obama.

As noted, Secretary Gates advocates increased funding for State, USAID, and other development organizations to empower them to cooperate on more equal ground in stabilization and whole-of-government (or fusion) activities—institution building, essential service delivery, governance assistance, and economic stabilization. Yet to be determined is the model for managing these disparate resources and the leadership role for foreign and security policy within the Washington departments. Focus would be on an interagency framework for aid with developed lines of authority, budgets, and strategies.

Collaboration between Defense and security agencies, development organizations, and diplomatic missions, the strengthening of civilian institutions and the reorientation of military structures are essential. Whole-of-government strategies bring the chronic shortages of civilian personnel in international development and human security to the fore. On February 8, 2008, USAID Administrator Henrietta H. Fore announced, "that the 2009 budget request will include an historic shift—the largest personnel increase USAID has ever requested . . . as we launch the Development leadership initiative."[31]

Central to the whole-of-government approach is a planning, fiscal monitoring, and evaluation process that crosses departments and agencies and breaks down bureaucratic barriers. Since September 11, Defense and State (and USAID) have found it difficult to coordinate their efforts.[32] There has been an institutional reluctance for USAID and State to cooperate with Defense for scarce resources.[33]

The downside of interagency cooperation may be to turn foreign aid and "development management tides back to a strong emphasis on technical fixes, standardized solutions, and effective management of donor project interventions but without the sensitivity to political realities and our historical understanding that critics demand."[34] Beyond this, critics worry about the long-term militarization of aid and foreign policy, particularly toward Africa, which is populated with fragile and collapsed states. The coming to power of a new administration with different policy priorities is an additional complicating factor. It is to this issue that we now turn.

The Creation of the Africa Command

Operationalizing Civic Action in AFRICOM

The move toward a whole-of-government approach to conflict mediation, stabilization, and reconstruction within the regional commands began with the strengthening of the regional commanders in Europe, the Western Hemisphere, Pacific command, and Central Command between 1995 and 2005.[35] Both Southern Command and Central Command pioneered the integration of civilian programs. Whole-of-government strategies are central components in Defense.

In 2001, Central Command leased land in Djibouti in the Horn of Africa and established the Navy-managed joint force facility, Camp Lemonier, occupied by 5,000 troops (rotating in and out of Djibouti) on 500 acres. Five years later on March 3, 2008, two US missiles hit a house in Somalia in what the United States claimed was directed at a well-known al Qaeda terrorist. Another attack followed on April 30, 2008. US foreign and security policy on Africa had become central in the war on terror.

Discussions about a unified African command began in 2002. Bush and Gates announced the establishment of AFRICOM on February 6, 2007. AFRICOM is a "unified combatant Command," combining both military and civilian-supported activities and headed by a military leader with a deputy appointed from State. It became operational on October 1, 2008.

The Africa Command (containing elements of Central Command, Pacific Command, and the European Command) completes the globalization of the regional military command system of the United States.

AFRICOM had about 1,300 civilian and military personnel as of December 2008. AFRICOM's goal was to have major civilian involvement in its activities through interagency task forces and to ensure civil-military cooperation between the military, State, and USAID. The goal was to promote stabilization activities through transformational development, humanitarian assistance, and the transformation of fragile and collapsed states, "through the far-reaching, fundamental changes in institutions of governance, human capacity, and economic structure that enable a country to sustain further economic and social progress."[36]

Institutional reform focuses on the civilian governance and security sectors of African states, encouraging them to operate under democratic and good governance principles.[37] Both the regular military and military Special Forces are said to be preparing to engage in the humanitarian and development field in their planning and training, much to the chagrin of USAID.[38] According to one critic, the geographical command "is being touted in Private Military Contractor (PMC) industry publications like *Soldier of Fortune* as ushering in a new market for employment."[39] The overall concern remains the extent to which a Defense-led initiative is the best way to approach underdevelopment (political, social, and economic) in Africa. We now turn to that issue.

AFRICOM and Whole of Government Challenges

We begin with the difficult challenges presented by the preponderance of fragile and collapsed states in Africa (representing more than 70 percent of all fragile states worldwide). Since 2001, as Jakkie Cilliers notes, many African states "present the 'shell' of the territorial state where national security is equated with that of the governing elite."[40] This is fertile ground for terrorism. Despite limitations of African governance systems, democracy, development, and security are said to be closely linked in Africa. US experience in Rwanda and Somalia illustrates the limits of US foreign policy in Africa given the problem of "blowback" in the continent.

The lessons of Liberia, Somalia, and Sierra Leone suggest that both domestic and international terrorism evolves out of collapsed states.[41] Focus must be on the hard knot of African problems—economic distress, ethnic and religious conflicts, fragile governance, weak democracy, rampant human rights abuses, and overall, the "ungoverned spaces" of the continent. Pentagon planners assumed that in preconflict situations combined action would pay huge dividends in conflict mediation where building capacity in governance, security, and community development are seen as essential to the reconstruction of weak and collapsed states.

US diplomats in mid-2007, perhaps naively, were surprised and disappointed at the depth of opposition to AFRICOM.[42] As one Africa-based critic put it, there was a fear in African circles (and among many international NGOs) that "the Pentagon is taking charge of US development policy and humanitarian assistance in Africa."[43] Yet widespread consultation with African leaders only started seriously in mid-2007, long after the AFRICOM policy had been decided.

At issue was the nature of the wider mandate sought by AFRICOM beyond the normal security brief defining geographical commands. There is significant skepticism about the nature of policy and concern for a militarization of foreign and development policy in Africa.[44] The US policy goal was to the ill-stated one of to "win hearts and minds in Africa," a phrase reminiscent of Vietnam.[45] The phrase was also unfortunate because many southern Africans remember that the goal of former South African President P. W. Botha, in his fight against the African National Congress, was "WHAM" or "Winning Hearts and Minds."

In taking the lead over stability operations in Africa, critics suggest that Defense is not well suited to and will usurp the role of USAID and State in diplomatic, humanitarian, and development activities. Questions remain about the extent to which the military services can and should engage in public diplomacy and international development activities without militarizing its foreign policy in Africa. Patrick and Brown, in their book on whole of government, question the efficacy of using Defense as a supervising agency in historically civilian activities, suggesting that the establishment of such a civilian cadre, as was the case in Iraq and to a lesser extent in Afghanistan, is akin to creating a colonial service.[46]

Critics of aid restructuring, from a USAID perspective, suggest that the traditional development goals will be replaced by shorter-term strategic considerations. Within Africa, there was an immediate and negative response to the AFRICOM announcement, with more than one group suggesting that AFRICOM had "malign intentions."[47] More broadly, there is a concern that policy analysts in Defense, State, and USAID neglected the forward planning on the nonsecurity side to implement whole-of-government proposals within AFRICOM.

Policymakers have yet to learn from the failure to plan for civilian administration in Iraq, in contrast to the more meticulous planning that occurred prior to the occupation of Germany and Japan. USAID continues to suffer under the yoke of a multitude of policy and priority areas. A USAID internal document estimated that it had thirty-three goals, seventy-five priority areas and 247 directives.[48] The result was a severe case of policy incoherence.

Historically, USAID's congressional mandate has been that goals are never eliminated but rather realigned. With an integrated mission, this incoherence may be transferred to a new military-led all-agency command. At present, there is an absence of incentives (and motivation) for whole-of-government strategies. The project mode still dominates in foreign aid, making it hard to imagine policy coherence required in the whole-of-government approach.

Even as it has become operational, there is little agreement on the organizational parameters of AFRICOM. Little detailed work exists on financial accountability procedures or civilian personnel systems. Recruitment of civilians to AFRICOM has seriously lagged behind. Also at issue is how the institutional imperatives of departmentalism (stove-piping) can be combated within AFRICOM.

Financially, despite mechanisms to transfer funds between Defense and State/USAID, there will be pressures to ensure independent reporting authorities. In terms of fiscal management, the government is behind the leaders in the field of whole of government—Sweden, Britain, Canada and Australia—in the use of pooled funds and joint budget lines.[49] Agencies have different agendas, dissimilar systems, and degrees of competence. Policy approaches of the actors—governmental, for-profits and NGOs—are likely to remain fragmented. USAID has been frustrated by an inability to get interagency buy-ins for its concept of fragile states.[50]

Experiences in Iraq and Afghanistan suggest that military blending into humanitarian activities can endanger civilian aid workers, either by using civilian vehicles (white SUVs), through the visible service of civilians on military dominated committees, or by dressing in civilian clothes. Many NGOs complain that security forces could co-opt humanitarian efforts.[51] There is queasiness among both aid workers and observers of foreign assistance about the blending of humanitarian and military missions. The civilian-military relationship (and for some, continued civilian control) is central to discussions about the whole-of-government approach to foreign assistance.

Overall, there is not a significant pool of civilian professionals, either within Defense or seconded from USAID, who can be drawn on for diplomatic and developmental work required under AFRICOM. The geographical command must choose from the same pool of contractors and grantees now used by State and the foreign aid agencies. The role of contractors remains ambiguous.

It is now expected that AFRICOM will have no central headquarters outside of Europe but will have several pods, hubs, and satellite facilities on- and offshore. Organizationally, it is not clear how this will work. It is to be highly mobile and use air and sea facilities rather than land bases.[52] It may have representative centers in Ethiopia, Liberia, and perhaps Botswana in Southern Africa. There will be some use of Cooperative Security Locations (CSLs), set up by Defense but owned by the host country. They locate at or near civilian airports to facilitate joint training. With a crisis, they can be used as a logistics hub and launching point for a US military intervention.[53]

A pitfall of community development assistance is that policy is to ensure the United States gets credit for the activity rather than ensure project success and community buy-ins.[54] The civic action mode and its managers also have to deal with issues of organizational co-optation by donors, contractors, and local elites. That is the fear among some African observers. Community development work requires long-term commitment and hard work. The project mode often seeks quick fixes through short (less than five-year) interventions.

With fifty-four countries on the continent, including two-thirds of the fifty or so weak and failing states of the world, the leadership in AFRICOM identified a subregional approach to security issues, focusing on the several regional economic commissions (RECs) such as Southern African Development Community (SADC) and Economic Community of Western African States (ECOWAS) as intermediaries.[55] RECs reflect the command's mandate to work on humanitarian and development projects as directed by a civilian Deputy Commander for Civil-Military Activities, currently Ambassador Mary Carlin Yates.[56] At this point, however, there are no subregional (or supranational) linkages envisioned by State along the lines of NATO, Association of Southeast Asian Nations (ASEAN), and the United States models.

Defense seeks input from Africans and will operate AFRICOM within these stated needs; however, the United States still operates without an overarching strategic framework for the command as it becomes operational. As it comes on line, AFRICOM intends to provide that framework, refocus US efforts on capacity building and the strengthening of good governance and democratic institutions, and the establishment of continent-wide stabilizing mechanisms. Finally, it is unclear whether military "social work" fits the program better than existing civilian programs and organizations.

Conclusion

Despite the challenges of underdevelopment, there is a "rich track record of over forty years of success in reducing infant and child mortality, raising agricultural production through scientific innovations, and spurring economic growth and the building of democracies in many regions of the world."[57] These successes created market opportunities and strategic alliances for the United States during the Cold War; however, the question is whether armed social work can contribute to foreign policy and the foreign aid agenda, and, of course, help to win the peace in Africa.

These changes likely require a staged process of public service reform, both lengthy and planned over time to avoid the distortions of a donor-funded, postconflict situation with its "parallel" administrative structures.[58] A primary lesson derived from US support for civil society and civic-action activities is that institutions and institutional processes matter. This perspective may not be reflected in the geographical command approach developed by the United States in Africa.

Historically, the focus of much of foreign assistance was on the support of civil society organizations that can undertake civic-action development projects, including community-based sanitation and cleanup efforts, rebuilding of schools and clinics, installation of water pumps, and establishment of community health service delivery. The purpose is to combat the hostility of ethnic, ideological, and/or religious-based grassroots organizations, NGOs, and other financial institutions that run counter to US interests.[59]

At issue is the extent to which AFRICOM's creation was more than a change of bureaucratic structures, reflecting a different methodology toward nonmilitary reconstruction and stability support for fragile and collapsed states, or whether it represented business as usual for Defense. Civilian involvement in AFRICOM assumes there is a link between poverty and terrorism. This remains unproven. Much of the leadership in religious terrorist groups is middle class, sometimes educated in Western Europe.

AFRICOM focuses on governance: physical security, political institutional development, economic management, and social service delivery. Most of the assistance will be civilian in nature. Yet to be determined is the extent to which the civilian structures blend with the military leadership in Defense.

Notes

1. And as of July 1, 2005, Commander of Central Command (CENTCOM).

2. See "Brains, not Bullets," *Economist* (October 25, 2007). Downloaded on February 29, 2008 and taken from Web site http://www.economist.com/opinion/displayStory.cfm?Story_ID=10024437. See also the *Counter-Insurgency Field Manual 3-24 MCWP3-33.5* (Washington, DC: Department of the Army, December 2006).

3. We are grateful to Dr. John W. De Pauw, who drew our attention to this term as a synonym for military civilian action or civil military operations; that is, the use of military forces on projects useful to a local population (community development) in areas of actual or potential military tension.

4. "Smart Power: Building a Better, Safer World: A Policy Framework for Presidential Candidates," *Occasional Paper* (Washington, DC: Center for US Global Engagement, July 2007), p. 2.

5. S. K. Obeng, "What Does AFRICOM Mean for Africa?" Paper Presented at the Africa Command (AFRICOM) Dialogue (Tswalu Kalahari Reserve, Northern Cape, South Africa, 13–15 July 2007), Obeng is a general in the Ghana Army.

6. See John W. De Pauw, "Winning the Peace," in *Winning the Peace: The Strategic Implications of Military Strategic Action,* John W. De Pauw, ed. (New York: Praeger, 1991), p. 198.

7. Nancy Birdsall, Dani Rodrik, and Arvind Subramanian, "How to Help Poor Countries," *Foreign Affairs* (July/August, 2005), pp. 136–152. See also Susan E. Rice and Stewart Patrick, "The 'Weak States' Gap," *Washington Post* (March 7, 2008), p. A17.

8. Thomas Dempsey, "Counterterrorism in African Failed States: Challenges and Potential Solutions" (Unpublished Paper, Army Strategic Studies Institute, April 2006).

9. Robert M. Pereito, "U.S. Police in Peace and Stability Operations," *United States Institute of Peace Special Report,* no. 191 (Washington, DC: United States Institute of Peace, August 2007).

10. Princeton N. Lyman and J. Stephen Morrision, "The Terrorist Threat in Africa," in *Foreign Affairs* (January–February 2004), p. 77.

11. Paul P. Cale, "African Command—The Newest Combatant Command," (Carlisle Barracks, PA: Strategic Research Project submitted in Partial Fullfillment of the Masters of Strategic Studies Degree, March 18, 2005), p. 2.

12. "What Would Military Security Look Like Through a Human Security Lens," Report of a NATO Advanced Research Workshop on "Reconciling the Requirements of Contemporary Operations with the

Needs of Human Security" (ARW 981712) held by Oxford Research Group, Oxfordshire, UK, September 2006.

13. Charles W. Kegley and Gregory A. Raymond, *After Iraq: The Imperiled American Imperium* (New York: Oxford University Press, 2007).

14. Ibid., pp. 26 and 32.

15. Brennan M. Kraxberger, "The United States and Africa: Shifting Geopolitics in an Age of Terror," *Africa Today*, 52, no. 1 (2005), pp. 47–58. See also the essays in James S. Wunsch and Dele Olowu, eds. *The Failure of the Centralized State: Institutions and Self-Governance in Africa* (San Francisco, CA: ICS Press, 1995).

16. Fred T. Krawchucj, "Combating Terrorism: A Joint Interagency Approach," *Landpower Essay Series* (Arlington, VA: Institute of Land Warfare Publication, no. 05-1, January 2005), p. 3.

17. *The National Security Strategy of the United States of America* (Washington, DC: US Government Printer, September 2002).

18. Larry Nowels and Connie Veilette, "Restructuring U.S. Foreign Aid: The Role of the Director of Foreign Assistance," *CRS Report for Congress* (Washington, DC: Congressional Research Service Library of Congress, June 16, 2006).

19. *U.S. Foreign Aid: Meeting the Challenges of the Twenty-first Century* (Washington, DC: U.S. Agency for International Development, January 2004), p. 5.

20. Ibid. USAID identified five categories of LDCs 1) rebuilding countries, 2) transforming countries, 3) sustaining partnership countries, 4) reforming countries and 5) developing countries. Sustaining development countries are the most developed countries.

21. "National Security Presidential Directive/NSPD-44," (Washington, DC: The White House, December 7, 2005).

22. Report to Congress, (Secretary of Defense, 2007).

23. Stewart Patrick, "U.S. Foreign Aid Reform: Will It Fix What Is Broken?" (Washington, DC: Center for Global Development, September 2006). p. 15.

24. Ibid.

25. James Jay Carafano and Nile Gardiner, "U.S. Military Assistance for Africa: A Better Solution," in *Backgrounder*, no. 1697 (October 15, 2003), pp. 1–6.

26. "Losing Hearts and Minds in Afghanistan: Canada's Leadership to Break the Cycle of Violence in Southern Afghanistan," *Policy Paper* (Ottawa, ON: The Senlis Council, October 2006), p. 10.

27. According to Stewart Patrick, "Phase Zero: The Pentagon's Latest Big Idea," *Global Development: Views from the Center* (Washington, DC: Center for Global Development, July 20, 2007).

28. *Conflict Mitigation and Management Policy* (Washington DC: Bureau for Policy and Program Coordination, US Agency for International Development, April, 2005), p. 4.

29. *U.S. Foreign Aid: Meeting the Challenges of the Twenty-First Century* (Washington DC: US Agency for International Development, January 2004).

30. Terry F. Buss and Adam Gardner, "The Millennium Challenge Account: An Early Appraisal," in Louis Picard, Robert Groelsema, and Terry F. Buss eds., *Foreign Aid and Foreign Policy* (Armonk, NY: M. E. Sharpe, 2008).

31. "Remarks by Henrietta H. Fore, Administrator, USAID and Director of U.S. Foreign Assistance—Foreign Assistance: An Agenda for Reform," (Washington, DC: USAID Speeches, February 1, 2008), www.usaid.gov/press/speeches/2008/sp80201.html.

32. Walter Pincus, "Taking Defense's Hand Out of State's Pocket," *Washington Post* (July 9, 2007), p. A13.

33. Brett D. Schaefer and Mackenzie M. Eaglen, "U.S. Africa Command: Challenges and Opportunities," *Backgrounder,* no, 2118 (Washington DC, Heritage Foundation, March 21, 2008), pp. 1–10.

34. Derick W. Brinkerhoff, "The State, the Citizen and International Development Management: Shifting Tides, Changing Boundaries, and Future Directions" (Washington, DC: Unpublished paper, February 2008), p. 22.

35. Dana Priest, *The Mission: Waging War and Keeping the Peace with America's Military* (New York: W. W. Norton, 2004).

36. U.S. Foreign Aid: Meeting the Challenges, p. 14. Also see Andrew S. Natios, "The Nine Principles of Reconstruction and Development," *Parameters* (Autumn 2005), pp. 4–20.

37. *Fragile States Strategy* (Washington, DC: US Agency for International Development, January 2005), p. 6.

38. Austin Merrill, "Letter from Timbuktu, *Vanity Fair* (September 10, 2007). http://www.vanityfair.com/politics/features/2007/09/sahara200709. Web site accessed March 13, 2008.

39. Gerald LeMelle, *Africa Policy Outlook 2008 Foreign Policy in Focus* (February 7, 2008), p. 3. Uploaded from www.fpif.org/fpiftxt/4949 on April 7, 2008.

40. Jakkie Cilliers, *Human Security in Africa: A Conceptual Framework for Review* (Johannesburg: African Human Security Initiative, 2004), p. 10.

41. Dempsey, "Counterterrorism."

42. Pincus, "Taking Defense's Hand Out of State's Pocket" and Craig Whitlock, "North Africa Reluctant to Host U.S. Command," *Washington Post* (June 24, 2007), p. A16.

43. Mark Malan, "AFRICOM: A Wolf in Sheep's Clothing," Testimony before the Subcommittee on African Affairs, Committee on Foreign Relations, US Senate (Washington, DC: August 1, 2007).

44. Personal communication to the author by E. Philip Morgan, February 11, 2008.

45. Padraig Carmody, "Transforming Globalization and Security: Africa and America Post-9/11." In *Africa Today*, 52, no. 1 (2005), pp. 97–120. Quote p. 101.

46. Patrick and Brown, *Greater Than the Sum of Its Parts*, p. 62.

47. Greg Mills, Terence McNamee, Mauro De Lorenzo, and Matthew Uttley, "AFRICOM and African Security: The Globalisation of Security or the Militarisation of Globalisation," *Brenthurst Discussion Paper* (Johannesburg: Brenthurst Foundation, April 2007).

48. According to ibid., p. 8.

49. Patrick and Brown, *Greater Than the Sum of Its Parts*.

50. Ibid., p. 37. Leading USAID to abandon the concept in 2007.

51. See, for example, the testimony by a representative of Refugees International (Washington DC), Mark Malan before the Subcommittee on African Affairs, Committee on Foreign Relations, US House of Representatives, at a hearing on "Exploring the U.S. Africa Command and a New Strategic Relationship with Africa" (Washington, DC: Refugees International, August 1, 2007).

52. There is speculation that the nominal headquarters will be in Liberia. A military base with 5000 troops already exists in Djibouti. Other nodes could be located in Botswana, Ghana, Kenya, Congo (DRC at the Lower Congo and Kamina), and Angola. US concerns include Somalia, the Great Lakes conflict, Sudan, and Liberia.

53. Schaefer and Eaglen, "U.S. Africa Command," p. 10.

54. Baker, "Quick Impact Projects," p. 11.

55. Seth Kaplan, "West African Integration: A New Development Paradigm," *The Washington Quarterly*, 29, no. 4 (Autumn 2006), pp. 81–97.

56. As of October 1, 2008, commander of AFRICOM was General William E. (Kip) Ward and the deputy commander for Military Operations was Vice Admiral Robert T. Moeller.

57. Baker, "Quick Impact Projects," p. 4.

58. On this, see Eklil Hakimi, Nick Manning, Satyendra Prasad, and Keir Prince, "Assymetric Reforms: Agency-Level Reforms in the Afghan Civil Service," *South Asia Region PREM Working Paper Series*, Report No. SASOR-3 (Washington, DC: World Bank, June 2004).

59. Anish R. Ghatt, "Jihadist Terror: Propaganda, Inspiration, and the Internet—Threat and Response" (Washington, DC: Unpublished Paper, December 17, 2005).

PART III

CONTEMPORARY AID IN HISTORICAL PERSPECTIVE AND BEYOND

I hated the bureaucracy, the silliness, the patronizing attitudes, the jargon, the sanctimony.

Paul Theroux, *Reminiscence*

Let's use bureaucratic inertia to our advantage.

Robert Klitgaard, *Tropical Gangsters*

Today we rank last among the advanced nations in the share of income devoted to foreign aid.

Matthew Miller, "Thinking Big"

Either the grants can be administered by experts from outside the depressed area or they can be turned over to representatives of the depressed group.

Ralph Linton, "An Anthropologist Views Point Four"

11

FROM POLICY TO PROCESS

The syllogism is a reliable form of logic.

Harlan Cleveland, Gerald J. Mangone, John Clark Adams,
The Overseas Americans

The truth is that, whether it likes it or not, USAID is just another of
the federal government's engines for redistributing revenue among the
citizenry. . . . The result is a racial spoils system.

Simon Barber, "US Foreign Aid Has Little to
Do with Philanthropy"

Institutional Development

Despite some of the assumptions of structural adjustment, the US foreign
aid process changed little since the 1950s. Specialists premise their actions
on this: development assistance operates on modernization theory, which
assumes that all societies need to modernize and grow economically in a
series of historically verified stages similar to that undergone by Western
nations during the past 300 years. This process of modernization and
growth can be accelerated in poor countries through resource and technology transfers from developed industrialized countries.[1] The LDC state
is the principal instrument of that development.

In the end, international development is about human security and
development. Foreign aid holds the promise of institutional development—
that is, the building of structures and processes capable of introducing and
supporting changes implied under modernization, allowing societies to
function in an age of globalization. To its critics, however, aid lacks an adequate conceptual basis beyond the imprecise term of modernization. Like
other foreign policies, aid suffers from an absence of reality among advocates and critics. This chapter looks at the institutional and organizational

arrangements of aid policy within the context of the domestic and international situation. We examine aid's impact on recipient countries and the way strategic planning became weakened with the project approach to development assistance. This *projectization* of foreign aid meant the United States was ill-equipped to address post–September 11 challenges.

Technical Assistance and Organizational Development

There are three types of technical assistance: employing foreign experts on a long- and short-term basis as operational experts or advisers; training for LDC public and NGO managers in country; and financing short-term training and long-term educational programs out of their own country—either in the United States or in a third country.[2] Crossing over these, bilateral aid in the late twentieth century involved use of a contracting process, grants, and employment of NGOs during the period 1989 to 2009. These define international assistance.

Aid is about organizations and their relationships with governments and societies. Historically, it was critical in improving the skills of managers in public and private enterprises. Such capacity building needs to address financial analysis, budgeting, revenue generation and administration, debt management, cash management and cash recovery, management of financial services, management information systems—including computer-based systems, and development of indigenous, in-country management, and consultancy services. Both sustainability and replicablility are dependent upon strengthening the capacities of sub-national governments, local administrative units, NGOs and emerging private sector institutions.

There are several high-priority capacity building activities requiring improved management:

First, there should be capacity to analyze development policy needs and provide public and private sector policy choices, including use, or at least understanding, of public choice and institutional analysis theory; institutional and transaction cost economics; and principles of international political economy.

Second, there should be capacity to assist national-level private, public, and *parastatal* sectors in the analysis of institutional and organizational factors that shape the sustainability of program or project benefits, including courses of action taken to improve the likelihood of sustainability after the host country assumes responsibility for projects.

Third, donor interventions should include the identification of appropriate strategies and approaches to privatization of government functions, as well as the effective and efficient reform of those functions that remain public. Social and economic costs of these reforms could be monitored through contractor services and research institutes. Support should also include design and introduction of effective monitoring systems to assess effects of policy changes and reforms on the socioeconomic patterns of the host country.

A fourth is development of a capacity among both educational and training institutions to provide (and, where appropriate, sell) services to governments, donors, and the private sector at an economically sustainable rate. Sales of services should be unsubsidized and allow competition. Ideally, regional institutes should be able to assist national ones in the development of their internal management systems where economies of scale exist.

There are four prerequisites to a successful development management strategy. First, development management must capture the most productive blend of national (government, nongovernmental organizations, and the private sector), local, and grassroots inputs into the program and project-planning process. This includes a commitment by host country and donor stakeholders to a strategy of *decentralization,* which takes into account both local conditions and national priorities. Planning should include development of management systems and skills development both at the national and subnational level. Planning activities need to ensure the participation of beneficiaries and target groups specified in the program or project, and they should provide mechanisms to advise on the utility of their design and implementation strategies.

Second, management training and human resource development must be part of a strategy for public sector reform and public-private partnerships. Rather than advocating privatization, such a strategy would define the proper role of government in economic and social development, specifically in the education and training areas. Also included would be policies for placing greater reliance on the private sector in food production, delivery of social services, and marketing of goods and services. Commercialization rather than privatization remains an option. Overall, such strategies should limit social costs of privatization. Management training and education should also include an understanding of the policy reform arguments and limitations.

Third, beyond privatization strategies, there must be a strategy for reforming and democratizing central and local government institutions and organizations. The state will not whither away. Strong, efficient, and accountable government is essential in creating a viable private sector. Such a strategy would include measures to make public sector organizations economically accountable for their actions and ensure creativity; a sensitivity to market principles and individual entrepreneurialism characterizes all sectors of the host country management system.

Experience with educational and training institutions suggests there must be financial and institutional autonomy from the civil service to ensure efficiency in performance. Ideally, focus should be on autonomous, nongovernmental educational and training institutions, (rather than on commercial programs) that would provide professional management education and training for all sectors.[3]

Four, the key to the long-term sustainability of donor-funded programs and projects (and in support of management training) must be the development of systems of cost recovery during the project or program period, ensuring the activity can be financially sustained. Effective recovery of recurrent costs is critical to ongoing programmatic activity, and attention needs to focus on developing innovative approaches to ensure this occurs before donor funding terminates. Success or failure of foreign aid depends upon how effectively and efficiently LDC program managers manage. Program managers require skills in needs assessment, negotiation, coordination, monitoring, and impact assessment.

Planning and the Failure to Institutionalize

Despite lip service to sustainability factors, the past fifty years has been about short-term projects, without concern for long-term sustainability. By the early 1950s, project managers learned they had to cope with ten- to twenty-year problems with three- to five-year projects staffed by one- or two-year contracted personnel. As David Sogge notes wryly, most donors stood "by their old, tested model: [t]ransferring resources through micro-projects."[4]

From the beginning, international assistance projects have meant "paperwork by the ream and very long lead times in planning ahead."[5] As early as 1952, Walter Sharp wrote, "Follow-up on the findings of country field projects . . . constitutes the weakest link in the implementation process."[6] Paper is what justified a project, and it is often assumed that development occurred with the commitment of funds, rather than through the impact on the LDC's capacity to deliver public services or increase its own productivity.

Bilateral and multilateral aid continues to be allocated to specific and narrow development activities. As a result, donors focus on short-term projects rather than longer-term programs. A continuing problem is that money is divided into large and small discrete projects, with universal procedures, reporting, and reimbursement schedules that dissipate aid's impact.

The project cycle system originated in the early 1960s. To garner and manage funding, federal agencies adopted Defense's planning, budgeting, and programming systems (PPBS). USAID's planning, budgeting, and review (PBAR) process was a variation of that process. Within the context of external requirements, however, USAID continued "to use in its own management procedures a control-oriented process that attempts to anticipate and plan for all aspects of a project prior to its approval and implementation."[7]

For planning reasons, conventional foreign aid is top down, based on process design that critics suggest is similar to drawing a blueprint for the construction of a building. Since the 1950s, the syllogism inherent in the donors' logical framework became the mantra of foreign aid. The project approach, Operation Blueprint by 1960, required logical relationships to be applied to all aid activities. While this may work on physical infrastructure or turnkey projects, codetermination of projects (by donor and recipient) are more appropriate for "building confidence and capacity, people, organizations and institutions, including capacity to learn, decide and mobilize resources in one's own unique situation."[8] Despite this, blueprint planning came to be applied to virtually all projects by 1975.

Ten years later, projects became the primary mode of aid delivery. While their purpose was benign, they were vehicles to manage activity over time with limited resources. The result was a rigid framework that made the system more compatible with USAID's programming strategy. This strategy called for each project blueprint to be approved in Washington. As a result, policymakers created organizations where institutions were needed.

A corollary was an irresistible pressure to move funding through the USAID mission system and out into the country through projects and grants. As John Montgomery put it, "Managing large controversial programs by using discrete, safe projects has become an art form in foreign aid administration."[9] A design system that produced a very large, safe, acceptable project that offered only limited discretion in the field was required.

By 1990, USAID and other donors had become stricter in the way they negotiated aid. The goal was to "use programme aid as a lever for bringing about changes in the policies of recipient countries towards the price of agricultural projects, public utilities and foreign exchange."[10] However, nonproject aid increased since the early 1990s, though much of it was small- and medium-sized "project" grants. Because of the nature of project management, donors often blame foreign aid recipients for failing to provide direction, follow-up sustainability, and a failure to manage aid properly.

Projectization's Impacts

Managers exhaust much of foreign aid in project administration. For example, Tanzania hosted 10,000 separate donor missions from 1995 to

2005. Critics see the project as the problem, not its solution. Within the recipient country, the disbursing of money, rather than strategic planning or even Cold War goals, motivated aid agencies.

It is fashionable in development to critique counterproductive effects of project-based assistance, especially for institutional development. Projects exist for donor convenience and "the advocacy purpose of project development derives from the incentive structures that move mission staff, the consultants they engage, and certain elements within the [LDC] central bureaucracy."[11] In addition, much criticism aimed at projects is focused on poor utilization of the project approach rather than the approach itself.[12] While there is some truth to this, there is also a rigidity built into the project approach, making institutional development difficult.

The problem is overdesign, both preprogramming and overoptimism. Preprogramming, or "pre-mature programming," refers to the confident statements made about distribution of benefits, economic return, positive institutional outcomes, replicability, and sustainability. All are supported by implementation schedules, as though uncertainty characterizing any development activity had been accounted for in advanced planning. Overoptimism describes a tendency to assume success with the design and allocation of funds, rather than through the implementation and impact of project activities.

Overall, the project approach has been unhelpful. It seems that "[p]ost project impact evaluations reveal that there continue to be negative social effects from AID's development efforts, regardless of project type."[13] This said, social analysis in practice has, "proven to be somewhat at odds with the way the findings are presented and the proviso that 'the data should be possible to obtain in two to three weeks.'"[14]

There are institutional development problems faced by both donors and host-country officials in the design and implementation of activities. "Transportability of the [project approach] concept," according to David Hirschman, "is the central characteristic of the foreign aid process."[15] This is the case in complex human resource development projects and in strategies of management development. Putting the human component into donor-supported activities is a first step to reorganizing international assistance.

Aid projects claim their purpose is to invigorate the economy, not provide social services; however, failure of a planned economic development model "has been accompanied by shifts in development thinking away from financial resources to human capital, social capital, policies and institutions."[16] Increasingly, economists suggest that productivity is not possible without human and social capital investment and higher levels of assistance than currently provided.

There are five factors that can affect sustainability. First, donors need to recognize economies of scale in institutional design. Cost effectiveness and market demands are important in designing training and human capital development programs. Regional collaboration, if national sensibilities can be overcome, can stretch scarce resources. Regional organizations work better in Asia and Latin America than in Africa and the Middle East, however.

Second, the planning process needs to include an institutional analysis of the context of the intervention and its impact on stakeholders. Social, economic, political, and cultural factors can all have an impact upon sustainability. Planning needs to include benefit-cost analysis and a more qualitative assessment of the societal environment.

Clearly, development planning works best when it assists government to do its work better rather than providing design as a part of technical assistance. It is critical to recruit field staff experienced in overseas work and sensitive to cultural differences and the nature of development activities. Successful planners often see their role more as facilitators than managers.

Third, planners need to allow enough time for institutionalization to occur. Institutional development in less than ten years is almost impossible. A three-to-five-year horizon to institutionalize systems makes a mockery of its intention. The project model severely limits the potential for institutionalization and sustainability.

Fourth, interventions should be of high quality. This means the decision to intervene should be selective and taken only after a needs assessment process. All foreign aid projects are full of good intentions. Mediocre interventions, however, backed by limited resources can do more harm than good and provide simple solutions for complex problems.[17]

Finally, there must be a correct definition of needs prior to intervention. This makes the design and appraisal process critical. Without this, activities will be ad hoc and random in impact.

The Changing Environment of Foreign Aid

Staffing USAID

Traditionally outside of ICA/USAID, Agriculture, Education, Labor, Commerce, and Treasury have all provided technical assistance. Agriculture's role in foreign aid has long been important. Elements of interagency involvement in foreign aid continued to exist in these agencies, funded out of the aid budget.

For much of the 1950s, while aid was allocated through MSA and later ICA and USAID, other foreign assistance was dispersed through the Development Loan Fund, the Food for Peace Program, USIA, and the Export-Import Bank, increasing involvement in international assistance.

In 1958, there were more than 2,235 Americans working overseas in private firms, universities, and NGOs and carrying out the work of ICA. In 1959, ICA had eighty-four active technical service contracts. During the same year, 184 universities carried out 382 international programs, 234 of which sent university faculty abroad.

Over time, especially after 1960, complaints about the quality of technical assistance experts heightened, one observer calling them "the bottom of the barrel."[18] Though unfair, such comments reflected dissatisfaction about quality of assistance. Politicization of aid during the Cold War likely contributed. One of the major problems for donors was the inability to recruit high-quality people.

Foreign aid became a large operation. In 1960, 40,000 people worked for the government worldwide. In Asia alone, there were 1,200 employed by ICA, 1,200 employed on ICA contracts, 420 employed by USIA, and 1,200 employed by State. By 1969, there were 5,324 direct-hire employees of USAID in service.

USAID and its contractors and cooperants employed more than 18,000 people annually around the world in 1971, a peak year for American foreign assistance. At any given time, more than 20 percent served in Vietnam alone. That said, USAID "had great difficulty in recruiting young development economists and all of the technicians that it need[ed]— agronomists, hydrologists, and mechanics."[19] The bulk were short-term contractors in that year. USAID hired 6,000 on direct or personal services contracts. Ten years later, that figure would shrink by 25 percent.

In 1990, USAID had about 4,300 direct-hire employees, a figure down from the 1971 high and a total that remained stagnant for twenty years. These administrators managed aid programs that were contingent on multiple external and internal factors. Few performed operationally. With the wholesale intervention in Eastern Europe about to begin, USAID was asked to do more with a capacity little different from that at the end of Vietnam. Those who made careers in Africa, Asia, or Latin America were transferred to the uncharted waters of Eastern Europe.

Contracts, Grants, and the NGO Conundrum

Private foundations have long played a major role in promoting international development. Private foundations have been most successful in supporting the educational sector. The Ford Foundation supported educational development in Indonesia and a number of other Asian countries and later played a role in post-apartheid South Africa. Given the Ford Foundation's $10 billion in assets, according to Joye Mercer, "what the foundation does is always analyzed, both by supporters—who applaud

Ford's efforts to promote diversity, for instance, and by detractors, who criticize what they call its attempts at social engineering."[20]

From the beginning, the foundations focused on programs with clearly defined goals. One of the more successful educational development interventions was the Rockefeller Foundation, the objective of which was to strengthen a few African, Asian, and Latin American universities over the course of fifteen to twenty years.[21] The Rockefeller experience, in both agriculture and education, illustrated the importance of "going first class" with a high-quality intervention of highly qualified people. The Green Revolution of the 1950s–1960s was initially financed by the Rockefeller and Ford foundations.

International donors see NGOs as an alternative to working through the state. Church-based organizations remained important in social services, relief work, and education throughout the twentieth century. Use of voluntary organizations and religious groups in international assistance goes back at least to the eighteenth century.

Prior to World War II, policymakers often directed international assistance contracts to religious missions and war-relief organizations. This early faith-based approach was taken for granted throughout the mid-1990s. NGOs, including faith-based groups, continued to play a major role in aid since the early 1950s, continuing to the present.

Later in the 1950s, ICA awarded aid contracts to American universities, particularly land grant colleges in the Midwestern states, for agricultural development. By July 1956, ICA had fifty-two universities on contract in thirty-eight countries. By 1960, it had contracts with sixty American universities involving "indispensable skilled human and institutional talent for the development program overseas."[22]

While private funds have remained important to international assistance, by 1970 private transfers of resources through NGOs accounted for only a small percentage of aid flows. Increasingly however, international assistance involved private-to-private aid transactions through a grants and subgrants process that allowed donors to allocate funding to a single cooperant, who would then parse it out to numerous small NGOs. The argument for using NGOs for aid was they could get assistance out more quickly and efficiently.

By 1975, with the shift to basic needs, aid began to flow to indigenous nongovernmental organizations [INGOs], modeled after Western charities, to build up civil society structures as a replacement for dissolving LDC governments; however, according to Fred Riggs, "[a]t another level, are there any American PVO's [private voluntary organizations] that could support this process?"[23] Riggs' skepticism points to the weakness of exporting ideas to LDCs that are not practical at home.

Aid-funded foundations and NGOs have received grant money from USAID and other donors since 1975. By the late 1990s, close to $20 million in Development Assistance funds were made available for the Inter-American Foundation alone and up to $11.5 million would be available for the African Development Foundation.[24] A 1996 article in the *Economist* argued:

> Most of the big agencies [large NGOs] now get about half their income from governments. Organizations that once saw themselves as the harbingers of an alternative and more altruistic form of human development are the tools of governments. They fear this "contract culture" will cost them their independence.[25]

By the late 1980s, the goal of INGOs was to become more businesslike, more professional, and more cost-effective. As part of this process, there were pressures placed upon NGOs to create larger bureaucracies and improve their financial management. This did not mean that they would necessarily carry out better relief and development work. In many countries, aid flowed through NGOs and nonprofit international agencies.[26]

By the early 1990s, USAID awarded three-fourths of its contracts and grants to US for-profit and nonprofit organizations. By 1997, $28.3 million in grants went to higher education partnerships alone. According to former USAID Director Brian Atwood, "You have heard us make a reference to 'franchising.' What it means is if the U.S. wants to have an assistance program in a country without a USAID mission, or where we have a minimal presence, we will be able to use NGO or contractor partners to achieve our objectives."[27]

With NGO proliferation, there were efforts to make them efficient service delivery agents. NGO absorption of programs associated with government and the pressing need for cost recovery take on added significance in understanding of aid. NGOs are also better equipped to support skills transfer and capacity building activities. NGOs are, according to advocates, less bureaucratic, smaller, and less constrained by rigid financial criteria. They also employ people who are more likely to live in poor communities.

Over the last decade, cynicism about NGOs has crept in. Of the NGO contractors and grantees utilized by USAID, many were US-based. Like the private sector, these NGOs followed the money, and often, aid workers attached to these organizations were aid entrepreneurs.[28] To critics, there is sometimes more than a little hucksterism among NGOs working in international development.

Humanitarian organizations are prone to send a message, "for the price of a cup of coffee, we can alter the lives of poor children in the Third World. It is bargain-basement charity."[29] For many within INGOs, because grant money is their primary goal, they rarely seem to meet a development project they do not like, in the process, losing their objectivity.[30]

With increased involvement in aid since the 1990s, NGO-based interest-group support under democracy and governance programs increased, though it remained weak. "Under the New Policy Agenda," according to Jennifer Brinkerhoff, "donors look to non-governmental organizations [NGOs] as implementers of donor-driven development policy, thereby bypassing government and co-opting NGOs, often destroying their organization identity and comparative advantages in the process."[31]

By the early 1990s, donor fatigue set in for NGOs as well. While Americans had given generously to private efforts, NGO fundraisers feared that the rash of disasters in the 1990s proved to be too much for the voluntary contributor.[32] In the end, Jennifer Brinkerhoff continues, "Regardless of the particular donor agency, partnership work necessarily varies with the partnership and project officers involved. . . . Some partnership initiatives encourage the use of more flexible mechanisms [e.g. USAID umbrella grants]."[33]

Both indigenous and international NGOs can and do play a controversial role at the community level. Historically, village elites often have benefited most from the NGO expatriate or volunteer's presence in the village in support of community-based organizations. Elites who most often interact with aid workers are often the most Westernized, speak an international language, are more educated than most in the village, and in material terms, live lives far from most of the people in the villages.

Local elites are often most able to manipulate the aid system. At the same time, mistakes made at the community level are seldom seen at higher levels of management. There are limits to responsibility in technical assistance. As Michael Maren notes, if "my project created a disaster, no one outside of the village would ever hold me accountable."[34] At the community level, NGOs will pull teachers out of the school system for the more lucrative salaries and benefits.

A further significant change is that NGOs are emerging with capacity to design and carry out programs in low-cost ways that conventional development programs have not.[35] Involvement of NGOs is not without its costs however:

> NGOs may lose their organization identity through a gradual and subtle "hardening of the arteries," as NGOs bureaucratize and become risk averse or reluctant to bear the costs of listening

to their constituencies. This has been particularly documented
with respect to donors. . . . The process begins with the acceptance of donor money; progresses to the adoption of donor techniques for programming, implementation, monitoring, and
evaluation; and begins to affect staff composition-recruitment,
selection, and valued skills; until the entire organization culture
is eventually attuned to donors.[36]

International NGOs have lost some of their luster.

Personnel Ceilings and Contracting Out

Historically, contracting out in foreign aid has not been adequately stud-
ied. Use of US-based foreign aid contractors became widespread as early
as the 1950s, initially for work done in the "neutral" countries in Asia. In
1958, the ICA had 3,328 people on its payroll and another 2,235 people
working for contractors. In the late 1950s, fifty-six nonprofit groups spent
more than $10 million in eighteen countries. Half of all technical assis-
tance went through contracts. There was widespread acceptance of no-risk
government contracts for specific projects abroad. By 1960, contracts with
universities and private consulting firms already had reached considerable
proportions.

As the Kennedy administration came into office, foreign aid budgets
were a year-to-year battle in Congress with no formalized continuity, making contracting out the only way to do business. Lack of continuity continues to plague aid. According to one practitioner, to "be successful as an
A.I.D. contractor, a firm is virtually required by A.I.D. contracting regulations to specialize in the A.I.D. market."[37]

By the middle of the 1960s, much technical assistance consisted of a
series of operational expert projects. USAID missions had flexibility in
how resources were used, and the mix of technical assistance, human
resource transfer, and financing was mission-directed. In the late 1960s,
concern over corruption in places like Vietnam led USAID officials to turn
toward competitive bidding and contracting out.

It was in Vietnam that USAID officials sometimes came to be corrupted
by contractors seeking funding. As early as 1968, one-half of USAID personnel were not direct hires. They were either on loan from other government agencies or on personal services contract.

Contracting was based on either cost plus a fixed fee or as a multiplier
of personnel costs. The assumption remains that contracts and business
procedures lead to more successful foreign aid. Into the 1970s, it was not
normal practice to hire non-Americans in technical assistance positions

without approval. This was resented by many Third World nationals and LDC program managers, who would like to use the best talent available. By the 1990s, the contracting process became internationalized with competition and merit selection. A significant number of personal and institutional contractors operated out of emerging market and other developing countries.

Ultimately, the implementation of foreign aid is a complex process involving multiple actors. By the 1970s, US missions became more restrictive in their operational framework and less able to take advantage of "targets of opportunity" identified in receptive departments and ministries. For this reason, as Judith Tendler points out:

> It is generally recognized that the transfer of a given amount of development assistance takes a long time. . . . This happens because of administrative complexities on both sides; because developing country governments may not be institutionally equipped to produce the kind of bureaucratic output required to qualify for and later monitor such assistance.[38]

Contracting out at the project level accelerated after 1975 with establishment of personnel ceilings in many aid agencies by the Carter and especially the Reagan administrations, with emphasis on privatization as a foreign policy. By the mid-1990s, USAID awarded 85 percent of its contracts and grants to US firms. Use of grants and contracts for technical assistance increased to close to 100 percent of bilateral US assistance over the next two decades.

Private sector for-profit organizations increasingly became involved in international development work. The reality of contacting out is that "profits and incomes are made by people whose responsibility it is to care for the victims of war and natural disasters. From a contracting perspective, a

> distinction needs to be made, however, between organizations that provide specialized services—computer training, map production, organization development, or distribution of pharmaceutical products—and full-service firms that assist A.I.D. in its heartland activities—the design, implementation, and evaluation of development projects.[39]

Increasingly, it has been the latter model that characterized aid.

Contracting out has significantly affected NGOs. "In this context," according to Jennifer Brinkerhoff, "an organization's power is determined not by its internal resources but by the set of resources it can mobilize through its contacts. Effectiveness is also enhanced through the innovation partnership can foster."[40] By 2000, NGOs in North America and Europe entered a contracting out era without appearing to plan for it.[41]

The problem with NGOs is they live with short institutional horizons and very small budgets. Their staffs are underpaid; they are often young returned Peace Corps or other volunteers with a newly minted master's degree in international development, or committed but poorly paid, part-time employees who work with meager resources for long hours at a go.[42] While this may allow for greater return to the organization, it may also result in a lack of professional standards.

Operationally, the distinction between the private sector and the non-profit sector is unclear and often unimportant. Increasingly, for-profit contractors employ a separate nonprofit-affiliated group or form a permanent alliance with a nonprofit to compete for grants. In the early 1980s, the TransCentury Corporation (a for-profit corporation) that bid on contracts and New TransCentury Foundation (a nonprofit) provided an example of this "twinning model."

The New TransCentury Foundation, which acted as private voluntary organization servicing the private voluntary organization community, doing immigration, research, and nutrition work, started by competing for a project that needed a NGO. Each had a separate board of directors.[43] Images of the two organizations tended to blend.

It is in the nature of donors, as with most bureaucracies, to seek standard operating procedures in the way that money is spent. Confidence develops through business expectations, rather than through ethics, and the organizational grounding in regulations, contracts, and standard operating procedures. US and international for-profits and NGOs have had to fit into this search for rational expectations based sometimes on the logical model or logical framework.

One issue often debated within and between NGOs is the allocation of program versus administrative funds for nonprofit and for-profit contractors. Save the Children, for example, allocates more than 82 percent of its money to program costs. Private for-profit contractors, on the other hand, allocate less than 50 percent of funds to program work. Their mark up can double or triple program costs.

By the late 1980s, there were two components to the donor business. On one side was the official donor community, the bilateral and multilateral aid organizations. On the other hand were the contractors, NGOs, and private voluntary organizations competing for donor grants and contracts. Critics complained about the contracting process as increasing the overall mediocrity of assistance efforts.

Ultimately, it took the foreign aid debacle in the former Soviet Union after 1989 to demonstrate what had long been known about Africa and Latin America. Contractors, including prestigious universities, could be as corrupt as the most despotic dictatorship. What allegedly happened in the former Soviet Union was that a clique formed between the Harvard Institute for International Development and a St. Petersburg-based group of Russian policy elites. It was an internally rigorous elite circle, both more widespread and monopolistic than an interest group, a faction, or a coalition.[44]

Since the mid-1980s, USAID prefers prebid indefinite quantity contracts (IQCs) to allocate resources. IQCs allow for the prebid of a small number of contractors and a more rapid response by limiting bids to those prequalified organizations. Ultimately, IQCs quash competition because they keep any organizations not inside the IQC loop, out of the bidding process. Price, not quality, largely determined the choice.

The importance of contracting out mechanisms increased as personnel ceilings decreased. As Amy Rubin pointed out in 1997, "Last month they recommended that the agency [USAID] limit overhead costs to 15 per cent of the total amount an organization receives from the U.S.I.A. for a program."[45] By the mid-1990s,

> the facts are that in five years our [USAID] direct-hire work force will be smaller-both in Washington and overseas. We have already cut our workforce over the past three years by a higher percentage—19 percent—than all but one other federal agency. This is down from some 11,500 employees to just over 9,000 today. And we will get smaller still-reaching a goal of less than 8,500 employees (U.S. and foreign nationals) by 1998.[46]

By 2000, USAID developed a "working relationship with more than 3,500 American companies, as well as more than 300 private voluntary and other nonprofit organizations in the United States.[47] Washington, DC, was the center of a "cottage industry of consultants, businessmen and lobbyists [that were] tapping into one of Washington's least-known pools of money, international development banks."[48] In the end,

> Donors may intentionally overexert their power, driving the process and destroying the spirit of partnership (along with many of its benefits), co-opting and compromising the organization identity of its partners, and even threatening national sovereignty. . . . More commonly, the negative impact on

partners' organization identity is caused by donors' lack of understanding of partners, their strengths and weaknesses; and the constraints posed by donor's administrative procedures and requirements and accountability to their constituents. The volume of resources and power a donor controls can influence incentive structures, diverting attention from value-based motivations, and, in the worst cases, inciting competition and corruption.[49]

Intragovernmental Agreements and Public-Private Partnerships?

Intragovernmental agreements within the federal system are part of contracting, sometimes referred to as "contracting in" agreements. As Raymond Hopkins noted, USAID established a number of Participating Agency Service Agreements (PASA) with other federal government departments, including Labor, Agriculture, the then–Health, Education and Welfare (HEW), and Justice to support its technical assistance programs.[50] Other co-operant agencies included Commerce, Education, USIA, the Peace Corps, and Environmental Protection. In addition, other government agencies, institutions of higher education, foundations, and NGOs are all stakeholders and have competence in the international development process.

Intragovernmental focus on aid became widespread, with Agriculture being active in this process. Agriculture and USAID have long been the beneficiaries of a partnership that goes back to 1950 when USAID's predecessor, TCA, was established. The partnership was renewed in the 1990s, with a new agreement to allow USAID access to agricultural expertise under PASAs and Resource Support Services Agreements (RSSAs).[51] Through the PASA/RSSA system, foreign aid funds and personnel ceilings sometimes can be hidden.

Increasingly, through the contracting-out process, for-profits, NGOs, and community-based sectors had public roles along with state actors, some competing with each other while others cooperated or partnered with the state. Public-private partnerships came into use to describe this process. Advocates have suggested that public-private partnerships, rather than contracts and competition, were the answer to aid failures. Public-private partnerships often involve significant investments in capacity building, targeting organizations that may have high personnel turnover.

In spite of their popularity, there is little agreement on what partnership really means. To its advocates, partnership using a grants mechanism is an alternative to contracting out. In a foreign aid context, "One partner's capacity can be enhanced through the experience of working with other partners and through training and staff exchanges."[52] USAID grants, according to their critics, lacked the flexibility needed for cooperating partners to provide professional judgment in project design and implementation.

NGOs justify strengthening their implementation capacity. "If a partner is looking for comparative advantages deriving from NGOs' philanthropic origins, the NGO should be able to articulate clearly its definition of development, mission, institutional goals, and identified constituency."[53]

Many NGOs cannot combine the ideals of advocacy and self-help with donor-stimulated (and funded) policies of structural adjustment and public sector reform. From the perspective of the donor's objectives, creation and sustainability of social capital is the foundation for any realistic exit strategy; however, according to critics, NGOs can also become bureaucratized and donor driven. NGOs receive what their critics call subsidies in the form of tax relief and privileges not available to the for-profit sector. Often nonprofits complain that USAID cooperative agreements often are no different than contracts. When government or international donors seek efficient service deliverers, agents contracting with nonprofits often could have contracted with private commercial entities.

To establish public-private partnerships, foreign aid must respond to real needs and to informed voices in developing countries. Developed countries need to strengthen the growth of pluralism and democracy in LDC societies. Over time, there has been a significant blurring of the role played by those competing agents that respond to international crises, particularly the NGOs involved in disaster-relief and other humanitarian assistance with that of development organizations.

Despite the criticism, donor interventions are most likely successful if they are collaborations between overseas and host-country actors. Institutionally, a bimodal contractual relationship between a technical assistance agency and an in-country institution is more likely to contribute to institutional development than is the traditional donor-recipient relationship. Finally, a support structure might need to provide for the internal management of LDC organizations.

Capacity Building for Sustainability?

Human Resources and Institutional Development

Since Point Four, technical assistance models have stressed human development approaches to international development, based on assumptions of indigenization of professional personnel and a phase-out of foreign overseas expatriates. Educational support for aid research objectives is an important component of university support for USAID activities. Education and training (and the technical assistance that went with it) were thought to be the keys to development after the Point Four announcement. At the beginning of the Eisenhower administration, Harold Stassen, President Eisenhower's director of FOA/ICA, advocated that American universities be tapped as human resource reservoirs for the extension of American technology abroad.[54] Professor Clark Kerr, of the University of California, later the embattled University of California at Berkeley president, first came up with a vision of the large university as a "service station" to government and society.[55]

Land-grant colleges and universities participated in USAID agricultural development projects "since the beginning of development assistance activities shortly after World War II, making monumental contributions on the food production front."[56] Aid advocates argue that the "sensible approach to development management was to nurture an understanding of the need for reform through analysis education."[57]

There has been a long-standing relationship between USAID and elements of higher education. As early as 1960, most of the education and training work internationally was assigned to colleges and universities. Use of contracting out had drawn both the private sector and universities into overseas technical assistance. Other than universities, by the late 1950s, there was an increasing focus on nonreligious NGOs and their employees.[58] It is important to keep in mind that prior to 1965 (and the heating up of the Vietnam war) the government had on tap the finest scholars available from the academic community to engage in thinking about international development.

After 1965, foreign aid increasingly functioned on the basis of low-trust management, which required time-consuming, and in some cases, humiliating supervisory procedures among foreign aid recipients. Sources of academic expertise dried up after Vietnam. Universities gradually began to withdraw from the foreign aid process, replaced by nonprofit and for-profit contractors.

The importance of higher education was based on its own institutional capacity. Throughout the world, education needs are high-quality needs because an educational system will be no more efficient than those who staff it. In the 1960s, staffing international centers and projects became a major component of university activity in foreign aid activities, both in the field and in the education and training of developing country students.

In the early 1960s, Michigan State University had assigned more than 200 faculty members annually implementing educational projects in thirteen countries, including Taiwan, Colombia, Turkey, Brazil, and Okinawa.[59] By the late 1970s, however, there was growing resistance within LDCs to learning from overseas. In the past twenty years, there has been increased interest in basic principles of the indigenous management of sector activities.

Between 1983 and 1995, under structural adjustment, there was almost a neo-Malthusian view of capacity building: "No governance [reform], no HRD, no social development."[60] This radical view ultimately led to calls to put a more human development face on structural adjustment, using such things as social and municipal funds to refocus on social needs.

Policymakers sometimes underestimate the importance of education and training. In the 1980s in Botswana, donors prematurely pulled out from secondary school education; however, the United States maintained an involvement with the Brigades (technical training programs) and the teacher training projects.[61] This was critical to the sustainability of Botswana's human resource development program, one of the most successful in Africa, even in the face of an increasingly virulent HIV/AIDs crisis.

From an international development perspective, the design and creation of effective organizations and systems staffed by capable managers requires a long-term investment that may require a decade or more;[62] however, USAID activities often did not target organizational development activities. From a capacity building perspective, there needed to be a greater degree of agreement on what the building blocks of development were. Prevailing notions are that they should be firmly based on both increasing human capacity and promoting with good governance, but with human security, physical capacity, and capital investment a necessary, but secondary, concern.[63]

Human resource development and training became predefined components of development efforts. Moreover, by targeting semi-skilled workers with bridging training, a human resource void could be filled. There was an explicit need to change values from a focus on economic restructuring and growth to human resource development. This position, in part, went back to the faith-based organizations that worked in health and education and that dominated technical assistance in the early 1900s. Changing norms required a minimum technical assistance commitment of more than the usual three to five years encompassed in the project model.[64]

In the late 1990s, once again American universities needed to play a greater role in improving basic education in developing countries. In making better elementary and secondary education one of the top goals for sustainable development overseas, Brian Atwood, stated in 1997 that USAID would dedicate greater resources to teaching programs that involved US colleges and universities.[65] The foreign aid managers and their clients would be better served if education were outsourced not to contractors but to universities able to provide professional-level analysis.

This did not happen, and since 1997 the gap between the academy and the development community has widened again, stimulated in part by the Iraq war after 2003. Despite a lack of clarity in the mission, in 1997, $28.3 million of USAID funds went to higher education partnerships. LDCs face enormous challenges in a short period of time, and it is important to remember that many "developing countries have achieved in 30 years what it took industrial countries nearly a century to accomplish."[66]

The human resource dilemma remains. Growth of enrollments and facilities at primary, secondary, and tertiary levels in LDCs is not accompanied by a corresponding increase in qualified administrative and managerial staff. In addition, educational planning in many developing countries focuses on central goals and objectives at the expense of regional, local, and community needs. Economic growth lags far behind support for higher education.

Training Realities

Initially, training within the foreign aid community often turned inward. Before 1960, focus was heavy, with the garnering of information about agencies' own internal procedures and advice badly out of date and with discussions about living conditions in the field. Only after states and organizations failed did donors examine fundamental flaws in institutional relationships. At that point, donors saw "themselves spending more on skill-building projects, like professional training programs and basic education."[67] International training programs resulted.

Many feel that the primary focus of donor training intervention should no longer be on overseas education and training; it should be on capacity building to develop regional and national management and professional-level institutions, and LDC university programs. American universities should build capacity and facilitate information technology, rather than retail training.[68] This is easier said than done, of course, as the physical state of many LDC training and education institutions leave a great deal to be desired. Physical plants have deteriorated, morale is low, and faculty and staff salaries are sometimes close to nonexistent. There are many elements to the capacity building conundrum.

Where economies of scale require it, regional (third country) and national training institutions must be able to provide the full complement of management development services for a country, meeting the needs of both the public and private sectors; these are services, which for the most part now, are provided by North American and European institutes, universities, and private nonprofit and for-profit companies. Focus is on the indigenous capacity to develop the leadership cadre of LDC managers, including the next generation of policy elites.

Technical transfer occurs in strategic interventions in support of increasing development management capacity. These include tools, techniques and technologies, skills in the analysis of the environment, principles of organization and management, and unstructured skills. It is the latter that Gabino Mendoza calls "the synthetic mode of thought."[69] The tools and techniques of administration transfer most rapidly through bridging training. They are not worth high levels of investment, as they can be best provided through the private sector. Unstructured skills, however, are the most difficult to transfer because they require that we have, following Mendosa, the "synthetic mode of thought . . . [where] something . . . is viewed as part of a larger system and is explained in terms of its role in that larger system."[70] At the upper levels of management and for development management, it is the unstructured skills of judgment and analysis (including abstract thinking) that make organizational management skills an art rather than a science.

Mendoza contrasts this with the quick fix, often a counter-productive strategy of short, inexpensive bridging training. A policy focus is important; however, according to one observer, "It is the contention [here] that the preoccupations of the leaders of the 'development' profession, in their role of experts, has led to an over-emphasis in teaching and research on policy recommendation rather than empirical work and conceptual analysis, which should properly include studies of the policy decisions [and the decision-making processes] of those in power."[71]

Donor interventions need to focus on the transfer of unstructured skills by strengthening educational and training capacity at the postgraduate level. The assumption here (as with any generalization, there are no doubt some exceptions) is that creative management cannot be practiced by those who have not experienced the intellectual development that occurs with university degree or its equivalent and a professional postgraduate masters' degree.

Assumptions on the importance of intellectual development are infrequent, especially in postcolonial Africa, where ten years of basic education contributes adequate preparation for even the most senior positions in the public and parastatal sectors. Bridging training strategies, however, simply do not foster the intellectual capacity that is critical for development management. Part of the failure of management systems, particularly in Africa, relates to invalid assumptions that such a stopgap management strategy is possible.[72]

At this level of debate, cultural factors may be important. According to Ian Clark, "The fundamental question concerning development and culture, in the anthropological sense of the word, has to be posed and re-posed if we of the North are not to be blinded by our own self-satisfaction and ethnocentricity, and fall into the error of dictating or imposing what we think is necessarily best for others."[73]

Organizations and programs can contribute to institution building at the national level through basic research and the development of pilot programs. Neither the LDC program manager nor the donor project officer, however, should expect international intervention to be the primary vehicle for the development of organizational capacity or training skills to increase management effectiveness. Rather, through a spread effect, indigenous institutions should be capable of providing support for national and local structures in enhancing their organizational capacity and training skills, particularly in the areas of applied research and consultancy.

There are four types of administration in LDCs—maintenance, scaffolding, praetorian, and development. Maintenance administration focuses on the preservation of patterns of management. Scaffolding administration is supportive of private sector initiatives and efforts. Praetorian administration is prescriptive, control-oriented, and involves use of (or the threat to use) force.

General management and leadership skills at the upper levels of an organization, and development administration/management specifically, are different than maintenance administration at the middle and lower levels. These, in turn, differ from sector management skills (health, education, agriculture, transport). It is the integration of these various components of management that are at the heart of the institution and capacity building.

Designer training and organizational development capacity are two key areas that must be addressed when considering sustainability and replicability. While training and organizational development can occur at the national and even subnational level, economies of scale suggest that regional/third country and international programs can contribute to the research, design, and delivery of such tailor-made programs, especially in small or medium sized countries.

An implementing agency in defining an intervention strategy can begin by determining what kind of skills need to be transferred to management training and other professional institutions. Once accomplished, the agency may develop a strategy to transfer the skills needed and to provide institutional development services to regional, and indirectly, to national-level training institutions. International support for enhancing management effectiveness should not replicate the support and human resource development to be provided at the national level.

There is an unfortunate growing trend in human resource development efforts and higher education coming out of September 11. "To prevent countries that support terrorist activities from gaining knowledge useful to their weapons programs, the United States [began to tighten] its screening procedures for granting visas to students from those countries."[74] Closing international access to American higher education, even temporarily, runs counter to the whole strategy of foreign aid policy and has begun to have an effect on US institutional development strategies in LDCs. International involvement in capacity building has become more problematic in post-September 11 foreign assistance strategies.

Conclusion

Any efforts by the United States or others at LDC institutional capacity building must begin with a serious commitment by USAID to its own self-defined international development themes. These have included (1) the commitment to a policy dialogue between the public and the private sector; (2) a commitment to real technology and skills transfer from more developed states to lesser developed states; (3) a firm commitment to an expanding but institutionalized (and legally defined) role for the private sector in economic activities; and (4) a concern for institutional development, capacity building and sustainability.[75]

The goal of the donor is often said to be to assist LDC postcolonial modernizers in carrying out the tasks of development while mass awareness and participation evolve. Even accepting the limits of this assumption, having such postcolonial modernizers available requires an emphasis on high-level human resource development. Given this, donors need to revisit the issues of expanded funding of nongovernmental organizations and private voluntary associations that support capacity building at the professional level.

To understand the prerequisites for sustainability, it is necessary to begin with an institutional analysis of the environment of the donor project, and it is important to understand the social, economic, cultural, and political framework within which the development intervention occurs. Human skills and institutional issues will increasingly come to the fore in the first decade of the twenty-first century. We will continue our discussion of institutional development in the next chapter.

Notes

1. Dennis A. Rondinelli, *Development Administration and U.S. Foreign Aid Policy* (Boulder, CO: Lynne Rienner Publishers, 1987), pp. 30–31, 40–45 and 214.

2. *Assessing Aid: What Works, What Doesn't, and Why* (Washington, DC: The World Bank and Oxford University Press, 1998), p. 100.

3. See *Management Training and Research for African Development* (Washington, DC: Economic Development Institute of the World Bank, January 1987) for a cogent summary of this argument. See also Kamala Choudhry, "Strategies for Institutionalizing Public Management Education: The Indian Experience," in Stifel, et al. *Working Papers— The Rockefeller Foundation,* pp. 107–108 makes the same point, drawing from the Asian experience.

4. David Sogge, *Give and Take: What's the Matter with Foreign Aid?* (London: Zed Books, 2002), p. 158.

5. Cleveland, et al., *The Overseas Americans,* p. 156.

6. Walter R. Sharp, "The Institutional Framework for Technical Assistance," *International Organization,* 7, no. 3 (August 1953), pp. 342–379. Quote, p. 372.

7. Rondinelli, *Development Administration,* p. 236.

8. Des Gasper, "Ethics and the Conduct of International Development Aid: Charity and Obligation," in *Forum for Development Studies* (Oslo), 1, no. 1 (1999), p. 36.

9. John D, Montgomery, *Aftermath: Tarnished Outcomes of American Foreign Policy* (Dover, MA: Auburn House Publishing Company, 1986), p. 98.

10. Paul Mosley, *Overseas Aid: Its Defense and Reform* (Brighton, UK: Wheatsheaf Books, 1987), p. 28.

11. Ibid., p. 12.

12. George H. Honadle and Jay K. Rosengard, "Putting 'Projectized' Development in Perspective," *Public Administration and Development,* 3, 1983, pp. 299–305. Quote, p. 304.

13. E. Philip Morgan, "Social Analysis, Project Development and Advocacy in U.S. Foreign Assistance" (Unpublished Paper, 1980), p. 1.

14. Ibid., p. 4.

15. David Hirschmann, "'Customer Service' in the United States Agency for International Development: An Example of Designing a Democracy Program in Bangladesh," *Administration & Society*, 31, no. 1, (March 1999), p. 114.

16. Hans Singer, "Preface," in Stephen Browne, *Beyond Aid: From Patronage to Partnership* (Aldershot, UK: Ashgate Publishing, 1999), p. ix.

17. Browne, *Beyond Aid*, p. 49

18. Rowland Egger, "Technical Assistance at Home and Abroad," in *Institutional Cooperation for the Public Service: Report of a Conference* (Chicago: Public Administration Service, 1963), p. 49.

19. John Franklin Campbell, *The Foreign Affairs Fudge Factory* (New York: Basic Books. 1971). p. 188.

20. Joye Mercer, "The Ford Foundation Shifts its Focus and Structure," *Chronicle of Higher Education* (August 15, 1997), A29.

21. Lawrence D. Stifel, Joseph Black and James S. Coleman, eds., *Education and Training for Public Sector Management in Developing Countries* (New York: Working Papers of the Rockefeller Foundation, April 1978), p. 1.

22. James P. Grant, "Towards a More Effective Domestic Political Base for American Economic Assistance Abroad—As Seen by a Practitioner" (Paper prepared for delivery at the Annual Meeting of the American Political Science Association, New York, September 8–10, 1960), p. 14.

23. Fred W. Riggs, "Memorandum: Suggested Discussion Topics based on Dennis Rondinelli, *Development Administration and Foreign Aid Policy*" (Unpublished Letter to the Author, Honolulu: University of Hawaii, March 1987), p. 2.

24. Marianne O'Sullivan, "President Signs FY 1996 Foreign Assistance Appropriations Act," *Front Lines, USAID* (April–May 1996), p. 2.

25. "New Tasks for the Aiders," *Economist* (June 22, 1996), p. 44.

26. According to a *New York Times* account in 1992, "The United States Agency for International Development, which pioneered the funneling of aid through nongovernmental or voluntary organizations, says that a substantial part of its annual spending of $7.5 billion is now channeled through nongovernmental organizations or the private sector." See Barbara Crossette, "Givers of Foreign Aid Shifting Their Methods," *New York Times* (February 23, 1992), p. A2.

27. Brian J. Atwood, "The Future of Foreign Aid." Speech, to the Advisory Committee on Voluntary Foreign Aid (Washington, DC: US Agency for International Development, March 12, 1996).

28. Mark Hertsgaard, *The Eagle's Shadow: Why America Fascinates and Infuriates the World* (New York: Picador Books, 2003), p. 27.

29. Michael Maren, *The Road to Hell: The Ravaging Effects of Foreign Aid and International Charity* (New York: The Free Press, 1997), p. 264.

30. As a result, according to Hertsgaard, "[i]n spite of their reservations, [donor funded NGOs] allowed themselves to be used, because they were dependent on government money and supplies; most were willing to do whatever was necessary—including distributing food in situations that were at best questionable and at worst harmful to recipients." Hertsgaard, *Eagle's Shadow*, p. 201.

31. Jennifer M. Brinkerhoff, *Partnership for International Development: Rhetoric or Results?* (Boulder, CO: Lynne Rienner Publishers, 2002), p. 23.

32. Celia W. Dugger, "International Disasters Tax America's Compassion," *New York Times* (May 12, 1991), p. A9.

33. Brinkerhoff, *Partnership for International Development*, p. 12.

34. Maren, *The Road to Hell*, p. 11.

35. Ralph H. Smuckler and Robert J. Berg, "New Challenges New Opportunities, U.S. Cooperation for International Growth and Development in the 1990s" (East Lansing: Michigan State University, August 1988), p. 5.

36. Brinkerhoff, *Partnership for International Development*, pp. 52–53.

37. Donald R. Mickelwait, "Terms of Reference: The A.I.D. Consulting Industry," (Unpublished Document, n.d.).

38. Judith Tendler, *Inside Foreign Aid,* (Baltimore: Johns Hopkins University Press, 1975), p. 86.

39. Mickelwait, "Terms of Reference: The A.I.D. Consulting Industry."

40. Brinkerhoff, *Partnership for International Development*, pp. 3–4.

41. Ian Smillie, *The Alms Bazaar: Altruism Under Fire—Non-Profit Organizations and International Development* (London: IT Publications, 1995), p. 167.

42. Ibid., p. 140.

43. Louis A. Picard, Personal Notes, June, 1980, Author's Research Diary.

44. See Janine R. Wedel, *Collision and Collusion: The Strange Case of Western Age to Eastern Europe, 1990–1997* (New York: St. Martin's Press, 1998) for a discussion of this.

45. Amy Magaro Rubin, "Senate Panel's Plan Would Limit Use of USIA Funds," *Chronicle of Higher Education* (August 8, 1997), p. A44.

46. Atwood, "The Future of Foreign Aid."

47. Eric Schmitt, "Helms Stipulates Private Channels for Foreign Aid," *New York Times* (Jan. 12, 2001).

48. Jeff Gerth, "In Post-Cold-War Washington, Development is a Hot Business," *New York Times* (May 25, 1996), p. A1.

49. Brinkerhoff, *Partnership for International Development*, p. 65.

50. Raymond F. Hopkins, "The International Role of 'Domestic' Bureaucracy," *International Organization*, 30, no. 3, (Summer 1976), p. 417.

51. "The Spirit and Intent of PASAs and RSSAs in a USDA/USAID Partnership," USDA/FAS/ICD/DRD (August 1997), p. 1.

52. Ibid., p. 5.

53. Brinkerhoff, *Partnership for International Development*, p. 51.

54. See Vernon W. Ruttan, *United States Development Assistance Policy: The Domestic Politics of Foreign Economic Aid* (Baltimore: Johns Hopkins University Press, 1996), pp. 506–507.

55. Both quotes from Warren Hinckle, "The University on the Make," *Ramparts*, 4, no. 12 (April 1966), pp. 11–22. Quote, p. 14.

56. "Report of the Task Force on the University Center Program" (Washington DC: The Agency Center for University Cooperation in Development, USAID, December 5, 1991), p. 4.

57. Martin Wolf, "Aid, hope and charity," *Financial Times*, November 11, 1998, p. 13

58. Typical of university programs was the University of Pittsburgh's Graduate School of Public and International Affairs, which was founded in 1957 on the principle of academic-practitioner linkages for both its degree and its executive programs for students from LDCs. Particular focus was given to the student's personal philosophy, and an understanding of the power structure and the bureaucratic processes in foreign and comparative perspective. In addition to degree granting programs, there was a strong capacity to provide executive training programs through the school's International Management Development Institute. There was a strong belief that those programs could bring professionalism to international development work that had been lacking in the early years.

59. Hinckle, "The University on the Make," p. 14.

60. Samuel W. Shoen, "USAID Africa Bureau; Strategic Analysis and Recommendations for the 1990's," Working Draft Internal Document (September 9, 1991), p. 12.

61. H.F. Lundburg, Desk Officer, Personnel, DANIDA, personal interview, June 26, 1980, Author's Research Diary.

62. Thomas Thorsen and Kenneth Kornher, "Draft Report of the Work Group for the Review of the Programs in Management

Improvement and Development Administration of the Agency for International Development" (Washington, DC: Department of State, US
Agency for International Development, n.d.), p. 4.

63. Clay Wescott and Abdul Majid Osman, "International Resources
and Policies" (New York: United Nations Development Program,
Unpublished Paper, 1992), p. 1.

64. However, as Robert Cassen has put it: "There is . . . a shortcom-
ing in the intellectual underpinnings of institution building, human
development, and associated cooperation, compared with the theoretical
and quantitative tools used to plan physical development. Work has
been done on manpower planning and the development of individual
institutions. But there is little guidance for planning the institutional
requirements of whole sectors, for matching institutional needs with
evolving economic structures, or for systematically defining intersectoral
institutional linkages. The basic objective of technical cooperation—to
promote self-reliance—has not been defined in terms that would aid the
planning of institutional needs and facilitate national decisions. This
subject warrants a major conceptual effort. Robert Cassen, "The Effectiveness of Aid," *Finance & Development* (Johanesburg, South Africa,
March 1986), p. 13.

65. Jeffrey Selingo, "U.S. Plans to Expand Role of Universities in
Helping Developing Nations," *Chronicle of Higher Education* (July 25,
1997), p. A50.

66. Wescott and Osman, "International Resources and Policies," p. 5.

67. Howard W. French "Donors of Foreign Aid Have Second
Thoughts," *New York Times* (April 7, 1996), p. A5.

68. Such universities as the University of Pittsburgh, through its International Management Development Institute, the University of Connecti-
cut through its Public Service Institute, and the University of Southern
California through its International Public Administration program have
long provided generic management training. A shift to capacity building
and applied research would better complement the broader university
agenda and would better utilize the development funds provided the
USAID, the World Bank and the UN Development Program.

69. Stifel, et al., "Models of Public Management Education for Development Sectors," *Working Papers—The Rockefeller Foundation*, op. cit.,
p. 44.

70. Ibid.

71. Edward Horesh, "Academics and Experts or the Death of the
High Level Technical Assistant," *Development and Change*, 12, no 4,
(October 1981), p. 615.

72. Wyn Reilly makes this point. See his *Training Administrators for Development* (London: Heinneman, 1979).

73. Ian Christie Clark, "From Crisis to Renaissance at UNESCO— Can the Struggle Be Won Without the USA?" *Newsletter of Americans for the Universality of UNESCO*, IV, issue 4, (September 1988), p. 16.

74. Karla Haworth, "Tighter Procedures Urged for Student Visas," *Chronicle of Higher Education* (October 24, 1997), p. A64.

75. Agency for International Development, *A.I.D. Policy Paper: Institutional Development* (Washington, DC: USAID, March 1983).

12

DONORS AND CLIENTS

She was in love with the idea of love and with the idea of sacrificing herself to it.

Deborah Scroggins, *Emma's War*

[I]t is the engineer and technician with an anti-political turn of mind who provide the solutions for all major problems.

Joseph Buttinger, "Fact and Fiction on Foreign Aid"

The sensible approach is to nurture understanding of the need for reform through education and analysis.

Martin Wolf, "Aid, Hope, and Charity"

Africans were "grant savvy." They were so used to getting grants, they were aware that the money would dry up in three to five years and assumed that they would have to look elsewhere for more money for their plans.

Paul Theroux, *Dark Star Safari*

Operational Limitations

The Not-So-New Missionaries

The missionary impulse continues to influence international assistance into the twenty-first century. "A common explanation for these so-called imperial effects or consequences of foreign technical assistance" according to E. Phillip Morgan, "attributes them to structures which perpetuate dependence in the international economic order."[1] There is modernity in assumptions about missionary influences on foreign aid. As Deborah Scroggins puts it, in speaking of the 1993 Somalia tragedy:

Was the U.S. "intervention" as journalists called it, a prelude to a UN takeover of Somalia? If so, wasn't that just another name for colonialism? Had we come full circle, back to the point one hundred years earlier when Britain had justified its conquest of places like Sudan and Somalia by arguing that they were saving the inhabitants from famine and slavery?[2]

Idealism was and is important to those working in technical assistance. Cleveland, et al., noted: "There is a sense in which all religious missionary workers have a belief in mission; their small cash incomes and the natural frustrations of their work require the highest conviction of purpose to keep the individual on the job at all."[3] Yet, life and death places—whether due to famine, drought, or human made disaster—are not always a high-donor priority. In 1989, only 27 percent of humanitarian staff travel was to disaster areas.[4]

Service overseas uncovered nationalistic feelings that Americans are different from and better than those they worked with. Sometimes, Americans measure their status by the "American-ness" of their privileges. Moreover, motivations of the overseas worker are mixed. According to Cleveland, et al., "Getting along with one's American peers and superiors is usually far more important to the individual's morale than getting along with the nationals."[5]

Expatriates have social and ego needs, as well as economic interests. Critics of technical assistance, such as Emery Roe, argue that experts sometimes use their expertise to "assert rights as 'stakeholders' in the land and resources of . . . Africa."[6] Not surprisingly, expatriates have often defined development needs of a country as needing more expatriates. While Roe's complaint is fair enough, it also misses the value of experts.

Distance is a component of international interventions, reflected in the way journalists, military officials, and expatriates define their involvement in aid. Blaine Harden expresses this problem as the emptiness of psychological distance between aid workers and recipient. According to Harden there is a vast

> distance between Sakarto [an Ethiopian nineteen-year-old starving mother holding a dead baby] and me, in language, culture, [which] made our interview a charade. She thought I was a doctor. I came no closer to the woman than if I had seen her on television. My feeling for [her] like the feelings of millions of Americans who saw television pictures of suffering in Ethiopia, had little to do with her, and even less to do with her country's poverty or its wretched government.[7]

Escape is sometimes part of the experience. The narrator in Graham Greene's *The Quiet American* could not live in his own country.[8] As Deborah Scroggins writes, speaking of the southern Sudan, "In truth the average aid worker . . . lived for the buzz, the intensity of life in the war zone, the heightened sensations brought on by the nearness of death and the determination to do good." She goes on, "The rush, the thrill, the excitement of living on the edge in itself gave the aid workers an excuse for all sorts of wildness that never would have been tolerated in their own countries."[9]

Even for those who eventually returned home, there are opportunities to go back, at least for a limited time. More and more LDCs' elections require international observers, and for a few months, "The pay is princely: a presiding officer at a polling station will get $800 for two months' work, [plus all expenses] in a country whose GDP per person is about $150 a year."[10] It is more exciting than a tourist cruise.

Given their numbers, expatriate aid workers and volunteers not surprisingly have critics and even enemies, especially among LDC intellectuals and elites. Campbell complained of the propaganda masters, the "surplus supply of propagandists, agronomists and returned Peace Corps Volunteers" all functioning as cheerleaders for foreign aid.[11] Theroux suggested that expatriates in Africa had a Tarzan complex.[12] Okot B'itek equated them to legions of white ants invading the Third World.[13] "Perhaps nothing irritates foreigners more," Mark Hertsgaard states, "than America's habit of thinking it has all the answers, and the right to impose them on everyone else." Above all, Hertsgaard goes on, there is a concern "that Americans think only of themselves."[14]

Graham Hancock questioned fundamental assumptions, motives, and mechanisms of official aid, though not necessarily those, especially within NGOs, that implement humanitarian and development activities. He felt expatriate aid workers, "had the power to make arbitrary decisions that may mean the difference between life and death for thousands of poor people."[15]

Many observers think of aid workers as developmental tourists or imperial-style elites with privileges. At worst, expatriate aid workers are a rear guard of colonialism or missionary endeavors, covering the retreat of the West from Africa and Asia. According to Campbell, "Like it or not, the donor-recipient relationship looks suspiciously like a new form of colonialism to many of the receiving countries."[16]

In the field, the aid worker is frequently the only foreigner in town. Yet, as Theroux described, speaking of workers in rural Africa, "[t]hey were, in general, oafish self-dramatizing prigs, and often complete bastards." In their field experience, there was, he goes on, "often a tone of melodrama among relief workers, charity in Africa frequently being a form of theater."[17]

Aid workers appear to those working with them as "infuriatingly self-righteous, [and] so ignorantly superior."[18] They often see themselves as fighting evil. At the same time, according to Scroggins, "it was often the complexity of the development conundrum that was most threatening. Sudanese leaders self-righteously have long complained about Western aid workers the arrogant young foreigners who ran so many of the refugee programs."[19] Though, from the architects of Darfur, the protest has a hollow ring.

Somalia, according to Michael Maren, "added a whole new dimension to my view of the aid business. My experience there made me see that aid could be worse than incompetent and inadvertently destructive. It could be positively evil."[20] He goes on, the "only Americans who spent time with Somalis were . . . young former Peace Corps volunteers who were hired as personal service contractors to do the dirty work of going out into the bush and telling career people what was going on."[21]

Motives and Dilemmas

Morale declined somewhat within the foreign aid community in the 1960s. Edward Weidner portrayed the donor environment as: "[Z]eal or enthusiasm is lacking. The missionary spirit, or more properly, the sense of mission is not present in most instances."[22] The combining of foreign aid and military conflict, particularly in Vietnam, was a major factor.

By 1970, an aid worker profile was developing. The Peace Corps experience demonstrates the variety of individual motives and the limits. Foreign aid is about people and the motivations they bring with them. Being in the international aid business is a life. According to Michael Maren:

> Many stay in it, become part of the system, and only resist it on occasion. They cling to the idea of aid. Aid redeems their lives and uplifts the lives of the poor. To them, the contradictions all stem from the West's not understanding or helping enough. Their answer is always more aid, bigger budgets, another project.[23]

The newly minted Peace Corps and/or other voluntary groups became a ticket to punch for those working in foreign aid. By the late 1970s, there were "on the staff of AID . . . [more than] five hundred former Peace Corps volunteers . . . and their presence clearly [or at least hopefully] promotes mutual understanding."[24] Volunteers often go to work in the Third World without training or experience.

Many ex–Peace Corps volunteers work for international organizations, foreign aid contractors, and NGOs. The typical foreign aid or technical assistance officer eventually becomes a part of an expatriate or emigrant lifestyle.[25] "To obtain one of these jobs," according to Scroggins, "certification from a Western university in development studies or refugee affairs was usually the ticket."[26]

Historically, development studies programs were defined by development administration programs, which in turn had their origins in anthropology departments and in training courses for colonial officials. Public and development administration programs of American and European universities in the postwar period shared many assumptions of these earlier ones. When the Peace Corps began to work in East Africa in 1961, it took over the Teachers for East Africa program, a joint British and American program, with its origins in the late British colonial system.[27]

Typically, the foreign aid worker starts off as a volunteer, working for the Peace Corps, Britain's Voluntary Service Overseas (VSOs), or one of the other European volunteer agencies. Volunteerism is fun at first though hard, and the novelty of deprivation wears out fast. After a few years in a hardship post—Southern Sudan or in the killing fields of Rwanda—workers often aspire to a better paying job.

Many workers become aid entrepreneurs in NGOs, grinding out proposals for projects or looking for design or evaluation opportunities. Others end up as a desk officer for a bilateral aid agency, or a contractor, serving as a consultant, or on a long-term overseas contract, serving as an operational expert in a ministry or NGO.

Operational experts and personal services contractors (PSCs) were at the heart of the technical assistance process by the 1980s. PSCs had long expanded the capacity of USAID and because "PSC's are contractors, they are not covered by RIF [reduction in force personnel] regulations."[28] USAID-sponsored OPEX (Operational Experts) workers took the place of an indigenous official while they went overseas to study.

In the late 1970s, the first OPEX team included more than one hundred to Ethiopia, and fifteen to Botswana, Lesotho, and Swaziland.[29] While the OPEX assignment was shorter, the expert had a habit of hanging on, either because of his quality of training or for more personal reasons. In addition, according to Gerald Helleiner:

> When a department, research station, school or Ministry find an expatriate employee who is effective, there is every reason for the relevant local decision-maker, who may himself have been placed in authority prior to his having acquired much skill or confidence, to retain the services of the expatriate for as long as possible; the success of his own career may even be or become dependent upon him.[30]

In 1990, there were more than 80,000 expatriate workers of all nationalities living in Africa alone.[31] These expatriates worked on development projects and private sector activities proliferating throughout the underdeveloped world. In Africa, more expatriates were living there than during the colonial period prior to 1960. The size of the international consulting and technical assistance community—official and unofficial—means that it had a network of advocates for its own agenda. As Hancock argues:

> After the multi-billion-dollar "financial flows" involved have been shaken through the sieve of over-priced and irrelevant goods that must be bought in the donor countries, filtered again in the deep pockets of hundreds of thousands of foreign experts and aid agency staff, skimmed off by dishonest commission agents and stolen by corrupt Ministers and Presidents, there is really very little left to go around.[32]

Stereotypes

Interaction with the developing world has been dominated by antagonisms of ideology, culture and race for sixty years.[33] By 1950, the United States emerged from the era of arms-length diplomacy and foreign policy to engage the postwar world. In that postwar world, work done by expatriates involved in activities formerly considered the domestic affairs of a foreign country.

Motivation for providing foreign aid throughout the world was a mixture of humanitarianism, idealism, and mercantilism. Some, even in the United States, had a quasi-imperialistic view. Foreign aid became a component of a larger security system precipitated by the Cold War. The United States in Asia, and later in Africa, operated within the ambient of this *domino theory*—the fall of one country to Communism would lead another to fall as well. The overall foreign policy goal became establishment of a non-communist stable world order.

Observers tend to isolate social and economic processes from the political ones that define foreign policy.[34] Donor values often reflect social norms or historical images. Frances FitzGerald, speaking of US foreign aid in the 1950s states, "Covered with righteous platitudes," the foreign aid adviser had, "an essentially colonialist vision, born out of the same insecurity and desire for domination that had motivated" many of the European colonial officers in Africa and Asia.[35]

Colonial impulses and cultural assumptions, ethnocentric values and misperceptions were sometimes part of the picture of foreign aid and expatriate life, especially in conflict situations. Racial assumptions are sad, ugly reminders of a *primordialism* within all societies, often swept under the rug. The counter-image is of a Pollyanna-style liberalism that assumed natives could do no wrong.

The reality is, however, that from its beginnings, assistance included assumptions of donor superiority. During Vietnam, for example, Vietnamese for many Americans were "gooks." According to FitzGerald, speaking of Vietnam:

> Americans had been brought up in a pluralistic world, where even the affairs of the family are managed by compromises between its members. In the traditional Vietnamese family [and in other traditional families throughout the Third World]—a family whose customs survived even into the twentieth century—the father held absolute authority over his wife (or wives) and children.[36]

In Iraq, some assume Arabs are lazy, dirty, and animalistic. The American, whether soldier or civilian, are most often people unfamiliar with the societies in which they work and often administer donor assistance. Because of language limitations, many donors are limited to dealing with those they feel comfortable with, who they describe as honest and trustworthy, that is, those who speak English. Foreign aid and technical assistance inevitably involves cultural strangers.

Some blame assistance problems on "the ethnocentricity of the developed-world technician, his insensitivity to other cultures, and his inability to meet the challenge of new situations."[37] So, aid workers give false hope to those they work among. Their presence alone suggests the possibility of change, a possibility that will most likely never materialize. As Lorraine Adams opines, speaking of one British aid worker, "She was British; she was in a poor and angry part of Africa; therefore she must be helping."[38] To Scroggins, foreign aid was both "the noble cause [and] the great saving illusion."[39]

Critics accuse aid administrators of not being adaptive, lacking innovation, and having a low learning capacity. Donors have two effects on LDCs: they depoliticize state power and poverty, while at the same time, reinforcing bureaucratic controls.[40] The individual administrator, contractor, or adviser is often "ground down and exhausted by their bouts with developing country environments."[41] Ultimately, many lose a sense of proportion between LDC political weakness and American political power.

As 2000 approached, little had changed from nineteenth-century colonial stereotypes of the developing world. Ten years later, with the United States bogged down in Iraq and Afghanistan, aid workers, academics, and practitioners alike blamed the intemperance and volatility of "tribal" culture for the failure of donor-sponsored democracy and governance programs.

Dealing with Donors

The Donor as a Problem

Despite massive foreign aid, however, state failure was common. The result, "more often than not, [was] bad government—in its broadest sense."[42] It is within the LDC institution that failure is clearly seen. Collapse of the public sector devastates the rural poor in Africa because "enhancing public service must itself be fundamental to undertaking rural development."[43] According to Daphne Eviatar, "Although some directed forms of aid have been highly effective—like health programs providing oral rehydration therapy or vaccinations for children—the key to the overall development puzzle has remained a mystery. When you're talking about development, you're talking about wholesale transformation of a society."[44]

Nowhere is aid failure more symbolic than in Africa because with "almost half a billion people, Africa [in 1989 had] a total GDP equivalent to that of Belgium, which only has 10 million inhabitants."[45] As Pierre Landell-Mills points out, "Few would dispute that responsibility for Africa's economic crisis is shared by donor agencies and foreign advisers as well as African governments."[46] That, however, tells us little about how to address the issue. In 1989, the *Economist* asked: "How else to explain a 10% fall in income per head in black Africa between 1980 and 1987, when it was receiving foreign aid worth an average of $13 billion a year?"[47] There has to have been some form of failure. In terms of foreign aid policy, "activities of USAID for the past 30 years in most of Africa are therefore best described as welfare."[48] Aid recipients "are customers only in a notional sense that they have been given that status for the time being by USAID."[49]

Linkage of issues relating to older, traditional components of economic and social development dominates the moral debate about aid. To critics, blame is wrongly placed at the feet of LDC leadership. In two problem countries, for example, "the United States has been less successful in Jamaica and Liberia due in part to lack of cooperation with AID from these governments' leaders."[50] By the early 1990s, the world community found it difficult to respond to disasters. As a result, those debating aid blamed the impoverished countries for their woes.

Despite the perception of domestic failures, USAID worries about promoting an image of intrusion through direct interventions. Rather, as one sarcastic view of LDC state power suggests, an "embassy official said . . . covenants were preferable since they did not impact on the 'sovereign image' of Jamaica and avoided having U.S. demands brought into the open for public debate."[51] According to one critic, "grant aid, adminis-tered through USAID is scattershot."[52] Little is planned strategically and the donor was at least part of the problem.

There is an American ideology "that combines the concepts of liberty and purpose [that] has led us throughout our national history to see our-selves as morally superior and others as deficient, an attitude of 'prophetic dualism.'"[53] According to Judith Hoover, "Both perspectives demanded that we aid regions resisting 'the enemy,' either because it was morally 'right,' or because it was technically 'smart.'"[54] Former USAID Adminis-trator Brian Atwood adds, "We talk of our experience in running the old-est development program in the world. We cite the extensive network of universities and think tanks, the creative and dynamic private sector and the effective and dedicated private voluntary agencies."[55] USAID assump-tions were clear because according to Martin Wolf, "There is no alterna-tive to rapid economic growth if the aim is the alleviation of poverty." "Second," he went on, "it is no good expecting improved policies from a complacent, corrupt or criminal regime."[56]

There are odd differences in how the United States distributes aid in dif-ferent parts of the world. From the *Economist*, "In 1994 the 2.5m people affected by war in former Yugoslavia got $288 each, the 2.1m in Liberia got $24.50."[57] In many countries, recurrent assistance was not enough to maintain preexisting capital investment. Despite this, recipients often could not say no to aid, even when ongoing maintenance revenue require-ments could not be met.

Dependency on donors to fund and manage projects did not occur out of project design but rather as part of organizational imperatives. Nonetheless, some critics suggested that the process resulted in corrup-tion, decay, or destruction of institutions of public policy and surrender of national sovereignty because "aid has tended to rob states and citizens of political power and self-determination."[58] Often, the result limits degrees of policy freedom within an LDC.

The LDC Program Manager

Time and time again, a weak and unstable LDC bureaucracy has had to deal with the donor community's massive pool of well-qualified people and complicated administrative processes. Public servants often juggled two jobs, the official one that involved sitting in a dimly lit office reading newspapers and the real one, as a consultant or a part-time embassy employee or entrepreneur who started at noon and finished at 8:00.[59] In the few hours they have each day working for government, they must deal with donors and projects.

Foreign aid created two new kinds of professionals, a donor official and a recipient program manager. Recipient countries increasingly have been characterized by fragmentation in aid planning and management. Management responsibility often falls among numerous ministries and departments. At the same time, recipients do not say no to even risky schemes because they need Western funds. These risky and unsustainable projects are often part of the same package as vital activities. LDC program managers, to quote Carol Lancaster, need to have "the ability to say no."[60]

Ideally, the LDC program manager should not have problems dealing with donors. The correct way to approach the problem is to ensure that donors deal fairly and rationally with LDC program managers. In reality, this is easier said than done, and it is usually left to the LDC program officer to manage donor activities involving multiple donors and a staggering number of policies and programs within the context of weak, and often corrupt, political leadership.

By 1985, a medium-size African country would have twenty-five to thirty donor representatives and eighty or more NGOs and private foundations interacting with it. The LDC program officer will spend a great deal of time negotiating with donors and international organizations that finance construction, social programs, management training, democracy projects, and education. Organizational development stimulated by foreign aid meant a formalized structure:

> A formalized structure reduces the need to develop ad hoc understandings and engage in constant negotiations and bargaining . . . . Formalization is required to ensure financial accounting; and transparency often necessitates the formalization of agreements and reporting requirements. When significant resource commitments are introduced, even previously informal organizations tend to formalize. Institutionalizing lessons learned through partnership work also typically rely on formal processes, such as the development of standard operating procedures.[61]

Dealing with multiple donors begins with the recognition that each donor can be identified by specific characteristics and operating procedures, including both bilateral and multilateral donors, where the "rules of the game" are different. Program managers also can deal with both grants and loans, often including structural adjustment social or municipal funds, which have different and perhaps contradictory impacts upon society. Often, politicians impose decisions about technical assistance on them. To improve the process, managers need more choice on the acceptability of donor projects within the context of national programs and priorities.

As foreign aid became more permanent, donor-client relationships became part of a broader dependency problem. Ultimately, aid weakened national institutions as they became more dependent on the donor. As Judith Tendler concludes, "Dependency results from the fact that decisions affecting a nation's destiny are frequently made outside its borders."[62] For aid recipients in Eastern Europe, one of the skills that developed quickly, according to Wedel, was the ritual of listening to the foreigners with a certain skepticism. What many in power in Eastern Europe would regret was their inability to "train" the donors.[63]

Coping Strategies

Sustainability and replicability are the keys to a successful donor-supported design and implementation strategy. LDC managers must develop the capacity to ensure project sustainability, where it is desired. Increasingly, donors such as USAID see projects as a pilot for self-sustaining activity, financed by host country institutions. LDC managers, however, more likely view projects as an integral part of an already existing program or a gap-filling activity that can eventually be dropped. In both scenarios, the project would best allow for ongoing assessment. LDC program managers are aware that donor-sponsored project interventions often do not necessarily pursue these goals.[64]

Those responsible for coordination and negotiations with donors should be the most capable managers available. They should be the "best and the brightest," to use the infamous Halberstam phrase, and should be paid accordingly.[65] Given the importance and potential for tension between donor missions and LDC institutions, it behooves the latter to recruit only the best. Of the variety of strategies available, the most important is the provision of host-country personnel as program managers.

Self-sufficiency is one answer to donor relations. Rhodesia, under its unilateral declaration of independence, and even black-ruled Zimbabwe in the 1990s, contained lessons for self-help. For many years, both were able to exist without foreign aid and international diplomatic help through a rigorous program of import substitution. Apartheid South Africa even functioned as a regional donor, while postapartheid South Africa is a major recipient of donor funds.

Regional cooperation is one strategy for self-sufficiency. While there are powerful regional groupings in Asia and Latin America, (Association of

Southeast Asian Nations—ASEAN and Southern Common Market—MERCOSUR), and potentially important groups in southern Africa (Southern African Development Community—SADC) and West Africa (the Economic Community of West African States—ECOWAS), no analogous regional organizations exist in east and central Africa (with the partial exception of the Preferential Trade Area, which partly overlaps with SADC, and the limited East African Community, which links Kenya, Uganda, and Tanzania and recent additions, Rwanda and Burundi). Regional cooperation could facilitate efficient management of donors.

Since independence, attempts at continental regional collaboration have met with limited success in Africa. The African Union, and its New Partnership for Africa's Development (NEPAD) have had few successes; nor did the Organization of African Unity before it. Current attempts at regional collaboration in Africa often do little other than make life more difficult for project managers dealing with them.

At the national level, LDC program managers must speak the donor's bureaucratic language of monitoring and design requirements.[66] This means understanding the way that the donor representative works domestically in his or her own country and the nature of the administrative and political environment within which the aid mission operates.

Bureaucratic procedures and language often are little understood among LDC program managers. There is a continual presence of resident, as well as visiting, consultants, working alone or in teams to influence the dynamics of a project, either positively or negatively. LDC program managers caught between donor expectations, project dynamics, and revolving consultants can very quickly become mired down.

Speaking the donor's language also means reading the donor's voluminous aid documents. Aid missions are veritable "paper mills," and donor documents come on top of a variety of LDC documents produced. Nonetheless, if a line program officer cannot read and understand the donor-generated project materials, then they likely have lost control of the project.

Program officers need to understand donor representatives. Donor mission technical assistance personnel are often isolated from the society within which they work, often for security reasons, locking donors in and LDC officials out. Even more likely, the barriers are cultural and linguistic.

Likewise, until events prove otherwise, the LDC manager should assume donors lack knowledge about the country generally, and in particular, about the host government's development programs. Donor officials, like senior colonial administrators before them, tend to move around, making it difficult to know about countries where they are stationed.

Donor representatives are primarily oriented toward their own internal management systems, rather than the project and program goals of the LDC state. For example, USAID's internal management and congressional regulations almost totally consume the USAID official. Thus, it behooves the program officer to be aggressive in meeting with donors. Where necessary, to enforce LDC priorities, it is useful to get quiet political backing for policy demands, a sensitivity for donors.

Also important is making a realistic assessment about donor intentions. Without over-stressing the overtly political nature of foreign aid, bilateral donors, whether from a large or a small country, represent an extension of the donor country's foreign, security, and economic policy. Regardless of the host-country's political ideology, the international economic regime remains "the only game in town" when it comes to conflicting public policy choices.[67]

To get beyond the agenda of the donors, it is important for program managers to push donor coordination. It is the absence of such coordination that pulls the program officer and the LDC in a variety of directions.[68] As newly emerging donor recipients, and often newer at the rules of the game, NGOs are susceptible to multiple donor monies and the problems this can cause for managers. Training would help.

Finally, an LDC program officer can influence the aid process in a number of ways; however, above "all else, the bargaining power of the aid-receiving government or department rests upon its capacity to say 'no' and to regulate its own requests."[69] The thesis here is that an acceptable aid allocation is the outcome of a bureaucratic decision-making process, which is "subject to both bureaucratic criteria and the economic, political and other relations between the donor and recipient."[70]

Coping with Clients

LDC Failures

Foreign aid sometimes seems to search for failure. Success is seldom rewarded. "As soon as a country sorts out its economic management it finds the assistance it has been receiving shrinks."[71] The fragile state "graduates" from the donor program and is in danger of losing aid funding. Most important, foreign aid to developing countries since 1970 has not had a significant impact on either the recipient's growth rate or the LDC's economic policies. In the end, foreign aid can make a significant difference, but it can only do so when there is a domestic constituency for change within the LDC and a system of good governance in place to manage the development process.[72]

Increasingly since 1990, there have been moral as well as technical debates regarding foreign policy. Foreign aid critics argue that foreign aid can be destructive, actually causing harm or, at best, has no impact. Foreign aid workers, though they toiled in the field for many years, sometimes made things worse. As the *New York Times* reported in 2002, "The vast majority of people living in Africa, Latin America, Central Asia and the Middle East are no better off today than they were in 1989, when the fall of the Berlin Wall allowed capitalism to spread worldwide at a rapid rate."[73]

In the past, donors weakened incentives for development by supporting centrally driven nonincentive-based programs, providing aid politically motivated and propping up nonreformist governments. As a result, aid programs often focused on internal bureaucratic politics and competition rather than on societal or group motivation. At the same time, as Severine points out, "There is growing evidence to suggest that not only has foreign aid failed to mitigate critical problems of underdevelopment but quite often it has help[ed] to debilitate rather than stimulate potential productive energies in Africa."[74]

Foreign aid failure rates are disturbing. According to Blaine Harden, "The World Bank . . . found the failure rate [of its projects] was 12 percent worldwide, while the West African failure rate was 18 percent and the East African rate was 24 percent."[75] Donor failure in Africa is painful to watch. Agriculture projects alone failed one-third of the time in West Africa and half the time in East Africa. Conference after conference questions African development over the past thirty years. In 1996, for example, much of a conference on African trade "was devoted to offering prescriptions for Africa. Topping the list was the need for more openness."[76] According to Paul Lewis, "The diplomats said a World Bank report just circulated to finance ministers of member governments meeting . . . painted the gloomiest possible picture of black Africa's prospects."[77]

In Liberia, during the Samuel Doe regime, the United States gave his government nearly $500 million in economic and military aid, approximately one-third of the country's operating budget. In Kenya, according to Theroux, donor funds often "went into the pockets of politicians."[78] In the Sudan, "[a] steady flow of U.S. aid greased the wheels of [the country's] patronage machine."[79] Fungible foreign aid allowed Sudan to purchase weapons to wage war on the south for close to twenty years. Over a thirty-year period, the United States gave Zaire and Mobutu more than $2 billion in foreign assistance. In Uganda, one of the darlings of the donors in the 1990s, more than half its budget came from donors.

These African failures—or, like Uganda, near successes—were hard on donor morale. As a result, "[f]rustrated by what they perceived as the inefficiency and corruption of African governments, they channeled an increasing amount of their aid through private, non-governmental organizations such as World Vision and Oxfam."[80] The UN intervention in Somalia brought in hundreds of NGOs, which then were told to develop grants programs to fund thousands of local NGOs to deliver humanitarian assistance.

Critics describe in the best-case scenario the uselessness of foreign aid, and at worse case, the serious harm caused by aid agencies. They claim that labor-intensive projects are so few because donors impose constraints, limiting access to grants and contracts to specialized, self-interested development organizations. All foreign aid is self-serving, and human and natural disasters are welcomed as a growth opportunity. Speaking of Africa in the 1990s, Theroux said, "Africa is materially more decrepit than it was when I first knew it." He goes on, saying it's "hungrier, poorer, less educated, more pessimistic, more corrupt, and you can't tell the politicians from the witch doctors." [81]

Tolerating Corruption

The reality of the debate about corruption suggests that LDC governments appear to live on underdevelopment to survive. Debt and poverty bring in aid. Civil service salaries barely sustain workers. It is NGOs and charities that pay what passes for middle class salaries. What passes for service delivery is project-based. In this environment, widespread corruption is rampant. Speaking of Malawi, Theroux has noted, "After decades of charitable diligence, there were more charities in Malawi then ever. Charities and NGOs are now part of the Malawi economy, surely one of the larger parts."[82] Within the African middle class, by contrast, there appeared to be little evidence of volunteerism, little desire to replace aid workers, and only a dim sense of futility with regard to the future of charity.

Corruption severely challenges aid. "The U.S. General Accounting Office evaluated the bank's [World Bank] anti-corruption effort and gave a mixed review," according to a US government study in 2003.[83] According to one USAID official in the former Zaire, "It is probably not corruption in the sense, to use a David Gould academic term, that is a 'fluctuating barter' relations, we are talking about essentially a contractual relationship of some kind."[84]

During the Cold War, corrupt countries often received the lion's share of foreign aid. Between 1965 and 1988, USAID was generous with Zaire under the corrupt Mobutu, giving more than $860 million. "Recipient governments or government departments ally themselves with external donors for the pursuit of their own domestic interests against other domestic (and foreign) actors."[85]

As a program officer in Kinshasa opined to one of the authors, Zaire was essentially a "'privatized government.' What we are dealing with is a government, which does not manage collective goods or collective welfare; therefore in that sense one is living or working in anarchy from a project point of view." The official continued:

> The project concept is ideal for what I call the premium paid option. What the premium paid option essentially is, to use polite words again, it creates government departments and organizations and individuals, as though they were operating in the 'for profit' private sector, which means for example, if USAID mission in Kinshasa wants to get demographic data, or let's say they are working on a major health project for HIV/AIDS [which is a major concern in Zaire], they need to get data from the census department. Normally what you would do is request the census department for that information, however what the USAID Mission does, rather than simply doing that is that they arrange payment for that information to the Office of Census in Kinshasa, in effect to the director of that office, who is then responsible for the distribution throughout the agency. This is how the formula works. Let's say there is a rolling scale.[86]

As Zaire collapsed in corruption and poverty, the donor community maintained a level of innocence and ignorance about conditions within the country. How else could one explain the level of foreign aid, $9.3 billion, between 1975 and 1997? To their critics, donors were the problem in Zaire. As Martin Wolf intones, "It is no good expecting improved policies from a complacent, corrupt or criminal regime."[87]

To aid's critics, it is donors who caused the waste and corruption by encouraging LDCs to aspire to a level of rapid industrialization impossible to achieve. As a result, huge capital projects gave ample scope for patronage, bribes, and huge Western contracts. Often, foreign aid was tied to the purchase of the donor country's exports and the use of its personnel.[88] According to Wolf, "The examples of wasted aid were all too depressing: in Tanzania, for example, $2bn went into roads but the network was no better afterwards because of poor maintenance."[89]

One academic thesis portrays the organizational environment as playing a central role in determining the context of development assistance. "Organizational turpentine" is the term sometimes used to describe the need for a cleansing process. It is within the LDC organization that corruption must be addressed. As Jeffery Sachs points out, "For developing countries to achieve rapid growth in today's global economy, they must embrace private, rather than state, ownership of business. They must be receptive to foreign trade, technology, ideas and investment, and they must have governments that accept the rule of law and curb corruption."[90] At the same time, amid the normality of corruption, there is much that functions normally even in the collapsed state.

Interactions between Donors and Program Officers

Effective control of aid by both program officers and donor officials assigned to manage it is essential to success. "Just as the 'policy adviser' cannot come to grips with the administrative process," according to Edward Horesh, "still less can the professional foreigner understand the most elementary social processes unless . . . there are 'enough local professional colleagues to save the outsider from most indiscretions.'"[91] LDC project managers must contend with is the variety of donor rules and regulations.

At a basic level, the manager faces donors who are "hard," as opposed to those who are "soft." For example, US technical assistance, with its congressional and administrative regulatory and reporting requirements, is often classified as a "hard," while Germany. Sweden, Norway, and Denmark are considered "soft," with very simple procedures for activating money.[92]

Just as there are hard donors, there are hard clients. India's judicious use of foreign aid in the 1960s and 1970s comes to mind. It is the LDC itself that can take the initiative to bring technical assistance activity under control. At that point, donors may become more conscious of the need to "cope with clients." One important set of skills and processes identified are the development of suitable donor, donor mission, and LDC participating agency procedures, and the teaching of those concepts and procedures to host country cooperants. This is a neglected area in management training and education.

The nature of the resident mission in the host country has an impact upon an LDC program manager as well. One factor is the size of the mission. A USAID mission in Mauritania will be a very different organization than the huge factory that is the USAID mission in Egypt or Pakistan or in post-Saddam Iraq. A small donor mission will often be much more attune to the local situation. In a small mission, technical assistance officials more likely will be personally close to program managers at the operational level, and relatively small amounts of money spent may have a greater impact than very large expenditures. In one small West African USAID mission in the late 1980s, the security door to the office was held open by a heavy brick to allow unfettered access. This sent a message to host country officials who visited the mission. In the wake of 9/11, of course, this would not be acceptable.

The LDC program officer will find it very difficult to communicate with large missions. With large missions, there is almost no potential for communications control, other than at the political and, in some cases, the head-of-state level. These donor "factories" often process money in the same way that oil refineries process fossil fuel (quick and dirty). Part of the hopelessness of dealing with donors in Iraq and Afghanistan has been the shear volume of donor and military officials interacting with Iraqi program officers, all in the pristine environment of the green zone.

Donor missions also differ in the extent to which they have delegated authority from their home capitals. Some donors, such as Swedish SIDA and USAID, delegate a great deal of authority to in-country personnel. Other donors, such as Canadian and German technical assistance, are highly centralized with little in-country discretion. In the case of German technical assistance, there is sometimes no field operation.[93] Donors also increasingly rely on personnel services contractors, including third-country (foreign) nationals. These personnel often have no institutional memory or administrative training in aid procedures, and their short-term narrow expertise precludes them from seeing the "big picture."

After more than a half-century of aid dependence, foreign aid has become a part of the LDC economic culture. In the 1970s through the 1990s, many countries tended to accept any aid, technical assistance, and loans that were offered. LDC governments often used aid to purchase items politically desirable but not necessary socially or economically necessary. As one World Bank report has put it, "[d]onors should take it for granted that their financing is fungible because that is reality."[94] In some cases, aid is simply used as a no-cost add-on to domestic funding.

Conclusion

From the perspective of the LDC manager, it is important that project design, implementation strategies, and assessment documents reveal both donor and host-country contextual factors that may impede successful and sustainable intervention. These include: (1) key stakeholders' concerns over the final product of the intervention; (2) a strategy for a replicability effect of design activities within the host country; and (3) a strategy for successor activities, where appropriate, after the completion of a project.

Several themes have characterized foreign aid since the 1950s. Thirty years of donor intervention in support of management and development taught us little about sustainability; however, it is sustainability that is often the key to program development. Secondly, human resource development (and particularly education and training) is often the key to sustainable program activity. Often, without human skills, the foreign aid project cannot be successful however.

Management skills as both art and science are important to development policy implementation. Handling the myriad problems resulting from intervention in the LDC development process is a neglected area of LDC management skills. Program managers need specific training to deal with donor-supported projects. Donor managers need to be aware of the skills needed to "cope with their clients," the recipients of technical assistance.

This chapter and the last has examined the role that international technical assistance plays in professional development, management training, and in improving management performance. Attention needs to be paid to intervention strategies that have an impact on the capacity of host country educational and training institutions.

In many LDCs, economies of scale preclude development of a full complement of national-level training and educational institutions in each country. In the African case, there would seem to be little option but to develop a strategy that targets the development of regional or even continental educational and training institutions as centers of excellence. This replicates a pattern of institutional development successfully applied to Latin America and Asia a generation ago.[95]

Strategic intervention strategies should have a greater impact upon LDC development-oriented educational and training institutions and on managerial personnel in the public and private sector. Given the "economies of scale" problem, a successful strategy of institutional development will be a human resource/management development strategy targeted at those regional organizations that have the potential to develop high-quality training, research programs, and services.[96] Such a strategy shows more potential than a pure economic growth or privatization one.

Three arguments need to be made. First, donor interventions will not be successful unless strong priority is given to institutional development and capacity building strategies. Secondly, institutional development can only occur if there is significant sectoral donor coordination between and among technical assistance missions. Finally, it is up to host-country program officers to set priorities between and among donors and to ensure that donor money reaches recipient country institutions. This in turn requires that LDC program managers have the skills to manage donor-financed projects.

Since the 1950s, both bilateral (particularly US donor agencies) and multilateral organizations have framed the foreign aid agenda and shaped the values, processes, and debates that came to dominate foreign aid though private, foundation, and nongovernmental involvement has remained important. The donor agenda assumed that both LDCs and the developed states would benefit from foreign aid and technical assistance. Effective foreign aid in a developing country requires a long-term vision of systematic change, support for knowledge generation, politically well-placed champions for aid in both donor and recipient countries, and the engagement of civil society. Specifically, effective foreign aid requires more space for civil society.

Development assistance is most successful when there are predictable internal institutions of governance, fair international rules of the game, and targeted foreign aid that includes support for human resource development. To be successful, foreign aid should be primarily focused on governance, incentives, educational support, and human resource development rather than economic growth.

An important aid goal should be development of a pool of trained professionals who are comfortable with competition for positions in government—the private or the nonprofit sectors—who operate in an environment that provides for incentives for action, and who can provide policy (and political) leadership for their countries. An action-oriented social-development component involving civil society in development programs is important.

The key to development, this book argues, is creation of sustainable human capital through investments in education, health, and social capital networks through support for democratic governance civil society. Only after a country has the human and social capital, good governance and the management skills to handle it, can (and should) a country seek out large capital infusions or make structural changes in economic patterns because the misuse of capital investment can lead to financial disaster.

Notes

1. E. Philip Morgan, "Why Aid Fails: An Organizational Interpretation," Public Lecture, Institute of Development Management (July 19, 1979), p. 1.

2. Scroggins, *Emma's War,* p. 307.

3. Harlan Cleveland, Gerard J. Mangone, John Clarke Adams, *The Overseas Americans* (New York: McGraw-Hill, 1960), p. 133.

4. Graham Hancock, *Lords of Poverty: The Power, Prestige and Corruption of the International Aid Business* (New York: Atlantic Monthly Press, 1989), p. 21.

5. Cleveland, et al., *The Overseas Americans,* p. 154.

6. Emery Roe, *Except-Africa: Remaking Development, Rethinking Power* (New Brunswick, NJ: Transaction Publishers, 1999), p. ix.

7. Blaine Harden, *Africa: Dispatches from a Fragile Continent* (Boston: Houghton Mifflin Company, 1990), p. 13.

8. Graham Greene, *The Quiet American* (Harmondsworth, UK: Penguin, 1973).

9. Both quotes from Scroggins, *Emma's War*, pp. 8–9 and 65.

10. "The Missionaries' Position," *Economist* (April 24, 1993), p. 36.

11. John Franklin Campbell, *The Foreign Affairs Fudge Factory* (New York: Basic Books, 1971), p. 77.

12. Paul Theroux, "Tarzan is an Expatriate," *Transition*, no. 21 (1967), pp. 13–19.

13. Okot p'Bitek, "Foreign 'Experts' and Peace Corps swarm the Country Like White Ants," *Transition*, no. 21 (1967), p. 20.

14. Both quotes from Mark Hertsgaard, *The Eagle's Shadow: Why America Fascinates and Infuriates the World* (New York: Picador Books, 2003), pp. 68 and 89.

15. Hancock, *Lords of Poverty*, p. 31. Others would point to the cynicism of Hancock, who it was allegedly discovered was on contract to Mengistu Haile Mariam, who was the Marxist dictator of Ethiopia when he wrote his book on foreign aid.

16. Campbell, *The Foreign Affairs Fudge Factory*, p. 179.

17. Both quotes from Theroux, *Dark Star Safari*, pp. 146 and 158.

18. Ibid., p. 148.

19. Scroggins, *Emma's War*, p. 66.

20. Michael Maren, *The Road to Hell* (New York: Free Press, 1997), p. 12.

21. Ibid., p. 40.

22. Edward W. Weidner, *Technical Assistance in Public Administration Overseas: The Case for Development Administration* (Chicago: Public Administration Service, 1964), p. 59.

23. Maren, *The Road to Hell*, p. 92.

24. M. Peter McPherson, "As a Development Agency," in *Making a Difference: the Peace Corps at Twenty-Five*, Milton Viorst, ed. (New York: Weidenfeld & Nicholson, 1986), p. 105.

25. Judith Tendler, *Inside Foreign Aid,* (Baltimore: Johns Hopkins University Press, 1975), p. 27.

26. Scroggins, *Emma's War*, p. 67.

27. Notes on the "Memories of Empire" Conference held at the Institute of Commonwealth Studies, University of London, Held on June 27–28, 2005. One of the current authors (Picard) participated in the first training program of the Peace Corps that evolved out of the TEA

program at Teachers College, Columbia University, August–December 1965.

28. "Administrator Announces Personnel Reductions," *Front Lines, USAID* (April–May 1996), p. 3.

29. Louis A. Picard, Personal Notes, June 1980, Author's Research Diary. One of the present authors (Picard) served as an OPEX specialist in Botswana from January 1980 to December 1981.

30. Gerald K. Helleiner, "Aid and Dependence in Africa: Issues for Recipients," *The Politics of Africa: Dependence and Development,* Timothy M. Shaw and Kenneth A. Heard, ed. (London: Longman, 1979), p. 239.

31. Severine M. Rugumamu, *Lethal Aid: The Illusion of Socialism and Self-Reliance in Tanzania* (Trenton, NJ: Africa World Press, 1997), p. 163.

32. Hancock, *Lords of Poverty*, p. 190.

33. Edmund Stillman and William Pfaff, *Power and Impotence: The Failure of America's Foreign Policy* (New York: Random House, 1966), p. 60.

34. John D. Montgomery, *The Politics of Foreign Aid: American Experience in Southeast Asia* (New York: Praeger, 1962), p. 3.

35. Frances FitzGerald, *Fire in the Lake: The Vietnamese and the Americans in Vietnam* (New York: Vintage, 1972), p. 462.

36. FitzGerald, *Fire in the Lake*, p. 19.

37. Tendler, *Inside Foreign Aid*, p. 23.

38. Lorraine Adams, review of *Emma's War* by Deborah Scroggins in *Book World Washington Post* (November 10, 2002), p. 3.

39. Scroggins, *Emma's War*, p. 344.

40. James Ferguson, *The Anti-Politics Machine: "Development," Depoliticization and Bureaucratic Power in Lesotho* (Cambridge: Cambridge University Press, 1990), pp. 255–256.

41. Tendler, *Inside Foreign Aid*, p. 13.

42. Barbara Crossette, "Givers of Foreign Aid Shifting Their Methods," *New York Times* (February 23, 1992), p. A2.

43. Roe, *Except-Africa*, p. 118.

44. Daphne Eviatar, "Do Aid Studies Govern Policies or Reflect Them?" *New York Times* (July 26, 2003), p. A19.

45. Pierre Landell-Mills, Ramgopal Agarwala, and Stanley Please, "From Crisis to Sustainable Growth in Sub-Saharan Africa," *Finance and Development* (Johannesburg, South Africa, December 1989), p. 26.

46. Ibid.

47. "Aiding Africa," *Economist* (November 25, 1989), p. 47.

48. Samuel W. Shoen, "USAID Africa Bureau; Strategic Analysis and Recommendations for the 1990's" (Working Draft, September 9, 1991), p. 3.

49. David Hirschmann, "'Customer Service' in the United States Agency for International Development: An Example of Designing a Democracy Program in Bangladesh," *Administration and Society*, 31, no.1 (March 1999), p. 116.

50. Frank C. Conahan, "Foreign Assistance: U.S. Use of Conditions to Achieve Economic Reforms," (GAO Report to USAID, August 1986).

51. Conahan, "Foreign Assistance," p. 30.

52. Janine R. Wedel, "Getting It Right in Aid to Russia," *New York Times* (April 5, 1992), p. A15.

53. Judith Hoover, "Ronald Reagan's Failure to Secure Contra-Aid: A Post-Vietnam Shift in Foreign Policy Rhetoric," *Presidential Studies Quarterly*, 24, no. 3, (Summer 1994), p. 536.

54. Ibid.

55. Brian J. Atwood, "The Future of Foreign Aid." Speech, to the Advisory Committee on Voluntary Foreign Aid (Washington, DC: U.S. Agency for International Development, March 12, 1996).

56. Both quotes from Wolf, "Aid, Hope and Charity," p. 12.

57. "Falling Fast," *Economist* (June 22, 1996), p. 44.

58. David Sogge, *Give and Take: What's the Matter with Foreign Aid?* (London: Zed Books, 2002), p. 178.

59. Michela Wrong, *In the Footsteps of Mr. Kurtz: Living on the Brink of Disaster in Mobutu's Congo* (New York: Harper Collins, 2001), p. 152.

60. Carol Lancaster, *Aid to Africa* (Chicago: University of Chicago, 1999) p. 226.

61. Jennifer Brinkerhoff, *Partnership for International Development* (Boulder, CO; Lynne Reinner, 2002), p. 84.

62. Tendler, *Inside Foreign Aid*, p. 109.

63. Janine R. Wedel, *Collision and Collusion: The Strange Case of Western Aid to Eastern Europe, 1989–1998* (New York: St. Martins Press, 1998), pp. 2–3.

64. The problem is not new. Back in 1962, John Montgomery pointed to what he called the problems of mutuality in donor-host country relationships. See Montgomery, *The Politics of Foreign Aid*.

65. David Halberstam, *The Best and the Brightest* (New York: William Morrow, 1972). Of course Halberstam used the term ironically.

66. This has nothing to do with whether or not officers in a donor mission speak French, English, German, or Russian as a first language, though these language skills are important as well.

67. William P. Avery and Louis A. Picard, "Collective Self-Reliance as a Counterdependency Strategy in Africa and Latin America," (Unpublished Paper, 1985).

68. India comes to mind as a country that takes a very strong management role vis-a-vis donors.

69. Gerald K. Helleiner, "Aid and Dependence in Africa: Issues for Recipients," in *The Politics of Africa: Dependence and Development*, T. Shaw and K. Heard, eds. (New York: Africana Publishing Group, 1979), p. 242.

70. Mark McGillivray and Howard White, "Explanatory Studies of Aid Allocation Among Developing Countries: A Critical Survey," Working Paper Series No. 148, (Institute of Social Studies, The Hague, April 1993), p. 68.

71. Wolf, "Aid, Hope and Charity," p. 13.

72. Stephanie Flanders, "Foreign Aid Has Little Impact, Says World Bank Study," *Financial Times* (April 14, 1997), p. 18.

73. Joseph Kahn, "Losing Faith: Globalization Proves Disappointing," *New York Times* (March 21, 2002), p. A3.

74. Rugumamu, *Lethal Aid,* p. 1.

75. Harden, *Africa*, p. 188.

76. Rose Umoren, "US Trade with Africa Grows, Aid Shrinks," *Citizen* (Johannesburg, June 19, 1996), p. 6.

77. Paul Lewis, "World Bank Plan for Aid to Africa Divides Members," *New York Times* (September 16, 1984), p. A1.

78. Theroux, *Dark Star Safari*, p. 159.

79. Bill Berkeley, *The Graves Are Not Yet Full* (New York: Basic Books, 2002), p. 212.

80. Scroggins, *Emma's War*, p. 66.

81. See Ibid., pp. 192–193.

82. Ibid., p. 291.

83. Jonathan Finer, "World Bank Focused on Fighting Corruption," *Washington Post* (July 4, 2003), p. E2.

84. Interview, USAID official, Kinshasa, Zaire, April 1989 Author's Research Diary. See David J. Gould, *Bureaucratic corruption and underdevelopment in the Third World: The Case of Zaire* (New York: Pergamon Press, 1980).

85. Gerald K. Helleiner, "Aid and Dependence in Africa: Issues for Recipients," p. 234.

86. Both quotes from Interview, USAID official, Kinshasa, Zaire, April 1989.

87. Wolf, "Aid, Hope and Charity," p. 13.

88. "The Rights and Wrongs of Aid," *Independent* (August 20, 1991), p. 14.

89. Wolf, "Aid, hope and charity," p. 13. Edward Horesh contended in 1981 that "the preoccupations of the leaders of the "development" profession, in their role of experts, has led to an overemphasis in teaching and research on policy recommendation rather than empirical work and conceptual analysis, which should properly include studies of the policy decisions of those in power. Edward Horesh, "Academics and Experts or the Death of the High Level Technical Assistant," *Development and Change*, 12, no.4 (October 1981) p. 615.

90. Jeffrey D. Sachs, "When Foreign Aid Makes a Difference," *New York Times* (February 3, 1997), p. A17.

91. Horesh, "Academics and Experts or the Death of the High Level Technical Assistant," p. 612.

92. David Jones, *Aid and Development in Southern Africa: British Aid to Botswana, Lesotho and Swaziland* (London: Croom Helm, 1977), pp. 139–141.

93. According to officials of the German Fund for Technical Cooperation, interviews with one of the authors (Picard), February, 1987, Author's Research Diary. In the development of the Management Resource Unit in 1985–1986, Picard recalls one case where a visiting German technical assistance delegation moved around the SADCC region with a German language project document that they referred to obliquely in discussions with SADCC program managers.

94. *Assessing Aid*, p. 80.

95. Samuel Paul, *Training for Public Administration and Management in Developing Countries: A Review* (Washington, DC: World Bank Staff Working Papers, 1983), pp. 18–21.

96. References to regional collaboration and to regional institutions should be understood to involve international cooperation between two or more countries in an area to training or education.

13

DEBATES INTO THE TWENTY-FIRST CENTURY

A rational government implies acceptance of institutional pluralism at a minimum.

Jennifer M. Brinkerhoff, *Partnership for International Development*

Experienced aid hands know that development concepts are generated at universities, accepted as profound by policy types in Washington, and declared as gospel.

Michael Maren, *The Road to Hell*

With Mr. Bush pressing other countries to knock down their trade barriers and expand open markets, his approval of an 80 percent increase in farm subsidies—with all the advantages that confers on American grain exports—is viewed as a move in the opposite direction.

Elizabeth Becker, "Raising Farm Subsidies, US Widens International Rift"

Contemporary Debates

This chapter looks at five contemporary issues that define the debates about foreign aid policy in the wake of September 11:

- Unilateralism and multilateralism divisions
- Human security, democracy and governance promotion
- Trade and investment approaches
- The Millennium Challenge Account as a new model
- The new triangulation between foreign aid, diplomacy, and security.

Unilateralism vs. Multilateralism

Despite the end of the Cold War in 1991, there were more than twenty-seven conflicts in twenty-six locations throughout the world during the

1980s and 1990s. All but two were civil wars. Policymakers dubbed several as terrorist incursions. While isolationist impulses remained, the United States after 1991 tended to swing back and forth between multilateralism and an isolationist-like interventionism referred to as unilateralism. To quote Mark Hertsgaard: "American elites sometimes talk of our nation's isolationist tendencies, but the correct adjective is unilateralist. The United States has hardly shunned overseas involvement over the years; we simply insist on setting our own terms."[1]

The story of foreign aid post–September 11 starts with Somalia, its links to Osama bin Laden, and the evolving unilateral role the United States first carved out at that time and then temporarily abandoned. After the collapse of the Somali government in 1991, the United States and the UN intervened with humanitarian programs. In addition to a temporary military force, the international intervention in Somalia (1993–1995) drew in hundreds of international NGOs to develop grant programs to fund thousands of local NGOs. The intervention began as humanitarian assistance but ended in confrontation with Somalia warlords.

"Blowback" was a CIA term "for how foreign policy can come back to haunt a country years after in unforeseen ways."[2] Blowback defined the intervention, and later the abandonment of Somalis, and the impact that the Somalia debacle would have on foreign policy for the next decade, leading to the capture of Somalia by Islamic fundamentalists and a US-sponsored Ethiopian intervention, and finally a dominant role for modern day pirates. The term "blowback," characterized the "Blackhawk Down" tragedy in Somalia, as well as US foreign aid policy. Nowhere was this pattern more clearly defined than in the months after September 11, 2001.

The Somalia incident was an exercise of control and overreach by the United States—which did not have sufficient force available—into a part of the world policymakers did not understand.[3] Somalia, like Iraq, was an international intervention quickly gone awry. According to a fierce critic of policy in Somalia:

> The violent events that occurred [in Somalia] in 1993 were not an aberration; they were, in fact, foreign aid carried out to its logical extreme. Foreign aid run amok. The desire to help had— as it almost always does—become the desire to control. In a routine foreign aid situation there is [a] local government, even a corrupt local government, to check the tendency of aid organizations toward control. There is a point at which the interests of the aid organizations clash with the interests of the government.[4]

By 1993, the Americans had become isolated from the Somalis that they hoped to save. Shortly after the Blackhawk Down massacre of nineteen of its soldiers, the United States announced it would withdraw from Somalia, a development seen as a victory for Osama bin Laden and al-Qaeda. The UN withdrew from Somalia on March 3, 1995. What followed was ten years of near anarchy, with modest humanitarian assistance.

After ten years of chaos, warlords and an orphan interim government (virtually unsupported by the United States and international community) were overthrown by the Islamic Court Union (ICU) whose leader, Sheikh Sharif Sheikh Ahmed, declared on June 2, 2006, that he would bring the Islamic revolution to Somalia. Three days later, the ICU wrested control of Mogadishu and about one-half the country. In December 2006, the United States sponsored an Ethiopian intervention to restore the provisional government.

Following Somalia, where bin Laden had sponsored one of the anti-American warlords in 1992, the al-Qaeda leader directed a series of other terrorist events, beginning with the first bombing of the World Trade Center on February 26, 1993. Bin Laden directed the 1998 American embassy bombings in Dar es Salaam, Tanzania, and Nairobi, Kenya, and sponsored, directly or indirectly, the USS Cole bombing, the Bali nightclub bombings in Indonesia, the Madrid and London train bombings, as well as bombings in the Jordanian capital of Amman and in Egypt's Sinai peninsula. Al-Qaeda was also said to be involved in the Lebanon conflict and in the confrontation between Israel and Hamas. Most importantly, bin Laden attacked the United States on September 11, 2001.

After September 11, the US reaction increasingly has been to strike back when its interests are threatened, refusing to accept international criticism, and in effect thumbing its nose at the UN.[5] To Robert Kaplan, "A great philosophical schism has opened within the West, and instead of mutual indifference, mutual antagonism threatens to debilitate both sides of the trans-Atlantic community."[6] The problem became more than a polemic, according to David Sanger, "The prevailing view focuses not on the dangers, but on the limited options for doing anything about them."[7]

In reality, according some observers, the Bush administration intended to promote unilateralism—influenced by neoconservatives who dominated Bush foreign policy (Bush himself, Vice President Dick Chaney, Secretary Rumsfeld, and Deputy Secretary Paul Wolfowitz among others)— independent of the terrorist attacks. The decision was not cluttered or haphazard; it was a deliberate choice. According to Rick Barton of the Clinton administration, "There was a clear choice [within the Bush administration]—unilateralism, occupation and change in the Middle East."[8] Iraq was the focal point. Observers and critics of the Bush administration predicted a deepening disorder throughout the world.[9] As William D. Hartung put it, "George W. Bush has adopted an aggressive, unilateralist foreign policy that reflects unbridled imperial attitudes not seen since the peak period of direct interventionism in Latin America in the early decades of the twentieth century."[10] Unilateralism unfolded in foreign and security policy and foreign assistance in the Middle East and Horn of Africa.

Bush's neoconservative unilateralism included "an ambitious reordering of the world through preemptive and, if necessary, unilateral action to reduce suffering and bring peace."[11] Since the al-Qaeda attacks, policymakers assumed only America could solve the political and security problems of the world, and increasingly the term unilateralism came to be widely debated. Unilateralism had become the other side of the coin to historical policies of isolationism.

This does not mean there was consensus within the Bush administration. There were "deep ideological schisms that had rent Bush's national security team throughout the first term."[12] State, headed by Secretary Powell, tended to be more multilateral in their worldview and cautious about military intervention. Unilateral pressures intensified, however.

Wherever it occurred, intervention led to increased foreign aid and intervention, a pattern illustrated by Iraq and NATO involvement in Afghanistan. Some unilateralists argue, in the context of the likes of Osama bin Laden, that there must be a new imperialism that will bring parts of the world again under Western control in the war on terrorism.[13] For Niall Ferguson, the issue raised by Somalia, Afghanistan, Iraq, and other crises is whether after 2001 there was a need to reorder the world in a way that replicates some elements of empire.[14]

For the United States, the choice came down to either a unilateral approach to international order or a return to collective leadership. As Ferguson, a radical unilateralist, has put it, "The hypothesis . . . is a step in the direction of political globalization, with the United States shifting from informal to formal empire much as late Victorian Britain once did." The United States should accept this global burden but fears that the American Empire "lacks the drive to export its capital, its people and its culture to those backward regions which need them most urgently and which, if they are neglected, will breed the greatest threats to its [and the world's] security."[15] Critics of unilateralism and aggressive multilateralism suggest that these conditionalities smacked of old-fashioned colonialism, a concept not necessarily rejected by the "neocons."

In the bridge between foreign, security, and foreign aid policy, we see a disproportionate power distribution between LDCs and Western countries. A system of aid chains, linkages of power, and influence have developed. They function as top-down mechanisms of control.[16]

Pulling Back from Unilateralism

There was political opposition in Defense, especially the military, and in State to the Iraq invasion since 2001; however, the Bush Administration made it clear that opponents of the invasion would be replaced with Republican Party loyalists. Loyalty was the key.

The Pentagon claimed politics were not a factor in replacing professional USAID and State officials with administration loyalists. The mainstream press remained skeptical. After troops found no weapons of mass destruction and the Pentagon admitted to having no plan for reconstruction, Secretary Powell concluded that the war had "gone sour."[17]

Despite the threat of military intervention, foreign aid influences remained informal or soft, exercised through economic, cultural, and in some cases, military means rather than through formal institutional (or colonial) structures. Foreign aid policy was central. Powell protected USAID at times, filling noncareer slots in the agency with career officers, most of whom held traditionalist views of foreign aid.

During the Bush administration, prior to when the Republican Party lost control of both the House and the Senate in November 2006, "the United States [exercised] power unimpeded by partnerships, alliances and rules—and without apology for its imperial [superpower] status."[18] Unilateralism became increasingly rigid, and part of what one writer called "a neo-imperial agenda." In both foreign aid and security terms, this neo-imperialism in allying the United States "with repressive regimes, overriding human rights conditionalities on U.S. aid, violating the conventions of international law, and standing behind a policy of 'regime changes' and first strikes [were] all acceptable means in Bush's endless war against evil."[19]

Within a few months of the Iraq invasion, the presumption of a long-term occupation, the basis of action until that time, evaporated. The Bush administration moved the timetable forward on the electoral and constitutional processes and on installation of an Iraqi government; however, despite this, and the commitment to obscene amounts of foreign aid, the United States became embroiled in quagmire as Americans became disenchanted with military casualties and financial burdens in what had become a three-sided civil war. The 2006 surge may have ameliorated the situation but has not addressed the fundamental political competition within in Iraq.

Within the Bush administration, muffled critics of Iraq policy, such as Colin Powell, believed that consequences of Iraq might bode ill for foreign policy and aid. Powell said, when speaking of Iraq, that the United States would end up owning this place and would have to assume the aspirations, hopes, and all the troubles and fears of the Iraqi.

Criticism of the war became partisan by 2004 once Democrats sent mixed signals. Democratic presidential candidate John Kerry (in voting against the first Gulf War) had criticized President Bush for assembling a Persian Gulf War coalition that amounted to a so-called "Pax Americana," though the 1991 Gulf War was clearly a multilateral intervention. Kerry then went on to vote for the Iraq war while criticizing the Bush administration for bungling it and failing to enlist the UN and key European allies in the conflict.[20]

Multilateralism versus unilateralism should have been debated but was not. Much of the international community saw Afghanistan differently from Iraq because "in contrast to Afghanistan, where reconstruction has been carried out under aegis of the UN, in Iraq it has been led almost exclusively by Americans—and not Americans . . . with long records of working with the international community in alien environments."[21] The Afghan intervention, from its beginning, had a strong international coalition, albeit led by the United States.

Iraq had been a US operation from the beginning. There was, according to Powell, a Bush White House machismo "that targeted any criticism of the administration or suggested weakness."[22] From a European perspective, as then–French foreign minister Dominique de Villepin put it, "The struggle was not so much about Iraq as it was about 'two visions of the world.'"[23] According to Robert Kaiser, "The [Iraq] war has damaged the good name of the United States in every corner of the globe, has cost unanticipated scores of billions [all of it borrowed] and now threatens long-term damage to our Army and National Guard."[24]

After the invasion, critiques of unilateralism began to appear. At issue was how to limit casualties, or the perception of them, and to "'accelerate' the handover of sovereignty to Iraq by the end of June [2004]—an adequate four months before the U.S. elections."[25] There was reluctance in "even defining the situation . . . perhaps the most telling indicator of a collective cognitive dissidence on part of the U.S. Army to recognize a war of rebellion, a people's war, even when they were fighting it."[26] The declining security situation neither allowed for foreign aid support at a level that would stabilize the country nor anticipated withdrawal.

Unilateralism already has a "retro" feel, as the United States moves haltingly toward a post-Iraq world. Instead of unilateralism, the world will require more "'internationalism' than before, and the novel experience of cooperating widely with associates who are no longer satellites or dependents—as well as with the enemy of the past forty years."[27] In 2007, despite the unfinished business in Iraq, the leaders of both Germany and France had reached out to the United States. In a post–September 11 world:

> The United States has a strategic problem: its war on terror, unlike its long fight against Communism, is not universally seen as the pivotal global struggle of the age. Rather, it is often

portrayed abroad as a distraction from more critical issues—as an American attempt to impose a bellicose culture, driven by the cultivation of fear, on a world still taken with the notion that the cold war's end and technology's advance have opened unprecedented possibilities for dialogue and peace.[28]

After the United States bogged down in Iraq, multilateralism made a comeback. As Glenn Kesler noted in late 2004, "Secretary of State Colin L. Powell [departed] on a weeklong trip to consult with an alphabet soup of European multilateral institutions and confabs, carrying a message that the second-term Bush administration [was] ready to work closely on forging what officials have dubbed 'effective multilateralism.'"[29] Foreign aid accompanied this shift as alternatives to unilateral intervention were proposed.[30] Jane Perlez has put it this way:

On the theory that ignorance and poor education are among the reasons that young people are drawn to radical Islam, the Agency for International Development has been revamping its programs in Muslim countries in the last two years to spend more on schools and less on other things, including family planning.[31]

As late as mid-2005, critics argued Iraq was still not ready for foreign aid.[32] Eventually, policymakers established the Office of Reconstruction and Humanitarian Assistance under Defense. In 2007, an "Iraq Czar" was established in the White House to spearhead policy. Military leadership in Iraq and in the Pentagon was replaced. State created an Office of Coordinator for Reconstruction and Stabilization. Nation-building came back on the agenda, but in critical countries it would either be exclusively managed by Defense or through triangulation between Defense, State, and USAID. The problem in Defense, according to the director of national security, was senior officials had independent fiefdoms and liked big concepts, but "[t]hey don't do implementation."[33] How to withdraw from Iraq without victory remains at the top of the agenda.

In 2007 and 2008, the Bush administration pursued multilateral approaches to foreign policy and foreign aid. When North Korea, a rough nation with nuclear weapons, tested them over the Pacific Ocean in an attempt to intimidate the United States, South Korea, and Japan, the United States insisted that the conflict be resolved through multiparty talks in the region with foreign aid—in the form of food and energy assistance—as incentives. Likewise, when Iran defied the UN and began producing weapons-grade plutonium, allegedly for use in its nuclear power facilities, the United States supported the UN and European diplomatic efforts rather than using force. Critics suggested, however, that US policies (or a neglect of multilateral cooperation with its European allies) have pushed Russia away from Europe and toward authoritarianism.

Human Security and Conflict Mediation

Jan Egeland of the UN argued in 2004 that there was global-wide declining support for humanitarian foreign aid. His solution to the dilemma was to ask countries to increase taxes to fund more aid, not a popular option. Neglect of genocide in Rwanda and Darfur are only the latest examples of this. Increasingly, debates about the nature of foreign aid and security assistance likely delayed a solution for human security. These were the views of a UN panel, chaired by Ernesto Zedillo, the former president of Mexico, including Robert E. Rubin, the former treasury secretary. Egeland went on, "Humanitarian aid workers who are impartial and needed to save thousands are often caught in the political crossfire. Terrorists and others are targeting us."[34]

After 1985, humanitarian aid became important, as ethnic conflict and economic pressures of structural adjustment led to state collapse in parts of Asia, the Middle East, Central America, and importantly, sub-Saharan Africa. By 1996 US emergency aid was increasing and took up 10 percent of the total aid budget. Back in 1991, it had been only 1.5 percent of the whole.[35] Some donor countries, including the United States, put human rights conditionalities into aid programs and focused, at least in rhetorical terms, on democracy and governance. Over time, humanitarian concerns led donors to support human rights, rule of law and democracy, and governance programs.

David Reiff explained the human rights emphasis in 1996: "From the civil wars in Somalia and Bosnia to the current crisis in Zaire, it has been the international aid agencies who have most strongly and consistently called for military intervention in humanitarian disasters."[36] Conflict resolution and human security issues became a part of the discourse on aid. In March 2002, President Bush advocated a three-year $5 billion increase in foreign assistance to poor countries that support human rights, adhere to strong systems of law, and were moving toward open markets.[37]

At the same time, those areas most in need are sometimes excluded from traditional foreign aid. In 2003, in the province of Aceh, Indonesia, where the UN estimated that 100,000 people had been displaced as a result of fighting, there were no foreign aid workers because Indonesia refused to give them permits.[38] Likewise, when a cyclone devastated Burma in 2008, its ruling military junta refused to allow aid workers into the country to deliver food and begin reconstruction. Months would pass before aid workers gained access. According to Mary B. Anderson, in an important book about foreign aid and conflict mediation, "[w]hen international assistance is given in the context of violent conflict, it becomes a part of that context and thus also of the conflict."[39]

USAID established the Office of Transition Initiatives (OTI) in the early 1990s to address conflict resolution, democratization, and the political change processes within in its institutional development framework. Prior to this, USAID negotiated political development, governance, and political elite-directed reforms. OTI focused on fragile states and sought a rapid on-the-ground entry in troubled countries, especially during political transitions. According to Rick Barton, OTI's first director, the Office was to pull failed and failing states back from the brink of collapse. The program represents, "the current best hope for development in many states. There is much denial in foreign aid/foreign policy circles regarding how we got into a situation like this [reconstructing states] but it is there and must be addressed."[40]

OTI has special crisis waiver authority to fund and execute its operations, including political interventions involving ethnic conflict in remote areas.[41] OTI works directly with indigenous, nonurban NGOs. Robert Rotberg calls OTI the "special forces of development assistance . . . , gave it an overall positive review and concluded that the organization has proved itself to be "nimble, imaginative and innovative."[42]

The program was not without its weaknesses. OTI suffered from tight budgets and a limited staff. OTI sustainability is a problem. Operationally, OTI functions in a country for three years or less. Contractors, grantees, and their staffs have not always been comfortable with OTI, especially with its short lead time, indeterminate goals, and short life span involvement.

Later, USAID created a separate Office of Conflict Resolution (OCR). According to Andrew S. Natsios, then administrator of USAID, "The nation-building challenge that follows . . . [the donor] switch to peacekeeping is daunting."[43] OCR also targeted fragile and collapsed states, because in the transition process, lawlessness, spotty oversight, and ethnic conflict have all blocked past rebuilding efforts.[44] Paul Lewis suggests, "The scope, cost and complexity of peacekeeping operations were [and are] likely to grow as more countries find themselves in the grip of violence, famine and civil war."[45]

The Governance Problem

Conflict resolution is an essential first step to democratic governance. Recognizing this, USAID established the Center for Democracy and Governance (CDG) (later an office) in 1994 to address the issue. CDG became

258   *A Fragile Balance*

the third component of the USAID triumvirate—reporting to the Bureau of Democracy, Conflict and Humanitarian Assistance—designed to support democratic governance. An early weakness in the approach was that historically it ignored political processes and legitimate political concerns of recipient country political leaders. USAID officials hoped the Bureau would correct that deficiency.

Concern about political development was not new. Throughout the Cold War, "aid allocations—by bilateral and multilateral donors—were dominated by politics—both the international politics of the Cold War and the internal politics of aid agencies."[46] According to an a USAID adviser in 1987, "Together, the three measures under the category of political issues are designed with the assumption that an assessment of political climate and political will to carry out reforms is essential to ultimate success and survival of any major policy reforms."[47] Commitment to support political reform and democratic governance was new.

By the late 1980s, the United States began to focus on basic human rights, democracy and governance. Ironically, this occurred when structural adjustment, public sector reform, and privatization were the order of the day, and LDC leaders might long for the day, in the height of the Cold War, when they had a political impact on donor policy. As a senior USAID official put it in 1991, "Successfully implemented, [public sector reforms] will have a bigger impact on democratization than anything else. In fact this will replace most of our 'democratization' efforts. No bourgeoisie, no democracy."[48]

Historically, USAID's record in democracy and governance is spotty, especially during the Cold War. A 1987 USAID survey of Zaire ignored the governance environment and the United States officially classified Zaire as a state transitioning to democracy down to the end of the Mobutu regime. There was resistance to policies purporting to expand democracy. The Zaire experience was exaggerated, but not uncommon. In Egypt, critics in 2004 complained that, "contrary to Bush's pronouncements, U.S. aid—nearly $2 billion per year over the past two decades—has propped up an unpopular government, its army and police, and helped suppress democracy."[49] And according to Steven Holmes, "The hard reality is that in the last few years, American financial aid to the fledgling democracies of Central America–and to much of the rest of the world—has fallen, as if off a cliff."[50]

Donors pushed for democratic processes while they required state systems to contract. Democratic governance was one of the set of conditionalities required by the international community as part of the policy reform process. According to USAID, "Democratization is an essential part of sustainable development because it facilitates the protection of human rights, informed participation, and public sector accountability."[51] In 1990, USAID encouraged outside input on democracy and governance issues. According to one USAID official, "I thought you [the author] would be interested from an academic perspective at least. Understand the administrator has initiated outside groups to get into the discussion and Ok'ed our sharing these papers."[52] This was different than earlier policies on political change completed in house and marked secret or confidential.

Military and security issues became part of the overall process having an impact on governance, as well as the movement toward economic and social development. Quantitative performance indicators for democracy and governance, a prerequisite for USAID's evaluation process, remain a problem.

Not all foreign aid recipients supported democratization. "Egyptian officials," as Glenn Frankel pointed out in 2004, "who have always wielded a veto over which private organizations are allowed to receive U.S. aid, are unhappy about an American proposal to earmark $20 million for democratization."[53]

Essential to aid success is working out "a mutually acceptable arrangement for joint control of the activity between donor and recipient, within the context of the two sides political processes."[54] If joint control was a concern, then in the future "the truly radical thing for the United States to do is to invest its resources and its credibility not in individual leaders but in the fledgling attempts . . . to build institutions of law and accountability."[55] This became the meat of democracy and governance. In Africa, for example, the declared goal of the foreign aid community focused on political stability, democratic governance, and conflict resolution combined with the development of the continent's economies.[56]

There are differences about the importance of democratic governance between those stressing political freedom and those arguing for economic libertarianism. "Where these two schools of thought come together," according to Howard French, "is in the need for foreign donors to give greater encouragement to countries where real democratization is taking place—places . . . where 'the poor are more empowered and where this induces governments to provide more basic services.'"[57]

With increased emphasis on democracy, the foreign aid catch phrase became good governance. Increasingly, officials concluded that without it, aid often is wasted.[58] Yet, for one critic, some bureaucrats in USAID's ODG talk "as if democracy were just a piece of technology, like a water pump, that needs only the right instillation to work in foreign climes."[59] "All elections, all the time," quipped one young USAID ODG official.[60] In emphasizing governance, especially in the Middle East, the Bush administration focused on national government structures. Critics accused the

Bush administration of being "hubristic, messianic, [and] imperialistic," particularly when funding committed to the Middle East for democracy and governance was very little.[61]

The Middle East remains a challenge for democracy and governance programs, particularly in the Levant and the Arabian Peninsula, where regimes are authoritarian. Elections, critics suggest, are held to impress donor countries and prove to the donors that the recipient country is doing the right thing. Palestine is an important, though troubling example.[62]

Almost all donors encourage decentralization as a way to reinforce democratic practices. In the past, donors only paid lip service to the issue. According to Raymond Hopkins, "within broad policy guidelines, the management of global political problems, especially those of a non-military nature, resides primarily in decentralized, partially-connected networks of executives in both national governments and private multinational business."[63]

In 2000, a major debate about groups centered on the relationship between civil society and political society, and whether or not the former is a prerequisite to the latter. Do civil society groups foster democracy, or do they advocate for special interests economic in nature? Much foreign aid reached NGOs whose advocacy work was social and economic and did not focus on political or human rights. In some situations, these special interest groups exercised inordinate influence over society. From a governance perspective, according to the *New York Times*:

> To supporters, the groups—better known in the diplomatic world as NGO's, or nongovernmental organizations—are essential to Africa's burgeoning democracy, giving communities the money and power to take part in their own development and circumvent ineffective or corrupt governments. To critics, they are new colonialists who instill dependency among Africans, and their contributions to Africa's development are hard to measure.[64]

As the millennium approached, former secretary Madeline Albright characterized international governance as "heightened interdependence, overlapping national interests, and borders permeable to everything from terrorists and technology to disease and democratic ideals."[65] Technical assistance was *internationalized* in a changing of the guard. Human rights advocates and aid workers from LDCs played an increasing role in assistance alongside of workers from Western nations. There were, for example, aid workers from LDCs involved in major human rights operations in Cambodia, Guatemala, and Haiti in the 1990s.[66]

Trade and Investment Debates

Despite the lack of private sector support for foreign aid and the annual legislative battle over it, programs survived because there is humanitarian concern within the broad electorate, executive branch, and Congress; however, political leadership was quick to see the commercial advantages of international assistance.[67] The United States had policies tying aid to purchases from US vendors. For many critics, aid became an expenditure designed to further donor country objectives in commercial and foreign policy.[68]

Trade liberalization, policy reform, and democratic governance as a package constituted a third stage of foreign aid (1983–2006) following an emphasis on growth and industrialization in the 1950s and 1960s and an emphasis on economic redistribution and basic needs in the 1970s.[69] As early as 1970, according to a presidential report on aid, private development in LDCs needed to "be encouraged by foreign investment, by appropriate domestic policies, and by an adequate public services and infrastructure."[70] The developed world needed to create new markets for goods and services in LDCs, with the goal to increase trade with them to promote growth opportunities and create more jobs within the developed countries.[71]

Recipient country officials increasingly note that aid favors special interests, particularly agriculture. Under aid regulations, the United States shipped goods on American carriers, required buy-American clauses in aid projects, and protected US small business and agribusiness from competition. In the modern foreign aid period, agricultural interests were very successful in carving out special privileges, particularly in provisions intended to encourage the export of US surplus agricultural commodities.[72] In the end, if foreign aid means international cooperation, this "cooperation has two essential aspects: creation of a vast economic area, in which trade is as free as possible, and the granting of development aid to the associated countries, mainly by means of [funds] specially set up for the purpose."[73]

Trade and not aid became the slogan of the 1990s among many critics of foreign aid. The African Growth and Opportunity Act (AGOA) of 2000 provided preferential access for selected African goods to US markets. It was, according to Theroux, a charitable idea that assumed African countries could not compete on their own.[74] However, AGOA failed to completely remove restrictions on LDC trade with the United States. By increasing public sector political power, LDCs may sometimes inhibit development of effective trade relationships and markets.[75] These market and trade reciprocities have not yet evolved between LDCs and the United States (and other more developed countries).

Trade policies are central to the development debate. In May 2002, President Bush signed the $190 billion ten-year farm bill. The farm granted the nation's biggest farmers $19 billion in subsidies, thus perpetuating a Depression-era program of direct financial aid to agriculture to encourage the production of cotton, dairy products, and grain.[76]

This was central: "If the United States is to open its wallet, poor nations must open their markets."[77] However, opening US markets to LDC products is another matter. Domestic lobbyists are reluctant to go that route. For example, in 2002, the World Trade Organization members (often hypocritically) debated European concerns that the United States used food aid to dump surplus commodities in foreign countries where the supply undercut LDC farmers' income.

Given the realities of US food policy, "it is also one that illustrates an expanding ideological consensus on the need to address poverty, disease, famine and conflict in Africa—as well as the remaining gulf between left and right about how best to do it."[78] The trade versus aid debate often appeared fraught with contradictions.

A chief complaint from LDCs is that rich nations are not consistent on trade liberalization. What was needed was less hypocrisy.[79] The "worst trade barrier [was] the $300 billion in agricultural subsidies given to farmers in the world's wealthy nations."[80] Increasingly, "the problem is the establishment of freer trade between North and South. That is something the West has promised but that has not materialized."[81]

Despite the critics, the claim that donors manipulate foreign aid for direct political or economic gains in trade and commerce remains exaggerated. There is little evidence that foreign aid supports a donor country's commercial or trade policy in any single situation. As Paul Mosley notes, quoting the OECD, "It is improbable that aid tying provides significant macro-economic benefits to any donor's domestic or balance of trade aggregates."[82] Nor is there evidence that foreign aid provides political leverage within an LDC, influences economic development, or serves as an instrument of export promotion. The process is more subtle than that. Moreover, it is a matter of perception and blurring of lines between commercial policy and protective tariffs influencing debate around trade and aid.

Because of northern tier trade barriers, millions of people in poor countries grow food and other agricultural products for a living, but they are frozen out (or perceived to be) of wealthy countries' markets by some of the highest trade barriers in the world, all imposed by the most wealthy nations on the most impoverished. The United States alone spends twice as much in subsidizing agribusiness than it does aiding poor countries. Debate is both rhetorical and real but has become part of an international belief system. According to Elizabeth Becker, "They [LDCs] complained that one minute the United States says it wants developing countries to rely on free trade rather than handouts, the next it enacts a law, which they say is the biggest impediment in the free trade of food, the one commodity all these countries produce."[83]

It remains that tariffs and subsidies are the problem. Increasingly, foreign aid experts express disappointment, noting that G8 members failed to acknowledge that it has been their agricultural subsidies that have squeezed out LDCs. A large farm bill that President Bush signed in 2002 took far more money away from Africans by blocking exports than the rich nations dole out in aid.[84]

The United States, Japan, and the European Union are all guilty parties. In the end, sometimes distinguishing foreign aid from export subsidies is not that easy.[85] The problem is that US unions oppose all duty-free access for Africa under any conditions.[86] As Tom Webb points out, "In caves and giant warehouses, the U.S. government is storing mountains of powdered milk that taxpayers were required to buy, even though nobody is sure what to do with it all."[87]

There is no justification for denying African states duty-free access for textiles, clothing, and other basic commodities. This should be a given. As Sebastian Mallaby opines:

> If Bush aspires to lead the world by the power of America's example, he should aim for nothing less than the top spot in the index. Or to put the same point more bluntly: If he is prepared to risk troops in the name of human advance, surely he should be ready to offend the protectionists who oppose trade and the nativists who hate immigrants and all the other interest groups who oppose making the world stable.[88]

LDC trade and industrial leaders make it clear that duty free access to the United States and other Western markets was much more important than foreign aid. According to one international union leader (Ebrahim Patel), speaking of a broad strategy for promoting development, "[we] support the concept of duty-free access for Africa in textiles and apparel."[89] One way to quickly raise development is for the United States (and the rest of the developed world) to grant LDCs preferential access to their markets. Ironically, as the United States and other developed countries approach trade questions,

> wealthy nations [such] as the United States continue to press the developing world to open its markets to free trade and turn over public utilities, such as water and electricity, to private companies to curb environmental abuses and improve basic service delivery. . . . [P]oor countries say their efforts have been undermined by the industrialized world's hypocrisy and corporate approach.[90]

A problem with foreign trade, from a developing country perspective, is that rivalries such as that between France and the United States, concern commercial, security, and foreign aid. The United States favors bilateralism and even unilateralism. France has long influenced multilateral aid and is often criticized as sole sourcing to favored French contractors. It favors a multilateral approach to security. As a result, multilateral loans have high interest rates, and overall costs are sometimes twice that awarded through competitive international bids.[91] Jean Chretien of Canada, the then–prime minister (1993–2003), has argued that developed states "must drop their trade barriers to African textiles, footwear and farm products."[92]

Occasionally, the United States offers trade preferences even when it is not in the national interest to do so. The United States granted Haiti tariff waivers for its apparel-exporting industry in the 2006 Hemispheric Opportunity through Partnership Encouragement Act (HOPE). The program was unusual because it not only went against U.S. domestic garment producers who are struggling, but also against U.S. interests in other countries that produce apparel. The program was even more unusual in that not only was there strong bipartisan support in Congress, but there was support from the Bush administration as well.

The Millennium Challenge Account

George W. Bush was the first president since John Kennedy to develop a new plan for foreign aid—the Millennium Challenge Account (MCA).[93] Under MCA, the United States "planned to increase foreign aid spending by 50 percent over three years beginning in the 2004 fiscal year. The proposal would raise development assistance to $15 billion, from $10 billion by 2006 . . . and would not decrease it thereafter."[94] The new plan included an initial $5 billion development fund that would disperse grants for antipoverty projects.

The MCA plan—announced by President Bush at the 2002 UN International Conference on Financing for Development in Monterrey, Mexico—derived from the work of Craig Burnside and David Dollar. After completing an elaborate statistical analysis, the researchers concluded that foreign aid promoted economic growth, so long as the recipient government had solid fiscal, monetary, and trade policies in place.[95]

"The fact is," Paul Blustein noted, "the president made a $10 billion, three-year promise called MCA—a program to target new aid to poor countries with sound policies—'and a $15 billion, five-year HIV/AIDS initiative, and he's received a lot of justified applause.'" What was new about MCA was the division of countries according to the quality of their economic policies and democratic governance patterns.

The assumption of MCA's designers was that in countries with good policies, foreign assistance, if it is significant, reduces poverty; in countries with bad policies it does not.[96] Foreign aid to poorly managed countries would not promote economic or social development but should rather focus on policy reforms and governance.

Countries with poor policies would not simply be left to their fate. By no means, MCA advocates argued that donors can still help by spreading technological or institutional knowledge in support of democratic governance and policy reform. Within the Bush administration, the theory behind the fund was that aid works well only in nations that embrace principles such as the rule of law, open markets, and the allocation of budget resources to health and education.[97]

President Bush pledged $5 billion for MCA annually, meaning that if it were fully financed, MCA would represent a doubling of aid.[98] MCA established a federal corporation,[99] separate from USAID, which would administer the fund given to countries that adopted sound economic policies, promoted democracy, and attacked corruption. In establishing the program, the

> Bush administration deliberately sidestepped the normal route
> of giving the money to USAID and, instead, created [the] new
> program called the MCA, which require[d] poor nations to
> meet criteria of good government to receive aid.[100]

In 2002, according to the *Washington Post,* the Bush administration's newly announced Africa initiative was to be included in the first segment of MCA.[101] Based on economic criteria, performance, and governance, MCA would be the closest thing to a development purist's model ever tried in the United States or elsewhere.[102] According to MCA's program statement: "The MCA is a partnership built on several key principles—including a focus on sustainable growth, country ownership, inclusiveness, accountability, and emphasis on results—that will be reflected throughout the development and implementation of MCA programs."[103]

MCA's beginnings were inauspicious and faltering. Though President Bush appointed well-respected businessman Paul Appelgarth as chief executive of a new enterprise, Millennium Challenge Corporation (MCC), "his tiny hovel is at the end of two rows of cubicles with no reception area in an Arlington office building. The staff, seven people at the beginning of the year (2004), [had] expanded to 42 in six months and [was] due to grow to 200 in a year."[104] Staffing for the fund was eventually capped at 100 people on limited term appointments.

The original idea was that the MCC would be small, independent, and driven by eligible LDC priorities. MCA was "designed to be independent of State [the State Department] and USAID, with as little bureaucracy as possible."[105] According to MCC, "When President Bush promised to channel billions of dollars in aid—but only to countries that were committed to 'ruling justly, investing in their people and encouraging economic freedom'—it was an extraordinary example of how an idea hatched by scholars could wend its way into mainstream politics."[106] The independence of the MCC was deliberate. Paul Blustein has put it this way:

> Secretary of State Colin L. Powell pushed hard for keeping the fund under his purview, according to sources familiar with the debate, but a compromise was reached in which he will chair a board consisting of other Cabinet-level officials who will make the final recommendations to the president about the countries to receive funding.[107]

Standards were strict but could change over time as political needs intervened. President Bush made it clear that "the increase in aid," according to James Dao, "will be contingent on the recipients' undertaking a range of economic, political and social reforms."[108] Under MCA, the administration would give more aid to a smaller number of countries that could pass a rigorous set of sixteen performance criteria.

Because of the limited capacity of LDCs to plan using US government formulas, however, there was a danger that MCA would revert to the normal USAID model, where the US government relied on an army of consultants, private companies, and NGOs to prepare proposals and design projects. That began to happen, to some extent, but not nearly as much as critics agonized. MCC had already stated that in some cases, "the next step may be for MCC to help the country identify appropriate technical assistance to further develop the proposal."[109] In the first year of operation, USAID identified potential consultants who could assist in the project development process, and some contractors were engaged to assist in the preparation of MCC and LDC documents. MCC rules were not always clear and were subject to change. MCC hedged and in its guidelines warned that the

> submission of a proposal by an eligible country does not guarantee that MCC will finalize a Compact with such country or fund the country's proposed program. MCC will evaluate proposals and make investment decisions based on a variety of considerations, including how well the proposal has demonstrated the relationship between the proposed program and economic growth and poverty reduction.[110]

Following its review of an eligible country's proposal, MCC would then contact the country's designated representative to discuss next steps in what was likely to be a long, difficult process.

By the end of 2002, however, the criteria, according to critics, appeared to change, giving more opportunity to make awards to middle income, politically strategic countries such as South Africa, Russia, Jordan, Peru, and Columbia.[111] This allowed the administration to use MCA for political or security purposes, weakening the program for some observers.

Congress initially was lukewarm to MCA. Republican lawmakers were hard to convince that this new foreign assistance fund would not be improperly spent on corrupt foreign governments. There was concern about the corruption in the conflict-prone countries of the Balkans.[112] Then-Senator Jesse Helms, (R-NC) was the most powerful critic of foreign aid in Congress. He stated that he would only champion an increase in foreign aid if all future US aid funneled to the needy through private charities and other faith-based groups instead of government agencies.[113] Adam Zagorin suggested, "According to Benjamin Gilman, chairman of the House International Relations Committee, widespread graft threatens to destabilize Bosnia and indefinitely postpone the departure of 6,000 U.S. peacekeepers from the troubled Balkan nation."[114]

In the planning for MCA, Congress directed it to concentrate its efforts on a few countries with potential for growth and commitment to economic reform. The fund was also to concentrate resources on certain vital sectors, including agricultural production, health, education, and voluntary family planning and to consider the impact of development assistance on the environment.[115] Over the next few years, however, the design process was slow, and to its critics, flawed.[116]

Very quickly it appeared the MCA initiative would fall short of expectations. For some critics, there would be both duplication with USAID and concern about mission drift. The problem was the preparatory work and the "contracting for, monitoring, and evaluating MCC programs would suggest a troubling misalignment of USAID staff's incentives and responsibilities as well as heavy MCC dependence upon USAID" in implementing the program in the field.

Delays in allocations caused some concern. According to the *Washington Post* in mid-2003, "Bush proposed the Millennium Challenge Account 16 months ago. . . . There's been some progress on the legislative front, getting bills marked up in the House and Senate, but in terms of getting the program running, there's been almost nothing."[117]

MCA changed over time as well. The president's initial budget called for allocating $1.3 billion to MCA in 2004, $2.6 billion in 2005, and $5 billion annually after the first three years.[118] In 2004, the MCC Board met for the first time. It established the rules for the grants that President Bush stated would total $5 billion annually by 2008. The goal posts kept moving.

By 2005, the MCA faced severe cuts in its proposed budget, halving it. These cuts were due to the burgeoning deficit and the out-of-control expenses for Iraq and Afghanistan. In what could only be called an understatement, the Bush administration admitted that the grant-making process was extremely slow. Virtually none of the money had been spent, other than for administrative costs; however, one program official cynically claimed that it didn't matter because "the program [was] as much about good government as about dispensing financial assistance."[119] The MCC director resigned after one year, having failed to ever really come to grips with the management of a complex, start-up program.

In the first year, just fifteen nations were projected to win awards. Only five countries qualified in 2005, with grants totaling less than $1 million. It was not until 2006 that MCC became fully operational, with eleven signed compact agreements and some $1.6 billion in programs. Ambassador John Danilovich, MCC's CEO, is universally credited with turning around MCC in a relatively short time. He reorganized the corporation, hired new staff where needed, improved the award-making process from start to finish, and effectively lobbied Congress and the administration for more time and funding.

Since its establishment in 2004, MCC had signed compacts totaling less than $6 billion with eighteen countries through 2008. This was far short of original estimates calling for the obligation of $15 billion up to this time.

In October 2008, the Senate rejected the president's budget submission for MCC, approving only $254 million, or just 13 percent of the administration's request. The Senate claimed that it had rejected the budget request because it doubted that the money expended was making a difference. The House Appropriations Committee and Subcommittee on State-Foreign Operations on both sides of the aisle protested the budget cut, stating that it felt that much progress had been made and that not granting funding now would seriously jeopardize relations with those countries participating in the program. At this writing (December 2008), the process remains deadlocked.

Triangulation—USAID, State, and Security

In 2006, discussions occurred within USAID about the future of foreign aid. Rumors abounded that USAID would be restructured, linked to military activities, and folded into State, thus ending forty-five years as an independent agency. Creation of MCA fueled these rumors.

The new component in the State Department would be headed by a deputy secretary of State for development (with the title of USAID Director) but perhaps shorn of much of its economic development functions. USAID would be directed away from long-term planning to short-term goals targeting conflict resolution, interagency cooperation with regard to security objectives, and transitional assistance. The rumors portended the likely end or fundamental realignment of more than a half a century of aid.[120]

Some of the rumors were true. From a policy perspective, the institutional changes reflected the new international environment within the foreign policy community and a triangulation between diplomacy, security, and foreign assistance. Ultimately, this would bring foreign policy and foreign aid much closer together and link both to defense and security concerns. While much of traditional foreign aid would continue, there would be a renewed focus on regime change, governance, and security issues, and over time perhaps, a decline in interest in economic and social development.

Natsios, the then-administrator, resigned January 13, 2006, possibly in protest against the decision to incorporate USAID into State. Secretary Condoleezza Rice, in a speech to the Department and USAID, announced on January 19, 2006, that a gradual process to integrate USAID into State had begun, one that would more closely link up foreign policy and foreign aid with Defense priorities. There were many foreign aid components already operating outside USAID at the end of 2006.

By 2006, central to the debate about international assistance was whether and/or when should USAID as a coordinating mechanism for foreign aid ultimately disappear? There was an autonomous HIV/AIDS office that fell outside of USAID, and in addition, there was MCC, organizationally independent from USAID and designed to transfer major financial resources to democratic progrowth and free trade–oriented LDCs. In all, there are at least eighteen to twenty foreign aid accounts, some in State, and some in USAID, plus assistance programs (including nonmilitary assistance in the Department of Defense). Estimates were that more than 22 percent of nonmilitary foreign assistance flowed through Defense.

Randall Tobias, who had headed one of those units—HIV/AIDs—that had been excluded from USAID control, replaced Natsios.[121] He wore two hats, also being appointed within State as deputy secretary and director of foreign assistance, as well as USAID administrator. It was not entirely clear what role he would play in coordinating the foreign aid units outside of USAID's span of control. In any event, Tobias resigned on April 27, 2007, for personal reasons under the cloud of a scandal.

Secretary Rice spoke of "Transformational Development"—reforms in governance, human capacity, and economic structures. This initiative was to build capacity for conflict management, reconstruction, and stabilization. Under Rice's transformational development policy, the United States' goal promoted "fundamental changes in governance and institutional capacity, human capacity, and economic structure that enabled a country to sustain further economic and social progress."[122]

The *2002 National Security Strategy* paper enunciated three security pillars: defense, diplomacy, and foreign aid.[123] The Rice doctrine sought to "build and sustain democratic, well governed states that will respond to the needs of their people and conduct themselves responsibly in the international system."[124] The new strategic framework created five categories of countries:

1. *Rebuilding countries:* These include collapsed, fragile (though the term was not used), and postconflict states.
2. *Transforming countries:* These are low- and middle-income states with the potential for meeting MCC performance criteria.
3. *Sustaining Partnerships:* These are countries with higher incomes, who have "graduated" from foreign assistance, with economic, trade, and security relationships with the US beyond foreign aid.
4. *Reforming Countries* (relabeled "Restrictive Countries"): These are made up of authoritarian countries ineligible for government-to-government relationships where the United States can only work through NGOs.
5. *Developing countries:* These are lower- and middle-income countries that are not able to meet MCC performance criteria.[125]

Critics of transformation diplomacy and the transition paradigm abound. Thomas Carothers criticizes the assumption that LDC states are moving away from authoritarianism toward democracy. Instead, many LDCs remain in a "gray zone" for long periods of time, neither authoritarian nor moving toward democracy. The move toward democracy, he argues, is an "extremely gradual, incremental process of liberalization."[126]

Ultimately, at issue in the organizational and policy reforms introduced in 2006 by Secretary Rice is whether the changes at USAID are the death toll for traditional foreign aid, what one critic calls a kind of "water torture" in which it was to be replaced by Rice's self-styled Transformational Diplomacy.[127] The end of the traditional foreign aid mission, if it is real, implicitly assumes that anti-poverty funds were ineffective and should be replaced by funding that promotes strategic and political interests.

In Afghanistan and Iraq, Provincial Reconstruction Teams (PRTs) were already functioning outside of the USAID system—a model likely replicated elsewhere.[128] The argument made by those advocating PRTs was that the US military can use social work techniques in order to win the hearts and minds of village dwellers. By March 2006, it was clear that there would be increasing linkages between State and USAID, on the one hand, and Defense on the other. Nation-building reforms came out of the debacle of postwar planning in Iraq. PRTs, according to Bob Woodward, involved "political and economic experts, aid workers and engineers who would go into the 18 provinces [in Iraq] set up posts, and help in the rebuilding."[129] There were discussions of a civilian reserve that would be available on short notice overseas (modeled on the military reserve).

Defense's intent is to create civil and military transition scenarios for field administration, based on models from Afghanistan, which would play an increased role in postconflict situations. The African Command described above is an example of this pattern of thinking. The control model in Iraq was the Afghanistan model of regional security teams of military and civilians, with each team consisting of State Department officials, a USAID representative, and one or more military officers. These PRTs were created by US Ambassador Zalman Khalizad, an Afghan-American, first in Afghanistan and later, in Iraq when he moved there in 2005. Policymakers considered this model in Africa, including Somalia, southern Sudan, and Darfur.

In the field, USAID and State had difficulties staffing civilian slots in the PRTs. It is unclear how much international support there is for the concept because outside Iraq, NATO and the European Union are involved in peacekeeping and human security activities. There were also financial constraints, particularly in Iraq, that delayed their implementation, and there were quarrels between State and Defense over control.

The foreign aid budget increased from $10 billion in 2000 to $27.5 billion in 2006, in part because of the transition model. FY2007 topped $29 million. However, the organizational reforms in foreign assistance to this point have been little more than a set of "modest stove-piped efforts."[130] The merger of USAID and State has been gradual; Carol Lancaster says it reflects a kind of "merger by stealth."[131]

The assistant secretary for foreign assistance, who now doubles as USAID administrator, exerts limited authority over foreign aid portfolios outside of USAID. USAID has only a limited assessment and informational coordination for the accounts in Defense, MCC, and the HIV/AIDS Office. The director has no oversight responsibilities over Agriculture, Health and Human Services, Labor, and Treasury, let alone Defense.

There remains much duplication of effort in foreign aid. An additional USAID problem is that programs and projects have too many restrictions. To what extent will foreign aid be increasingly militarized and linked to political goals? Where will the leadership role in nation-building be located, within civilian or military institutions?

Defense's foreign aid role expanded in areas of postconflict reconstruction, counterterrorism, antinarcotics efforts, and humanitarian assistance. The extent to which the reform process would continue after the December 2006 resignation of Rumsfeld and collapse of support for Iraq was not clear.[132]

Conclusion

In the wake of the Iraq debacle and the downward spiraling of events in Afghanistan and the Horn of Africa, strategic analysis came back into vogue with the recognition there is a role that the cool thinking of academics and intellectuals can play in foreign aid and foreign and security policy process beyond the policy implementation process. This approach is likely to predominate in the incoming Obama administration under the leadership of incoming Secretary of State Hillary Rodham Clinton. According to Edward Horesh, as early as 1981, "The proper role of academics in development studies . . . is to analyze economic and social conditions in less developed countries, not to take responsibility for increasing the rate of economic growth in those countries."[133]

Changes occurring in aid at this time (2009) make this an opportune moment to examine foreign aid issues from a policy perspective, this chapter's goal. There are policy problems and a lack of political and, even at times, ethical clarity, plaguing technical assistance and foreign aid during the past sixty years. It may continue well into the next century.

Under the Rice doctrine, there was very little commitment of involving USAID beneficiaries in policy development. There remained few mechanisms to monitor and evaluate foreign aid in terms of impact rather than output; however, there was agreement about the basic premise of reform of foreign aid and nation-building—that institutions matter.

Policy and implementation concerns are rooted in the evolution of foreign aid policy but also in the ideological and cultural assumptions, antecedents of state-to-state foreign aid as they developed after World War II. Much of this baggage continues into the twenty-first century. In the next chapter, we speculate about the future of international assistance.

Notes

1. Mark Hertsgaard, *The Eagle's Shadow* (New York: Picador, 2003) p. 71. This is ably demonstrated in Stephen Kinzer's recent book, *Overthrow: America's Century of Regime Change from Hawaii to Iraq* (New York: Times Books, 2006).

2. Hertsgaard, *The Eagle's Shadow*, p. 80.

3. Mark Bowden, *Black Hawk Down: A Story of Modern War* (New York: Penguin, 1999).

4. Ibid., p. 218.

5. See Ian Christie Clark, "From Crisis to Renaissance at UNESCO— Can the Struggle be won without the USA?" *Newsletter of Americans for the Universality of UNESCO* iv, issue 3 (September 4, 1988), p. 13.

6. Robert Kagan, "A Tougher War for the U.S. Is One of Legitimacy," *New York Times* (January 24, 2004), p. A19.

7. David E. Sanger, "Hawk Sightings Could Be Premature," *New York Times* (November 21, 2004), p. A1.

8. Rick Barton, "Failed and Failing States: Exploring New Directions for International Development," Paper Presentation (Washington, DC: George Washington University Development Management Network Workshop, October 30, 2004).

9. Carol Lancaster, *Transforming Foreign Aid: United States Assistance in the 21st Century* (Washington, DC: Institute for International Economics, 2000), pp. 58–59.

10. William D. Hartung, "Military," in *Power Trip: U.S. Unilateralism and Global Strategy after September 11*, John Feffer, ed. (New York: Seven Stories Press, 2003), p. 60.

11. Bob Woodward, *Bush at War* (New York: Simon & Schuster, 2002), p. 341.

12. Karen de Young, "Falling on His Sword," *Washington Post Magazine* (October 1, 2006), pp. 13–27. Quote p. 14.

13. Deborah Scroggins, *Emma's War: An Aid Worker, A Warlord, Radical Islam, and the Politics of Oil—A True Story of Love and Death in the Sudan* (New York: Pantheon Books, 2002), p. 351.

14. Niall Ferguson, *Empire: The Rise and Demise of the British World Order and the Lessons for Global Power* (New York: Basic Books, 2003).

15. Both quotes, Ibid, pp. 368 and 370.

16. David Sogge, *Give and Take: What's the Matter with Foreign Aid?* (London: Zed Books, 2002), p. 65.

17. De Young, "Falling on His Sword," p. 15.

18. Tom Barry, "How Things Have Changed," in Feffer, ed., *Power Trip,* p. 30.

19. See Feffer, "Introduction," in Feffer, ed., *Power Trip,* pp. 18–27 and Barry, "How Things Have Changed," in Feffer, ed., *Power Trip,* p. 28 for both quotes.

20. Glenn Kessler, "Engagement Is a Constant in Kerry's Foreign Policy," *Washington Post* (March 21, 2004), p. A1.

21. Michael Massing, "Appoint the Best to Iraq, Not the Best-Connected," *Washington Post* (July 6, 2003), p. B4.

22. DeYoung, "Falling on His Sword," p. 26.

23. Kagan, "A Tougher War for the U.S.," p. A19.

24. Robert G. Kaiser, "A Foreign Policy, Falling Apart," *Washington Post* (May 23, 2004), p. B4.

25. William Langewiesche, "Welcome to the Green Zone," *The Atlantic Monthly,* (November 2004), pp. 61–88. Quote, p. 87.

26. Thomas E. Ricks, "Army Historian Cites Lack of Postwar Plan," *Washington Post* (December 25, 2004), p. A18.

27. Stanley Hoffmann, "What Should We Do in the World?" *Atlantic Monthly* (October 1989), p. 96.

28. Roger Cohen, "An Obsession the World Doesn't Share," *New York Times* (December 5, 2004), p. A1.

29. Glenn Kessler, "Revived Policy Traveling Abroad," *Washington Post* (December 5, 2004), p. A17.

30. David E. Sanger, "In Global Shift, Bush Rethinks Going It Alone," *New York Times* (March 13, 2006), pp. A1 and A6.

31. Jane Perlez, "Enlisting Aid to Education in the War on Terror," *New York Times* (October 12, 2003), p. A12.

32. Despite the Claims of the Iraqi Government. See James Glanz, "Iraq is Ready for Foreign Aid, Minister Says," *New York Times* (June 20, 2005), p. A10.

33. Quoted by Woodward, *Bush at War,* p. 321.

34. The above is based on Nora Boustany, "An Insistent Appeal for Aid to Africa," *Washington Post* (December 22, 2004), p. A18.

35. "Falling Fast," *Economist* (June 22, 1996), p. 44

36. David Reiff, "Intervention Has a Price," *New York Times* (November 14, 1996), p. A17.

37. Elizabeth Bumiller "Bush Plans to Raise Foreign Aid and Tie It to Reforms," *New York Times* (March 15, 2002), p. A5.

38. Jane Perlez, "Indonesia Bans Foreign Aid Workers From Embattled Province," *New York Times* (September 21, 2003), p. A8.

39. Mary B, Anderson, *Do No Harm: How Aid Can Support Peace— or War* (Boulder, CO: Lynne Rienner Publishers, 1999), p. 1.

40. Barton, "Failed and Failing States."

41. *Office of Transition Initiatives: A Decade of Transition— 1994–2004* (Washington DC: US Agency for International Development, 2004), pp. 3–4.

42. Robert I. Rotberg, "The First Ten Years: An Assessment of the Office of Transition Initiatives" (Paper prepared by the Befer Center for Science and International Affairs, Kennedy School of Government, Harvard University, 2005), pp 1–3.

43. As noted by Joe Stephens and David B. Ottaway, "Postwar Reconstruction Efforts Have Had Dicey History," *Washington Post* (April 28, 2003), p. A13.

44. "Conflict Mitigation and Management Policy" (Washington, DC: US Agency for International Development, April, 2005), pp. 1–7.

45. Paul Lewis, "Panel Predicts Growing U.N. Peacekeeping Role," *New York Times* (February 27, 1993), p. A4.

46. David Dollar, *Assessing Aid: What Works, What Doesn't, and Why* (Washington, DC: The World Bank and Oxford University Press, 1998), p. 40.

47. Patricia J. Vondal, "Improving Non-Project Assistance Through Better Social and Institutional Analysis: Suggestions from Africa Bureau Experience" (Washington, DC: US Agency for International Development, December 1987), p. 10.

48. Samuel W. Shoen, "USAID Africa Bureau; Strategic Analysis and Recommendations for the 1990's" (Working Draft, September 9, 1991), p. 11.

49. Glenn Frankel, "Egypt Muzzles Calls for Democracy," *Washington Post* (January 6, 2004), p. A12.

50. Steven A. Holmes, "A Foreign Aid of Words, Not Cash," *New York Times* (December 5, 1993), p. A5.

51. "Building Democracy," USAID's Strategies for Sustainable Development" (Washington, DC: US Agency for International Development, 1996), p. 2.

52. Jeanne North, Cover Note to USAID Documents Given to Louis A. Picard (n.d., 1991).

53. Frankel, "Egypt Muzzles Calls for Democracy."

54. George Liska, *The New Statecraft: Foreign Aid in American Foreign Policy* (Chicago: University of Chicago Press, 1960), p. 19.

55. Bill Berkeley, *The Graves Are Not Yet Full: Race, Tribe and Power in the Heart of Africa* (New York: Basic Books, 2001), p. 240.

56. Francis Kornegay, Chris Lansberg and Steve McDonald, "Participate in the African Renaissance," in *What Does the World Want from America? International Perspectives on U.S. Foreign Policy,* Alexander T. J. Lennon, ed. (Cambridge, MA: MIT Press, 2002), p. 50.

57. Howard W. French, "Donors of Foreign Aid Have Second Thoughts," *New York Times* (April 7, 1996), p. A5.

58. Barbara Crossette, "Givers of Foreign Aid Shifting Their Methods," *New York Times* (February 23, 1992), p. A2.

59. Michal Ignatieff, "Who Are Americans to Think that Freedom Is Theirs to Spread?" *New York Times Magazine* (June 26, 2005), p. 47.

60. Source requested anonymity. Washington, DC. Author's Research Diary (Picard), June 11, 2007.

61. Ignatieff, "Who Are Americans," pp. 42 and 44.

62. As Stephen R. Weisman has put it, "The United States, Europe and Arab countries are considering greatly increasing—maybe even doubling—aid to the Palestinians on the condition that they and Israel take certain steps toward reducing their conflict, U.S. and Palestinian officials say." Steven R. Weisman, "Increase in Aid Discussed," *Pittsburgh Post-Gazette* (December 17, 2004), p. A8.

63. Raymond F. Hopkins, "The International Role of 'Domestic' Bureaucracy," *International Organization,* 30 no. 3, (Summer 1976), p. 413.

64. Norimitsu Onishi, "Nongovernmental Organizations Show Their Growing Power," *New York Times* (March 22, 2002), p. A5.

65. Albright, *Madame Secretary,* p. 429.

66. Seth Mydans, "U.N. Aide Left Legacy of Asia Role on Rights," *New York Times* (February 12, 1997), p. A5.

67. Edward K. Hamilton, "Toward Public Confidence in Foreign Aid," in *World Affairs,* 132, no. 4 (March, 1970), pp. 287–304. Quote, p. 291.

68. Paul Mosley, *Overseas Aid: Its Defence and Reform* (Brighton, UK: Wheatsheaf Books, 1987), p. 85.

69. Stephen Browne, *Beyond Aid: From Patronage to Partnership* (Aldershot, UK: Ashgate Publishing, 1999), pp. 29–30.

70. Rudolph A. Peterson, et Al., "U.S. Foreign Assistance in the 1970s: A New Approach," *Report to the President from the Task Force on International Development* (Washington, DC: March 4, 1970), pp. 19–20.

71. Clay Wescott and Abdul Magid Osman, "International Resources and Policies" (United Nations Development Programme, 1992), p. 2.

72. John D. Montgomery, *The Politics of Foreign Aid: American Experience in Southeast Asia* (New York: Praeger, 1962), pp. 130–131.

73. "How the European Community is Helping the Developing Countries," *European Development Aid* (Brussels: Commission of the European Communities, n.d.), p. 8.

74. Paul Theroux, *Dark Star Safari: Overland from Cairo to Cape Town* (New York: Houghton Mifflin, 2003), p. 188.

75. Michael Prowse, "The Twilight of Foreign Aid," *Financial Times* (September 28, 1992), p. 30.

76. Elizabeth Becker, "A New Villain in Free Trade: The Farmer on the Dole," *New York Times* (August 25, 2002), p. A10.

77. Tim Weiner, "More Aid, More Need: Pledges Still Falling Short," *New York Times* (March 24, 2002), p. 5.

78. Richard W. Stevenson, "2 Stars of Rock and Heavy Policy Seek Answers to Africa's Poverty," *New York Times* (May 22, 2002), pp. A1 and A4.

79. Dirk Olin, "Washington Consensus," *New York Times Magazine* (May 25, 2003), p. 21.

80. Elizabeth Becker, "World Bank and I.M.F. Say They'll Send Experts to Iraq to Investigate Postwar Needs," *New York Times* (April 14, 2003), p. A3.

81. David E. Sanger, "G-8 Adopts African Aid Package, With Strict Conditions," *New York Times* (June 28, 2002), p. A10.

82. Mosley, *Overseas Aid*, p. 228.

83. Becker, "A New Villain in Free Trade," p. A10.

84. Karen DeYoung, and DeNeen L. Brown, "G-8 Approves an Aid Package for Africa," *Washington Post* (June 28, 2002), p. A19.

85. "Linking Exports to Aid," *New York Times* (October 19, 1993), p. A14. In Europe, "[e]xports from the associated states to the Community have risen less on average than their exports to other countries, and there has been a similar trend for their imports." According to David Sanger, in March of 2002, then "Secretary General Kofi Annan of the United Nations warned Mr. Bush and other leaders of the industrial world, 'We can no longer continue to give with one hand and take with the other.'" See "How the European Community is Helping the Developing Countries," p. 24 and Sanger, "G-8 Adopts African Aid Package," p. A10.

86. Thomas Friedman, "Africa: Aid or Harm?" *New York Times* (March 28, 2000), p. A27.

87. Tom Webb, "Growing Powdered-Milk Surplus Is Blamed on Price Support Policy," *Washington Post* (August 20, 2003), p. A19.

88. Sebastian Mallaby, "Visions of U.S. Aid," *Washington Post* (April 19, 2004), p. A19.

89. Quoted by Friedman, "Africa: Aid or Harm?" p. A27.

90. Jon Jeter, "Rich, Poor Further Apart as Earth Summit Nears," *Washington Post* (August 25, 2002), pp. A22 and A23.

91. Blaine Harden, *Africa: Dispatches from a Fragile Continent* (Boston: Houghton Mifflin Company, 1990), p. 209.

92. Clifford Krauss, "Chretien is Hoping to Aid Africa by Mobilizing Rich Nations," *New York Times* (June 23, 2002), p. A5.

93. Terry Buss discusses MCA in his work, "The Millennium Challenge Account: A New High Performance Program," in Steve Redburn, Robert Shea and Terry Buss (eds.), *Performance Management and Budgeting* (Armonk, NY: M. E. Sharpe, 2008).

94. Joseph Kahn, "White House Adds Billions to an Increase in Foreign Aid," *New York Times* (March 30, 2002), p. A4.

95. See a discussion of this by Daphne Eviatar, "Do Aid Studies Govern Policies or Reflect Them?" *New York Times* (July 26, 2003), p. A17. See Craig Burnside and David Dollar, "Aid, Policies, and Growth," *American Economic Review,* 90, no. 4, (September 2000), pp. 847–869.

96. "Making aid work," *Economist* (November 14, 1998), p. 88.

97. Paul Blustein, "Bush to Call for New Foreign Aid Agency," *Washington Post* (November 26, 200), p. A4.

98. Christopher Marquis, "New System Begins Rerouting U.S. Aid For Poor Countries," *New York Times* (February 22, 2004), p. A1.

99. Terry F. Buss, "The Millennium Challenge Account," in Steve Redburn, Robert Shea and Terry Buss (eds.), *Performance Management and Budgeting* (Armonk, NY: M. E. Sharpe, 2008) pp. 262–274.

100. Elizabeth Becker, "With Record Rise in Foreign Aid Comes Change in How it is Monitored," *New York Times* (December 7, 2003), p. 10.

101. "Mr. O'Neill's Opportunity," *Washington Post,* editorial (June 14, 2002), p. A24.

102. Lael Brainard, "Compassionate Conservatism Confronts Global Poverty," *Washington Quarterly* vol. 26, no. 2 (2003), pp. 149–169.

103. "Guidance for Developing Proposals for MCA Assistance in FY 2004" (Arlington, VA: Millennium Challenge Corporation, April 29, 2004).

104. Glenn Kessler, "Reinventing U.S. Foreign Aid at Millennium Challenge Corp." *Washington Post* (August 10, 2004), p. A17.

105. Ibid.

106. "Guidance for Developing Proposals for MCA Assistance in FY 2004" (Arlington, VA: Millennium Challenge Corporation, April 29, 2004).

107. Blustein, "Bush to Call for New Foreign Aid Agency," p. A4.

108. Elezabeth Bumiller, "On the Eve of Latin Trip, Bush Ties Aid to Reforms," *New York Times* (March 21, 2002), p. A7.

109. "Guidance for Developing Proposals for MCA Assistance in FY 2004."

110. Ibid.

111. Brainard, "Compassionate Conservatism," p. 151.

112. Elizabeth Becker, "With Record Rise in Foreign Aid Comes Change in How it Is Monitored," *New York Times* (December 7, 2003), p. 6.

113. Eric Schmitt, "Helms Stipulates Private Channels for Foreign Aid," *Pittsburgh Post-Gazette* (January 12, 2001), p. 1.

114. Adam Zagorin, "More Losses in Bosnia; This Time It's Aid Money," *Time* (September 20, 1999), p. 18.

115. Raymond W. Copson, Brenda M. Branaman and Ted S. Dagne, "Africa: U.S. Foreign Assistance Issues," *CRS Issue Brief* (June 2, 1992), p. 4.

116. Brainard, "Compassionate Conservatism," pp. 149–169.

117. Blustein, "U.S. Aid Plan Comes Up Short."

118. James Dao, "With Rise in Foreign Aid" *New York Times* (February 3, 2003), p. A5.

119. See "Chief of 'Millennium' Aid Fund is Quitting," *New York Times* (June 16, 2005), p. A5 and Celia W. Dugger, "Bush Aid Initiative for Poor Nations Faces Sharp Budget Cuts and Criticism of Slow Pace," *New York Times* (June 17, 2005), p. A8.

120. This information was taken from "Notes from an Interaction Meeting on Restructuring" with USAID Director Andrew Natsios, December 14, 2005. Material provided to the authors by a colleague who has asked for anonymity.

121. See Steven R. Weisman, "Rice to Group Foreign Aid in One Office in State Dept." *New York Times* (January 19, 2006), p. A8.

122. White Paper on U.S. Foreign Aid Policy—2004, p. 14. (Washington, DC: US Agency for International Development).

123. *The National Security Strategy of the United States of America* (Washington, DC: US Government Printer, September 2002), p. 5.

124. Robert Nolan, "In Focus—The Rice Doctrine: A Look at 'Transformational Diplomacy,'" (Unpublished Paper, Foreign Policy Association—Global Views, January 26, 2006).

125. See Larry Nowels and Connie Veillette, "Restructuring U.S. Foreign Aid" (Washington, DC: Congressional Research Service, Report to Congress, June 16, 2006), pp. 7–8 for a discussion of this.

126. Thomas Carothers, "The End of the Transition Paradigm," *Journal of Democracy*, 13, no. 1 (January, 2002), pp. 5–21. Quotes p. 15. See

his debate with Gerald Hyman of USAID on this. Gerald Hyman, "Debating the Transition Paradigm: Tilting at Straw Men," *Journal of Democracy*, 13, no. 3 (July, 2002), pp. 26–32. Hyman argues that USAID really does not use a transition paradigm with an overemphasis on elections, as Carothers claims, but rather they see the move to democracy in realistic perspective, with increased focus on the development of civil society, institutions, local government, anti-corruption, and conflict resolution. While the USAID bureaucracy may have a more sophisticated view of democratization, the political rhetoric over the six years since September 11 clearly has assumed a transition framework.

127. William Fisher, "The End of U.S. AID," *Jordan Times* (February 2, 2006), www.menafen.com.

128. Reuben E. Brigety, *Humanity as a Weapon of War: Sustainable Security and the Role of the U.S. Military* (Washington, DC: Center for American Progress, June, 2008).

129. Bob Woodward, *State of Denial* (New York: Simon and Schuster, 2006), p. 421.

130. Stewart Patrick, "An Integrated U.S. Approach to State Failure" (Working Paper, Center for Development, December 2008), p. 5.

131. See Stewart Patrick, "U.S. Foreign Aid Reform: Will It Fix What is Broken?" (Working Paper, Center for Global Development, September 2006), p. 10.

132. See Patrick, "U.S. Foreign Aid Reform," p. 8. The predominance was especially visible in Iraq and Afghanistan. See also Robert McMahon, "Transforming U.S. Foreign Aid," *Background Paper: Council on Foreign Relations* (Washington, DC: Publication 10176, March 17, 2006), www.cfr.org.

133. Edward Horesh, "Academics and Experts or the Death of the High Level Technical Assistant," *Development and Change*, 12, no. 4 (October 1981), p. 611. Horesh goes on, "An academic social scientist cannot take a direct hand in policy making and simultaneously remain an academic because 'academic research is general whereas policy is usually specific and in addition requires . . . knowledge of the institutions and processes in which it is to be applied.'" See p. 612.

14

CHALLENGES FOR THE FUTURE

Aid is not development; it doesn't do diddley-squat.

Michael Maren, *The Road to Hell*

The modern American empire colonizes minds, not territory.

Mark Hertsgaard, *The Eagle's Shadow*

[A] U.S. tactical military defeat can result in strategic political victories in the long run.

Jerry Mark Silverman, "Winning by Losing in Vietnam"

Into the Twenty-First Century

Two conflicting models of foreign aid policy compete in the marketplace of theory and practice: a top-down process of structural reform emphasizing political and economic transformation, and bottom-up activities associated with NGOs and emphasizing poverty reduction, community-based self-governance, and social empowerment through small-scale activities targeted at primary communities and directed at the individual poor family. As an organization, USAID at various times has relied on both.[1] The motivation for foreign aid has remained a combination of diplomacy and security, commercialism with a modicum of *moralism,* in part stimulated by an increasing involvement in aid debates within a multiplicity of issues among policy elites.

Ostensibly, the goals of foreign aid in 2009 remain what they were sixty years ago:[2]

- Reduction of material poverty through economic growth and the delivery of social services
- Promotion of good governance through democratically selected, accountable institutions

281

- Reversal of negative environmental trends through strategies of sustainable development[3]

The reality, however, is that current priorities focused on economic growth efforts implemented through MCA, political efforts at democratization, and finally a narrow focus on health issues, especially HIV/AIDs, tuberculosis, and malaria.

In this chapter, we briefly examine the foreign aid record. We look at the limited successes, trying to explain aid failures. Finally, we close with a survey of where international assistance might succeed. We are mindful of the limits of flexibility programmed into the aid process, given the program restrictions, congressional earmarks, and standard operating procedures that make policy choices scarce.[4]

Limited Successes in Foreign Aid

By 2000, there were some successes in foreign aid. As the Congressional Budget Office puts it, "With respect to development, [foreign] aid helped eradicate polio, greatly reduce the incidence of smallpox, increase life expectancy, and reduce fertility rates around the world."[5] Between 1948 and 2006, according to the USAID *2004 White Paper,* there was much progress in reducing infant mortality, raising agricultural production through scientific innovations, spurring economic growth, and spreading democracy.

Even where mistakes were made, some things got better. While aid in the past financed metropolitan hospitals used by urban middle classes or not-so-low-cost housing that the poor could not afford, "it is more likely today to be used for rural health clinics and paramedical workers, or 'sites-and-services' schemes which do benefit poor people."[6]

Policymakers attempted to untie bilateral foreign aid from commercial and trade preferences through international agreements, though these have not all covered technical assistance or food aid. An overall goal of USAID remains the stimulation of markets and promotion of expanded markets for US exports, a task accomplished at least in part. The key to market expansion is creation of successful market economies in LDCs. Foreign policy and aid policy made steady progress, according to USAID's own analysis, in providing increased potential for US exports. That said, Africa (and parts of Asia and the Middle East) remains underdeveloped and "nearly one in every two people in Latin America and the Caribbean live in poverty today and one in five in extreme poverty."[7]

There are countries that successfully responded to foreign aid, including South Korea, Taiwan, Poland, Chile, and Botswana to name a few. Aid for global health services (the elimination of smallpox, polio, and other childhood diseases; nutrition; family planning; education; housing; and microcredit) are areas where donors learned from experience.[8] There are several countries—such as India, China, South Africa, and Brazil—that expanded their capacity and productivity or have "emerging" economies.

Food and agricultural development has significantly improved through the Green Revolution and related agricultural development activities. A dozen or so former LDCs—Singapore, Taiwan, Korea, and perhaps India and China—are entering the ranks of the developed world. Some countries approached self-sufficiency in basic foods. Overall, it also should be kept in mind that it took several hundred years for Europe and North America to achieve what LDCs have accomplished in a generation.

Incremental changes in the foreign aid process are abundant. After September 11, there was increased cooperation internationally in aid, although some of this reversed because of the United States' unilateral intervention in Iraq. In the aftermath of the terrorist attack, the United States, after years of ignoring it, began to address some poverty, provided that it can determine the manner of its involvement and the cost to the American taxpayer. In the end, it is the U.S. view that "there is no alternative to rapid economic growth if the aim is the alleviation of poverty."[9]

Policymakers in both donor and recipient countries need to better focus on impacts, benefits, and costs. Costs rather than benefits from a policy result if the donor fails to "avoid interference that is needless or irrelevant to major foreign policy purposes."[10] So often, aid lacks strategic planning. Quality control in foreign assistance is important.

Policymakers must look at costs and benefits, balancing the two. In Iraq, for example, USAID was "hopelessly behind" in the development of a democracy and governance plan in September 2004, relying instead on operating procedures.[11] Two years later, the impact of those failures became apparent as Iraq policy edged toward collapse by the end of 2006.

Foreign service officers are successful and "frequently cited by contemporary diplomats as an example of the Foreign Service at its best. But the idea that diplomatic professionalism is synonymous with expertise is under challenge by a new generation of management-oriented officials."[12] Of concern is the implementation of foreign aid as standardized in complex contracts and tied to grants that focus on statistical niceties rather than qualitative change.

One foreign aid theme links volunteerism to assistance and to development. Those involved in foreign aid have noneconomic motives. The Peace Corps ideology plays an important role in transferring these values. By 2000, work in the Peace Corps became like a union card for the development business. Volunteerism remains important, both in nonofficial and official assistance in the United States, Europe, and to a lesser extent Japan. This is an important legacy of the history of foreign aid.

NGOs continue to have an impact on foreign aid policy. Missionaries and faith-based organizations remain an important component of this influence. The intersection between government and NGOs occurred in nineteenth-century Asia and Africa, where missionaries were a major factor in the development of the British Empire. It was in this empire that the values of foreign aid were defined. This interaction of faith-based organizations, philanthropy, private and government funding, and indigenous peoples continued around the world, beginning in the 1990s.

American education is a factor in the success or failure of foreign aid programs; many education programs yielded positive results. According to a report from the 1980s, "Mission directors assigned to the more developed of the developing countries testified that large numbers of the senior policy and mid-level officials had received management training in the United States through US or international training programs."[13]

However, the basic assumptions of foreign aid are in question. Foreign aid supports economic growth, innovative technology, human resource development, organizational capacity, and investment.[14] But, there is no evidence, according to Easterly, of a relationship between foreign aid and either economic growth or investment and there may be a negative relationship between the wrong kind of foreign aid and economic progress in developing countries.[15] This brings into question the assumptions of MCA. Ultimately, economists argue, universal models of growth failed. Almost all foreign aid goes for either individual or collective consumption. Much of it seems to have an impact upon the urban middle class rather than the rural poor in LDCs.

When Foreign Aid Fails?

Despite limited foreign aid successes, much of foreign aid fails. Critics often blame aid failures on the capacity limitations within LDCs rather than on the aid process. The donor community must share the blame.[16] In many cases, however, the overwhelming donor demands overstretched the organizational and management capacity of the LDC state. This is illustrated by LDC governments' inability to cope effectively with the detailed aid processing and management procedures that aid projects require. Cynically, according to Steve Weissman, "the aid-givers coordinate their beneficence with other levers of control, from diplomatic pressure and private 'philanthropy' to military intervention."[17]

Historically, three motivations attributed to donor foreign assistance are self-interest, a concern for national security, and a sense of obligation and charity as some form of humanitarian responsibility. Donors, as individuals, work toward achievement both in terms of conscience-salving and through the performance of what Gasper calls "accountability rituals." Finally, there is a commitment to a "maturation process" that is sometimes referred to in foreign aid circles and suggests that people in poor countries are not quite adults. According to Gasper, international aid assistance should work with those in the developing world and "treat them as people, adults, and in collegial fashion, not in general as children or delinquents."[18] Nonetheless, the image of childishness remains a part of the LDC image.

Policymakers assumed that US development models best served LDCs. Criticisms of this position abound. As Riggs points out, "Nevertheless, one forms the impression . . . that AID persists in thinking that American administrative technology ought to be exported, and that we have in our experience satisfactory solutions for the problems of developing countries."[19] Because of this, domestic social issues intruded into foreign aid policy, especially in health. Not surprisingly, antiabortion bills and antibirth control concerns are linked to foreign aid. For twenty years, for instance, "[i]n the latest tactical victory by a resurgent anti-abortion movement in the United States, Congress has forced a drastic cut in aid that is the mainstay of family planning programs around the world."[20] This has implications for the fight against HIV/AIDs. Policymakers and domestic lobbyists both claim to know the needs of LDC people, even better than they do.

As early as the 1950s, donors assumed that foreign aid would provide a short-term boost to LDCs, by filling the "finance gap" a country lacked to take off toward sustained economic growth. The search was for a growth-formula-centered debate about development assistance ever since. "Many times over the past fifteen years," according to William Easterly, "we economists thought we had found the right answer to economic growth."[21] MCA is but the latest iteration in the illusive search for the growth magic bullet.

Initially, the Harrod-Domar model—that aid finance should be invested in large-scale infrastructure, such as dams, harbors, roads, and machinery—seemed to be the answer.[22] At various times, capital investment, population control, human resource development, policy reform, structural adjustment, and debt forgiveness have been employed as the elixir of international development. Despite massive amounts of foreign aid in the twentieth century, many countries remained among the poorest.

While some argued that education should be an important variable in international development, historically, researchers failed to find a direct correlation between economic growth and development and human capital growth. "The growth response to the dramatic educational expansion," in LDCs, according to Easterly, "has been distinctly disappointing."[23]

Economic development occurs only when education grows within the context of political stability and good governance.

Official development aid (ODA) has been weak when it has come to technological discoveries and the support of economic growth. Most of the former, in terms of international assistance, historically have come from large private foundations.[24] According to Rondinelli, "AID's technical assistance for development administration during the 1950s and early 1960s was heavily influenced by the prevailing concepts and theories of economic development, [which originated in the private foundations but] reflected in the Marshall Plan and Point Four Program, which were primarily aimed at rehabilitating physical infrastructure and industrial plants, temporarily feeding large numbers of people whose sources of income had been destroyed during the war, [and] re-establishing the economies of industrial societies."[25]

US policymakers tended to see their actions as charitable and even, as in the case of Afghanistan and Iraq, as a way to justify force to meet ideological and developmental goals. Academics and practitioners, when they intervene as consultants, affect LDC policy choices. Often, there is denial of the obvious: that foreign aid has implications for trade and commercial development.

For the past sixty years, foreign aid was governed by "the structural control patterns in the globalized world. Foreign aid, like diplomacy, propaganda, or military action is an instrument of statecraft. Foreign aid is a component of diplomacy and ultimately "a sophisticated instrument of control."[26] Domestic influences in donor countries also play a role in the agricultural sector, as well as in the pharmaceutical and energy industries.

Over time, USAID contractors, nonprofit grantees, and the domestic bureaucracies that operated these programs live off foreign aid and are a major source of opposition to and support for foreign aid and, in some cases, for its reform. Some of those who advocate the reform of aid call for a shift from bilateral to multilateral assistance. Others entreat for the complete separation of aid from State and a move to Treasury, the creation of a separate cabinet department, or a presidential agency headed by a person of stature. Others argue aid should be linked to US security and economic needs. Still others bemoan a loss of mission in the aid community. From this perspective, "[m]obilizing diverse energies means fostering decentralized development and selecting local initiatives [local government, private groups, individuals] over central initiatives."[27]

The mixed motives of foreign aid also relates to process. Given the realpolitik of foreign aid, just as there are populist and elitist views of the Foreign Service so are there populist and elitist views of foreign aid policy.[28] Populist views correspond roughly to the bottom-up approach, while the elitist perspectives refer to the top-down, planning methodology within the donor's power nexus. Populist formulas are popular in techni-cal assistance circles and should be examined within the context of foreign aid program managers' policy choices.[29] Elitist views tend to predominate in foreign policy circles.

It is important to separate the process of foreign aid policymaking in Washington with the way that foreign aid is planned and administered in the field. Too often, policy analysis focuses on the bureaucratic processes and neglects the situation on the ground. In the field, "[e]ach mission director likes to make a personal mark with a cluster of new activity reflecting his/her own initiative. . . . Consequently mission staffs are project advocates."[30] Congress, like USAID field staff, insisted on its prerogative to preapprove individual USAID programs, projects, and activities.[31]

To its critics, foreign aid is part of a broader problem of state weakness because assistance almost always is directed at or gone through inefficient central government structures even though local governments, NGOs, and the private sector provide social services more effectively than the state. Too often, aid has not only defined the nature and patterns of the donor-client relationship, but it also determined what interests were served and the ways in which those modalities were achieved. Corruption, bad gov-ernment, and traditional values are often the problem.

Foreign aid failures result both from international pressures and LDC domestic weakness. Our approach recognizes the responsibility of domes-tic LDC leaders in the management of foreign aid. LDC decision makers do make meaningful choices; however, it is important to place domestic leadership within a complex web of international and domestic factors that define foreign aid. "Just as the 'policy adviser' cannot come to grips with the administrative process," according to Edward Horesh, "still less can the professional foreigner understand the most elementary social processes unless . . . there are 'enough local professional colleagues to save the outsider from most indiscretions.'"[32]

Aid often seems "intellectually disorganized, practically ineffective in too many cases, and insensitive to the political implications and social consequences of foreign interventions."[33] The wholesale spending of huge amounts of foreign aid, in and of itself, "without serious plan, is not a moral spectacle."[34] Foreign assistance policy demonstrates an absence of policy coherence. USAID operates under a multitude of goals and direc-tions. In its *2002 White Paper,* as observed above, USAID admitted it had thirty-three goals, seventy-five priority areas and a whopping 247 direc-tives.[35] And yet, despite this concern, the USAID *White Paper* failed to discuss any way to eliminate any of these goals and objectives.

The foreign aid system, as it evolved in the United States and in other bilateral and multilateral organizations during the last sixty years, has largely been bureaucratic in nature, projectized in operation, and at times, has allowed for the implementation of foreign aid policies contrary to a country's national interests. As Henry Kissinger noted in the late 1960s, there was

> a sort of blindness [in terms of foreign aid] in which bureaucracies run a competition with their own programs and measure success by the degree to which they fulfill their own norms, without being in a position to judge whether the norms made any sense to begin with.[36]

The motivation for foreign aid has been political and economic, as well as ethical and humanitarian, in nature. There remains a predictability to foreign aid policy, and by 1980 "like an emergency room doctor who gives every patient an appendectomy regardless of the symptoms, the institutions treated almost every developing nation the same—with a package often referred to as 'structural adjustment.'"[37]

For the past sixty years, donors seem remarkably ignorant of the impact of political conflict and ethnic diversity on foreign aid and technical assistance. Few understand that one or more ethnic groups are likely to benefit disproportionately from economic advances, often increasing ethnic tensions. In addition, corruption is likely to increase precipitously with increases in foreign aid "in an ethnically divided society though not in an ethnically homogeneous one. Foreign aid is a common resource that each ethnic group will try to divert to its own pockets."[38] By the early 1990s, issues related to ethnic identification were important factors in the success or failure of foreign aid policy.

Development specialists point to concerns about corruption, ethnic patronage, and an "entitlement mentality," along with a generalized aid dependency among Third World elites; however, a great deal of the ineffectiveness of foreign aid rests with the donors, including their choice of methodologies and priorities. Likewise, senior donor representatives can have a "board of directors" mentality in their approach to controlling their host country's public policy choices, becoming in effect authoritarian collective decision makers. A major thrust of this book has been on ways that recipient countries can manage or "deal" with the donor process.

In 2004, USAID had three overall concerns: conflict resolution, development of civil society, and relief and development from social and economic perspectives. Policymakers increasingly saw these in the broader context of homeland security and counterterrorism policy. This context linked development assistance tightly to US foreign and security policy, including domestic security. Mark McGillivray and Howard White explain:

> From the donor's point of view, aid is seen as an instrument of foreign policy, serving to: promote political and diplomatic relations with developing countries; enhance stability within countries of strategic importance; expand export markets; procures strategic imports, and; gain kudos in international fora by being seen to be a responsible, caring member of the international community helping countries in need and seeking to promote international development. Indeed, there is reasonably wide acceptance that political, strategic, commercial and (albeit often begrudgingly) humanitarian motives offer a reasonable a priori basis for explaining patterns of aid allocation among developing countries.[39]

A Potential for Success

In the wake of September 11, George W. Bush, having found "a grandiose purpose" in foreign policy, announced his preemption doctrine, threatening a military first strike against an international threat. Foreign aid would help set the agenda in a postconflict situation. Increasingly, policymakers required international organizations to intervene during periods of social upheaval and political or economic collapse. Whether "striking first" can contribute to international development, however, remains problematic.

Historically, as we have seen, there are several motivations for foreign aid, including individual and collective altruism, particularly in terms of humanitarian assistance; military and strategic; political and diplomatic; commercial, and collective or multilateral. Self-interest defines the motives of actors in the aid process. Leaders in recipient states sometimes have private ambitions and interests on their agendas. There is a mutual but asymmetrical dependence to the relationship, and from the recipients' perspective, opportunity costs to foregoing foreign aid.

Official foreign aid and technical assistance ultimately are vehicles of a country's foreign policy. Foreign aid agencies are thus "part of an institutional framework . . . that continues to fall short of its potentials. [Foreign aid is] about politics and, crucially, the relationship between donors and recipients—not only at the higher echelons, but at all levels of contact."[40] Foreign aid as John Montgomery ruefully notes, "as a political instrument of U.S. policy is here to stay because of its usefulness and flexibility."[41]

Both official foreign aid and technical assistance harbor modernization assumptions wherein a transformation of society from ascriptive to meritorious and from rural to urban occurs. From a modernization perspective, a book on foreign aid and development should ideally focus on two levels of analysis: the relationship between the individual and a primary socialization process and the extent to which national ethical, normative, and moral values have an impact upon the individual.

Perhaps it is true that all of those involved in the development debate are *modernists*. From a policy perspective, the debate about foreign aid and development revolves around two issues: cultural transformation and what used to be called modernization, based on the assumption there is a set of characteristics that defines world culture in the twenty-first century, the former at two levels. First, there is the concept of identity and how one identifies oneself in relationship to family, language, religion, and culture. Second, there is the issue of social morality that ultimately is defined, at least in part, by national policy. According to Richard Sandbrook, "The new democratic [foreign aid] missionaries are perceived as ethnocentric in assuming the innate superiority of Western-style, liberal-democratic institutions."[42]

At issue in discussing foreign aid is the chain of forces having an impact on individual and social values as a means of promoting international development. Focus is on the full spectrum of foreign aid impacts, from individual to nation. History makes it clear that institutions and institutional relationships cannot realistically be transplanted from one society to another.

It was not until the 1980s that development specialists focused on the role of institutions in development, "not only the formal organizations of government and private-sector entities but the 'humanly devised constraints that shape human interaction.'"[43] "Aid donors," according to Lancaster,

> have found efforts to strengthen African institutions among the least effective of their activities. Indeed, evidence suggests that technical assistance has become part of the problem of institutional weakness, not the solution. . . . Despite 30 years of a heavy technical assistance present and much training, local institutions remain weak.[44]

Even with outside input, it is difficult to introduce organizational change. Unfortunately, however, organizational change is sometimes seen as a given by the donor. As a former USAID administrator once put it, "At this meeting, we received a briefing by a respected management consulting group, which had been engaged to assist in framing solutions to organizational concerns."[45] While change is often recognized, little is done. Organizational development is difficult and remains a central problem for successful development. Institutional development is even more difficult and is central to the foreign aid process; according to Des Gasper, "If one's theory of development centers not on volumes of investment but on building confidence and capacity, people, organizations and institutions, including capacity to learn, decide and mobilize resources in one's own unique situation, then co-determination in projects and policies is vital in place of conventional modes of aid."[46]

Donor intervention to improve management and organizational performance will not be successful without a sustained commitment to institutional development, particularly for institutions involved in education and training. Moreover, such interventions should be unencumbered by the unrealistic time bound constraints in the project cycle. The time phasing provided in donor project documents has been hopelessly unrealistic and has called for donors to shift their assistance from financing projects to financing a time-slice of sector or subsector programs.[47]

Ultimately, implementing foreign aid is a management problem. An early implementation issue relates to debates about coordination and specialization. Delegating responsibility to other departments or contractors in some situations could weaken control over the distribution of funds between functional fields. There was also a fear that proposals of special interest to individual governments could monopolize available program resources. Overall, the foreign aid dilemma often centers on the question of whether to co-opt or coerce.

Development management services involve design, monitoring, and evaluation methodologies; the development of suitable donor, donor mission, and LDC participating agency procedures; and teaching these concepts and procedures to host country cooperants.[48] To be successful, interventions need to include assistance to strengthen local- and national-level public management systems, and private sector management capacity, including: program and project analysis, project identification, design, evaluation/assessment, implementation, and monitoring activities. Public policy concerns include: policy analysis and choice, personnel systems development, organizational development, accountancy, human resource development and planning, and project management.

This adds up to operating within a very restricted project framework. Since the development of the project methodology, foreign aid has been trapped in rigid procedures that limit effectiveness and creativity. Opting for technical solutions ignores the need to address governance issues, including the management, monitoring, and if necessary, the whistle-blowing process because good governance broadly defined is the prerequisite to avoiding bad and poorly implemented economic and social policies.

Four policy areas can make a difference in terms of international development: transportation, competitive markets, agricultural extension, and transparent policymaking and good governance. In addition, a developing country needs a well-functioning credit system, stable property rights, and effective incentives for public sector employees. It is important to recast the agencies dealing with commerce and agriculture. "The Chamber of Agriculture," according to Robert Klitgaard, "should get out of the import-export business and certainly not aspire to be a marketing board. Instead, it should become an autonomous body [providing] service [to] the private sectors and functioning as its voice vis-à-vis the government."[49]

Neo-imperial control models, such as those exhibited in Iraq (and to a lesser degree in Afghanistan and in many African countries), are difficult to maintain. The limited resources available means that, in the contemporary era, the Western powers could not sustain the colonial style structures, so sadly represented by the Green Zone in Iraq, which had been maintained a generation earlier. For this to change would require a massive infusion of both military and foreign assistance. Iraq and Afghanistan clearly illustrate the difficulties of this. The resources and the political will in both cases were not there to maintain intervention models long term.

There is a common assumption that aid concentrates on expanding choices for individuals and families in society. "In some ways," according to Paul Blustein, foreign aid continues to be fixated at the macro level on large institutions and resembles "the insistence on structural adjustment in the 1980s, though with less emphasis on cutting budget deficits and more emphasis on developing clean, healthy institutions such as courts."[50] A more microapproach may be wise. More attention should be given to the impact of foreign aid on individuals and groups, which collectively will have a favorable impact on those countries that are able to establish and maintain patterns of good governance.

Since 2001, the developed/developing dichotomy increasingly became a false one. Instead, a foreign aid community is made up of several interrelated groups and increasing interdependence mechanisms that cross developmental, foreign, and security policy lines. Ability to manage and take advantage of information technology is central in twenty-first century development.[51] Both China and India have demonstrated their ability to do so without significant involvement of foreign assistance.

That does not mean there are not differences in economic and political status in the global political economy. An increasing division occurred between the developing countries that will be able to join the industrial world (mostly in Asia, with a few in Latin America and eastern Europe) and whose economic takeoff was spectacular and the many other LDCs (mainly in Africa, some in Latin America, and a few in Asia and south central Europe), whose policies failed. The latter fell more deeply into international debt. There remain, however, severe obstacles in the United States around the disjointed, incremental, and unplanned way in making international assistance policy. Beyond this, there is growing consensus that solid economic policies and economic management matters more to developing counties than international assistance does.

In foreign aid policy, there is a problem of what John Montgomery calls "consistent outcomes," that is, large policy decisions lead to disappointing results.[52] As Montgomery suggests, "Boldness [is] followed by indifference, greatness [is] permitted to degenerate into mediocrity."[53] In foreign aid policy, greatness in decision making can be followed by indifference in the aftermath of that decision, and as John Montgomery warns us, "the best decisions can have consequences harmful to someone."[54]

Ultimately, both individuals and groups of people respond to incentives. The assumption is that donors should need to link foreign aid to prior country performance, giving the LDC government incentives to pursue growth-creating policies; however, policies that encourage incentives and entrepreneurialism require a public policy process that is both rational at the individual level and based on societal rather that narrow interests. Development occurs

> when government incentives induce technological adaptation, high-quality investment in machines, and high-quality schooling. It happens when donors face incentives that induce them to give aid to countries with good policies where aid will have high payoffs, not to countries with poor policies where aid is wasted.[55]

Long term, there is a consensus that foreign aid should be directed at supporting efforts by LDCs to reform their own economies and political systems. Beyond this, the donor countries should move toward cooperative mechanisms that facilitate global access and connectivity in terms of trade, the movement of people, and productivity, which also contribute to a more benign invasion of the more-isolated and less-informed individuals and communities.

Successful international development should involve trade and tariff reform and a trade environment favorable or at least equitable to LDCs. It should allow LDC citizens access to education, training, information, and communications technology that, if not equal to more developed countries, is appropriate. Sustainability issues remain important as does "sustainability generated in circumstances of good national governance; which does not mean large government, but strong institutions which facilitate the provision of goods and services by the most appropriate means."[56]

Structuralist critics assume that foreign aid is set up to widen the economic disparities between wealthy states and LDCs. Inadvertent disparity might be a better way to put it. The perception is real, however. According to Stephen Hook, the "perceived effects of [such a] manipulation of foreign assistance include the increased reliance of LDCs on the monetary policies, consumption patterns, and export policies of core states."[57] In 1992, according to one South African observer, the Great Powers simply makes it known that if the small nation does not do what it is told "then its aid will be cut off."[58]

This may be overexaggerated. There is room for ethical, moral, and humanitarian concerns in international assistance; however, the realist position remains alive and kicking and can be detrimental to the international development process. Ethics are a part of the framework for international assistance. To illustrate the logic of this ethical dimension, according to an early Presidential Task Force, the United States should "create a U.S. International Development Bank to carry out the bilateral lending program. The Bank should be an independent government corporation, with a full-time president serving also as chairman of a board of directors, which would be composed of government officials and private members."[59] This suggests that in time,

> U.S. international development policies may well prove to be the most important—and the most rewarding—determinant of America's role in the world. . . . The United States has a profound national interest in cooperating with developing countries in their efforts to improve conditions of life in their societies. . . . This country should not look for gratitude or votes, or any specific short-term foreign policy gains from our participation in international development.[60]

This is an ideal position but does it also represent a realpolitik?

Conclusion

There has been one constant defining foreign aid during the last sixty years. Critics from lesser developed states suggest that the humanitarian and development goals of development policy are distorted by aid for donor country commercial, political, or military purposes. Given the nature of government in the twenty-first century, for foreign aid to succeed, it would have to be perceived as in the self-interest of a country's leadership and its societies in both donor and recipient nations. That, and a perception of the realities of the need for multilateralism, are, if not a blueprint, a start in the debate about international assistance in the twenty-first century.

In the end, as we stress here, foreign aid is above all an instrument of foreign and security policy. Part of that motive is political and military; part of it is economic. There remains a component of idealism in international development efforts, however. Without that, foreign aid is no different than seeking commercial advantage, political alliance, or combating military threats.

To conclude, if not to caution, we can go back to Ralph H. Smuckler and Robert J. Berg's wise words in 1988: "The world of the 1990s, and that of the 21st century, will be substantially different from one in which a worldwide enterprise known as 'foreign aid' was launched forty years ago. New circumstances make the concept of foreign aid less appropriate. To much of Asia and Latin America, the concept of 'cooperation for development' fits better."[61] By development cooperation, they suggest that responsibilities are widely and roughly equally shared between the two parties.

It is important to remember that the goals of the development policy can get mixed up because of the need of the organization to gain control over its social environment. There is also a need to reshape the organization and management of foreign aid. By 2000, "USAID [had] one of the most elaborate and time consuming programming systems of any aid agency."[62] Yet, despite or because of this, aid is ineffective.

The compelling mode for foreign and security policy, and hence foreign aid, is the national self-interests of the donor, as defined by the political leadership of a country, and in consultation with the broader international community as well as the recipient[s] of that assistance. In foreign aid, there is often a lack of mutual exchange. There are strings attached, but historically they have not always been one-sided. Unfortunately, in a post–September 11 world, most lesser developed countries have little to offer prospective donors other than markets and peace.

There remains a middle ground among critics of foreign aid. According to Larry Chang, "Between these critics and a steadily decreasing number of aid proponents are some analysts who contend that aid should not be terminated, but be concentrated on those countries that 'can be saved,' rather than on those desperately in need of it."[63] A saving model, however, according to Rondinelli, "consisted merely of transferring American administrative technology and 'know how' to less developed countries, much in the same way that industrial and agricultural technology and 'know how' were transferred through the Marshall Plan" (and the Point Four Model).

The view espoused here is that donors should provide foreign aid other than humanitarian assistance only when the recipient national and local authorities are clearly capable of both receiving and using this aid effectively through its own institutions in a manner that benefits the majority of its citizens. Policy is a complex combination of motives involving a variety of actors, interest groups, and members of the public. Developed countries do need to see that their self-interests are being met. In addition, civil society, nonprofit, or private-sector organizations should utilize foreign aid to foster social, economic, or political development.

Notes

1. Carol Lancaster, *Foreign Aid: Diplomacy, Development, Domestic Politics* (Chicago: University of Chicago Press, 2007).

2. Steven W. Hook, ed. *National Interest and Foreign Aid to the Millennium* (Boulder, CO: Lynne Rienner Publishers, 1996) provides a good discussion of several of these foreign aid issues.

3. David Sogge, *Give and Take: What's the Matter with Foreign Aid?* (London: Zed Books, 2002), p. 8.

4. A reality admitted by USAID itself. See "White Paper—U.S. Foreign Aid: Meeting the Challenges of the Twenty-First Century" (Washington, DC: US Agency for International Development, January 2004). Hereafter referred to White Paper on U.S. Foreign Aid-2004.

5. *The Role of Foreign Aid in Development* (Washington, DC: Congressional Budget Office, May 1997), p. 8.

6. Robert Cassen, "The Effectiveness of Aid," *Finance & Development* (March 1986), p. 11.

7. Marcela Sanchez, "Better than Foreign Aid," *Washington Post* (January 2, 2004), p. A21.

8. Robert McMahon, "Transforming U.S. Foreign Aid," *Council on Foreign Relationships Publication no. 10176* (New York: Council on Foreign Relations, March 17, 2006) www.cfr.org/publications/10176, pp. 1–5.

9. Martin Wolf, "Aid, hope and charity," *Financial Times* (November 11, 1998), p. 12.

10. John Montgomery, *The Politics of Foreign Aid: American Experience in Southeast Asia* (New York: Praeger, 1962), p. 250. See also Walter R., Sharpe, "The Institutional Framework for Technical Assistance," *International Organization*, 7, no. 3 (1953) p. 342.

11. That is according to a senior level USAID official who requested anonymity.

12. John M. Goshko, "Tradition Bows to the Demand for Management Skills," *Washington Post* (April 27, 1987), p. A1.

13. Thomas Thorsen and Kenneth Kornher, "Draft Report of the Work Group for the Review of the Programs in Management Improvement and Development Administration of the Agency for International Development" (Washington, DC: Department of State, US Agency for International Development, n.d.), p. 4.

14. See William Easterly, *The Elusive Quest for Growth: Economists' Adventures and Misadventures in the Tropics* (Cambridge, MA: MIT Press, 2001), p. 41.

15. Ibid. and William Easterly, *The White Man's Burden: Why the West's Efforts to Aid the Rest Have Done So Much Ill and So Little Good* (New York: Penguin Press, 2006).

16. For a detailed analysis of this point, see an analysis of aid to Haiti in Terry Buss, *Haiti in the Balance* (Washington: Brookings Institution Press, 2008).

17. Steve Weissman, "Inside the Trojan Horse," *The Trojan Horse: A Radical Look at Foreign Aid*, Steve Weissman, ed. (Palo Alto, CA: Ramparts Press, 1975), p. 11.

18. Des Gasper, "Ethics and the Conduct of International Development Aid," Notes from a Speech at Graduate School of Public and International Affairs, University of Pittsburgh (Pittsburgh, March 30, 1999), p. 1.

19. Fred W. Riggs, "Memorandum: Suggested Discussion Topics Based on Dennis Rondinelli, on Rondinelli's book, *Development Administration and Foreign Aid Policy*" (Personal Communication with the author from University of Hawaii, March 1987), p. 5.

20. Barbara Crossette, "U.S. Aid Cutbacks Endangering Population Programs, U.N. Agencies Say," *New York Times* (February 16, 1996), p. A6.

21. See Easterly, *The Elusive Quest for Growth* p. 23.

22. See John Martinussen, *Society, State and Market: Guide to Competing Theories of Development* (London: Zed Books, 1995), pp. 25, 80, and 229.

23. Easterly, *The Elusive Quest for Growth*, p. 73.

24. Milton J. Esman and John D. Montgomery, "Systems Approaches to Technical Cooperation: The Role of Development Administration," *Public Administration Review* (September/October 1969), pp. 507–539. Quote, p. 516.

25. Dennis A. Rondinelli, "Development Administration and American Foreign Assistance Policy: An Assessment of Theory and Practice in Aid," *Canadian Journal of Development Studies*, 6, no. 2 (1985), p. 213.

26. Weissman, "Inside the Trojan Horse," p. 11. According to Paul Glastris, speaking of foreign aid policy, "Even if these hearings were to lead Congress to tighten laws governing foreign influence, that wouldn't diminish the impact of some of the most effective advocates for foreign governments: the ethnic compatriots and their descendents who have immigrated into the United States." Paul Glastris, "Multicultural Foreign Policy in Washington," *U.S. News and World Report* (July 21, 1997), pp. 30–34.

27. Ralph H. Smuckler and Robert J. Berg, "New Challenges New Opportunities, U.S. Cooperation for International Growth and Development in the 1990s" (East Lansing: Michigan State University, August 1988), p. 24.

28. John Franklin Campbell, *The Foreign Affairs Fudge Factory* (New York: Basic Books, 1971).

29. Steven W. Hook, *National Interest and Foreign Aid* (Boulder CO: Lynne Rienner Publishers, 1995), p. 35.

30. E. Philip Morgan, "Social Analysis, Project Development and Advocacy in U.S. Foreign Assistance" (Unpublished Paper, 1980), p. 9.

31. *Office of Transition Initiatives: A Decade of Transition— 1994–2004* (Washington, DC: US Agency for International Development, 2004).

32. Edward Horesh, "Academics and Experts or the Death of the High Level Technical Assistant" *Development and Change* vol. 12, no. 4 (October, 2008), pp. 611–618, quote.

33. Edmund Stillman and William Pfaff, *Power and Impotence: The Failure of America's Foreign Policy* (New York: Random House, 1966), p. 220.

34. Ibid., p. 218.

35. White Paper on U.S. Foreign Aid-2004, p. 8.

36. Quoted in Campbell, *The Foreign Affairs Fudge Factory,* p. 8.

37. Daniel Altman, "As Global Lenders Refocus, a Needy World Waits," *New York Times* (March 17, 2002), p. A11.

38. Easterly, *The Elusive Quest for Growth,* p. 249.

39. Mark McGillivray and Howard White, "Explanatory Studies of Aid Allocation Among Developing Countries: A Critical Survey," *Working Paper Series No. 148* (The Hague: Institute of Social Studies, April 1993), p. 2.

40. Janine R. Wedel, *Collision and Collusion: The Strange Case of Western Aid to Eastern Europe, 1989–1998* (New York: St. Martins Press, 1998), p. 6.

41. Montgomery, *The Politics of Foreign Aid*, p. 9.

42. Richard Sandbrook, *The Politics of Africa's Economic Recovery* (New York: Cambridge University Press, 1993), p. 103.

43. Douglass North, *Institutions, Institutional Change, and Economic Performance* (New York: Cambridge University Press, 1990), quoted by Carol Lancaster, *Aid to Africa, So Much to Do, So Little Done* (Chicago: University of Chicago Press, 1999), p. 18.

44. Ibid., p. 57.

45. Ronald W. Roskens, Letter to USAID Colleagues (Washington, DC: January 23, 1991).

46. Gasper, "Ethics and the Conduct of International Development Aid," p. 2.

47. Jon R. Moris, *Managing Induced Rural Development* (Bloomington, IN: International Development Institute, 1981), p. 33.

48. This was a major thrust of the recommendations made in the 1984 SADCC study *Improving Management in Southern Africa* (Washington, DC: National Association of Schools of Public Affairs and Administration, July 1, 1985).

49. Robert Klitgaard, *Tropical Gangsters: One Man's Experience With Development and Decadence in Deepest Africa* (New York: Basic Books, 1990), p. 229.

50. Paul Blustein, "The Right Aid Formula This Time Around?" *Washington Post* (March 24, 2002), p. A27.

51. See Thomas L. Friedman *The World Is Flat: A Brief History of the Twenty-first Century* (New York: Farrar, Straus and Giroux, 2005), for a discussion of this trend.

52. John D. Montgomery, *Aftermath: Tarnished Outcomes of American Foreign Policy* (Dover, MA: Auburn House Publishing Company, 1986), p. ix.

53. Ibid., p. x.

54. Ibid., p. 116.

55. Easterly, *The Elusive Quest for Growth*, p. 289.

56. Ibid., p. 166

57. Hook, *National Interest and Foreign Aid*, p. 38.

58. Gerald L'Ange, "Aid Diplomacy: the New Persuasion," *Star* (Johannesburg, May 20, 1992), p. 14.

59. Rudolph Peterson, et al., "U.S. Foreign Assistance in the 1970s, A New Approach," *Report to the President from Task Force on International Development for FY1972* (Washington, DC: U.S. Government Printer, March 4, 1970), p. 28.

60. Ibid., p. 2.

61. Smuckler and Berg, "New Challenges New Opportunities," p. 1.

62. Lancaster, *Aid to Africa,* p. 107.

63. Larry Chang, "Foreign Aid and the Fate of Least Developed Countries" (Unpublished Paper, 1986), p. 6.

SELECTED BIBLIOGRAPHY

Anderson, Mary B., *Do No Harm: How Aid Can Support Peace—or War* (Boulder, CO: Lynne Rienner Publishers, 1999).

Brigety, Reuben E., *Humanity as a Weapon of War: Sustainable Security and the Role of the U.S. Military* (Washington, DC: Center for American Progress, June 2008).

Browne, Stephen, *Beyond Aid: From Patronage to Partnership* (Aldershot, UK: Ashgate, 1999).

Butterfield, Samuel Hale, *U.S. Development Aid—An Historic First: Achievements and Failures in the Twentieth Century* (Westport, CN: Praeger, 2004).

Campbell, John Franklin, *The Foreign Affairs Fudge Factory* (New York: Basic Books, 1971).

Collier, Paul, *The Bottom Billion: Why the Poorest Countries Are Failing and What Can Be Done About It* (New York: Oxford University Press, 2007).

Destler, I. M., *Presidents, Bureaucrats and Foreign Policy: The Politics of Organizational Reform* (Princeton, NJ: Princeton University Press, 1972).

Dollar, David. *Assessing Aid: What Works, What Doesn't and Why* (Washington, DC: World Bank, 1998). Eland, Ivan, *The Empire Has No Clothes: U.S. Foreign Policy Exposed* (Oakland, CA: The Independent Institute, 2004).

Easterly, William, *The Elusive Quest for Growth: Economists' Adventures and Misadventures in the Tropics* (Cambridge, MA: MIT Press, 2002).

Easterly, William, *The White Man's Burden: Why the West's Efforts to Aid the Rest Have Done So Much Ill and So Little Good* (New York: Penguin Press, 2006).

Etzioni, Amitai, *Security First: For a Muscular Moral Foreign Policy* (New Haven, CT: Yale University Press, 2007).

Hancock, Graham, *Lords of Poverty: The Power, Prestige, and Corruption of the International Aid Business* (New York: Atlantic Monthly Press, 1989).

Hook, Steven W., ed. *Foreign Aid Toward the Millennium* (Boulder, CO: Lynne Rienner Publishers, 1996).

Hook, Steven W., *National Interest and Foreign Aid* (Boulder CO: Lynne Rienner Publishers, 1995).

Hoopes, Townsend, *The Limits of Intervention: An Inside Account of How the Johnson Policy of Escalation in Vietnam Was Reversed* (New York: David McKay Company, 1969).

Kissinger, Henry, *Diplomacy* (New York: Simon and Shuster, 1994).

Lancaster, Carol, *Aid to Africa: So Much to Do So Little Done* (Chicago: University of Chicago Press, 1999).

Lancaster, Carol, *Foreign Aid: Diplomacy, Development, Domestic Politics* (Chicago: University of Chicago Press, 2007).

Lancaster, Carol, *Transforming Foreign Aid: United States Assistance in the 21st Century* (Washington, DC: Institute for International Economics, 2000).

Lancaster, Carol and Ann Van Dusen, *Organizing U.S. Foreign Aid: Confronting the Challenges of the Twenty-First Century* (Washington, DC: Brookings Institution Press, 2005).

Lennon, Alexander T. J., ed. *International Perspectives on U.S. Foreign Policy* (Cambridge, MA: MIT Press, 2002).

Liska, George, *The New Statecraft: Foreign Aid in American Foreign Policy* (Chicago: University of Chicago Press, 1960).

Maren, Michael, *The Road to Hell: The Ravaging Effects of Foreign Aid and International Charity* (New York: The Free Press, 1997).

Montgomery, John D., *Aftermath: Tarnished Outcomes of American Foreign Policy* (Dover, MA: Auburn House Publishing Company, 1985).

Nye, Joseph S., *Soft Power: The Means to Success in World Politics* (New York: Public Affairs Perseus Books, 2004.

Patterson, Robert G., J. Garry Clifford, and Kenneth J. Hagan, *American Foreign Policy: A History to 1911* (Lexington, MA: D. C. Heath and Company, 1983).

Picard, Louis A., Robert Groelsema, and Terry F. Buss, *Foreign Aid and Foreign Policy: Issues for the Next Half Century* (Armonk, NY: M. E. Sharpe, 2008).

Rondinelli, Dennis A., *Development Administration and U.S. Foreign Aid Policy* (Boulder, CO: Lynne Rienner Publishers, 1987).

Rossiter, Caleb, *The Bureaucratic Struggle for Control of U.S. Foreign Aid: Diplomacy vs. Development in Southern Africa* (Boulder, CO: Westview Press, 1985).

Rugumamu, Severine M., *Lethal Aid: The Illusion of Socialism and Self-Reliance in Tanzania* (Trenton, NJ: Africa World Press, 1997).

Ruttan, Vernon, *United States Development Assistance Policy: The Domestic Politics of Foreign Aid* (Baltimore: Johns Hopkins University Press, 1996).

Smillie, Ian, *The Alms Bazaar: Altruism Under Fire—Non-Profit Organizations and International Development* (London: Intermediate Technologies Publications, 1995).

Smith, Steve, Amelia Hadfield and Tim Dunne, eds. *Foreign Policy: Theories, Actors, Cases* (Oxford: Oxford University Press, 2008).

Sogge, David, *Give and Take: What's the Matter with Foreign Policy* (London: Zed Books, 2002).

Stillman, Edmund and William Pfaff, *Power and Impotence: The Failure of America's Foreign Policy* (New York: Random House, 1966).

Tendler, Judith, *Inside Foreign Aid* (Baltimore: Johns Hopkins University Press, 1975).

Weidner, Edward W., *Technical Assistance in Public Administration Overseas: The Case for Development Administration* (Chicago: Public Administration Service, 1964).

Wittkopf, Eugene R. and James M. McCormick, eds. *The Domestic Sources of Foreign Policy* (New York: Rowman and Littlefield Publishers, 2008).

INDEX

Achebe, Chinua, 26
Advisory Committee on Voluntary
  Foreign Aid, 74
Afghanistan
  aid failures in, 292
  compared to Iraq, 254
  de facto U.S. colony, 51
  Provincial Reconstruction Teams,
    271
  U.S. invasion of, 158
Africa
  aid failures in, 136–137,
    236–237
  aid to, 114, 124–125
  debt burden, 126
  early humanitarian work in, 24
  expatriates in, 227–228
  export efforts by, 261
  opposition to AFRICOM, 182
  regional organizations needed,
    234
  responsibility for crisis in,
    230–231
  rural development programs,
    122
  trade polices, 263–264
  U.S. strategy for, 181–185
Africa Food Security Initiative
  (AFSI), 122
African Command (AFRICOM),
  173, 180–185
African Growth and Opportunity
  Act (AGOA), 261

AFRICOM (African Command),
  173, 180–185
Agency for International
  Development. See US Agency
  for International Development
  (USAID)
Agricultural development aid
  aid success in, 283
  in China, 57–59
  failures of, 121–123
  subsidies effect, 261–263
  university-based programs, 201
Agricultural surplus, U.S., 67, 94
AID. See US Agency for
  International Development
  (USAID)
AIDS funding, 158, 164
Aid tying, 16, 141–142, 261–264
Alliance for Progress in Latin
  America, 95, 98
American Colonization Society,
  51–52
American Friends Service
  Committee, 44, 66
American Relief Administration
  (ARA), 67
Anti-war movement, Vietnam,
  108–110
Appelgarth, Paul, 266
ARA (American Relief
  Administration), 67
Asymmetric warfare, 173–174, 175
Authoritarianism, 69

305

future of, 177–180
merger with State Department,
  269–272
military advisors, 111–112
NGOs and, 202
origins of, 89
personnel levels, 145, 180, 184,
  199–200
project cycle weaknesses,
  196–198
reorganization of, 144
university contracting with, 136,
  209–212

Vann, John Paul, 111–112
Vietnam
  anti-Communist battles,
    104–106
  anti-war movement in US,
    108–110
  foreign aid success in, 106
  French colonial rule impact, 104

impacts of US actions in,
  112–115
Kennedy policies, 107–108
military intervention linked to
  foreign aid, 110–112
USAID activities in, 111–112

War Relief Control Board, 74
Washington Consensus, 124, 127
Whole-of-government strategy,
  176–180, 181–185
Wilson, Woodrow, 66–67
Wood, Leonard, 48–49
World Bank, 84, 121–124, 236–237
World University Service, 68
World Vision, 69

Yen, Y. C. James, 58–59
Young Men's/Women's Christian
  Association, 66

Zaire, 236, 237–238, 258

ABOUT THE AUTHORS

Louis A. Picard is professor and former (founding) director of the International Development Division of the Graduate School of Public and International Affairs (GSPIA) at the University of Pittsburgh. Picard served as senior research associate at the Africa Center for Strategic Studies while on sabbatical in 2007. In this role, he designed, supervised, and conducted research on strategic developments in the areas of conflict mitigation, human security, and international development, as well as governance, and foreign and military assistance in Africa. Picard has served as associate and acting dean of the Graduate School of Public and International Affairs (GSPIA) and has taught at the University of Nebraska and Gustavus Adolphus College. From 2002 to 2005, he served as president of Public Administration Service, an international research and consulting firm. Picard has accumulated more than forty years of research and consulting experience in both US and comparative politics and governance, international public administration, foreign assistance, and management development agencies, working in more than forty countries in Africa, the Middle East, and Latin America. His recent research concerns the political transformation in South Africa, a three-volume study, focusing on the "local state" and development policy in post-apartheid South Africa. A second project examines capacity building for policy change, decentralized development, and sustainable transformation in Africa. A third looks at the future of foreign and security policy and international assistance in the United States and on the triangulation of policy management between the Department of Defense, the Department of State, the US Agency for International Development and other US foreign aid agencies. Picard is the author or editor of nine books and more than fifty articles and book chapters on foreign aid, human security, development policy, and governance. His latest book is *Foreign Aid and Foreign Policy: Lessons for the Next Half-Century* (Louis A. Picard, Robert Groelsema, Terry F. Buss, eds., New York: M. E. Sharpe, 2007). His book, *The State of the State: Institutional*

Transformation, Capacity and Political Change in South Africa, was recently published in South Africa and the United States (Johannesburg and Rutgers, NJ: University of Witwatersrand Press and Transaction Books, 2005). He is the author and editor of two books on Botswana, coauthor of a book on policy reform in Africa, and editor of books on federalism and decentralization and the negotiated transition in South Africa, as well as a book on policy reform in the Caribbean. Picard sees his applied research, consulting, and practical work, and his academic research as two halves of the same coin and not mutually contradictory. His consulting work feeds into his academic research, and his academic research informs his consultancies. In all of his work, he tries to bridge the gap between the academic and the practitioner and the university community and international technical assistance.

Terry F. Buss is currently Distinguished Professor of Public Policy at the Heinz School of Public Policy and Management, Carnegie Mellon University, in Adelaide, Australia. Buss earned his doctorate in political science and mathematics at Ohio State University. During the past thirty years, Buss has built his career in both academe and government. In an immediate past position, he directed the program in International, Security and Defense Studies at the National Academy of Public Administration for five years. From 2000 to 2003, Buss served as dean of the School of Policy and Management at Florida International University (FIU) in Miami. In 2000, Buss worked as a senior policy adviser at the US Department of Housing and Urban Development in Washington, DC. From 1997 to 2000, Buss chaired the Department of Public Management in the Sawyer School of Business at Suffolk University in Boston. While on leave from Suffolk, Buss spent one year at the World Bank as a senior strategy adviser to the vice president for training and technical assistance and as the secretariat for the development of the World Bank's Global Distance Learning Network (GDLN). From 1987 to 1997, Buss directed the PhD program and chaired the Department of Public Administration and Urban Studies at the University of Akron in Ohio and he was also director of research at the St. Elizabeth Hospital Medical Center/Northeast Ohio College of Medicine. During this period, Buss, while on leave from Akron, directed the US Information Agency technical assistance program in Hungary for three years immediately following the fall of communism in Eastern Europe; he replicated this program in Russia from 1993 to 1996. In addition, he worked on leave with the Council of Governors Policy Advisors, an affiliate of the National Governors Association as a senior adviser. He did so as an unprecedented two-time Fulbright Scholar winner in Hungary, working with the Minister of the Interior and Budapest School of

Economics. He also received two fellowships with the Congressional Research Service, where he authored policy studies mandated by Congress. Buss has published twelve books and nearly 300 professional articles on a variety of policy issues. His latest book is *Haiti in the Balance* (Washington: Brookings Institution Press, 2008). Buss has won numerous awards for research and public service. Throughout the years, Buss has worked overseas on major projects in Russia, England, Wales, Italy, Czech Republic, Slovakia, Hungary, Romania, Bulgaria, Albania, Ghana, Haiti, Canada, Colombia, Jamaica, Bahamas, and Australia. He also directed projects in Iraq, South Africa, and Botswana from the United States.

 **Also from Kumarian Press . . .**

Foreign Aid and Development:

The World Bank and the Gods of Lending
Steve Berkman

Development Brokers and Translators: The Ethnography of Aid and Agencies
Edited by David Lewis and David Mosse

The Charity of Nations: Humanitarian Action in a Calculating World
Ian Smillie and Larry Minear

Players and Issues in International Aid
Paula Hoy

New and Forthcoming:

How the Aid Industry Works: An Introduction to International Development
Arjan de Haan

Strategic Moral Diplomacy: Understanding the Enemy's Moral Universe
Lyn Boyd-Judson

Civil Society Under Strain: Anti-Terrorism Policy, Civil Society and Aid Post-9/11
Edited by Jude Howell and Jeremy Lind

Freedom From Want: The Remarkable Success Story of BRAC, The Global
Grassroots Organization That's Winning the Fight Against Poverty
Ian Smillie

Visit Kumarian Press at **www.kpbooks.com** or
call **toll-free 800.232.0223** for a complete catalog

 *Kumarian Press, located in Sterling, Virginia, is a forward-looking,
scholarly press that promotes active international engagement and
an awareness of global connectedness.*